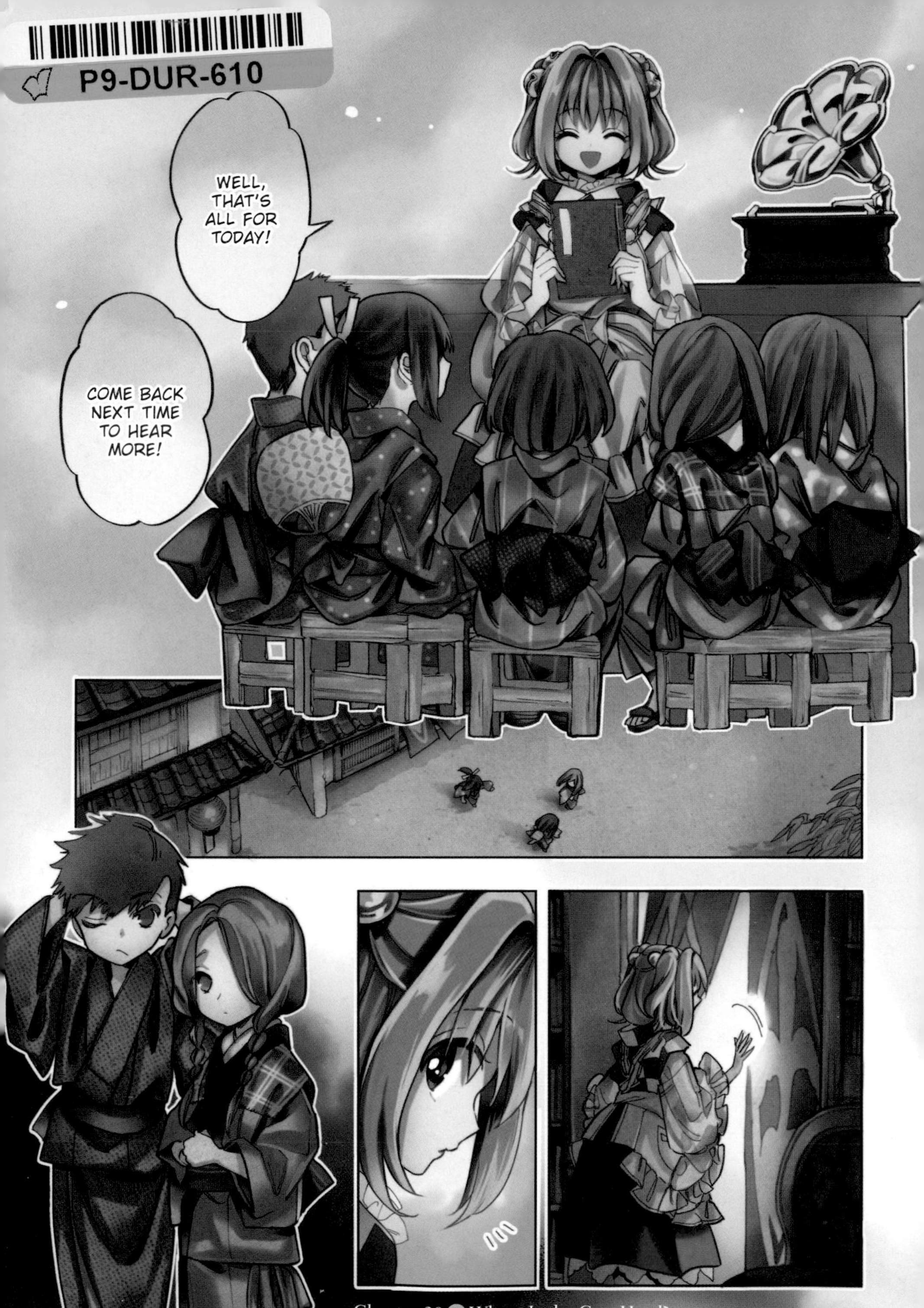
WELL, THAT'S ALL FOR TODAY!
COME BACK NEXT TIME TO HEAR MORE!

Chapter 30 Where Is the Cow Head? Part 1

Chapter 30 Where Is the Cow Head? Part 1

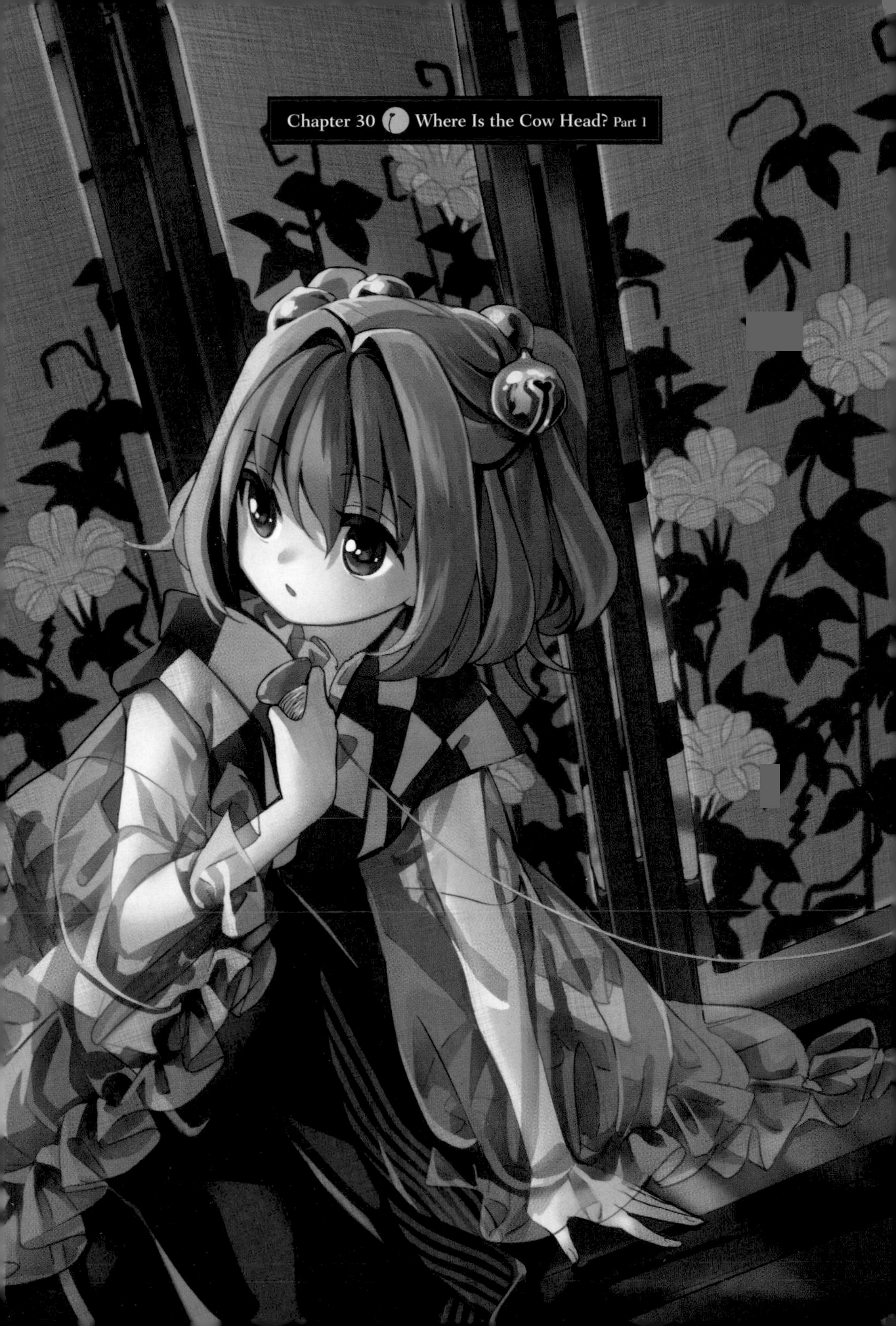

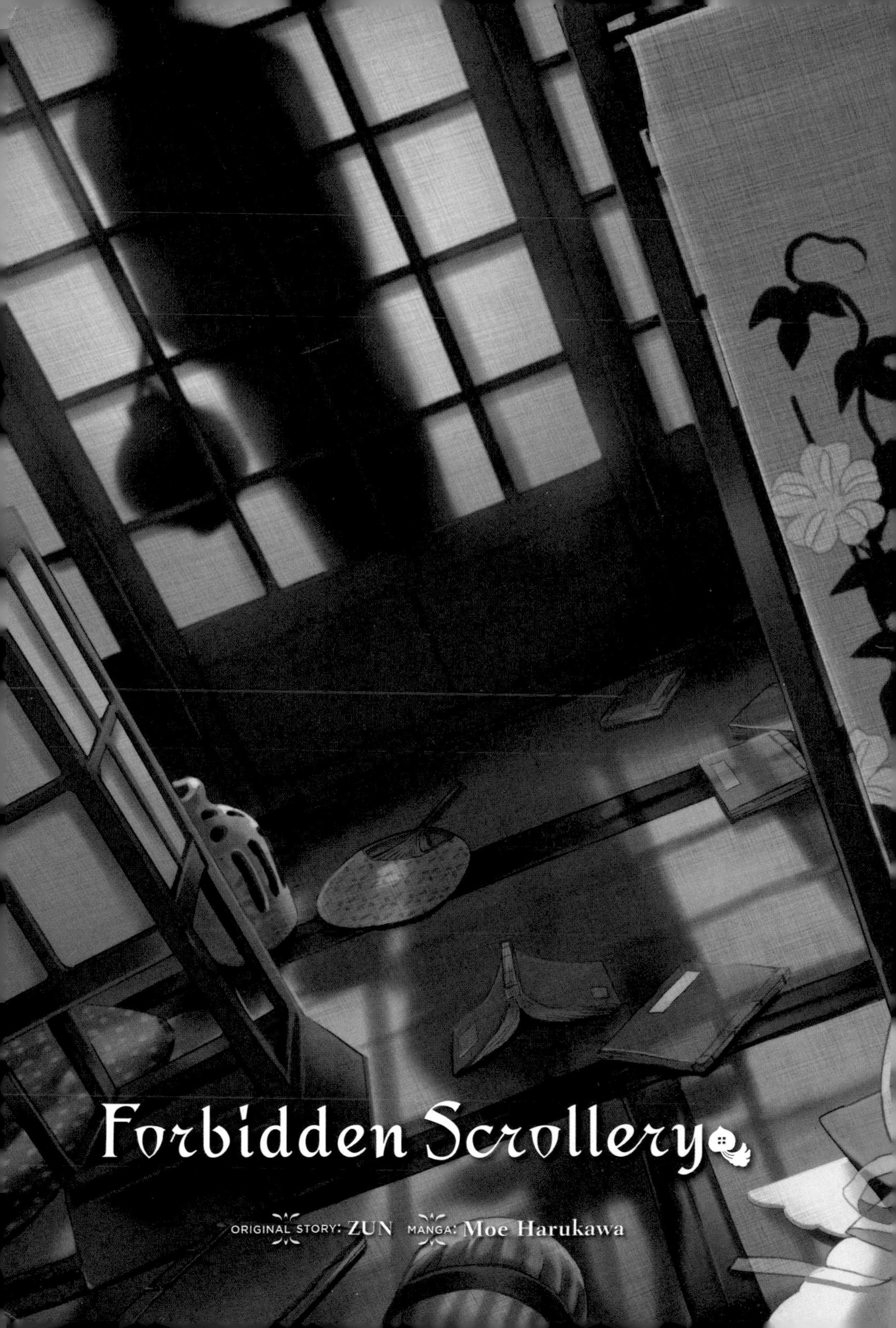
Forbidden Scrollery
ORIGINAL STORY: ZUN MANGA: Moe Harukawa

CONTENTS

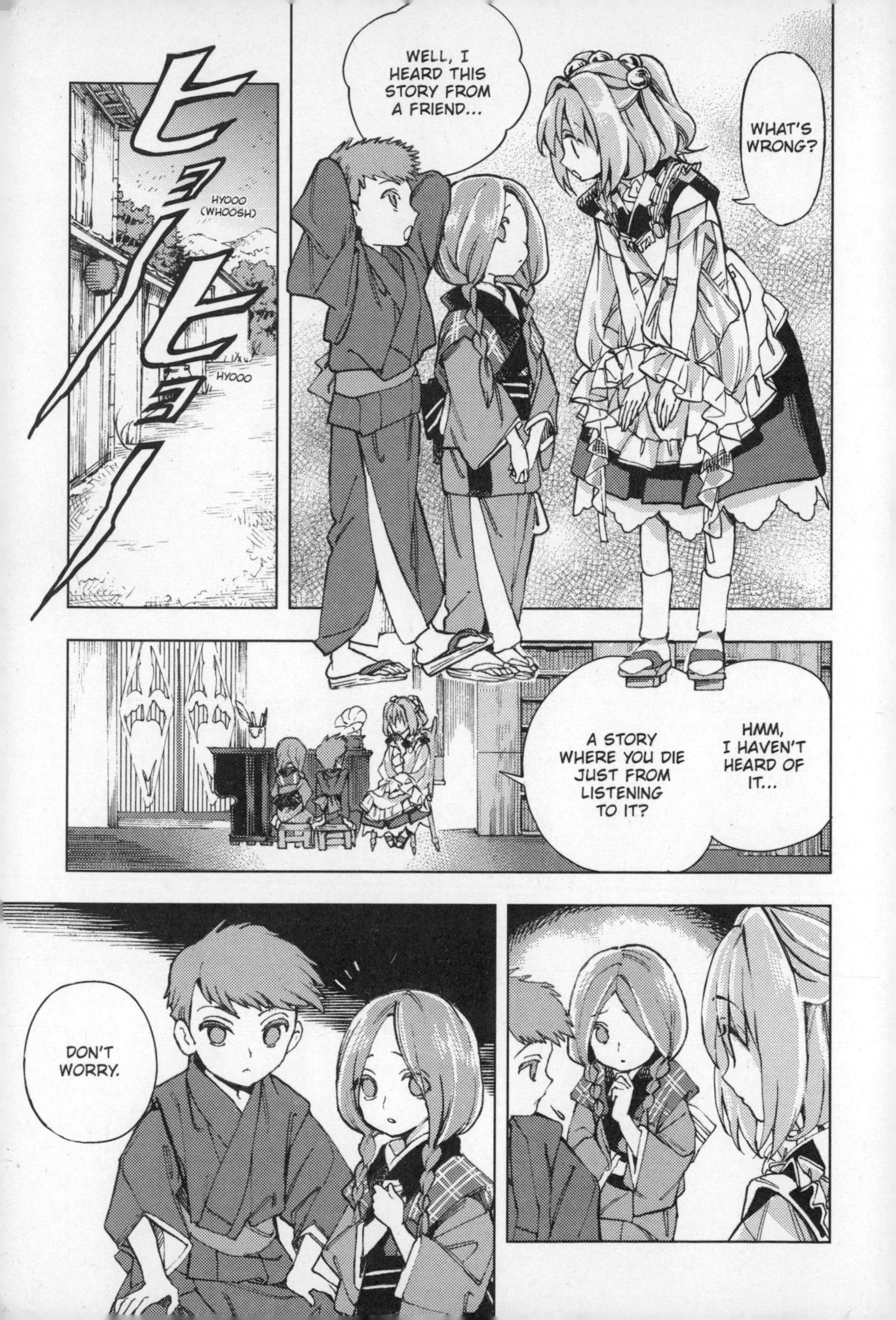
WHAT'S WRONG?
WELL, I HEARD THIS STORY FROM A FRIEND...
ヒョーヒョー
HYOOO (WHOOSH)
HYOOO
HMM, I HAVEN'T HEARD OF IT...
A STORY WHERE YOU DIE JUST FROM LISTENING TO IT?
DON'T WORRY.

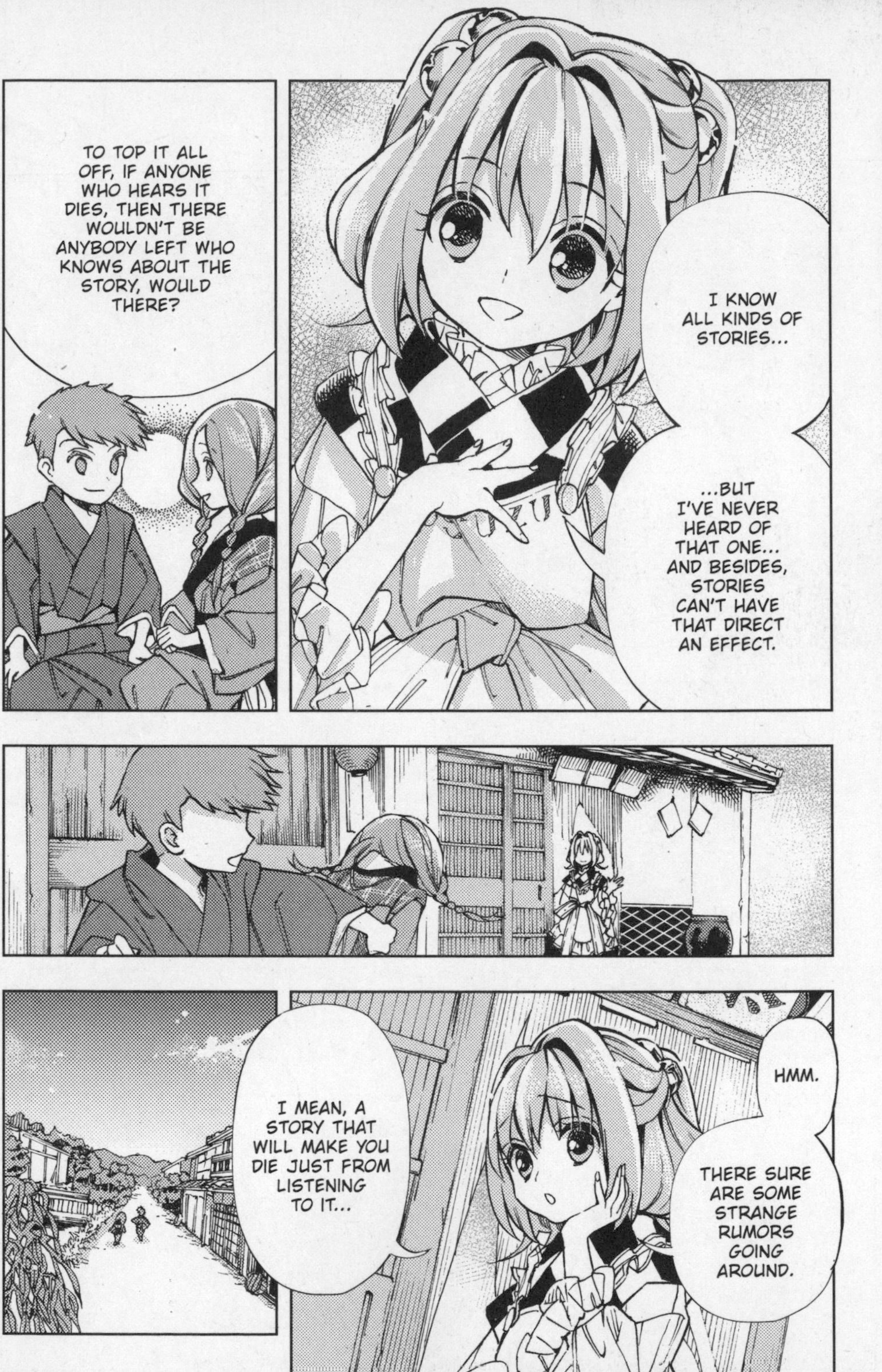
I KNOW ALL KINDS OF STORIES...
...BUT I'VE NEVER HEARD OF THAT ONE... AND BESIDES, STORIES CAN'T HAVE THAT DIRECT AN EFFECT.
TO TOP IT ALL OFF, IF ANYONE WHO HEARS IT DIES, THEN THERE WOULDN'T BE ANYBODY LEFT WHO KNOWS ABOUT THE STORY, WOULD THERE?
HMM.
THERE SURE ARE SOME STRANGE RUMORS GOING AROUND.
I MEAN, A STORY THAT WILL MAKE YOU DIE JUST FROM LISTENING TO IT...

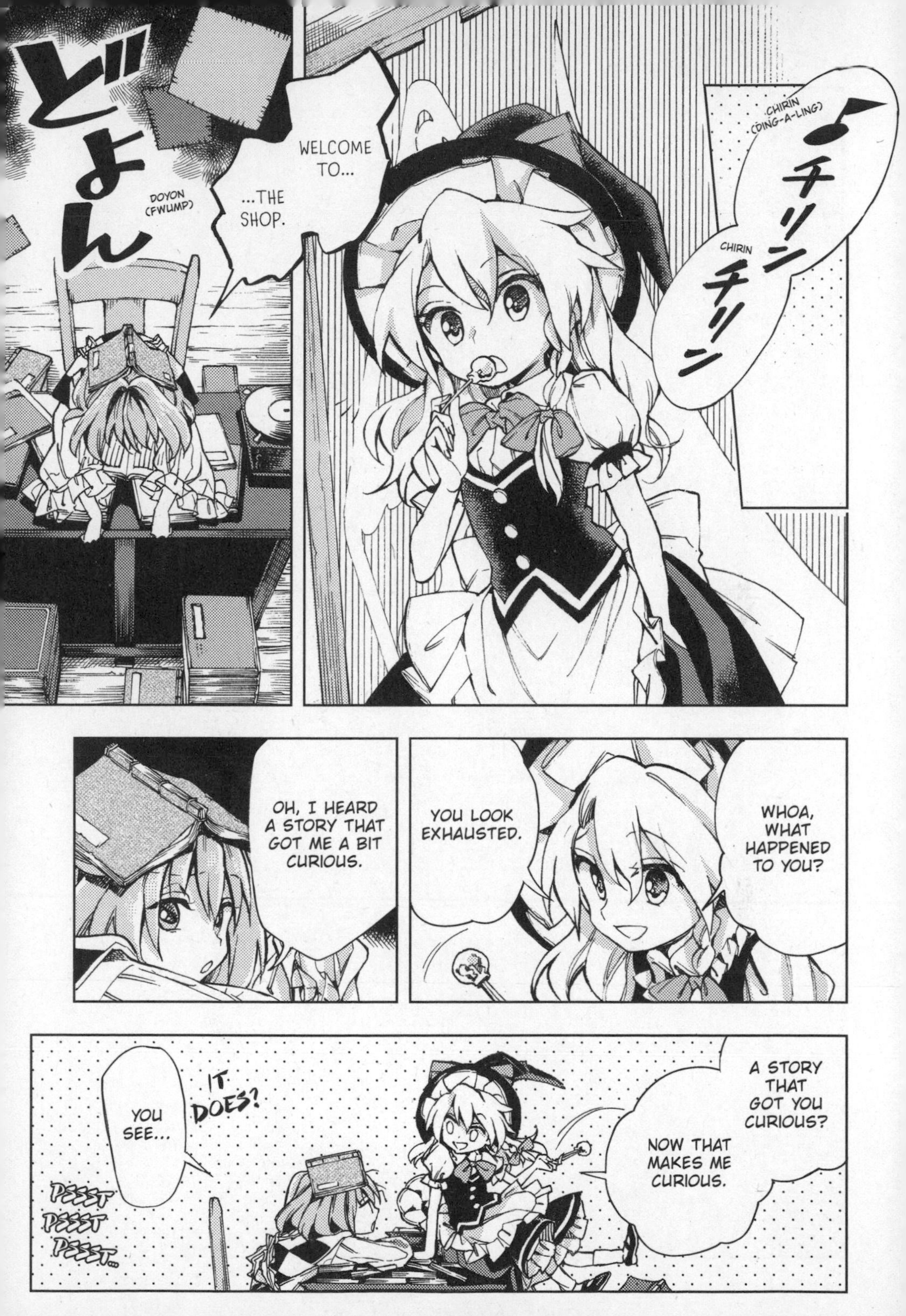
♪チリン
CHIRIN (DING-A-LING)
チリン
CHIRIN
どよん
DOYON (FWUMP)
WELCOME TO...
...THE SHOP.
WHOA, WHAT HAPPENED TO YOU?
YOU LOOK EXHAUSTED.
OH, I HEARD A STORY THAT GOT ME A BIT CURIOUS.
A STORY THAT GOT YOU CURIOUS?
NOW THAT MAKES ME CURIOUS.
IT DOES?
YOU SEE...
PSSST PSSST PSSST...

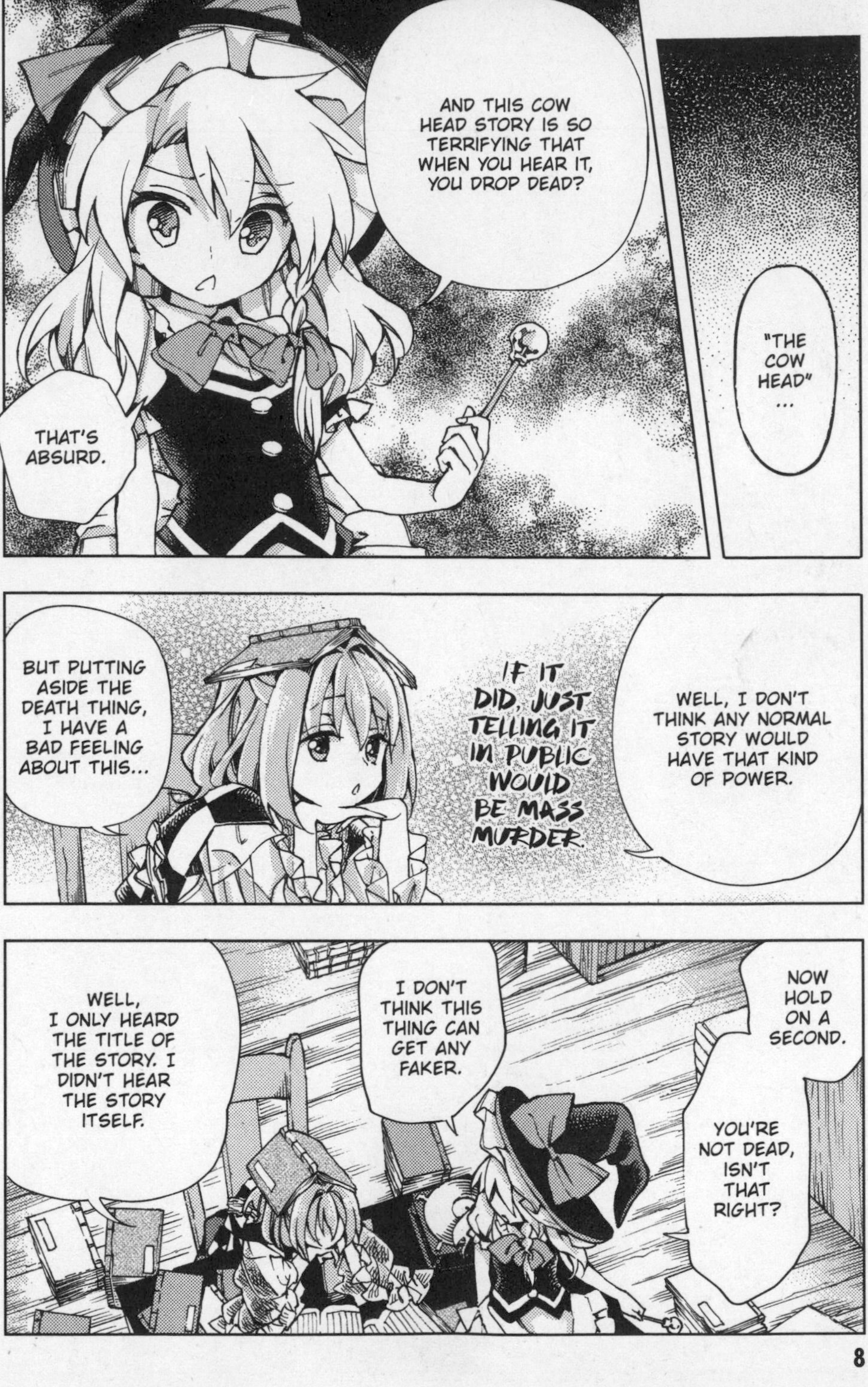
"THE COW HEAD"...
AND THIS COW HEAD STORY IS SO TERRIFYING THAT WHEN YOU HEAR IT, YOU DROP DEAD?
THAT'S ABSURD.
WELL, I DON'T THINK ANY NORMAL STORY WOULD HAVE THAT KIND OF POWER.
IF IT DID, JUST TELLING IT IN PUBLIC WOULD BE MASS MURDER.
BUT PUTTING ASIDE THE DEATH THING, I HAVE A BAD FEELING ABOUT THIS...
NOW HOLD ON A SECOND.
YOU'RE NOT DEAD, ISN'T THAT RIGHT?
I DON'T THINK THIS THING CAN GET ANY FAKER.
WELL, I ONLY HEARD THE TITLE OF THE STORY. I DIDN'T HEAR THE STORY ITSELF.

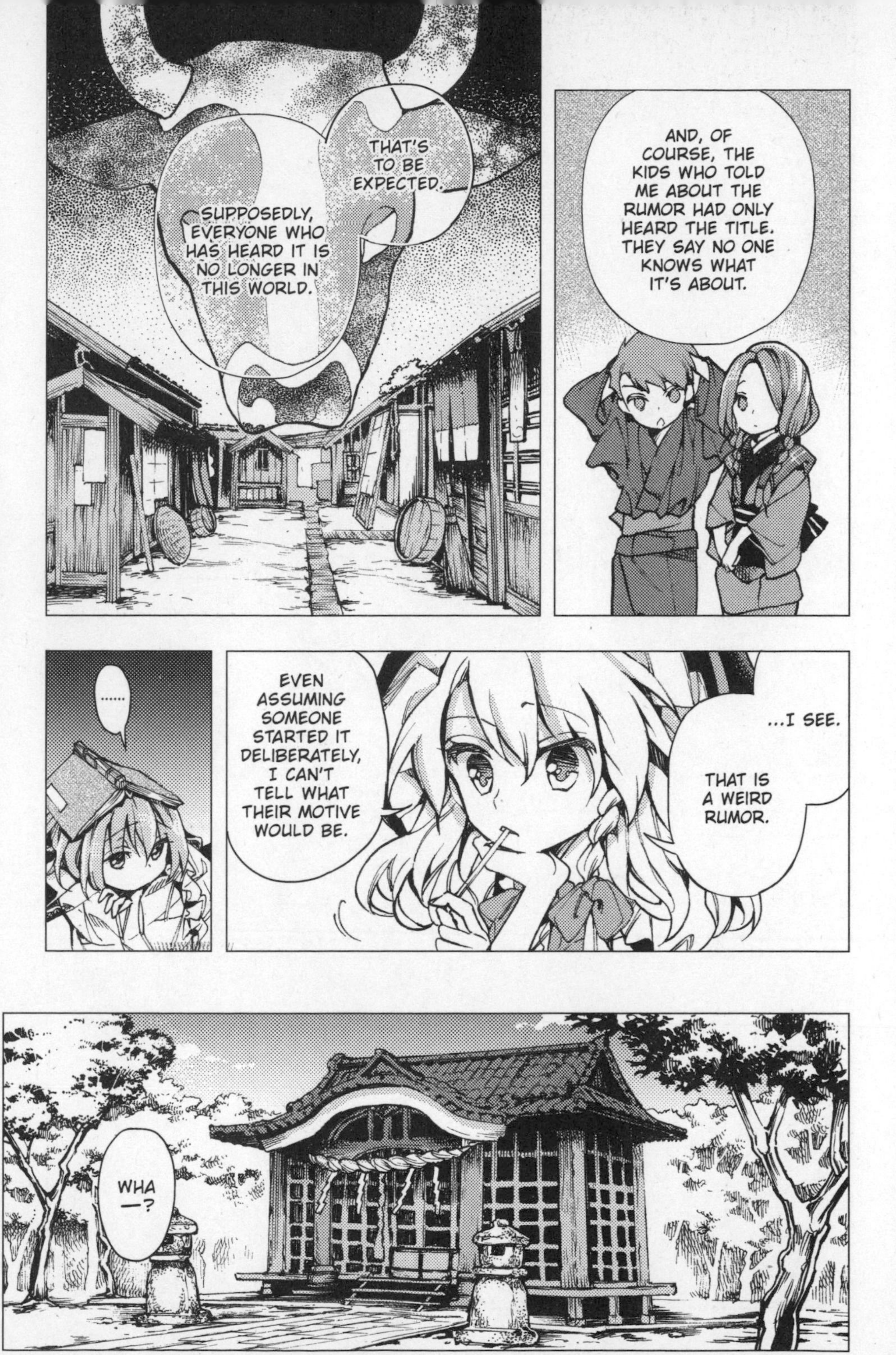
AND, OF COURSE, THE KIDS WHO TOLD ME ABOUT THE RUMOR HAD ONLY HEARD THE TITLE. THEY SAY NO ONE KNOWS WHAT IT'S ABOUT.
THAT'S TO BE EXPECTED.
SUPPOSEDLY, EVERYONE WHO HAS HEARD IT IS NO LONGER IN THIS WORLD.
...I SEE.
THAT IS A WEIRD RUMOR.
EVEN ASSUMING SOMEONE STARTED IT DELIBERATELY, I CAN'T TELL WHAT THEIR MOTIVE WOULD BE.
......
WHA—?

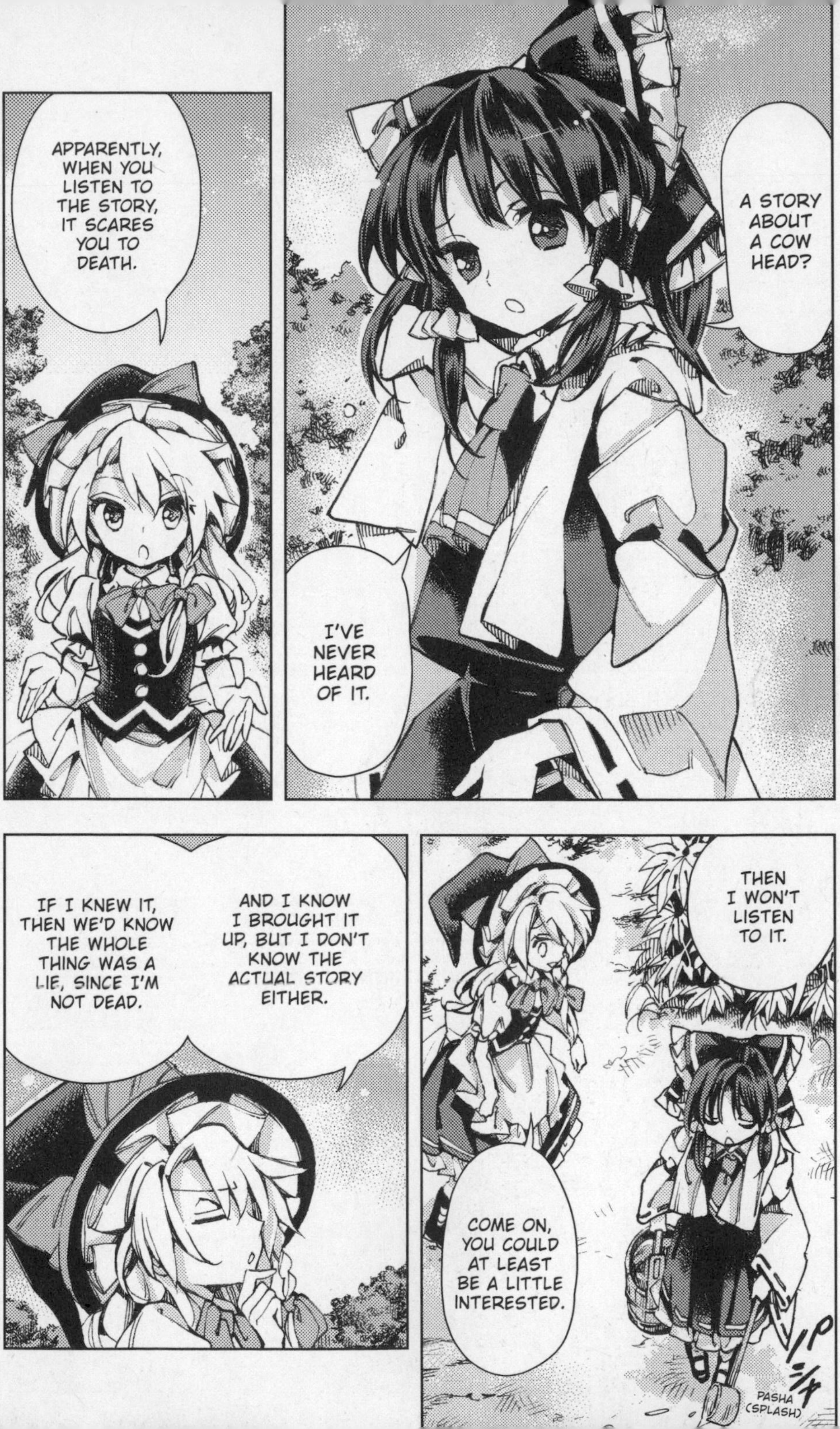
A STORY ABOUT A COW HEAD?
I'VE NEVER HEARD OF IT.
APPARENTLY, WHEN YOU LISTEN TO THE STORY, IT SCARES YOU TO DEATH.
THEN I WON'T LISTEN TO IT.
COME ON, YOU COULD AT LEAST BE A LITTLE INTERESTED.
PASHA (SPLASH)
AND I KNOW I BROUGHT IT UP, BUT I DON'T KNOW THE ACTUAL STORY EITHER.
IF I KNEW IT, THEN WE'D KNOW THE WHOLE THING WAS A LIE, SINCE I'M NOT DEAD.

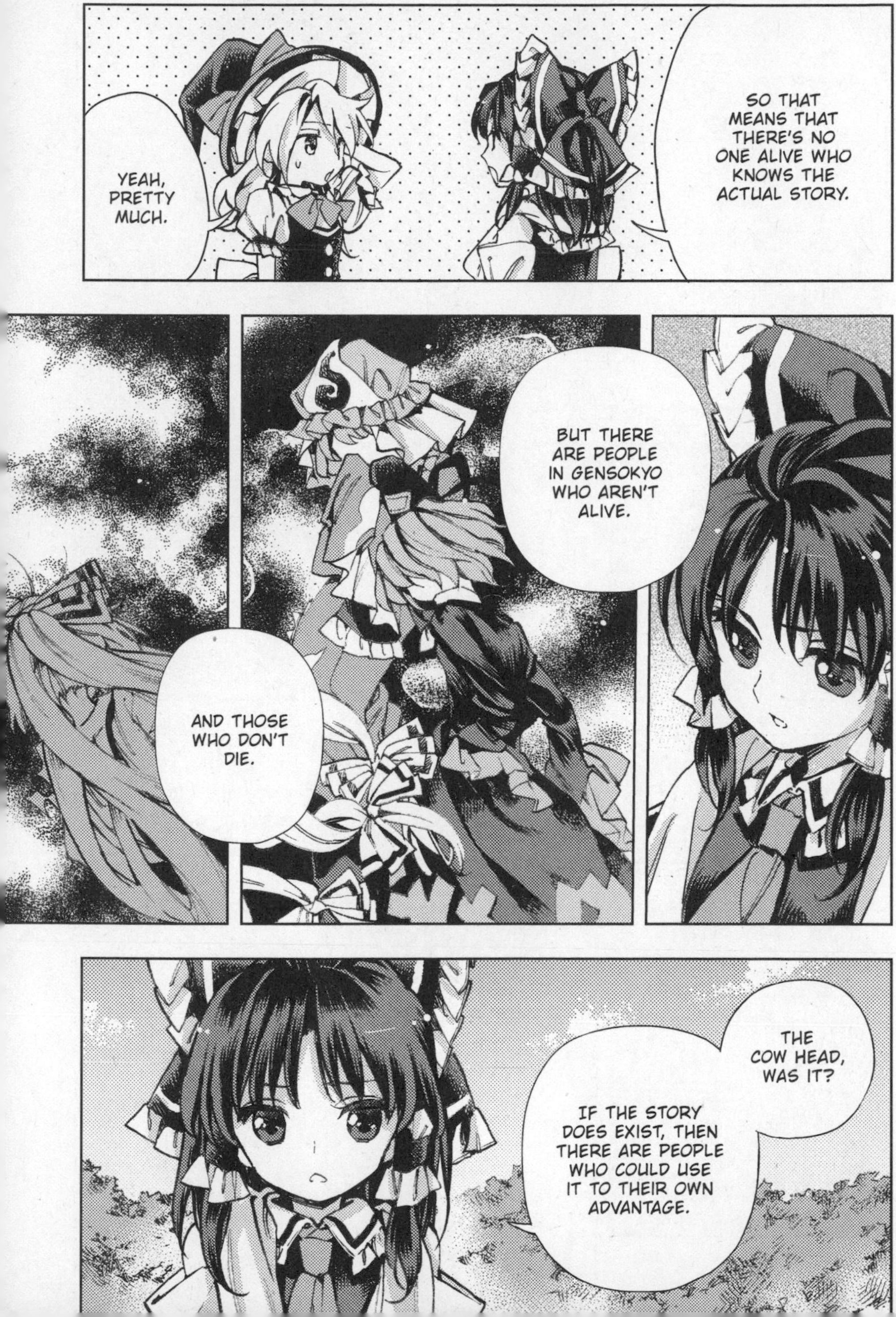
SO THAT MEANS THAT THERE'S NO ONE ALIVE WHO KNOWS THE ACTUAL STORY.
YEAH, PRETTY MUCH.
BUT THERE ARE PEOPLE IN GENSOKYO WHO AREN'T ALIVE.
AND THOSE WHO DON'T DIE.
THE COW HEAD, WAS IT?
IF THE STORY DOES EXIST, THEN THERE ARE PEOPLE WHO COULD USE IT TO THEIR OWN ADVANTAGE.

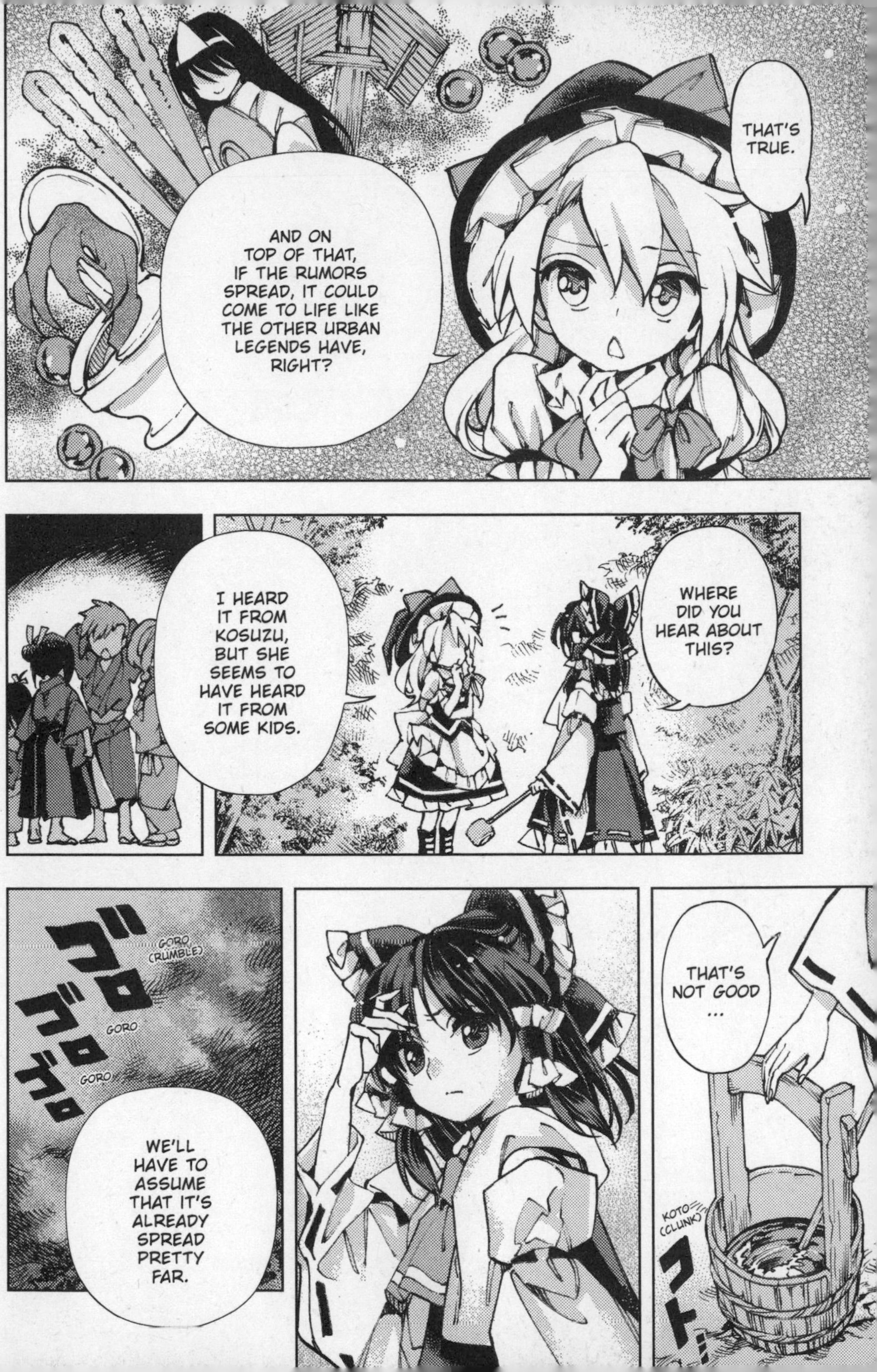
THAT'S TRUE.
AND ON TOP OF THAT, IF THE RUMORS SPREAD, IT COULD COME TO LIFE LIKE THE OTHER URBAN LEGENDS HAVE, RIGHT?
WHERE DID YOU HEAR ABOUT THIS?
I HEARD IT FROM KOSUZU, BUT SHE SEEMS TO HAVE HEARD IT FROM SOME KIDS.
THAT'S NOT GOOD ...
KOTO (CLUNK)
GORO (RUMBLE)
GORO
GORO
WE'LL HAVE TO ASSUME THAT IT'S ALREADY SPREAD PRETTY FAR.

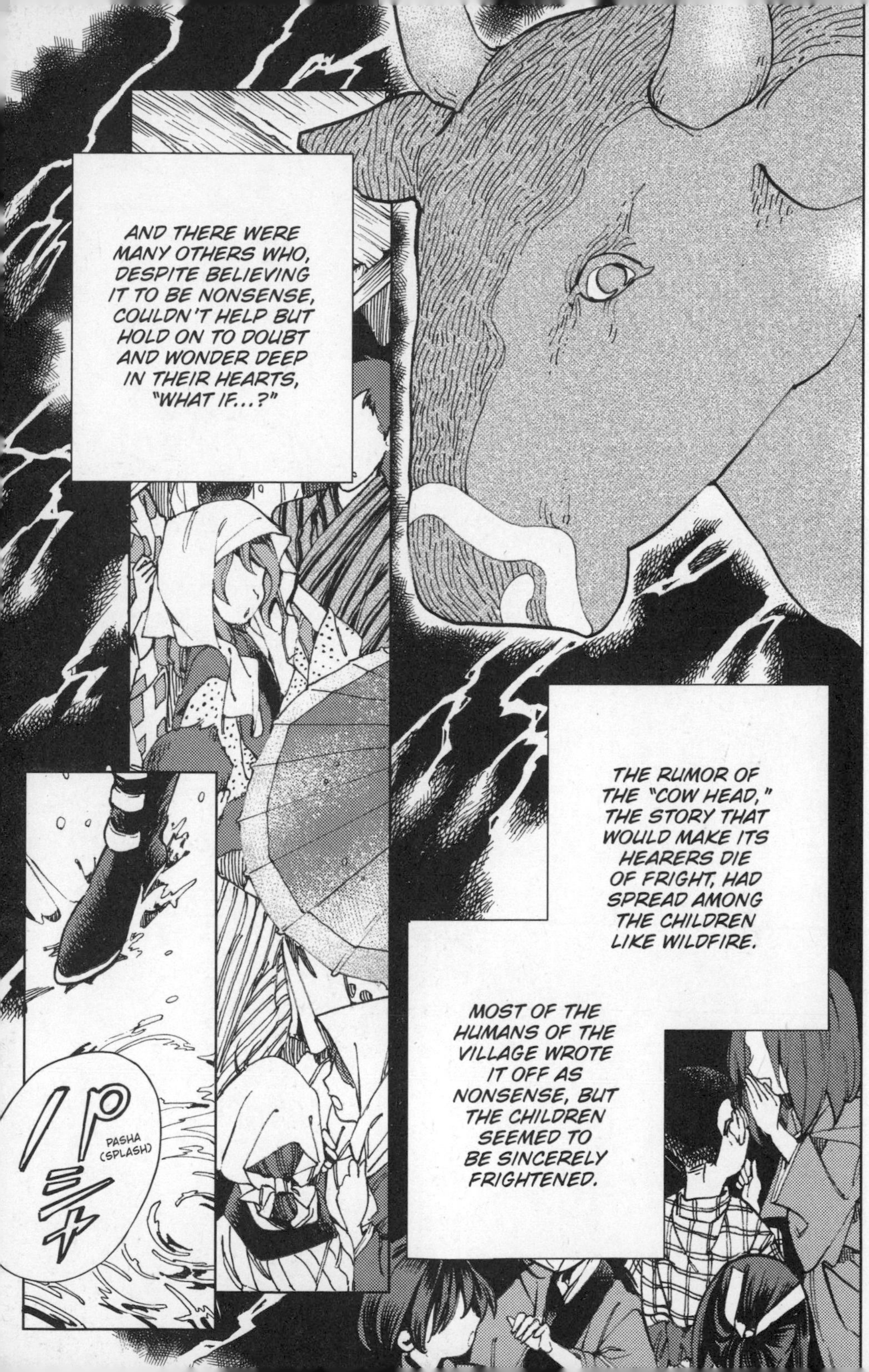
THE RUMOR OF THE "COW HEAD," THE STORY THAT WOULD MAKE ITS HEARERS DIE OF FRIGHT, HAD SPREAD AMONG THE CHILDREN LIKE WILDFIRE.
MOST OF THE HUMANS OF THE VILLAGE WROTE IT OFF AS NONSENSE, BUT THE CHILDREN SEEMED TO BE SINCERELY FRIGHTENED.
AND THERE WERE MANY OTHERS WHO, DESPITE BELIEVING IT TO BE NONSENSE, COULDN'T HELP BUT HOLD ON TO DOUBT AND WONDER DEEP IN THEIR HEARTS, "WHAT IF...?"
PASHA (SPLASH)

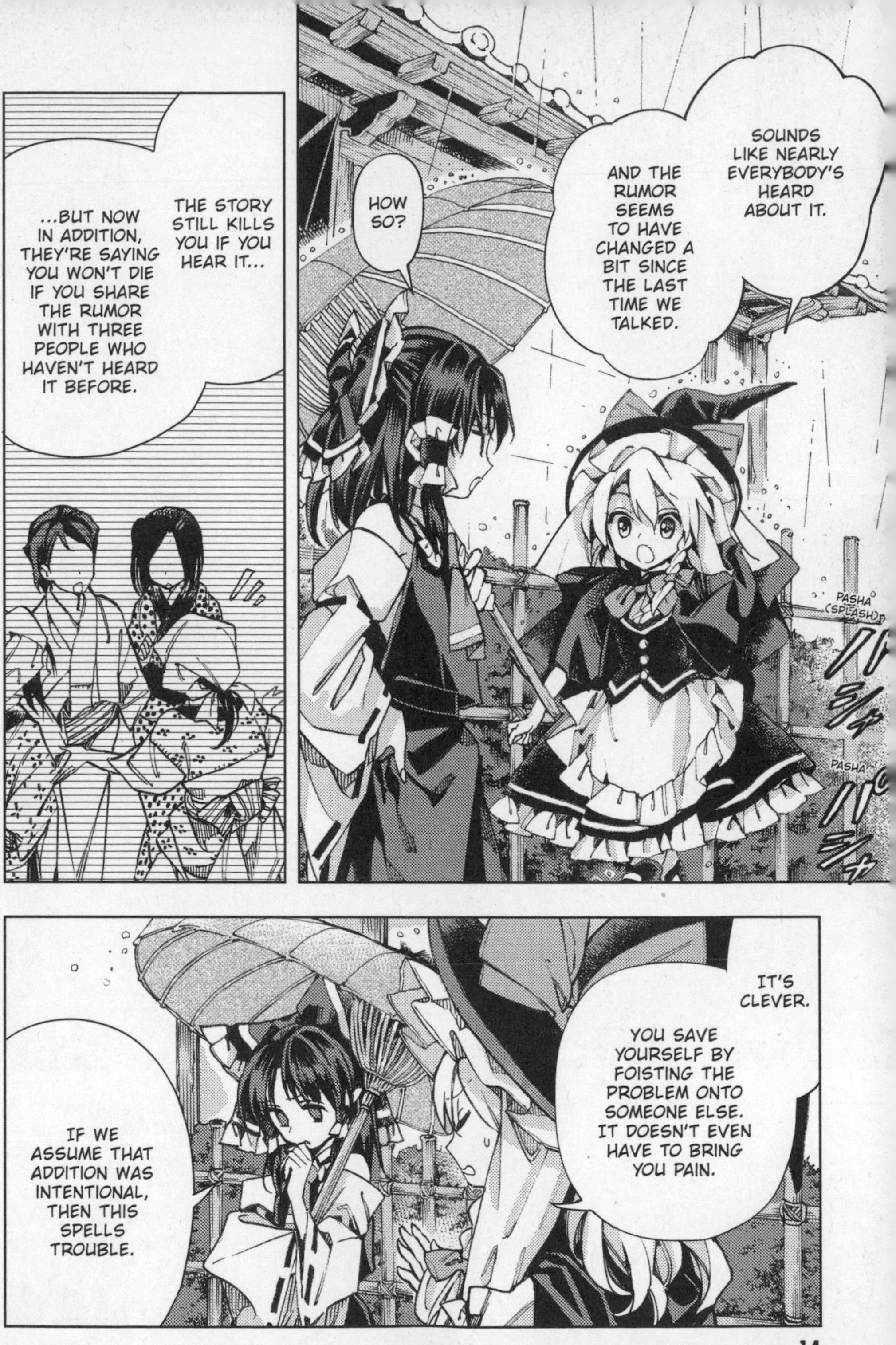
SOUNDS LIKE NEARLY EVERYBODY'S HEARD ABOUT IT.
AND THE RUMOR SEEMS TO HAVE CHANGED A BIT SINCE THE LAST TIME WE TALKED.
HOW SO?
PASHA (SPLASH)
PASHA
THE STORY STILL KILLS YOU IF YOU HEAR IT...
...BUT NOW IN ADDITION, THEY'RE SAYING YOU WON'T DIE IF YOU SHARE THE RUMOR WITH THREE PEOPLE WHO HAVEN'T HEARD IT BEFORE.
IT'S CLEVER.
YOU SAVE YOURSELF BY FOISTING THE PROBLEM ONTO SOMEONE ELSE. IT DOESN'T EVEN HAVE TO BRING YOU PAIN.
IF WE ASSUME THAT ADDITION WAS INTENTIONAL, THEN THIS SPELLS TROUBLE.

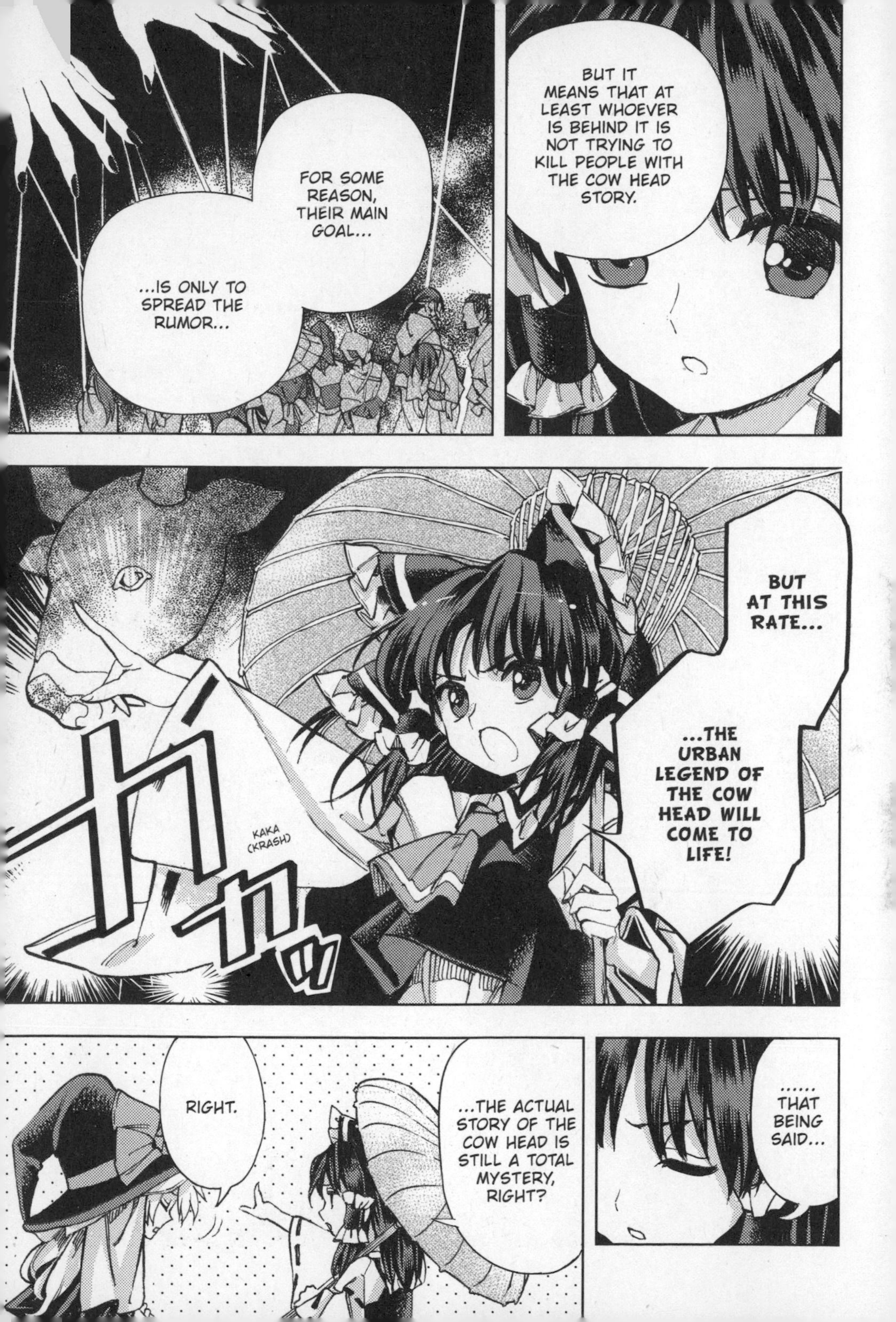
BUT IT MEANS THAT AT LEAST WHOEVER IS BEHIND IT IS NOT TRYING TO KILL PEOPLE WITH THE COW HEAD STORY.
FOR SOME REASON, THEIR MAIN GOAL...
...IS ONLY TO SPREAD THE RUMOR...
BUT AT THIS RATE...
...THE URBAN LEGEND OF THE COW HEAD WILL COME TO LIFE!
KAKA (KRASH)
...... THAT BEING SAID...
...THE ACTUAL STORY OF THE COW HEAD IS STILL A TOTAL MYSTERY, RIGHT?
RIGHT.

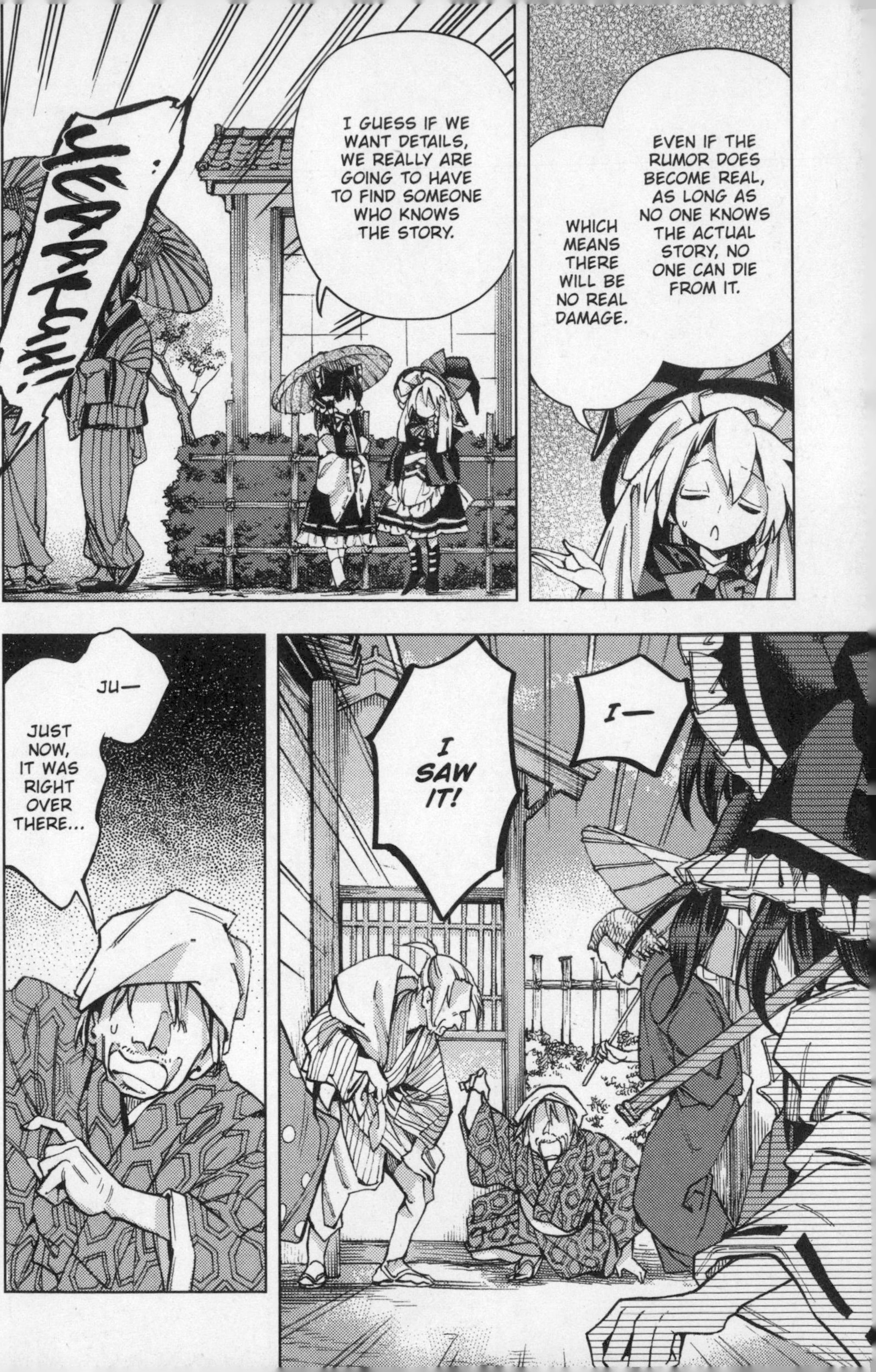
EVEN IF THE RUMOR DOES BECOME REAL, AS LONG AS NO ONE KNOWS THE ACTUAL STORY, NO ONE CAN DIE FROM IT.
WHICH MEANS THERE WILL BE NO REAL DAMAGE.
I GUESS IF WE WANT DETAILS, WE REALLY ARE GOING TO HAVE TO FIND SOMEONE WHO KNOWS THE STORY.
YEAAAUGH!
I—
I SAW IT!
JU—
JUST NOW, IT WAS RIGHT OVER THERE...

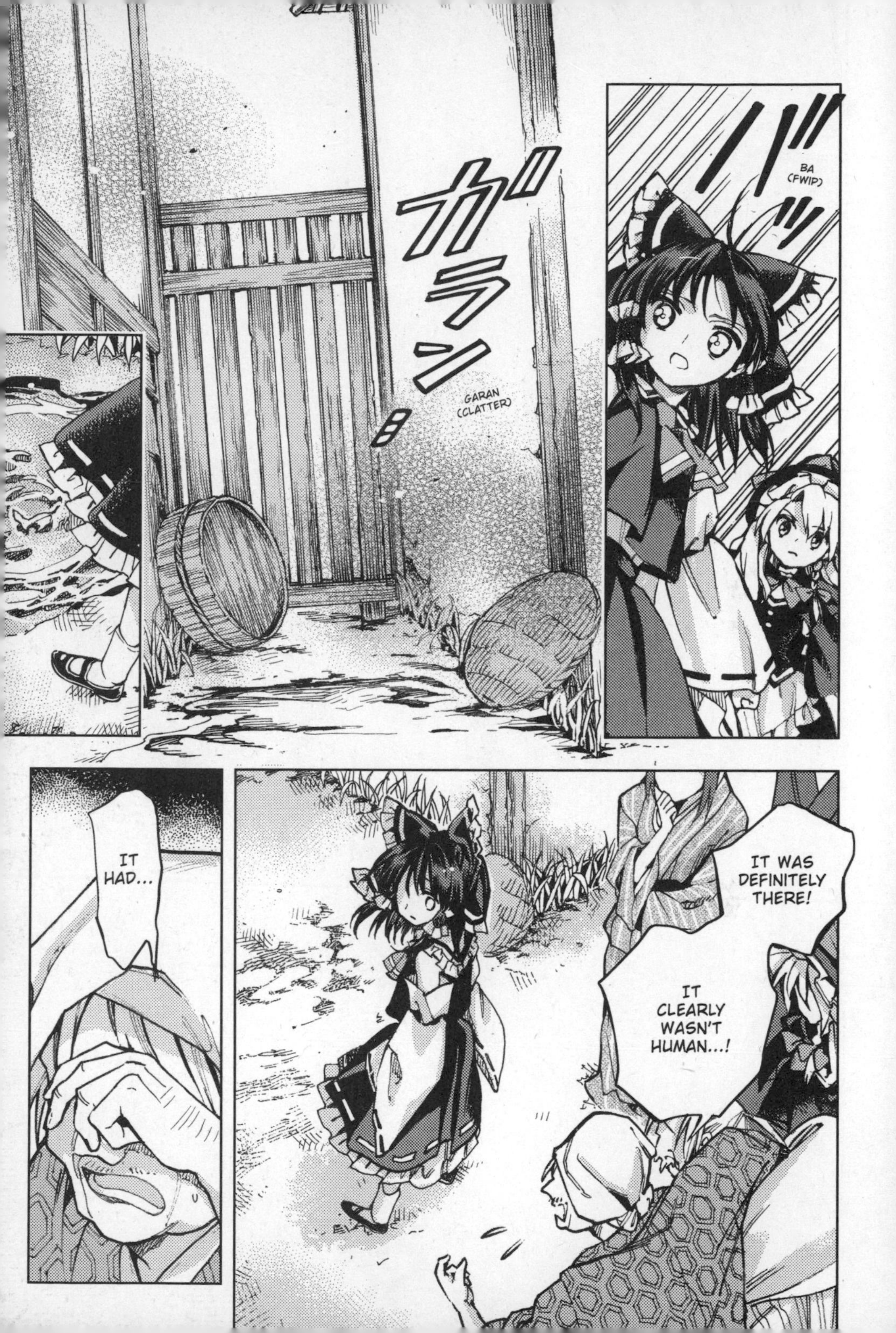
バッ
BA
(FWIP)
ガラン…
GARAN
(CLATTER)
IT WAS DEFINITELY THERE!
IT CLEARLY WASN'T HUMAN...!
IT HAD...

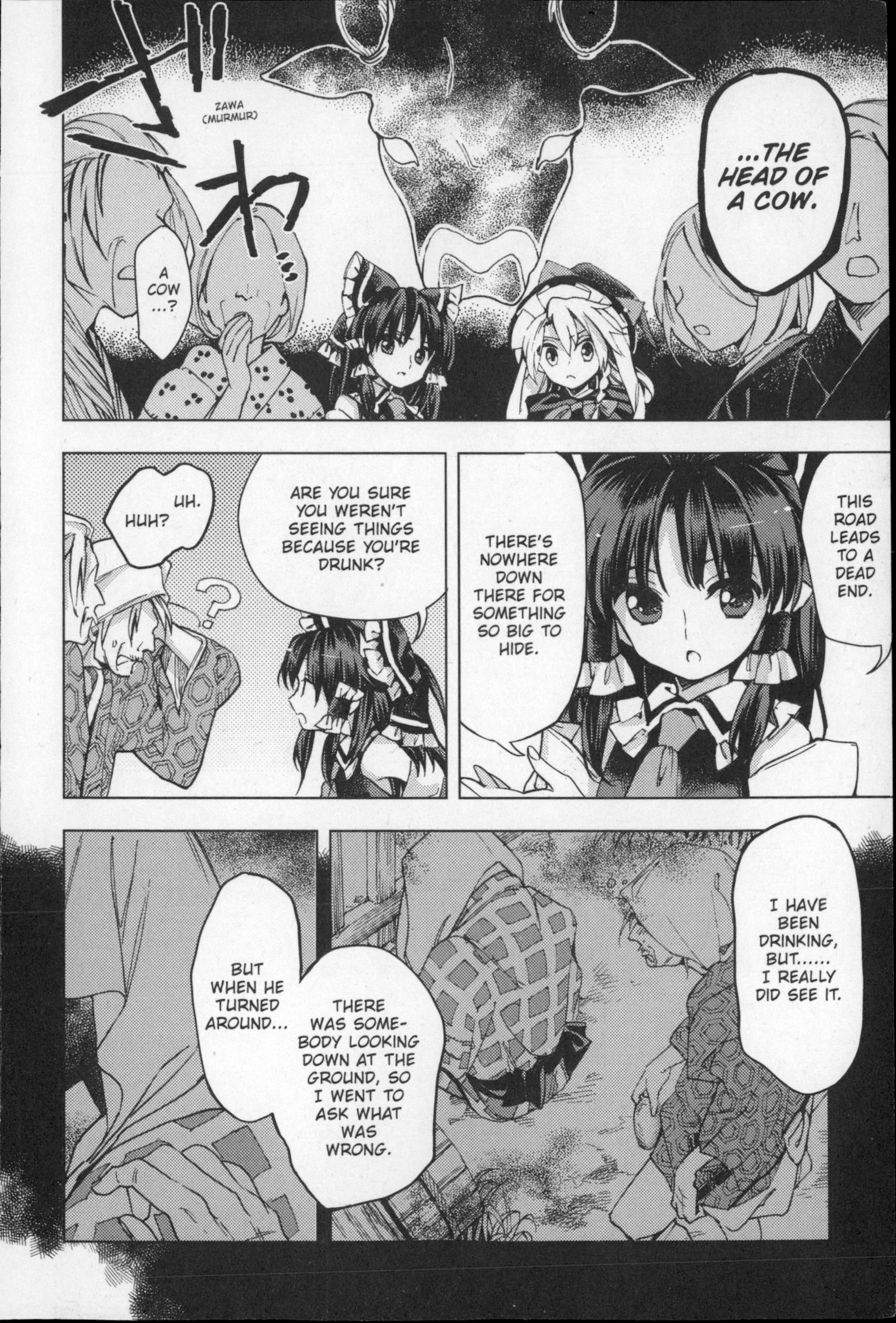
...THE HEAD OF A COW.
ZAWA (MURMUR)
A COW ...?
THIS ROAD LEADS TO A DEAD END.
THERE'S NOWHERE DOWN THERE FOR SOMETHING SO BIG TO HIDE.
ARE YOU SURE YOU WEREN'T SEEING THINGS BECAUSE YOU'RE DRUNK?
UH. HUH?
I HAVE BEEN DRINKING, BUT...... I REALLY DID SEE IT.
THERE WAS SOME-BODY LOOKING DOWN AT THE GROUND, SO I WENT TO ASK WHAT WAS WRONG.
BUT WHEN HE TURNED AROUND...

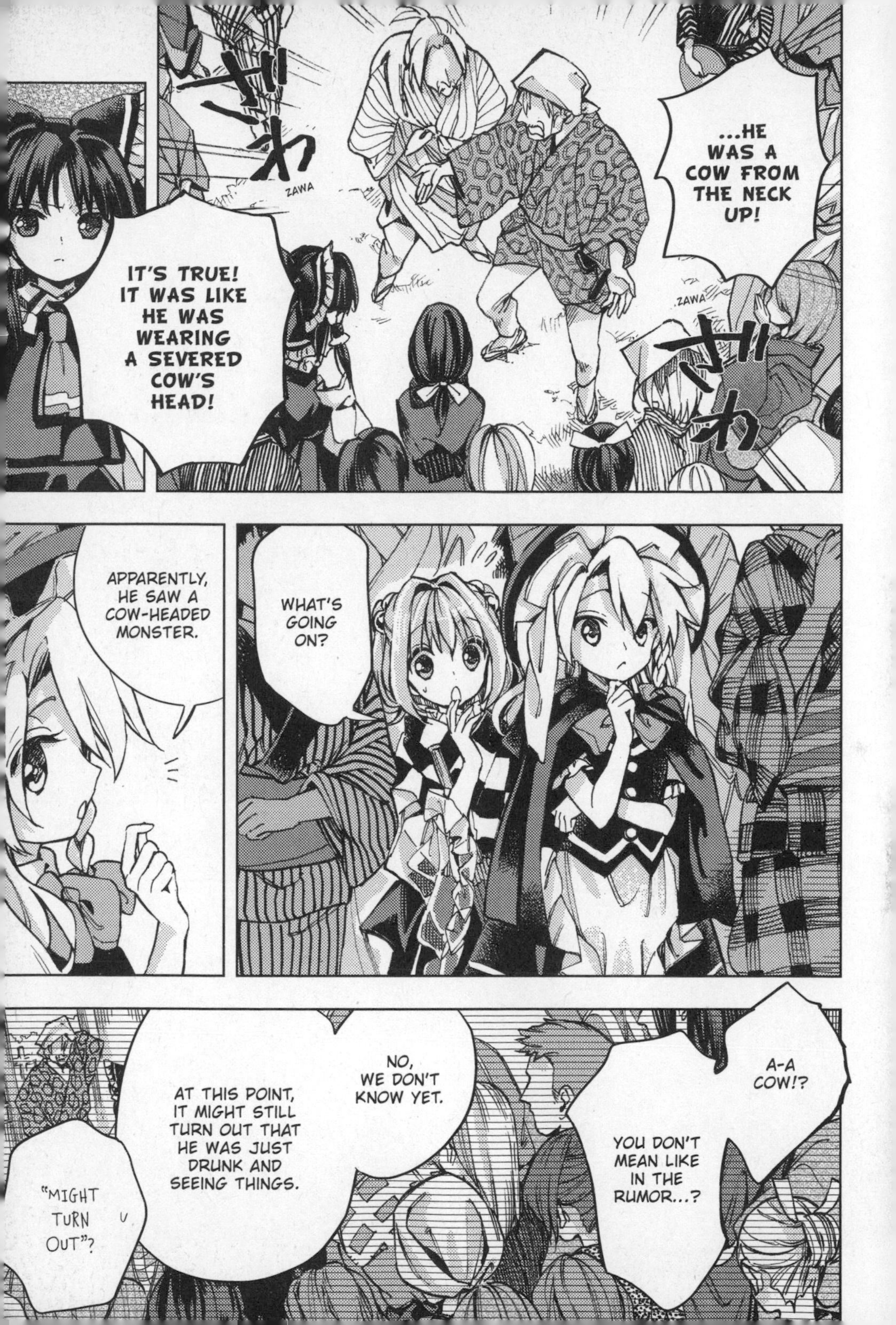
...HE WAS A COW FROM THE NECK UP!
ZAWA
ざわ
IT'S TRUE! IT WAS LIKE HE WAS WEARING A SEVERED COW'S HEAD!
ざわ
ZAWA
WHAT'S GOING ON?
APPARENTLY, HE SAW A COW-HEADED MONSTER.
A-A COW!?
YOU DON'T MEAN LIKE IN THE RUMOR...?
NO, WE DON'T KNOW YET.
AT THIS POINT, IT MIGHT STILL TURN OUT THAT HE WAS JUST DRUNK AND SEEING THINGS.
"MIGHT TURN OUT"?

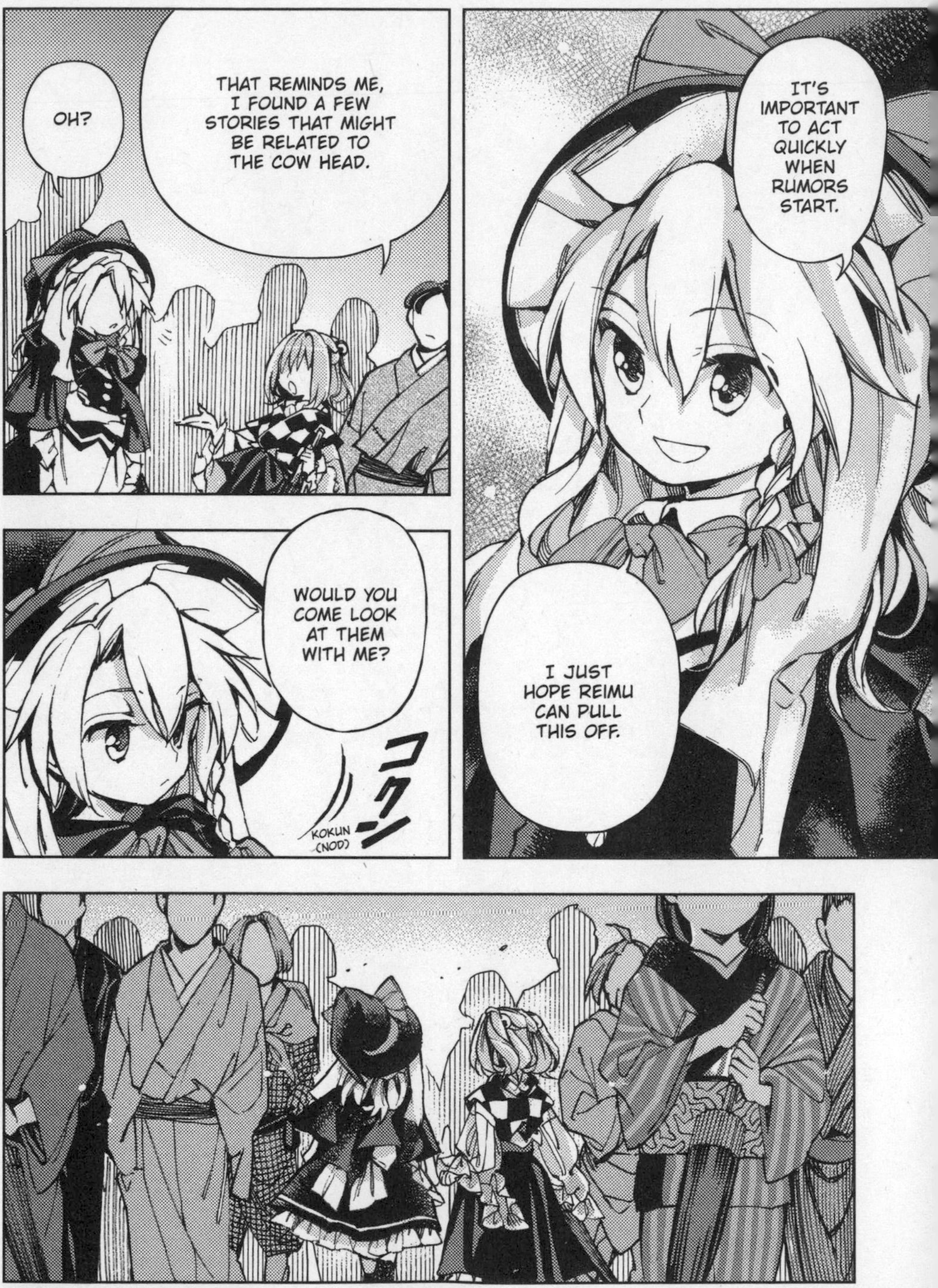
IT'S IMPORTANT TO ACT QUICKLY WHEN RUMORS START.
I JUST HOPE REIMU CAN PULL THIS OFF.
THAT REMINDS ME, I FOUND A FEW STORIES THAT MIGHT BE RELATED TO THE COW HEAD.
OH?
WOULD YOU COME LOOK AT THEM WITH ME?
コクン
KOKUN (NOD)

Chapter 30 To be continued

Forbidden Scrollery

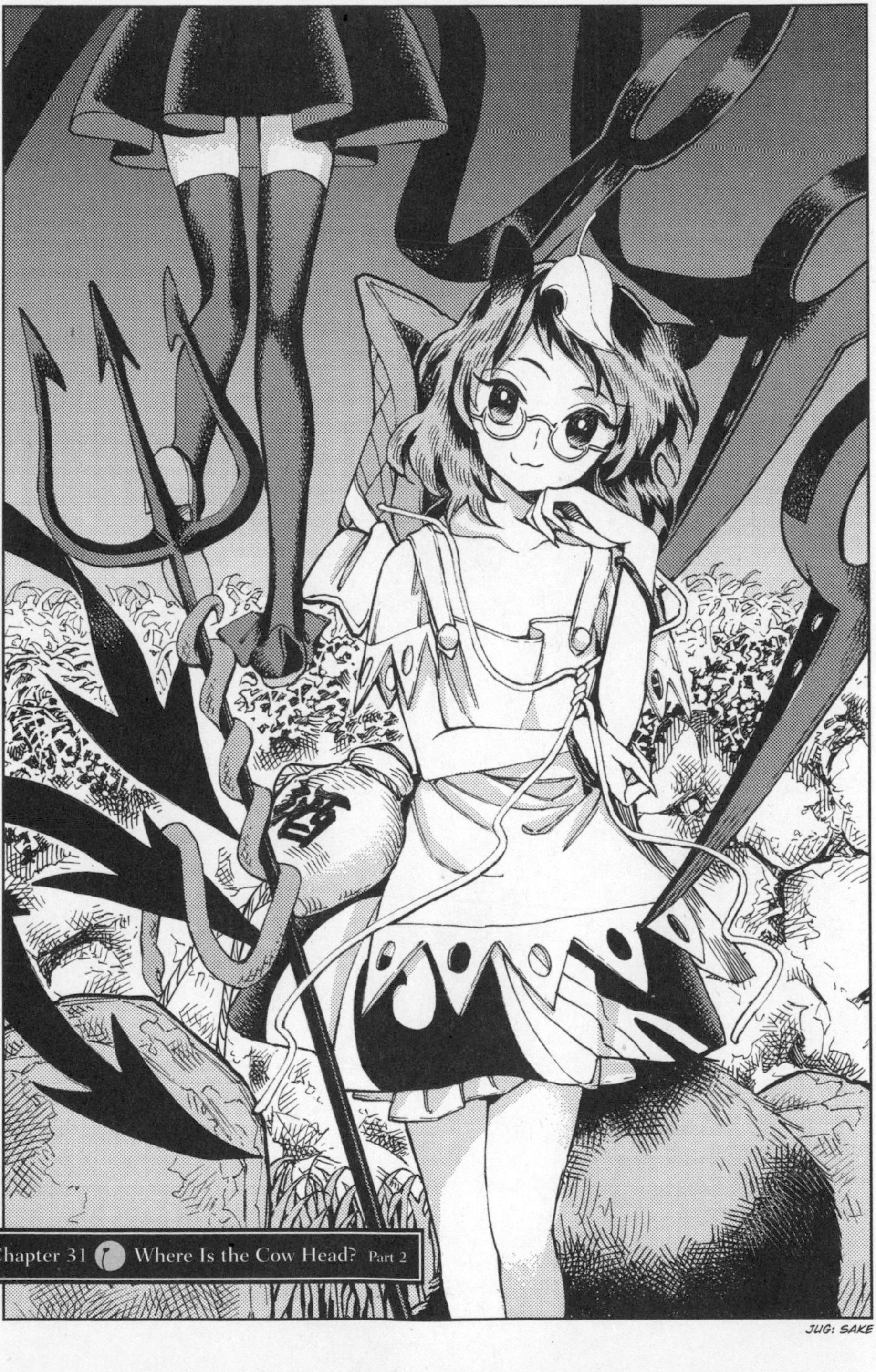
Chapter 31 Where Is the Cow Head? Part 2
JUG: SAKE

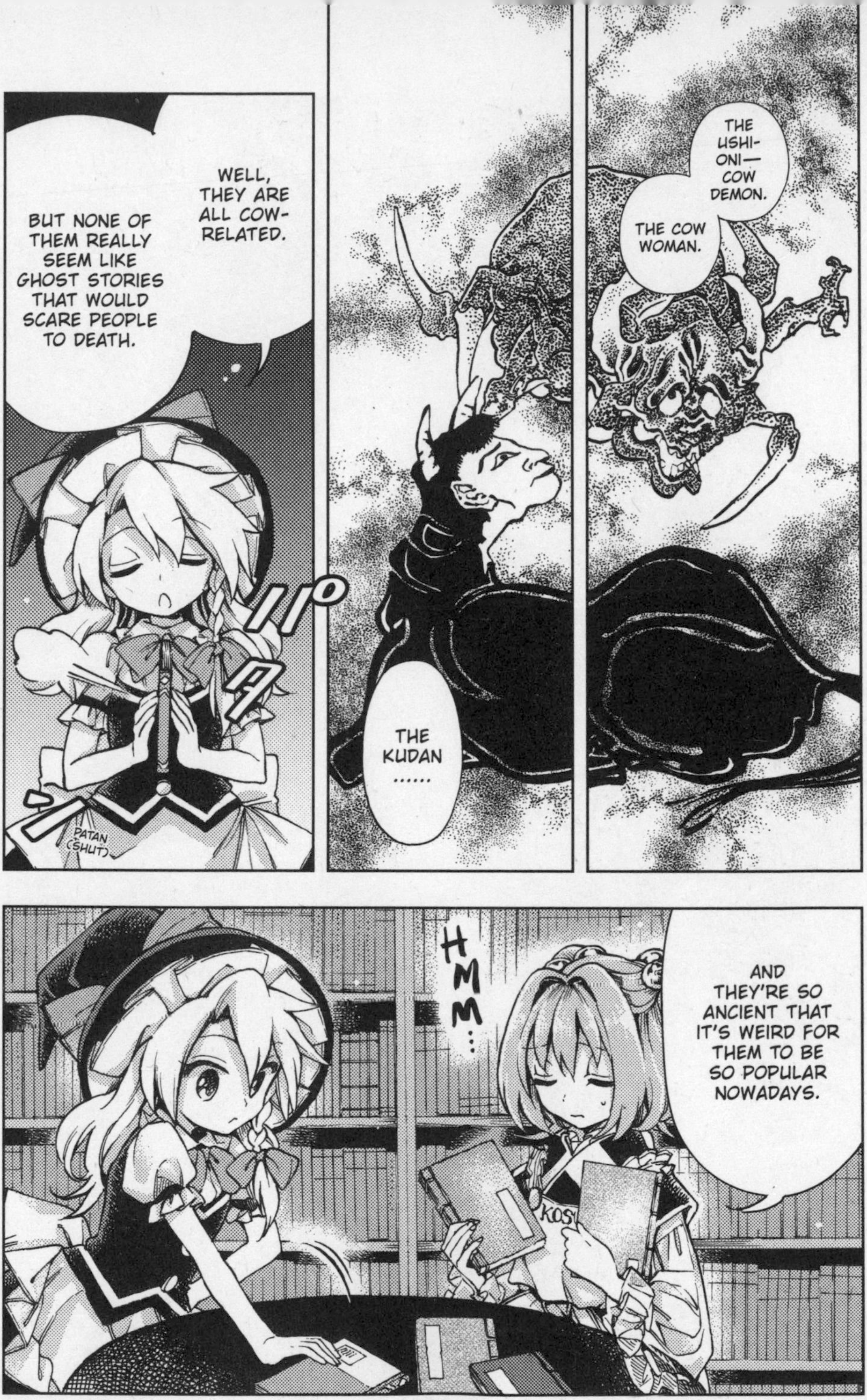
THE USHI-ONI—COW DEMON.
THE COW WOMAN.
THE KUDAN ......
WELL, THEY ARE ALL COW-RELATED.
BUT NONE OF THEM REALLY SEEM LIKE GHOST STORIES THAT WOULD SCARE PEOPLE TO DEATH.
PATAN (SHUT)
AND THEY'RE SO ANCIENT THAT IT'S WEIRD FOR THEM TO BE SO POPULAR NOWADAYS.
HMM...

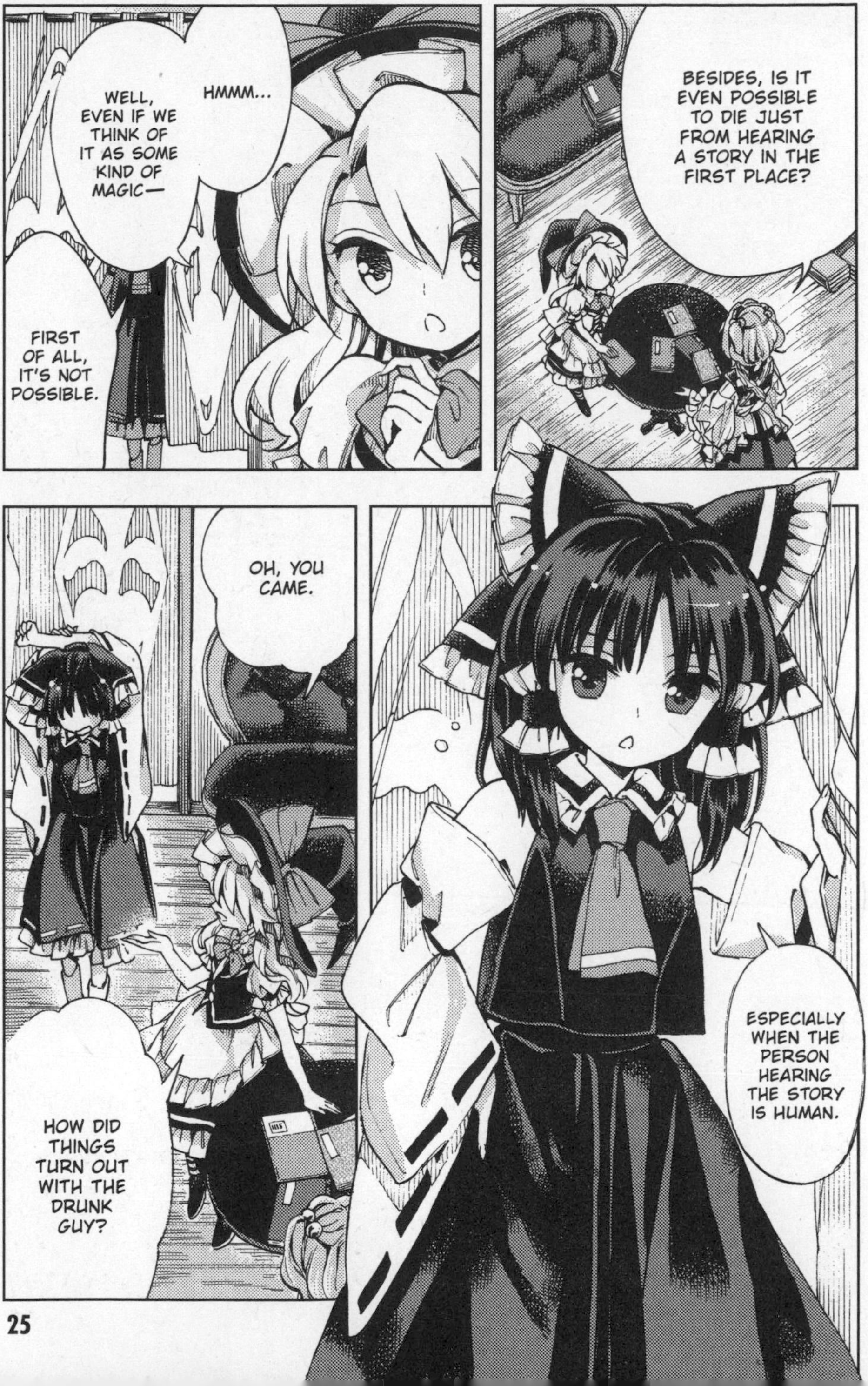
BESIDES, IS IT EVEN POSSIBLE TO DIE JUST FROM HEARING A STORY IN THE FIRST PLACE?
HMMM...
WELL, EVEN IF WE THINK OF IT AS SOME KIND OF MAGIC—
FIRST OF ALL, IT'S NOT POSSIBLE.
ESPECIALLY WHEN THE PERSON HEARING THE STORY IS HUMAN.
OH, YOU CAME.
HOW DID THINGS TURN OUT WITH THE DRUNK GUY?

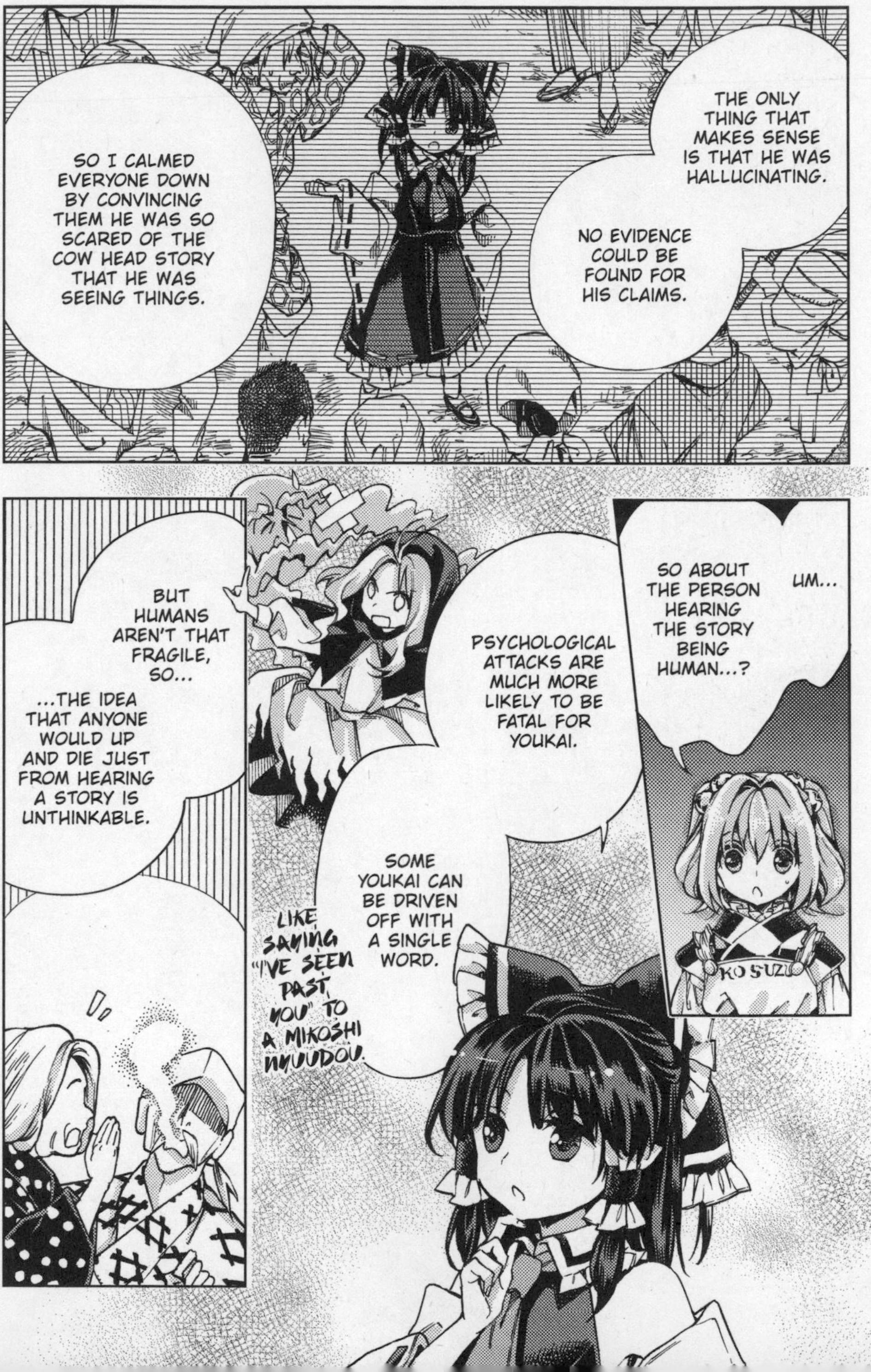
THE ONLY THING THAT MAKES SENSE IS THAT HE WAS HALLUCINATING.
NO EVIDENCE COULD BE FOUND FOR HIS CLAIMS.
SO I CALMED EVERYONE DOWN BY CONVINCING THEM HE WAS SO SCARED OF THE COW HEAD STORY THAT HE WAS SEEING THINGS.
UM...
SO ABOUT THE PERSON HEARING THE STORY BEING HUMAN...?
PSYCHOLOGICAL ATTACKS ARE MUCH MORE LIKELY TO BE FATAL FOR YOUKAI.
SOME YOUKAI CAN BE DRIVEN OFF WITH A SINGLE WORD.
LIKE SAYING "I'VE SEEN PAST YOU" TO A MIKOSHI NYUUDOU.
KOSUZU
BUT HUMANS AREN'T THAT FRAGILE, SO...
...THE IDEA THAT ANYONE WOULD UP AND DIE JUST FROM HEARING A STORY IS UNTHINKABLE.
!!

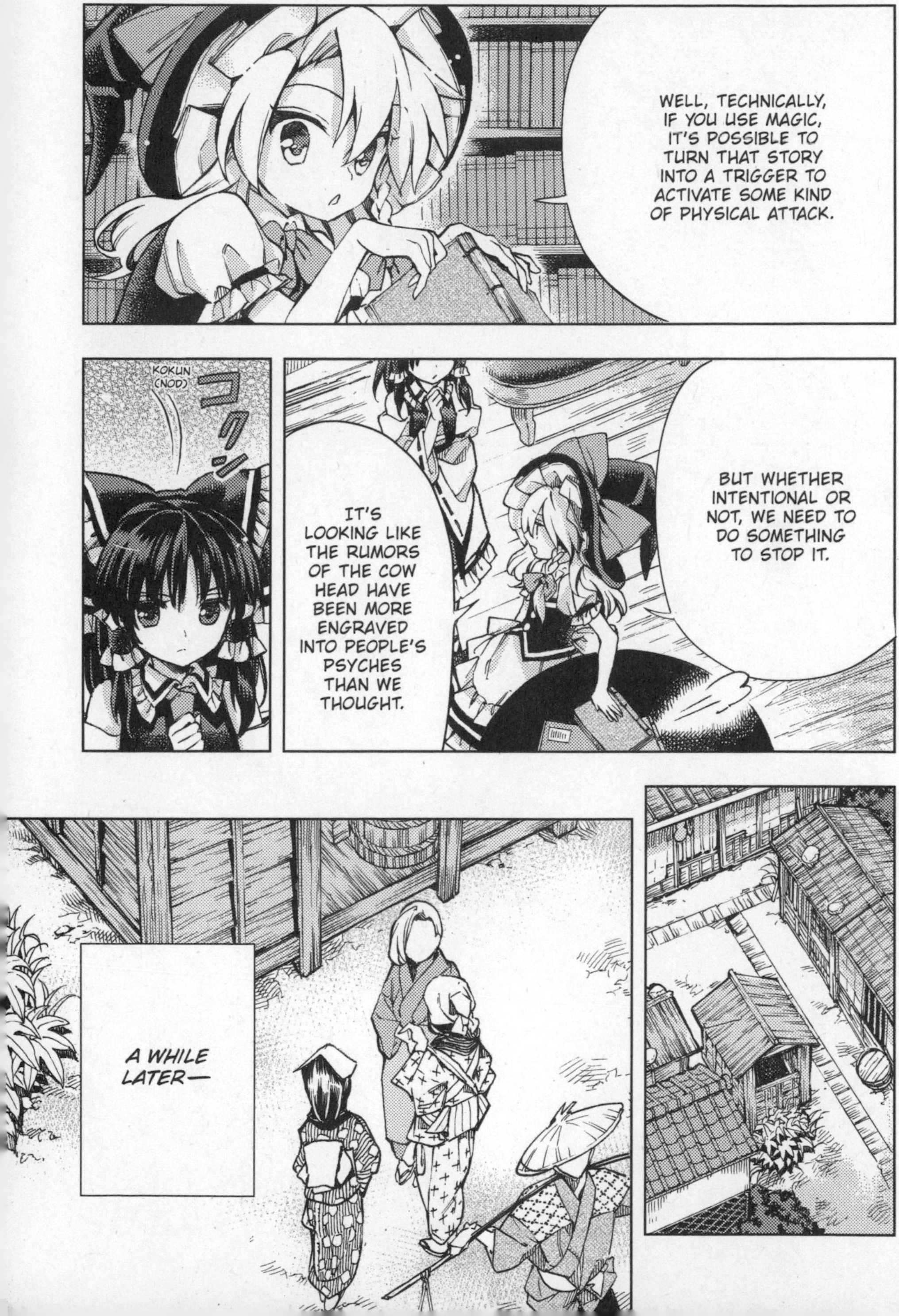
WELL, TECHNICALLY, IF YOU USE MAGIC, IT'S POSSIBLE TO TURN THAT STORY INTO A TRIGGER TO ACTIVATE SOME KIND OF PHYSICAL ATTACK.
BUT WHETHER INTENTIONAL OR NOT, WE NEED TO DO SOMETHING TO STOP IT.
IT'S LOOKING LIKE THE RUMORS OF THE COW HEAD HAVE BEEN MORE ENGRAVED INTO PEOPLE'S PSYCHES THAN WE THOUGHT.
KOKUN (NOD)
A WHILE LATER—

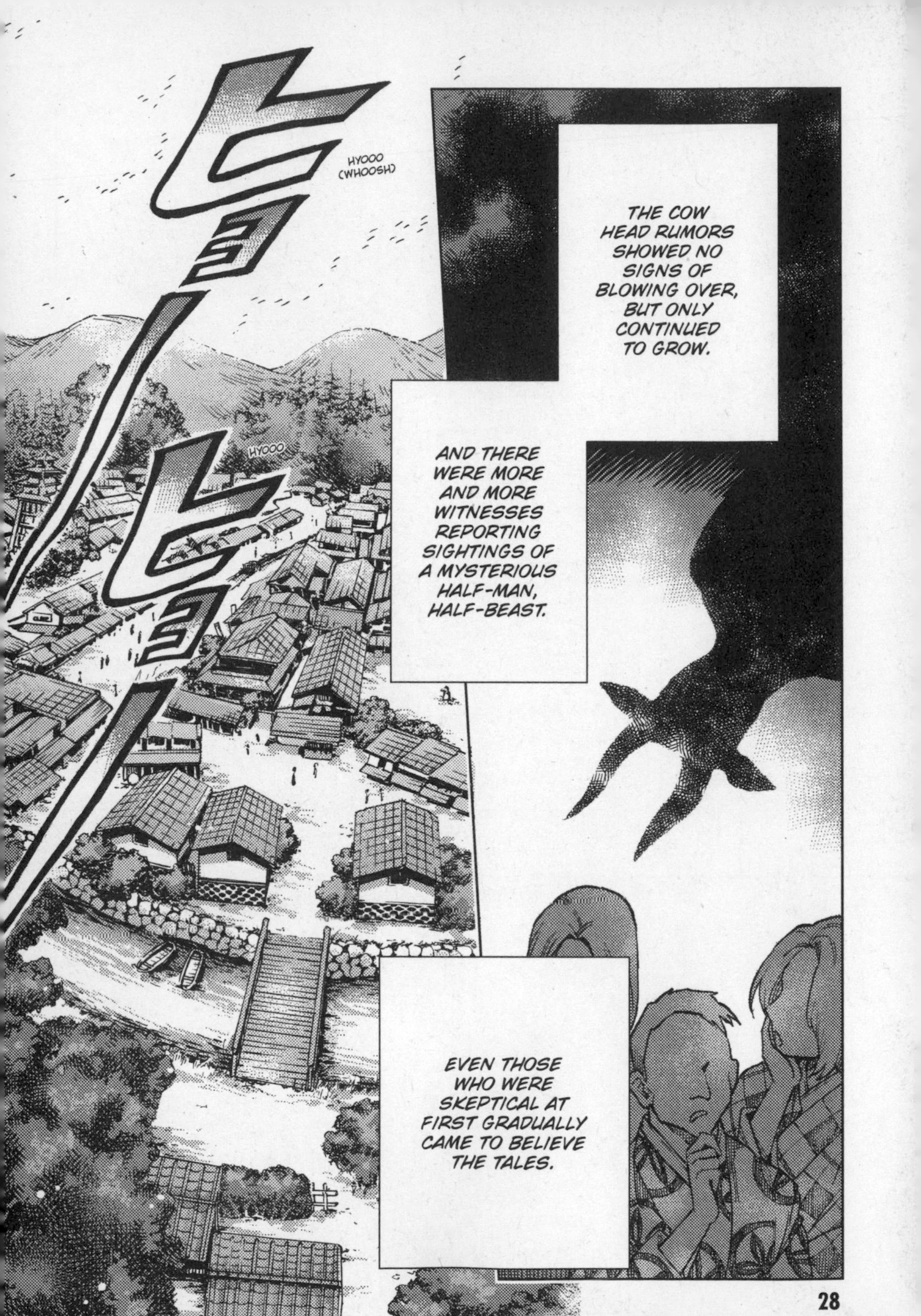
THE COW HEAD RUMORS SHOWED NO SIGNS OF BLOWING OVER, BUT ONLY CONTINUED TO GROW.
AND THERE WERE MORE AND MORE WITNESSES REPORTING SIGHTINGS OF A MYSTERIOUS HALF-MAN, HALF-BEAST.
EVEN THOSE WHO WERE SKEPTICAL AT FIRST GRADUALLY CAME TO BELIEVE THE TALES.
HYOOO (WHOOSH)
HYOOO

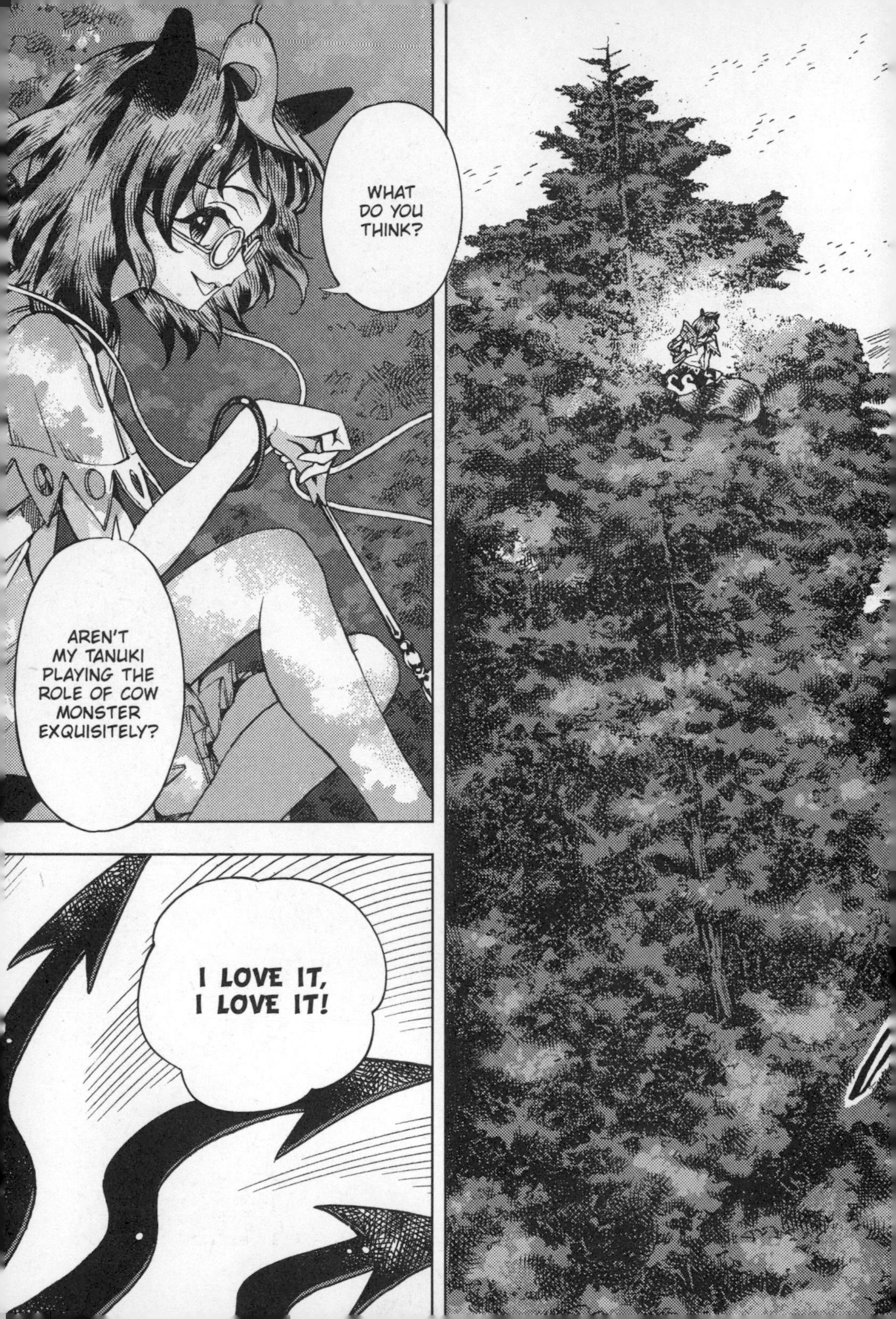
WHAT DO YOU THINK?
AREN'T MY TANUKI PLAYING THE ROLE OF COW MONSTER EXQUISITELY?
I LOVE IT, I LOVE IT!

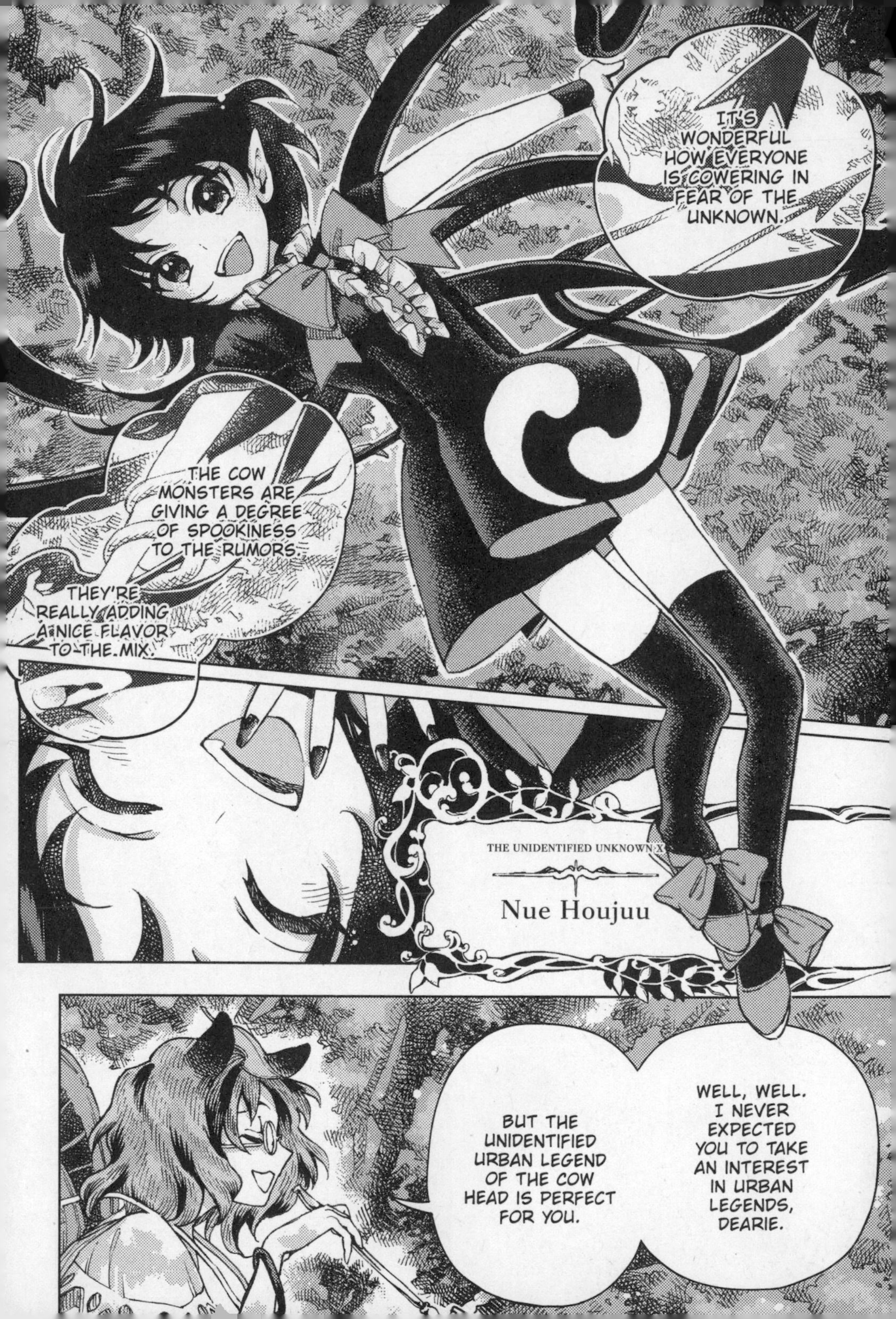
IT'S WONDERFUL HOW EVERYONE IS COWERING IN FEAR OF THE UNKNOWN.
THE COW MONSTERS ARE GIVING A DEGREE OF SPOOKINESS TO THE RUMORS.
THEY'RE REALLY ADDING A NICE FLAVOR TO THE MIX.
THE UNIDENTIFIED UNKNOWN X
Nue Houjuu
WELL, WELL. I NEVER EXPECTED YOU TO TAKE AN INTEREST IN URBAN LEGENDS, DEARIE.
BUT THE UNIDENTIFIED URBAN LEGEND OF THE COW HEAD IS PERFECT FOR YOU.

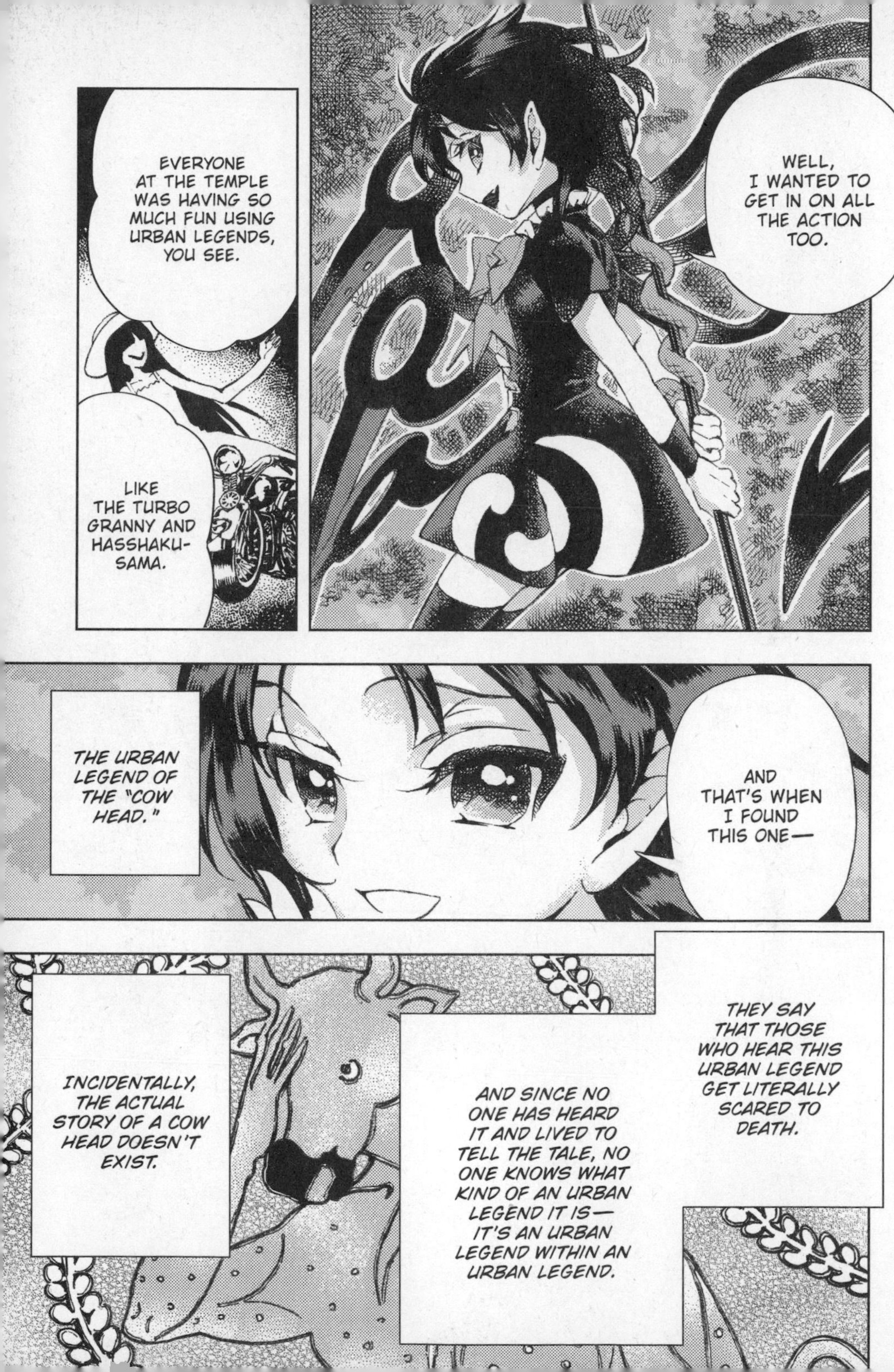
WELL, I WANTED TO GET IN ON ALL THE ACTION TOO.
EVERYONE AT THE TEMPLE WAS HAVING SO MUCH FUN USING URBAN LEGENDS, YOU SEE.
LIKE THE TURBO GRANNY AND HASSHAKU-SAMA.
AND THAT'S WHEN I FOUND THIS ONE—
THE URBAN LEGEND OF THE "COW HEAD."
THEY SAY THAT THOSE WHO HEAR THIS URBAN LEGEND GET LITERALLY SCARED TO DEATH.
AND SINCE NO ONE HAS HEARD IT AND LIVED TO TELL THE TALE, NO ONE KNOWS WHAT KIND OF AN URBAN LEGEND IT IS— IT'S AN URBAN LEGEND WITHIN AN URBAN LEGEND.
INCIDENTALLY, THE ACTUAL STORY OF A COW HEAD DOESN'T EXIST.

AS THEY COME TO FEAR THE UNKNOWN URBAN LEGEND...

...THE COW MONSTER GRADUALLY TAKES ON A SENSE OF REALITY.

BUT THAT REALITY IS ALSO UNKNOWN.

AND SO WE CAN SOAK THE WORLD IN FEAR WITHOUT ACTUALLY HURTING ANY-BODY, ISN'T THAT RIGHT?

IT'S A FINE IDEA.

WE BAKE-DANUKI WANT THE HUMANS TO FEAR THE UNKNOWN TOO.

BUT THERE ARE TOO MANY OUT THERE WHO WILL NOT STAY QUIET IF THERE ARE ANY REAL VICTIMS......

IT'S THE CLOSEST WE *OUTCASTS* CAN GET TO THE LINE WITHOUT CROSSING IT.

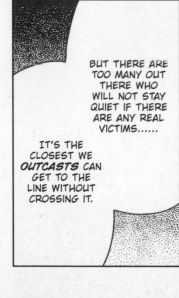

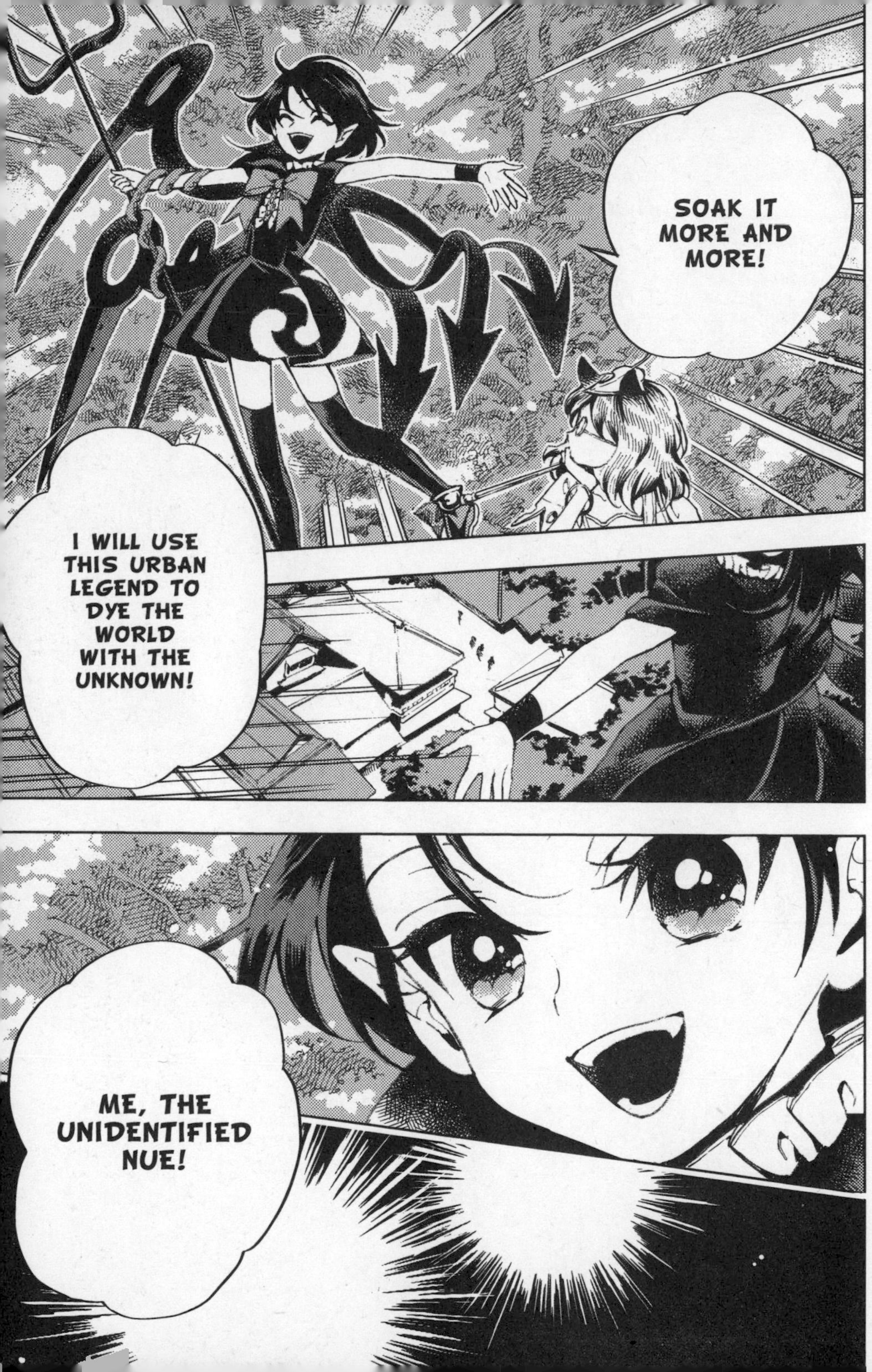
SOAK IT MORE AND MORE!
I WILL USE THIS URBAN LEGEND TO DYE THE WORLD WITH THE UNKNOWN!
ME, THE UNIDENTIFIED NUE!

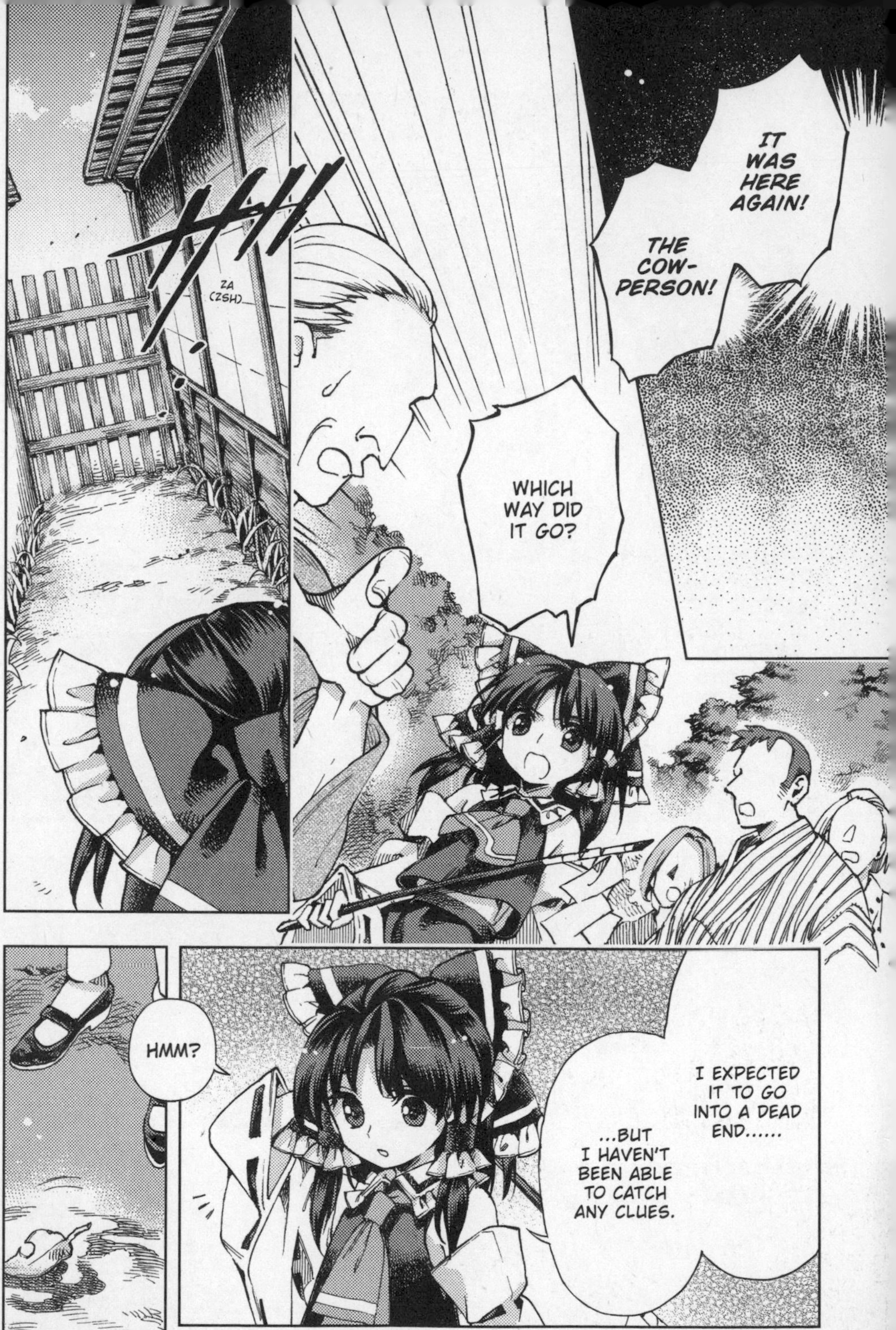
IT WAS HERE AGAIN!
THE COW-PERSON!
WHICH WAY DID IT GO?
ZA (ZSH)
I EXPECTED IT TO GO INTO A DEAD END......
...BUT I HAVEN'T BEEN ABLE TO CATCH ANY CLUES.
HMM?

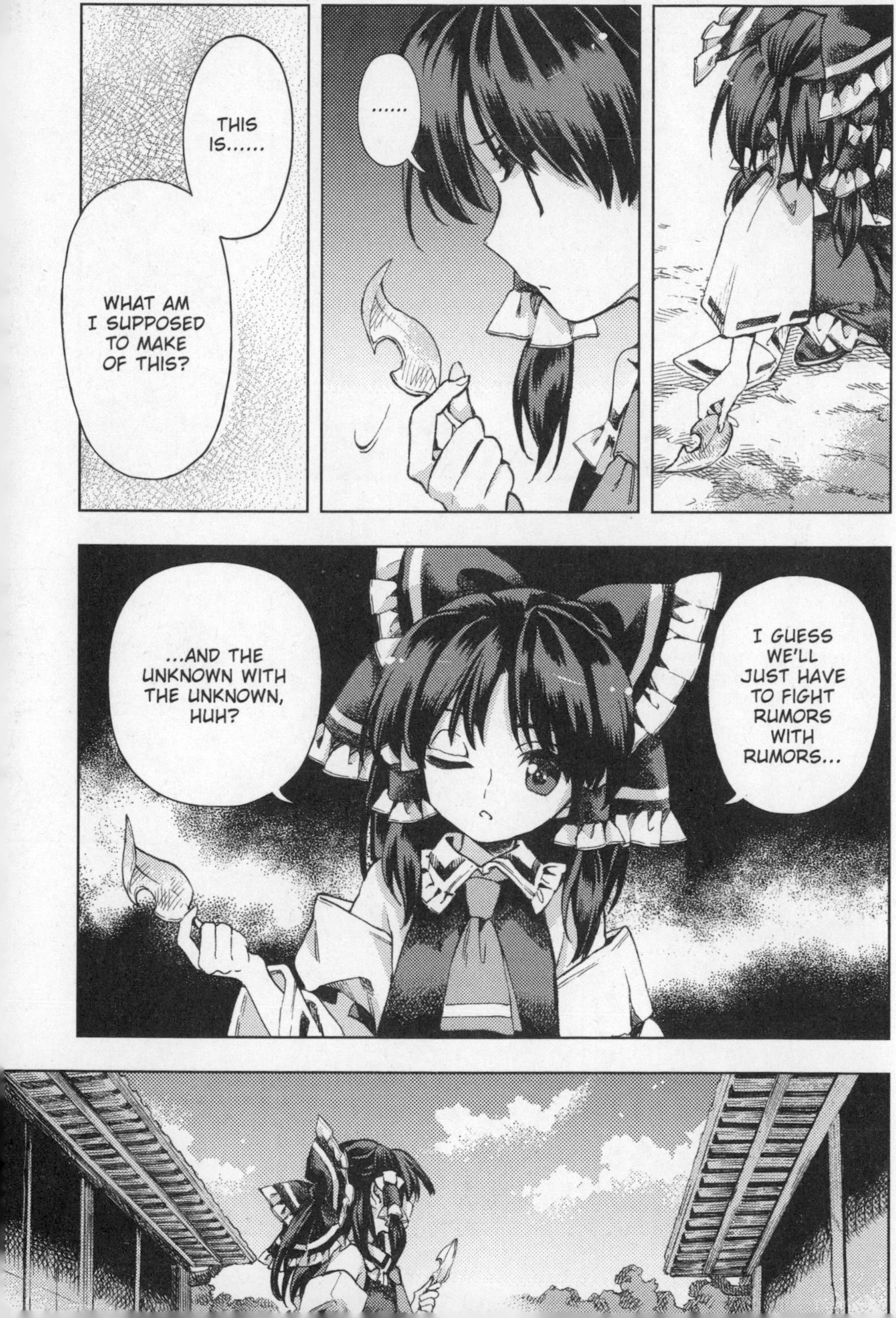
......
THIS IS......
WHAT AM I SUPPOSED TO MAKE OF THIS?
I GUESS WE'LL JUST HAVE TO FIGHT RUMORS WITH RUMORS...
...AND THE UNKNOWN WITH THE UNKNOWN, HUH?

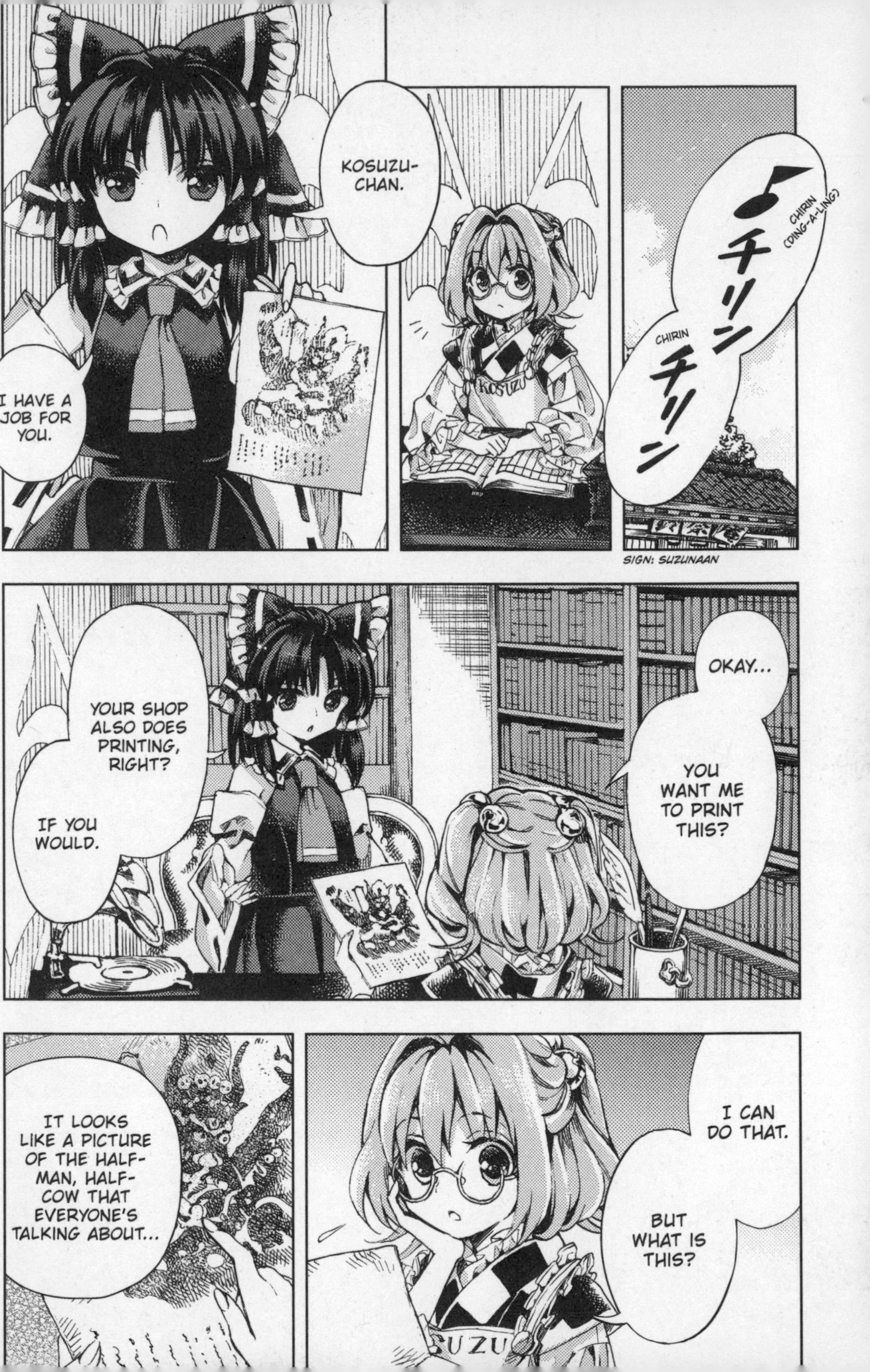
チリン
CHIRIN (DING-A-LING)
チリン
CHIRIN
SIGN: SUZUNAAN
KOSUZU-CHAN.
I HAVE A JOB FOR YOU.
OKAY...
YOU WANT ME TO PRINT THIS?
YOUR SHOP ALSO DOES PRINTING, RIGHT?
IF YOU WOULD.
I CAN DO THAT.
BUT WHAT IS THIS?
IT LOOKS LIKE A PICTURE OF THE HALF-MAN, HALF-COW THAT EVERYONE'S TALKING ABOUT...

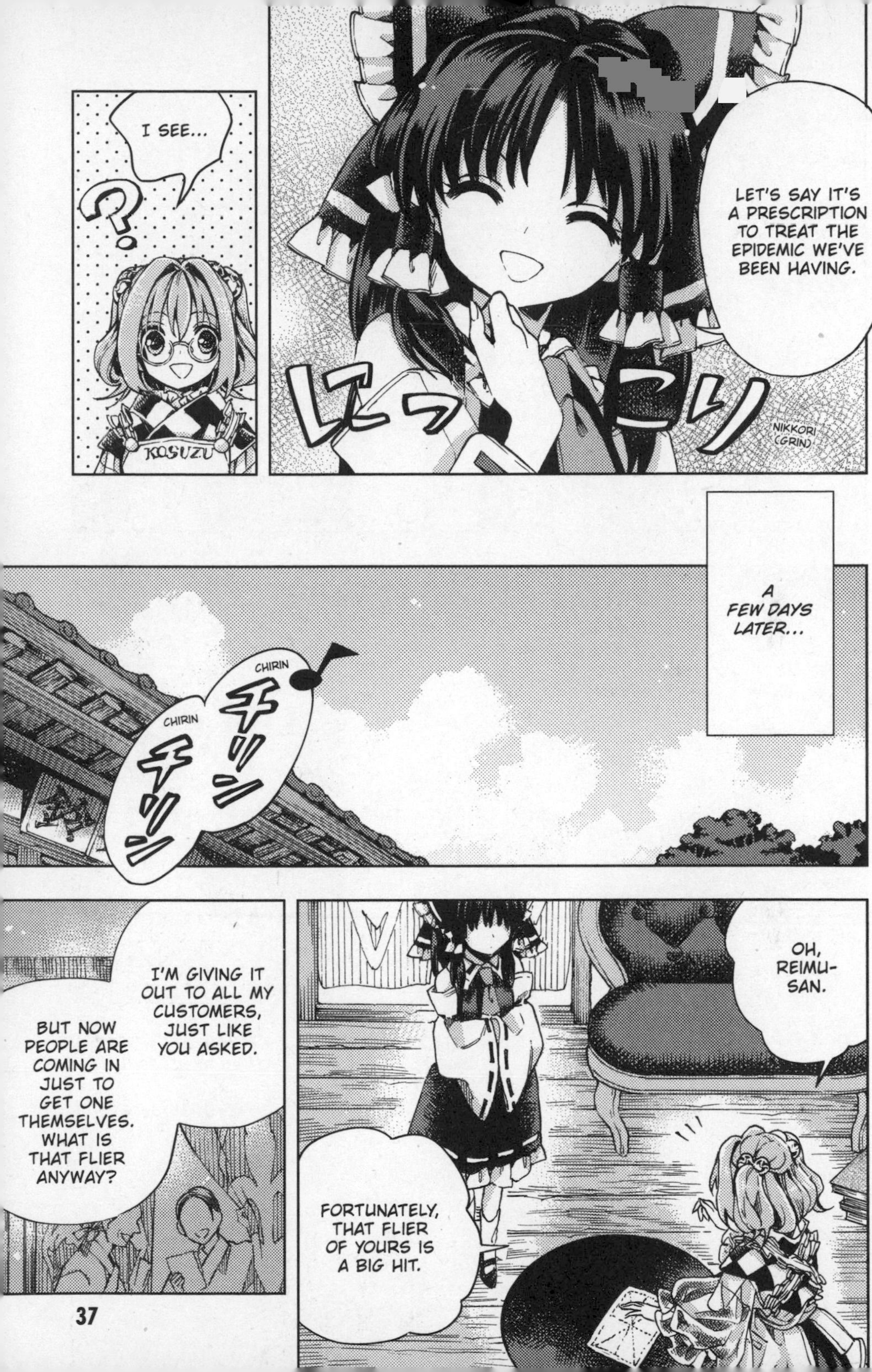
LET'S SAY IT'S A PRESCRIPTION TO TREAT THE EPIDEMIC WE'VE BEEN HAVING.
NIKKORI (GRIN)
I SEE...
KOSUZU
A FEW DAYS LATER...
CHIRIN
CHIRIN
OH, REIMU-SAN.
FORTUNATELY, THAT FLIER OF YOURS IS A BIG HIT.
I'M GIVING IT OUT TO ALL MY CUSTOMERS, JUST LIKE YOU ASKED.
BUT NOW PEOPLE ARE COMING IN JUST TO GET ONE THEMSELVES. WHAT IS THAT FLIER ANYWAY?

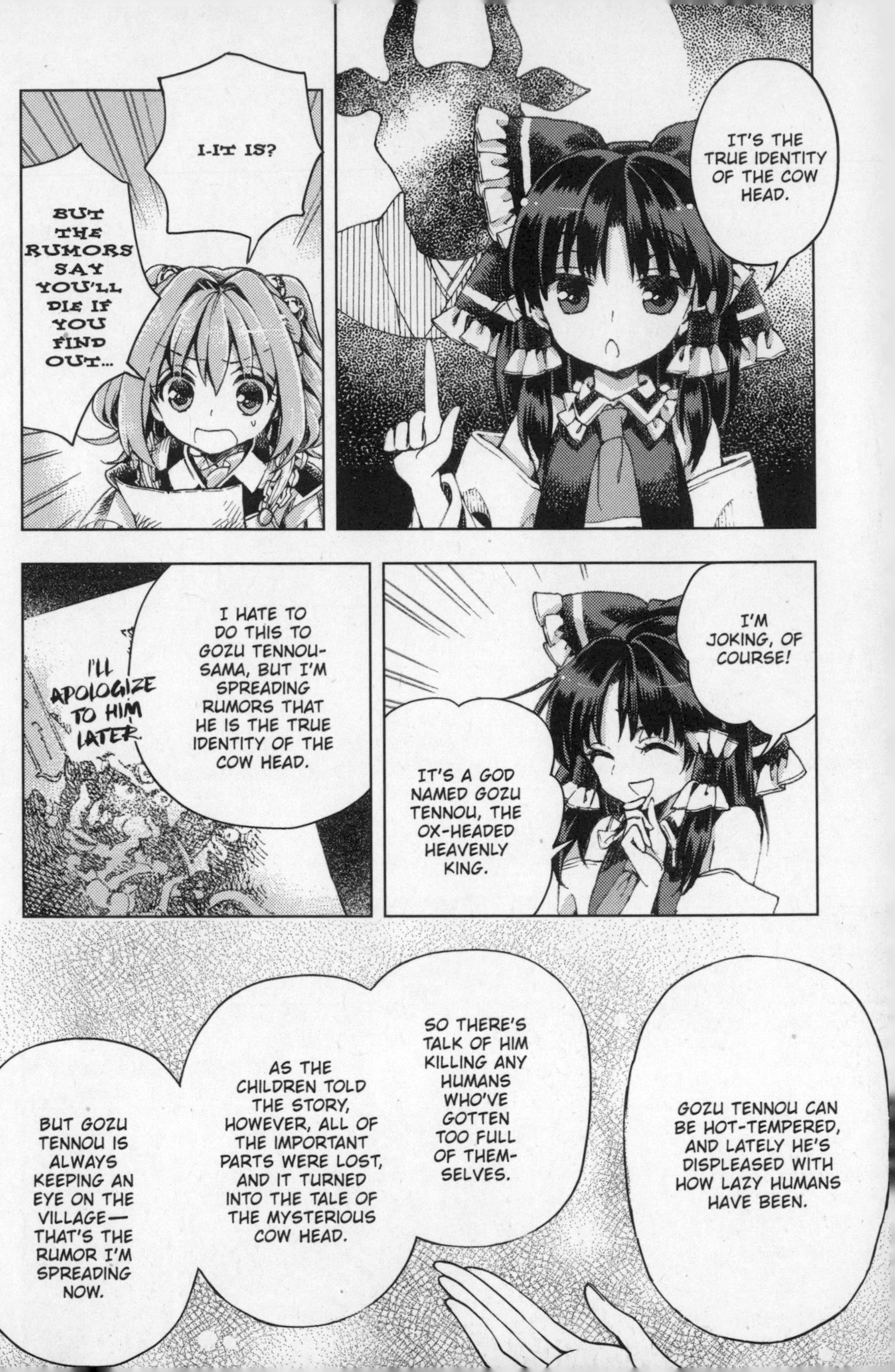
IT'S THE TRUE IDENTITY OF THE COW HEAD.
I-IT IS?
BUT THE RUMORS SAY YOU'LL DIE IF YOU FIND OUT...
I'M JOKING, OF COURSE!
IT'S A GOD NAMED GOZU TENNOU, THE OX-HEADED HEAVENLY KING.
I HATE TO DO THIS TO GOZU TENNOU-SAMA, BUT I'M SPREADING RUMORS THAT HE IS THE TRUE IDENTITY OF THE COW HEAD.
I'LL APOLOGIZE TO HIM LATER.
GOZU TENNOU CAN BE HOT-TEMPERED, AND LATELY HE'S DISPLEASED WITH HOW LAZY HUMANS HAVE BEEN.
SO THERE'S TALK OF HIM KILLING ANY HUMANS WHO'VE GOTTEN TOO FULL OF THEMSELVES.
AS THE CHILDREN TOLD THE STORY, HOWEVER, ALL OF THE IMPORTANT PARTS WERE LOST, AND IT TURNED INTO THE TALE OF THE MYSTERIOUS COW HEAD.
BUT GOZU TENNOU IS ALWAYS KEEPING AN EYE ON THE VILLAGE—THAT'S THE RUMOR I'M SPREADING NOW.

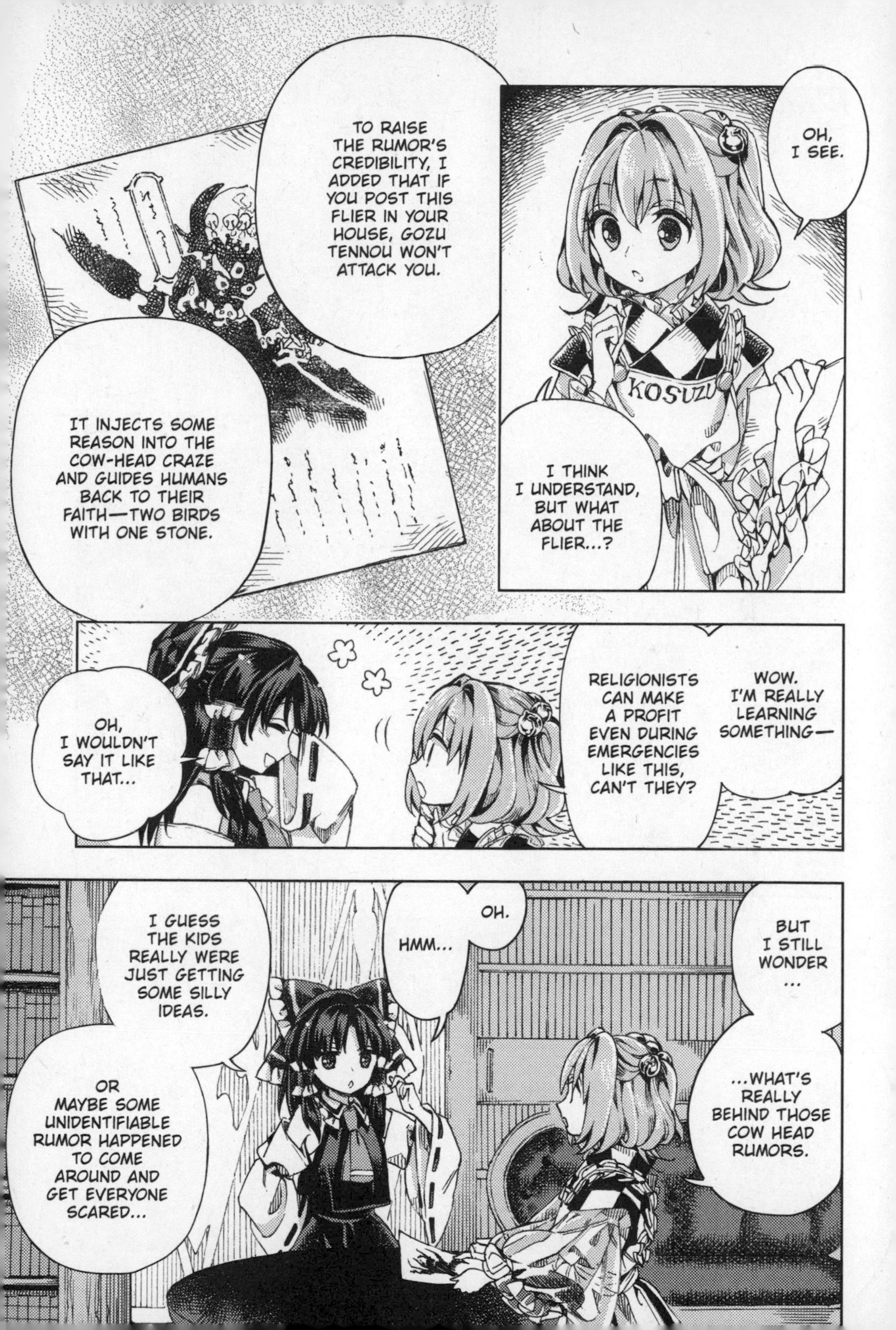
OH, I SEE.
I THINK I UNDERSTAND, BUT WHAT ABOUT THE FLIER...?
TO RAISE THE RUMOR'S CREDIBILITY, I ADDED THAT IF YOU POST THIS FLIER IN YOUR HOUSE, GOZU TENNOU WON'T ATTACK YOU.
IT INJECTS SOME REASON INTO THE COW-HEAD CRAZE AND GUIDES HUMANS BACK TO THEIR FAITH—TWO BIRDS WITH ONE STONE.
WOW. I'M REALLY LEARNING SOMETHING—
RELIGIONISTS CAN MAKE A PROFIT EVEN DURING EMERGENCIES LIKE THIS, CAN'T THEY?
OH, I WOULDN'T SAY IT LIKE THAT...
BUT I STILL WONDER ...
...WHAT'S REALLY BEHIND THOSE COW HEAD RUMORS.
OH.
HMM...
I GUESS THE KIDS REALLY WERE JUST GETTING SOME SILLY IDEAS.
OR MAYBE SOME UNIDENTIFIABLE RUMOR HAPPENED TO COME AROUND AND GET EVERYONE SCARED...

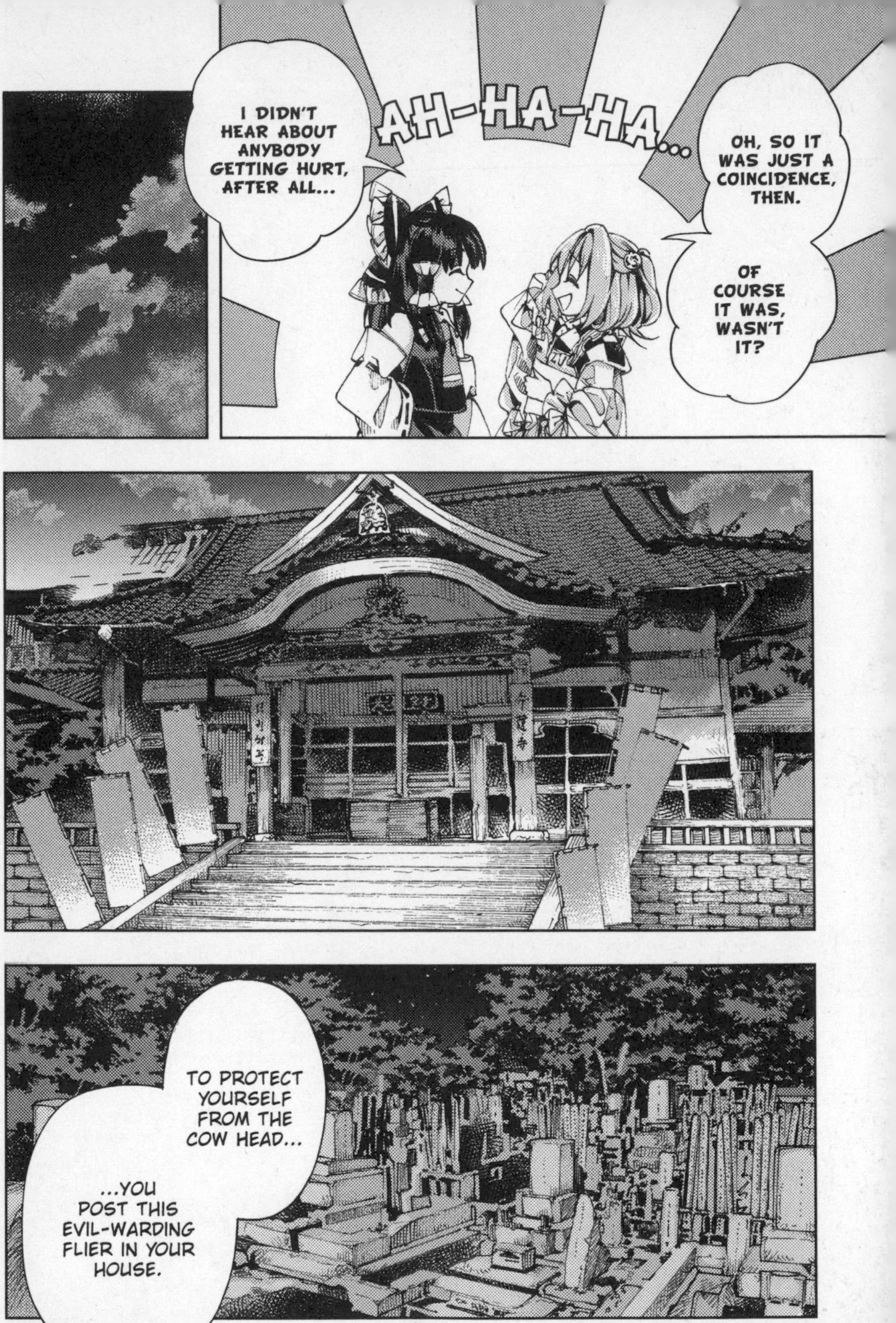
OH, SO IT WAS JUST A COINCIDENCE, THEN.
OF COURSE IT WAS, WASN'T IT?
AH-HA-HA...
I DIDN'T HEAR ABOUT ANYBODY GETTING HURT, AFTER ALL...
TO PROTECT YOURSELF FROM THE COW HEAD...
...YOU POST THIS EVIL-WARDING FLIER IN YOUR HOUSE.

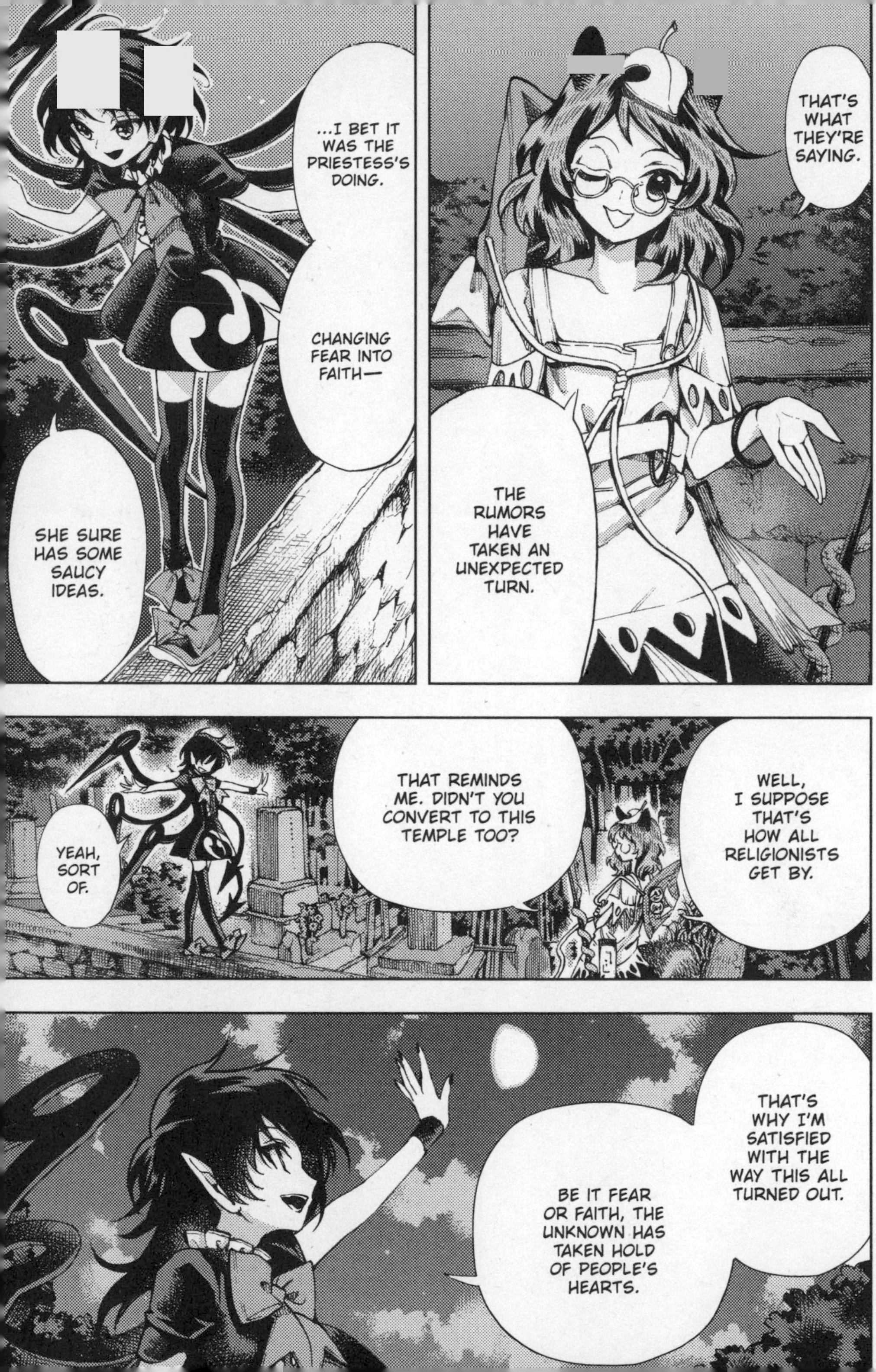
THAT'S WHAT THEY'RE SAYING.
THE RUMORS HAVE TAKEN AN UNEXPECTED TURN.
...I BET IT WAS THE PRIESTESS'S DOING.
CHANGING FEAR INTO FAITH—
SHE SURE HAS SOME SAUCY IDEAS.
WELL, I SUPPOSE THAT'S HOW ALL RELIGIONISTS GET BY.
THAT REMINDS ME. DIDN'T YOU CONVERT TO THIS TEMPLE TOO?
YEAH, SORT OF.
THAT'S WHY I'M SATISFIED WITH THE WAY THIS ALL TURNED OUT.
BE IT FEAR OR FAITH, THE UNKNOWN HAS TAKEN HOLD OF PEOPLE'S HEARTS.

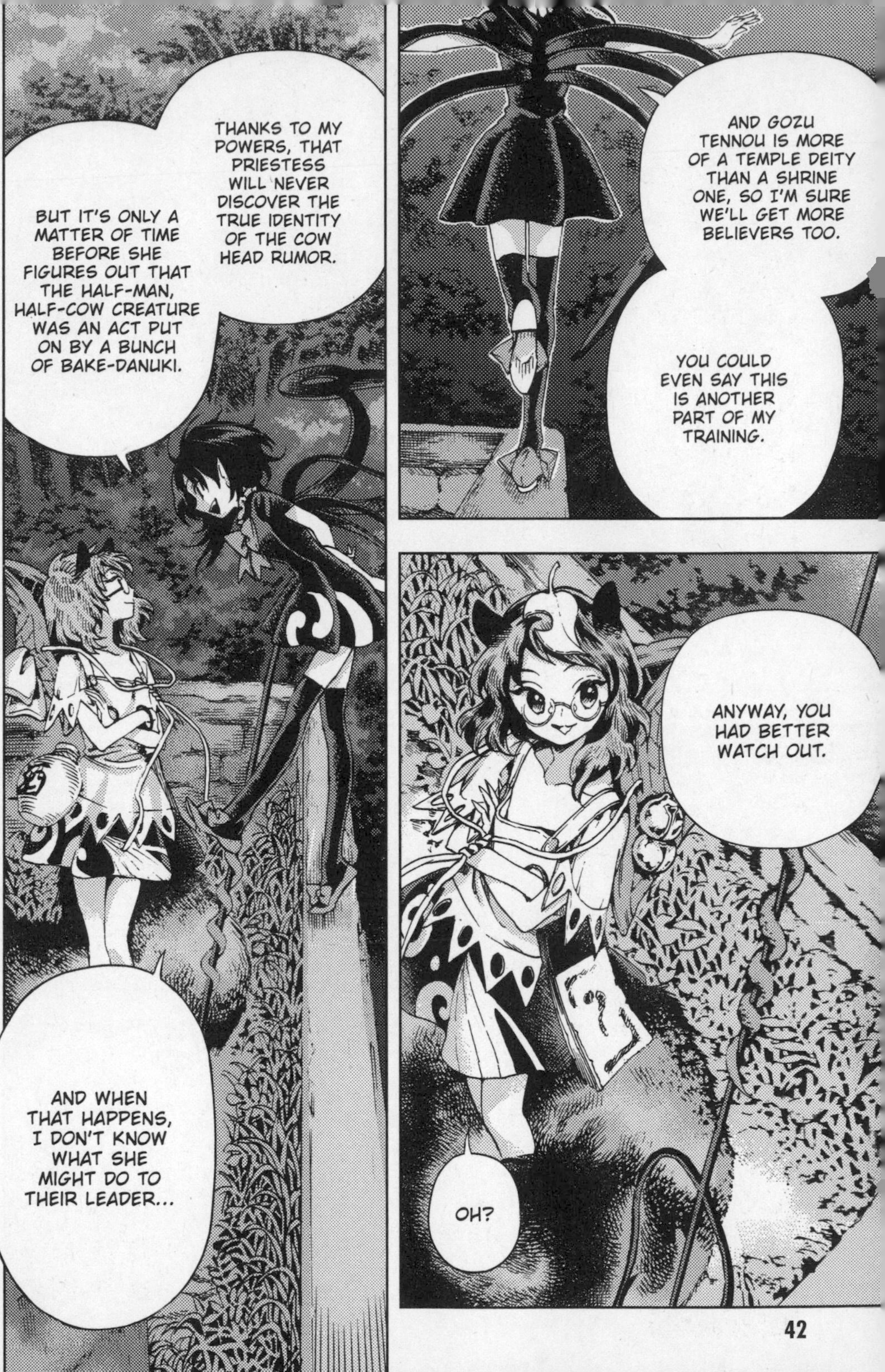
AND GOZU TENNOU IS MORE OF A TEMPLE DEITY THAN A SHRINE ONE, SO I'M SURE WE'LL GET MORE BELIEVERS TOO.
YOU COULD EVEN SAY THIS IS ANOTHER PART OF MY TRAINING.
ANYWAY, YOU HAD BETTER WATCH OUT.
OH?
THANKS TO MY POWERS, THAT PRIESTESS WILL NEVER DISCOVER THE TRUE IDENTITY OF THE COW HEAD RUMOR.
BUT IT'S ONLY A MATTER OF TIME BEFORE SHE FIGURES OUT THAT THE HALF-MAN, HALF-COW CREATURE WAS AN ACT PUT ON BY A BUNCH OF BAKE-DANUKI.
AND WHEN THAT HAPPENS, I DON'T KNOW WHAT SHE MIGHT DO TO THEIR LEADER...

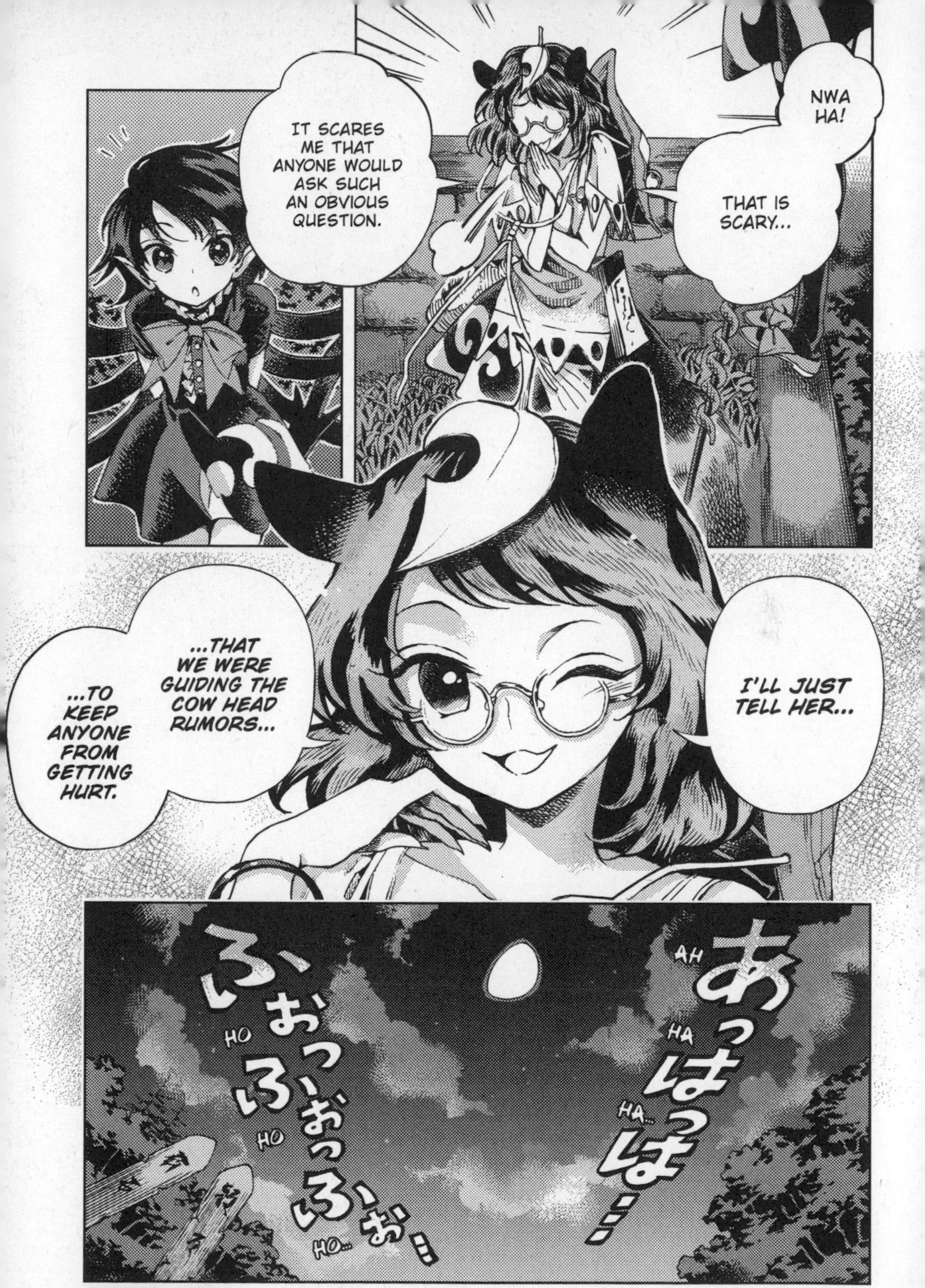
NWA HA!
THAT IS SCARY...
IT SCARES ME THAT ANYONE WOULD ASK SUCH AN OBVIOUS QUESTION.
I'LL JUST TELL HER...
...THAT WE WERE GUIDING THE COW HEAD RUMORS...
...TO KEEP ANYONE FROM GETTING HURT.
あっはっは…
AH HA HA...
ふぉっふぉっふぉ…
HO HO HO...

Chapter 31 End

Forbidden Scrollery

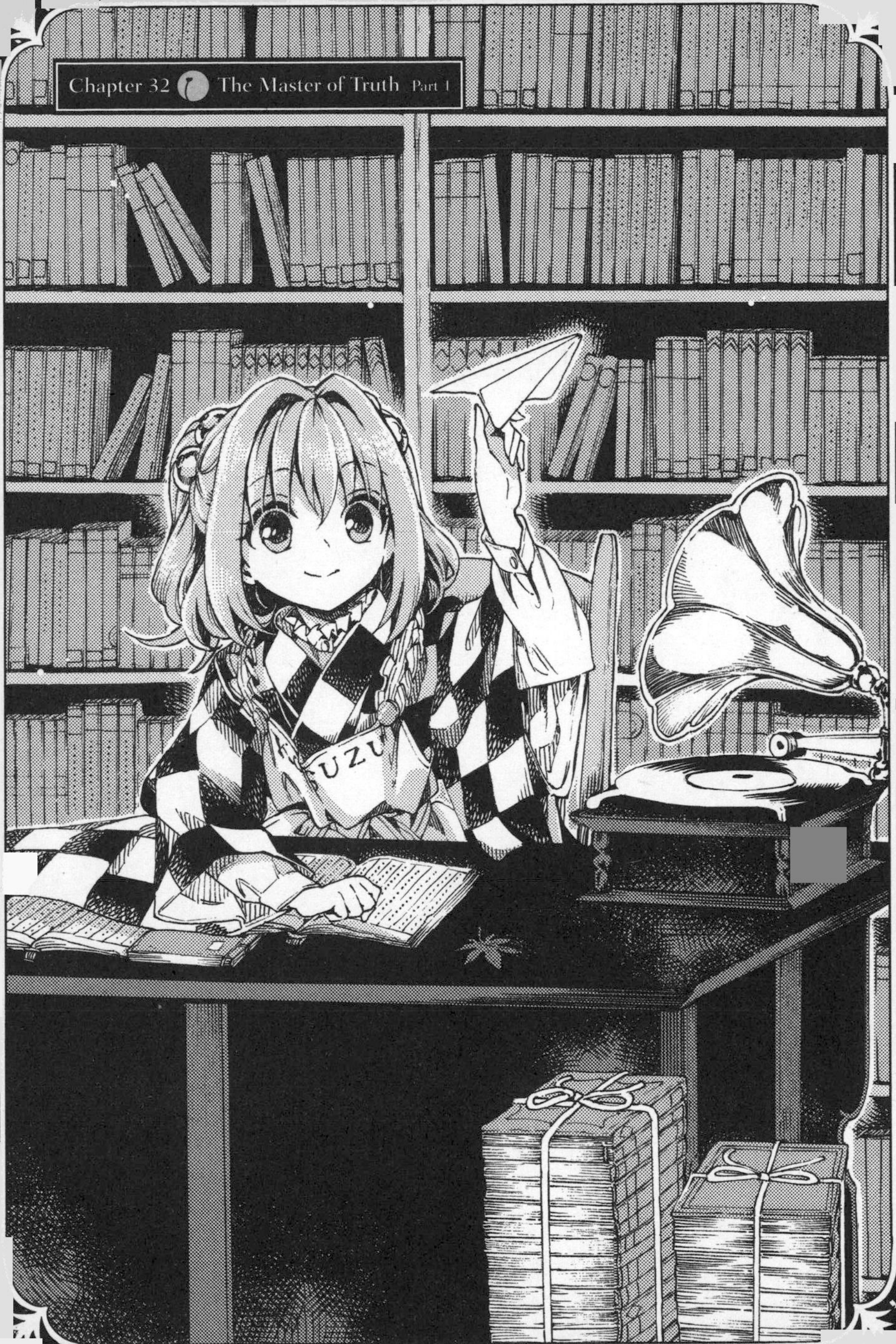
Chapter 32 The Master of Truth Part 1
SUZU

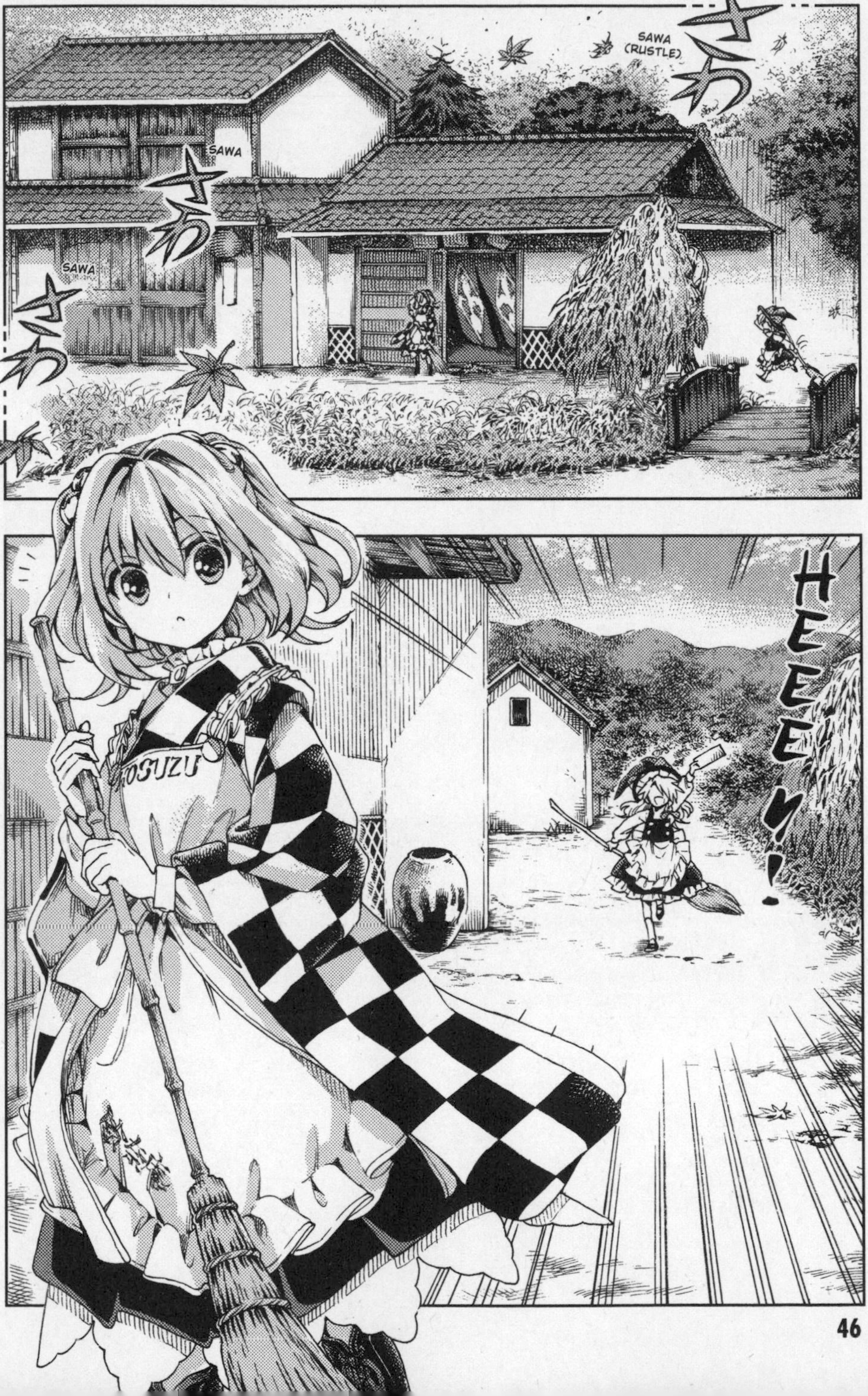
さわ
SAWA (RUSTLE)
さわ
SAWA
さわ
SAWA
HEEEY!!

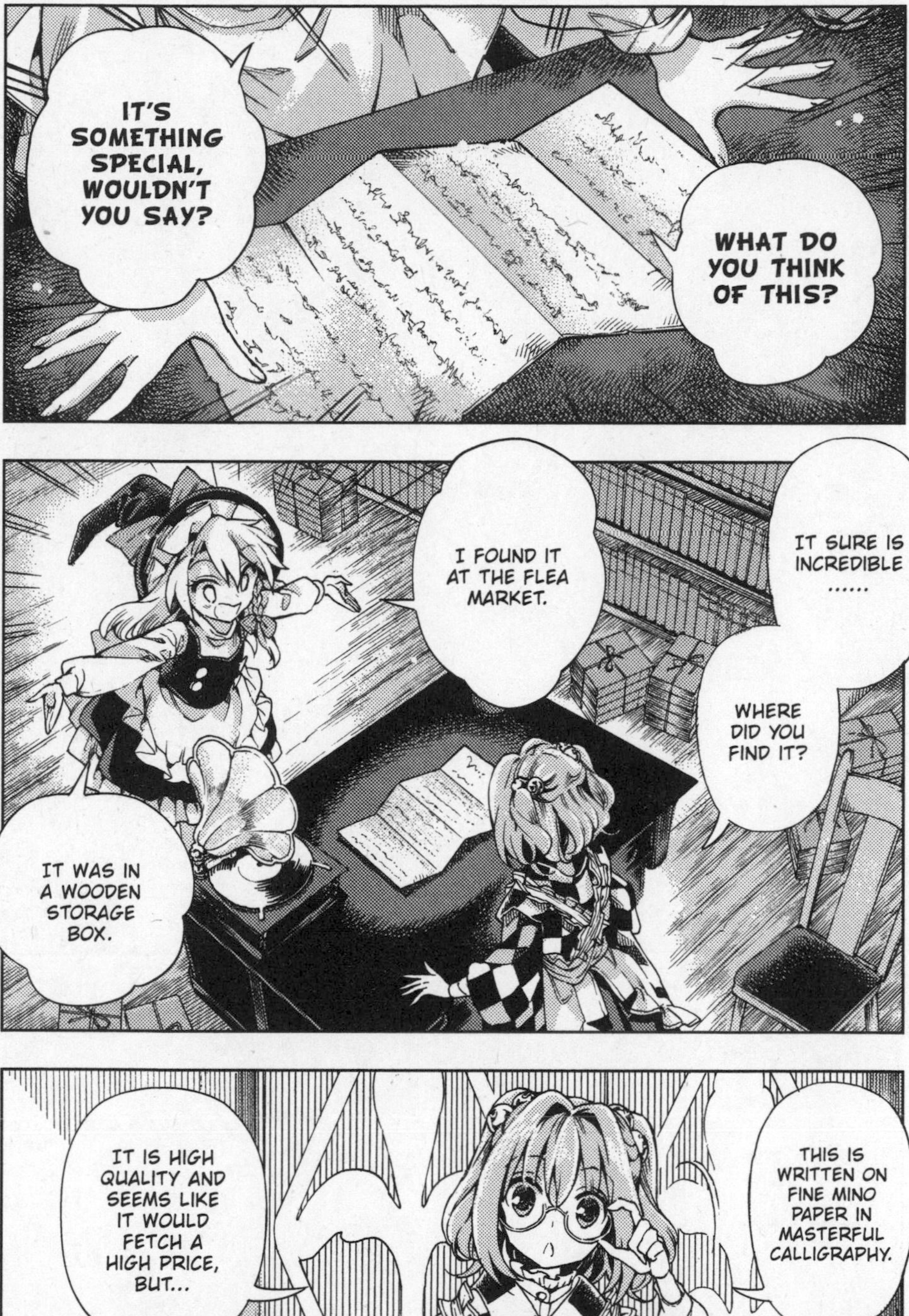
WHAT DO YOU THINK OF THIS?
IT'S SOMETHING SPECIAL, WOULDN'T YOU SAY?
IT SURE IS INCREDIBLE ......
WHERE DID YOU FIND IT?
I FOUND IT AT THE FLEA MARKET.
IT WAS IN A WOODEN STORAGE BOX.
THIS IS WRITTEN ON FINE MINO PAPER IN MASTERFUL CALLIGRAPHY.
IT IS HIGH QUALITY AND SEEMS LIKE IT WOULD FETCH A HIGH PRICE, BUT...

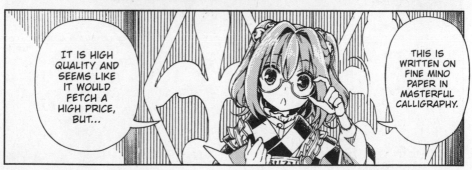

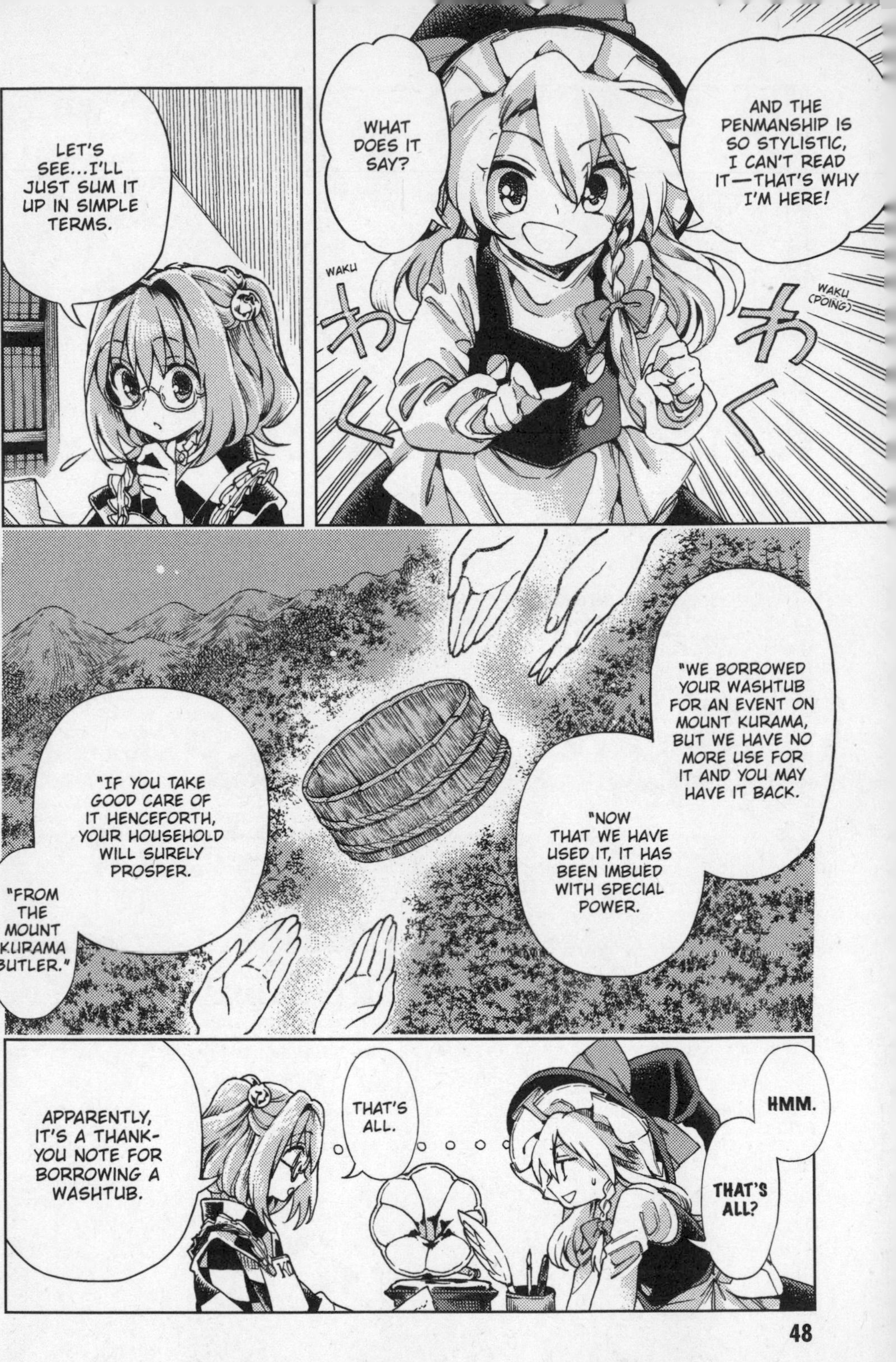
AND THE PENMANSHIP IS SO STYLISTIC, I CAN'T READ IT—THAT'S WHY I'M HERE!
WHAT DOES IT SAY?
WAKU (POING)
わく
WAKU
わく
LET'S SEE...I'LL JUST SUM IT UP IN SIMPLE TERMS.
"WE BORROWED YOUR WASHTUB FOR AN EVENT ON MOUNT KURAMA, BUT WE HAVE NO MORE USE FOR IT AND YOU MAY HAVE IT BACK.
"NOW THAT WE HAVE USED IT, IT HAS BEEN IMBUED WITH SPECIAL POWER.
"IF YOU TAKE GOOD CARE OF IT HENCEFORTH, YOUR HOUSEHOLD WILL SURELY PROSPER.
"FROM THE MOUNT KURAMA BUTLER."
HMM.
THAT'S ALL?
THAT'S ALL.
APPARENTLY, IT'S A THANK-YOU NOTE FOR BORROWING A WASHTUB.

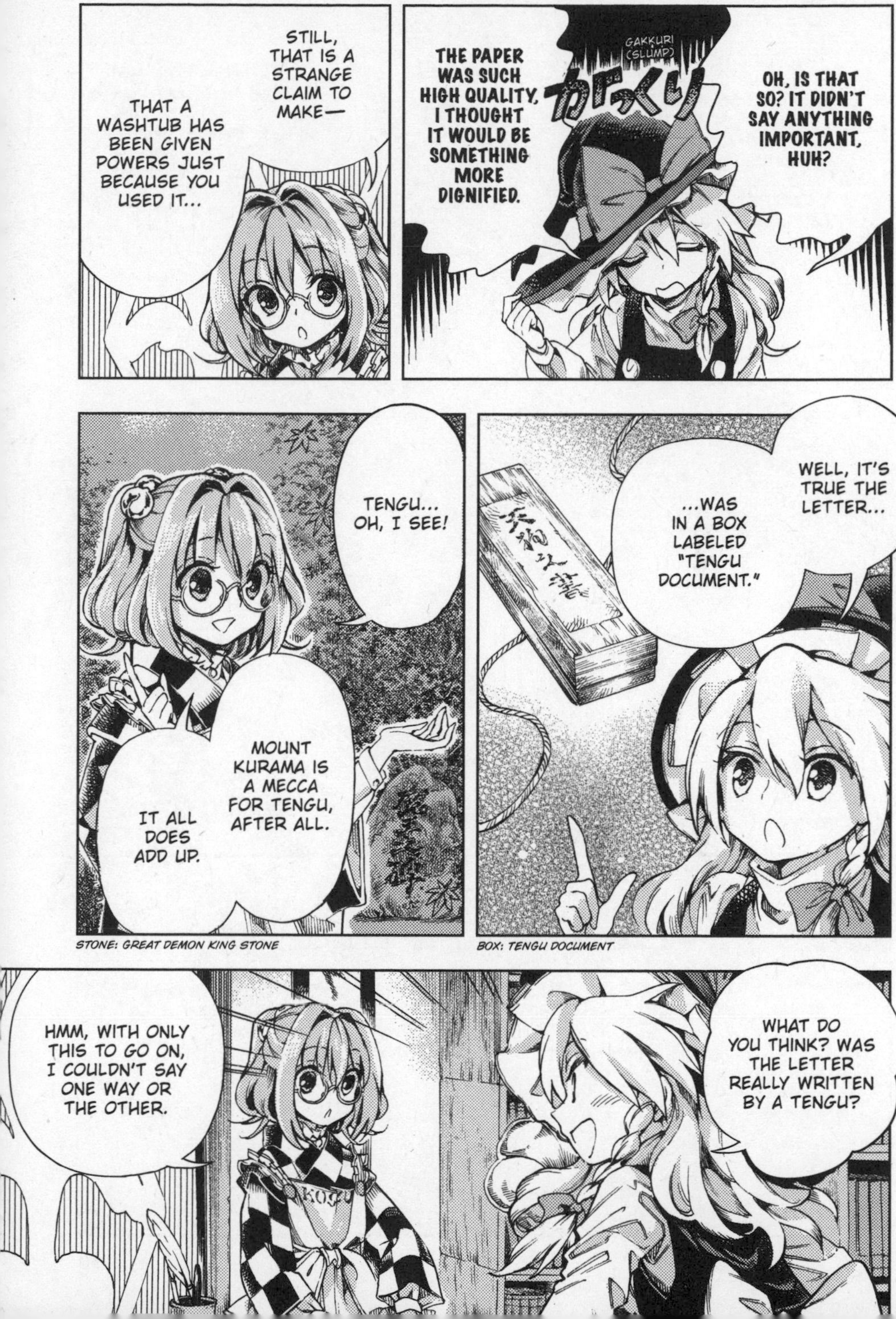
OH, IS THAT SO? IT DIDN'T SAY ANYTHING IMPORTANT, HUH?
GAKKURI (SLUMP)
THE PAPER WAS SUCH HIGH QUALITY, I THOUGHT IT WOULD BE SOMETHING MORE DIGNIFIED.
STILL, THAT IS A STRANGE CLAIM TO MAKE—
THAT A WASHTUB HAS BEEN GIVEN POWERS JUST BECAUSE YOU USED IT...
WELL, IT'S TRUE THE LETTER...
...WAS IN A BOX LABELED "TENGU DOCUMENT."
BOX: TENGU DOCUMENT
TENGU... OH, I SEE!
MOUNT KURAMA IS A MECCA FOR TENGU, AFTER ALL.
IT ALL DOES ADD UP.
STONE: GREAT DEMON KING STONE
WHAT DO YOU THINK? WAS THE LETTER REALLY WRITTEN BY A TENGU?
HMM, WITH ONLY THIS TO GO ON, I COULDN'T SAY ONE WAY OR THE OTHER.

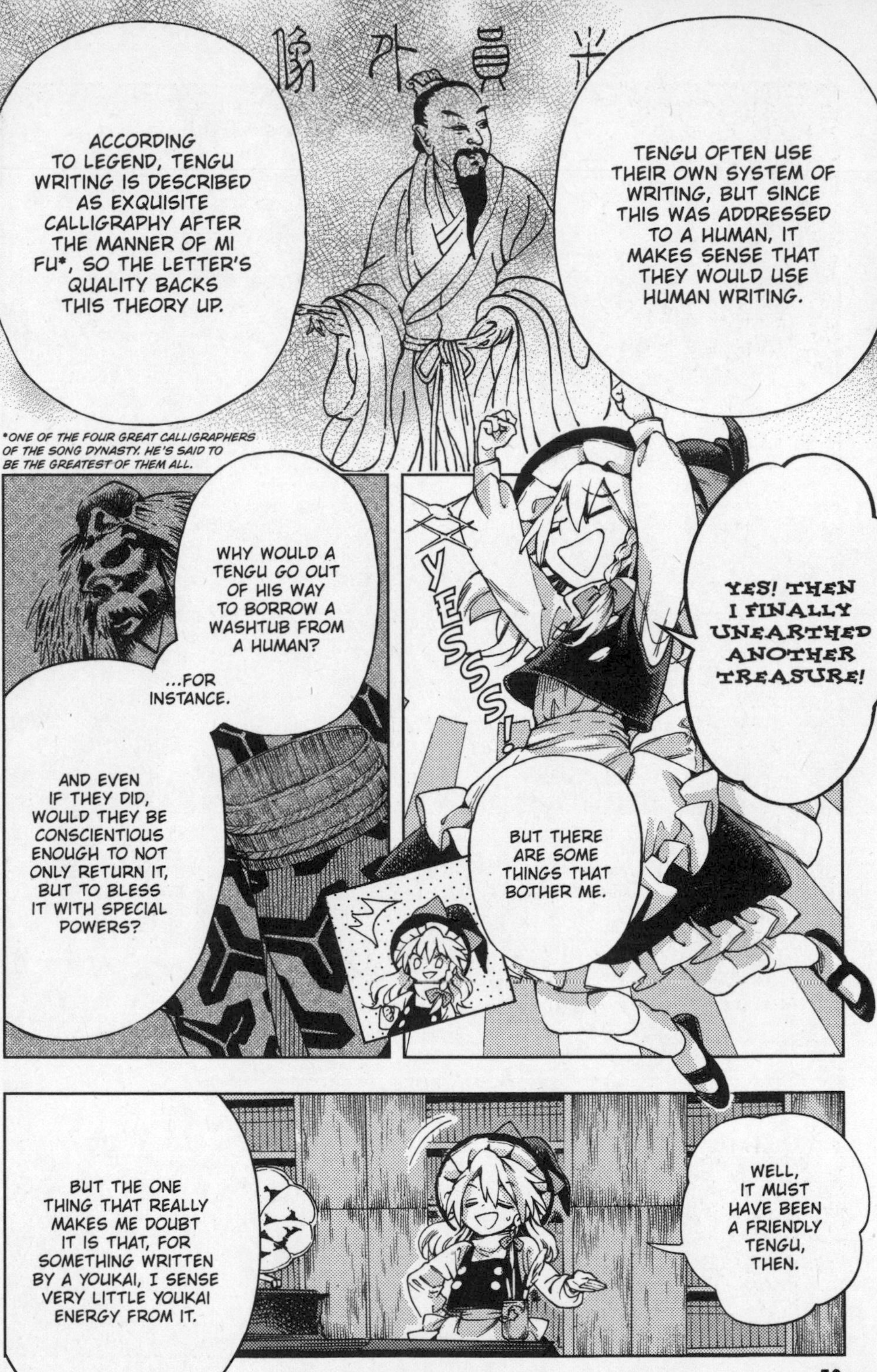
米員外像
TENGU OFTEN USE THEIR OWN SYSTEM OF WRITING, BUT SINCE THIS WAS ADDRESSED TO A HUMAN, IT MAKES SENSE THAT THEY WOULD USE HUMAN WRITING.
ACCORDING TO LEGEND, TENGU WRITING IS DESCRIBED AS EXQUISITE CALLIGRAPHY AFTER THE MANNER OF MI FU*, SO THE LETTER'S QUALITY BACKS THIS THEORY UP.
YES! THEN I FINALLY UNEARTHED ANOTHER TREASURE!
YESSS!
BUT THERE ARE SOME THINGS THAT BOTHER ME.
WHY WOULD A TENGU GO OUT OF HIS WAY TO BORROW A WASHTUB FROM A HUMAN?
...FOR INSTANCE.
AND EVEN IF THEY DID, WOULD THEY BE CONSCIENTIOUS ENOUGH TO NOT ONLY RETURN IT, BUT TO BLESS IT WITH SPECIAL POWERS?
WELL, IT MUST HAVE BEEN A FRIENDLY TENGU, THEN.
BUT THE ONE THING THAT REALLY MAKES ME DOUBT IT IS THAT, FOR SOMETHING WRITTEN BY A YOUKAI, I SENSE VERY LITTLE YOUKAI ENERGY FROM IT.

*ONE OF THE FOUR GREAT CALLIGRAPHERS OF THE SONG DYNASTY. HE'S SAID TO BE THE GREATEST OF THEM ALL.

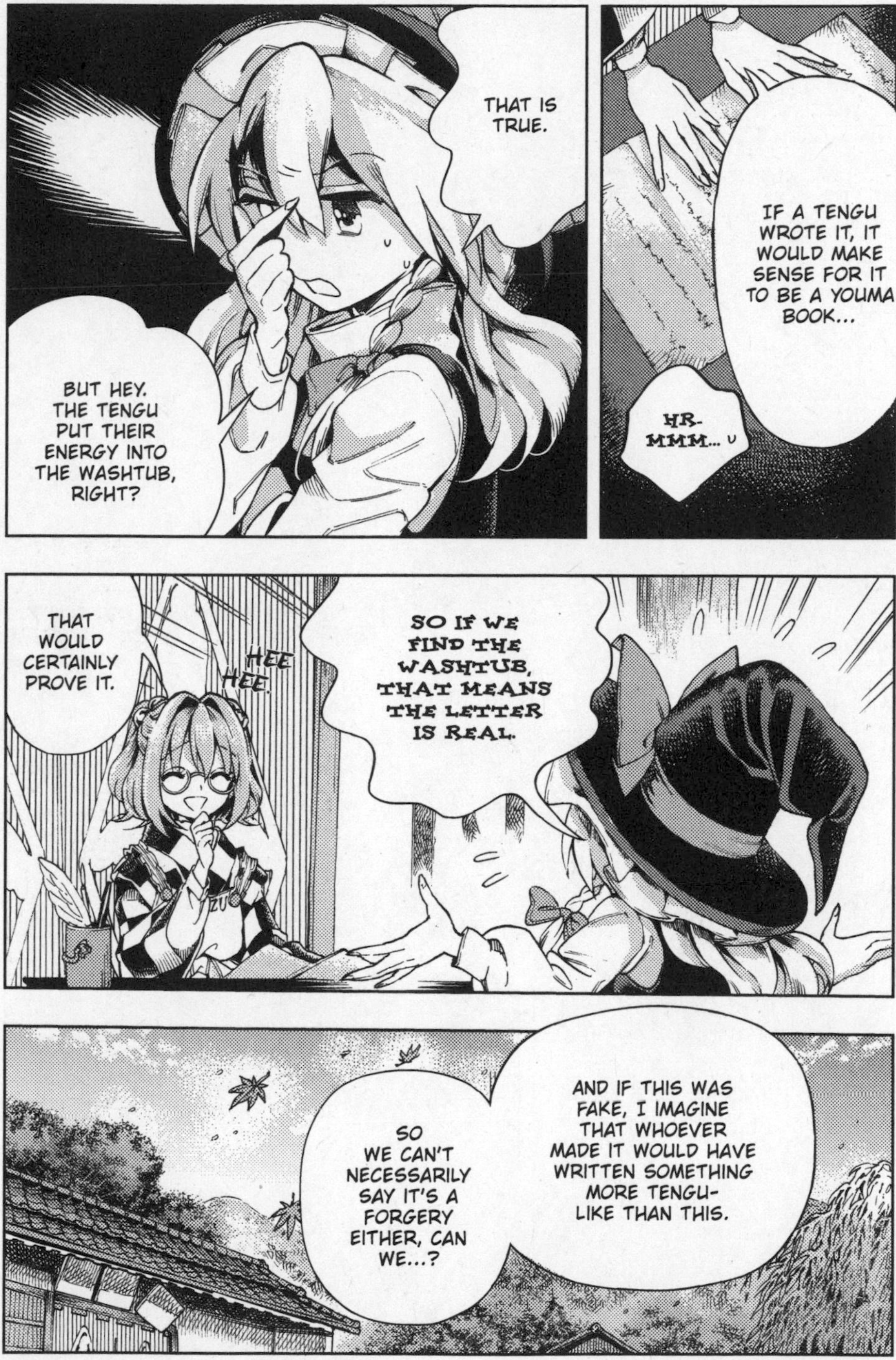
IF A TENGU WROTE IT, IT WOULD MAKE SENSE FOR IT TO BE A YOUMA BOOK...
HR-MMM...
THAT IS TRUE.
BUT HEY. THE TENGU PUT THEIR ENERGY INTO THE WASHTUB, RIGHT?
SO IF WE FIND THE WASHTUB, THAT MEANS THE LETTER IS REAL.
HEE HEE.
THAT WOULD CERTAINLY PROVE IT.
AND IF THIS WAS FAKE, I IMAGINE THAT WHOEVER MADE IT WOULD HAVE WRITTEN SOMETHING MORE TENGU-LIKE THAN THIS.
SO WE CAN'T NECESSARILY SAY IT'S A FORGERY EITHER, CAN WE...?

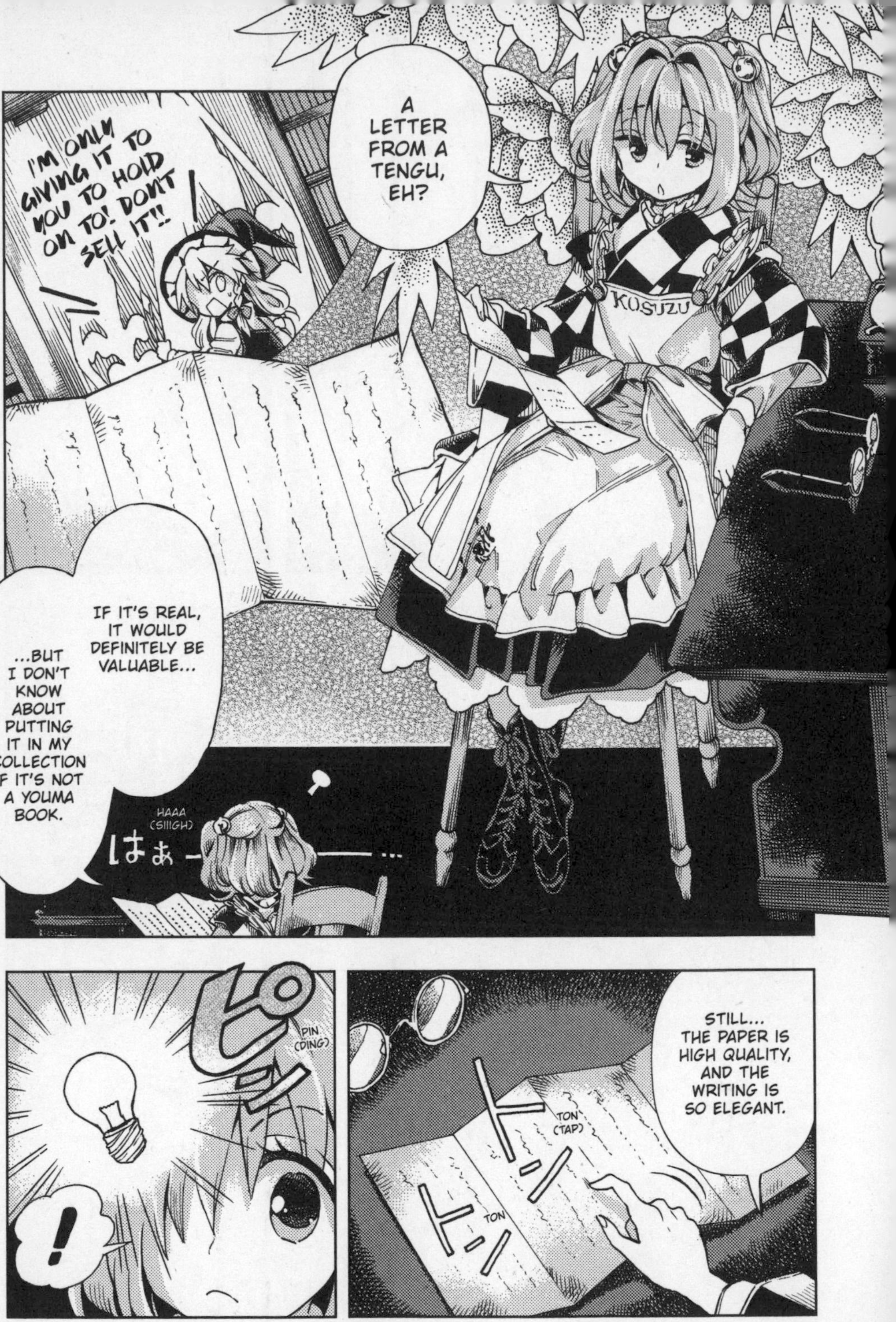
A LETTER FROM A TENGU, EH?
I'M ONLY GIVING IT TO YOU TO HOLD ON TO! DON'T SELL IT!!
KOSUZU
IF IT'S REAL, IT WOULD DEFINITELY BE VALUABLE...
...BUT I DON'T KNOW ABOUT PUTTING IT IN MY COLLECTION IF IT'S NOT A YOUMA BOOK.
はぁーーー…
HAAA (SIIIGH)
STILL... THE PAPER IS HIGH QUALITY, AND THE WRITING IS SO ELEGANT.
TON (TAP)
TON
PIN (DING)
!

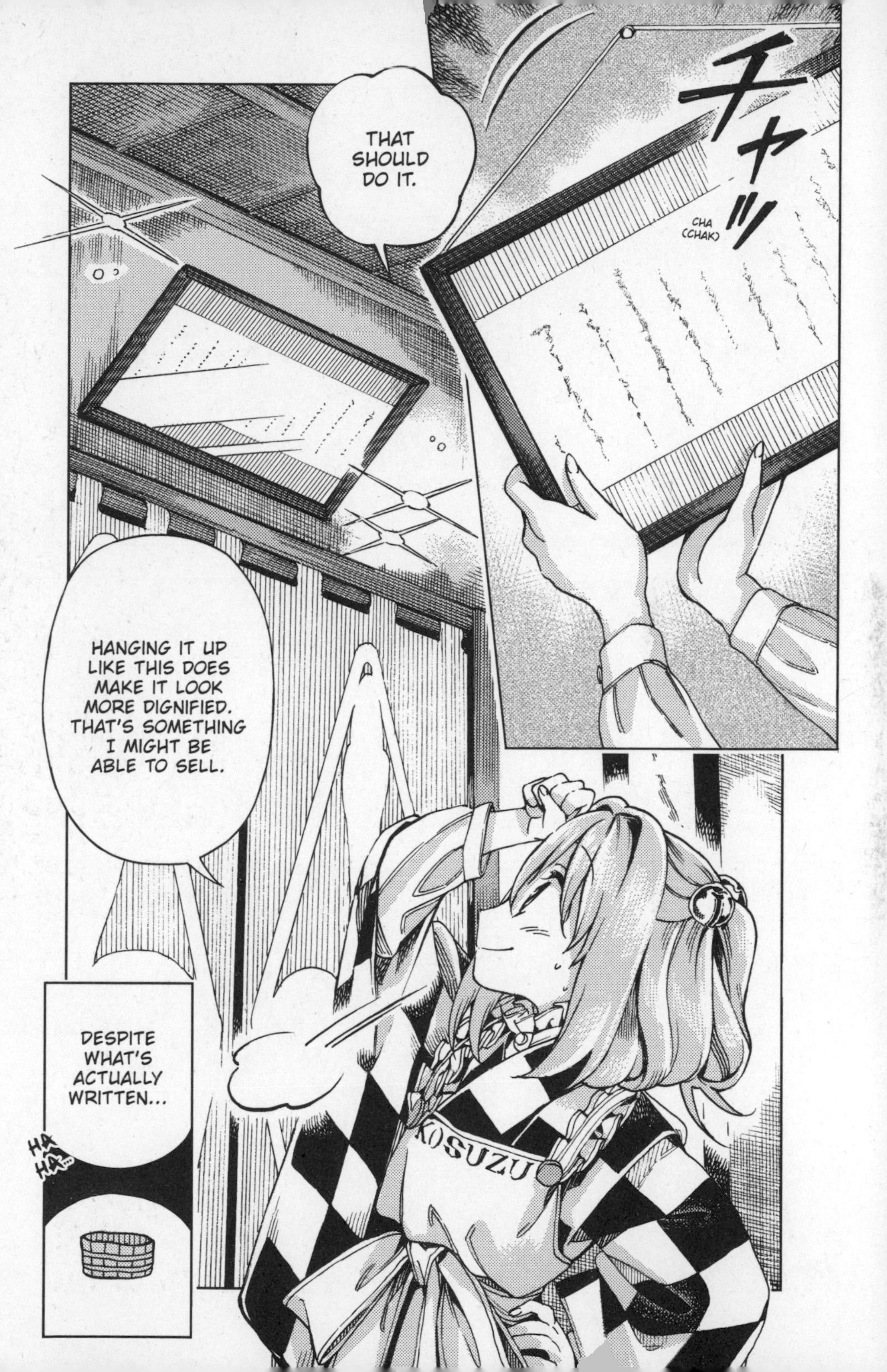

CHA (CHAK)
THAT SHOULD DO IT.
HANGING IT UP LIKE THIS DOES MAKE IT LOOK MORE DIGNIFIED. THAT'S SOMETHING I MIGHT BE ABLE TO SELL.
KOSUZU
DESPITE WHAT'S ACTUALLY WRITTEN...
HA HA...

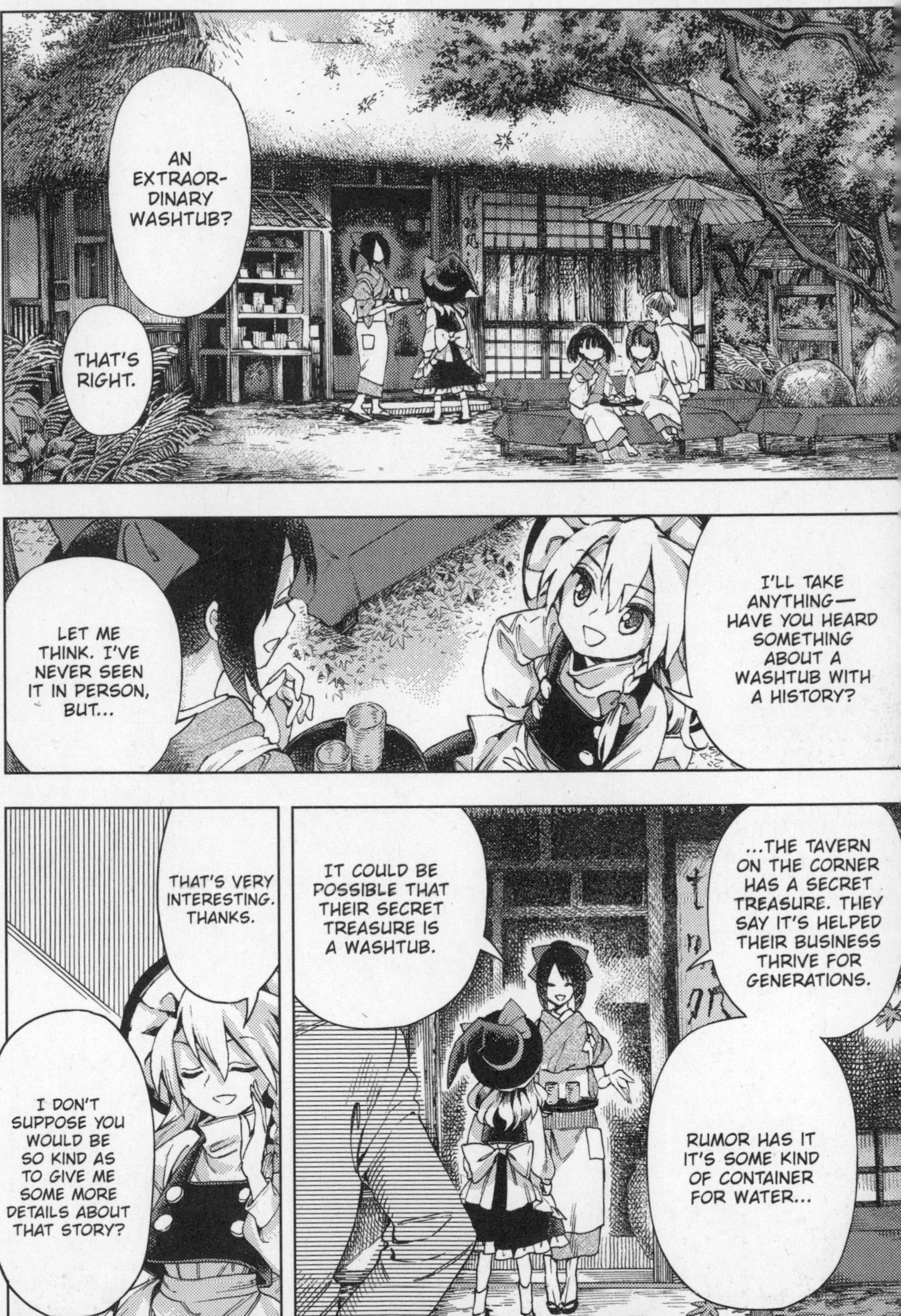
AN EXTRAOR-DINARY WASHTUB?
THAT'S RIGHT.
I'LL TAKE ANYTHING— HAVE YOU HEARD SOMETHING ABOUT A WASHTUB WITH A HISTORY?
LET ME THINK. I'VE NEVER SEEN IT IN PERSON, BUT...
...THE TAVERN ON THE CORNER HAS A SECRET TREASURE. THEY SAY IT'S HELPED THEIR BUSINESS THRIVE FOR GENERATIONS.
RUMOR HAS IT IT'S SOME KIND OF CONTAINER FOR WATER...
IT COULD BE POSSIBLE THAT THEIR SECRET TREASURE IS A WASHTUB.
THAT'S VERY INTERESTING. THANKS.
I DON'T SUPPOSE YOU WOULD BE SO KIND AS TO GIVE ME SOME MORE DETAILS ABOUT THAT STORY?

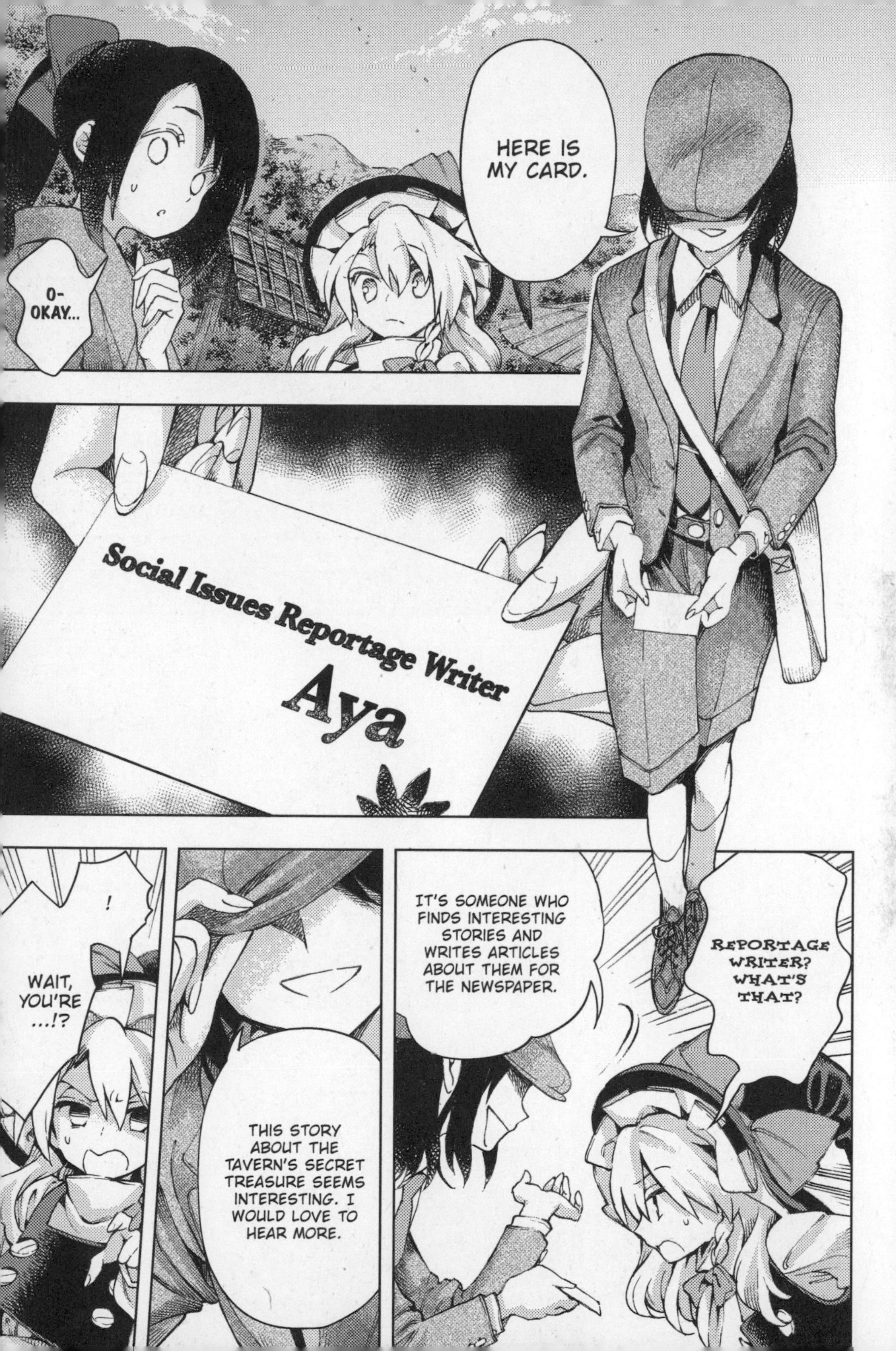
HERE IS MY CARD.
O-OKAY...
Social Issues Reportage Writer
Aya
REPORTAGE WRITER? WHAT'S THAT?
IT'S SOMEONE WHO FINDS INTERESTING STORIES AND WRITES ARTICLES ABOUT THEM FOR THE NEWSPAPER.
THIS STORY ABOUT THE TAVERN'S SECRET TREASURE SEEMS INTERESTING. I WOULD LOVE TO HEAR MORE.
!
WAIT, YOU'RE ...!?

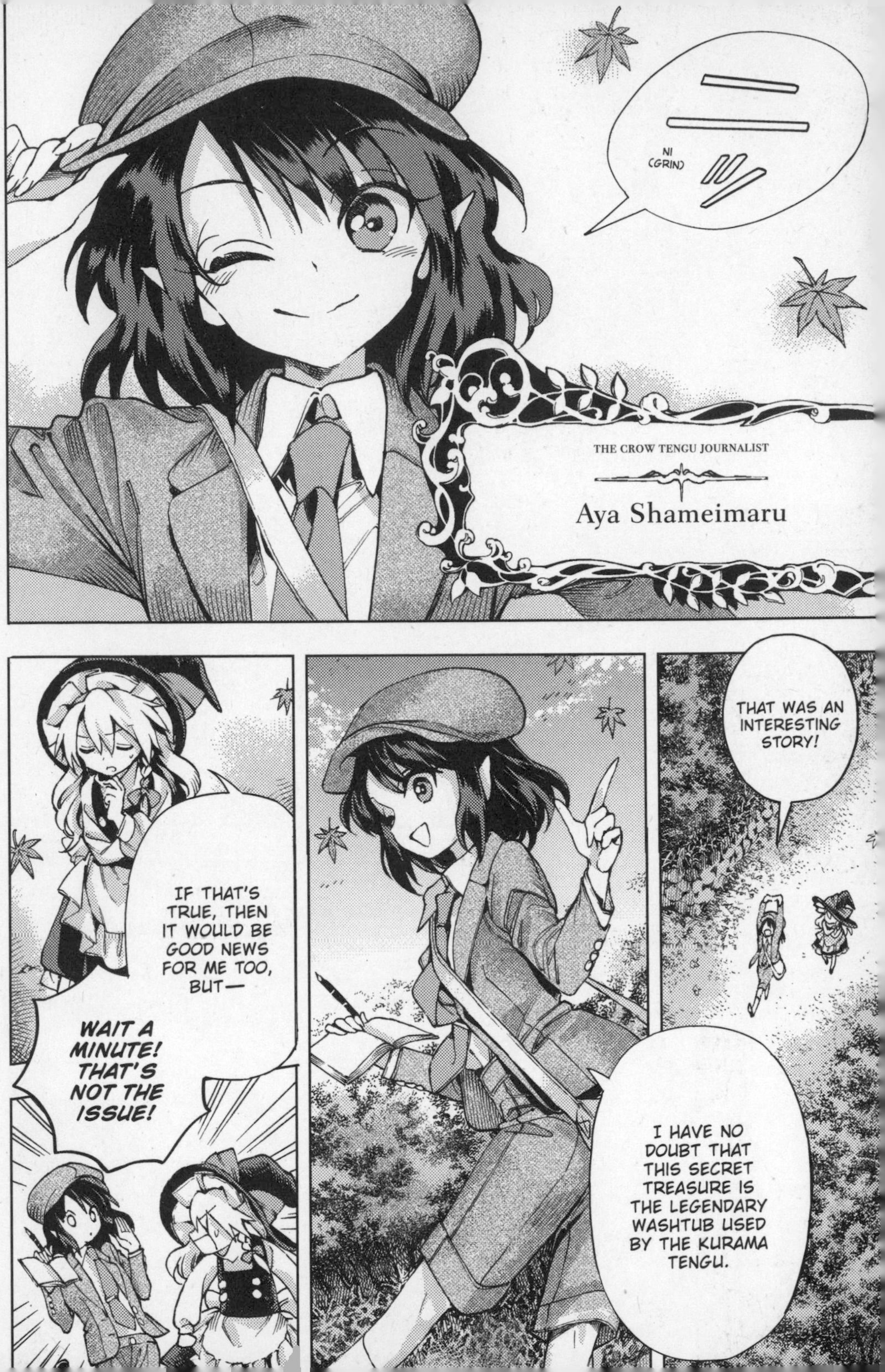
NI (GRIN)
THE CROW TENGU JOURNALIST
Aya Shameimaru
THAT WAS AN INTERESTING STORY!
I HAVE NO DOUBT THAT THIS SECRET TREASURE IS THE LEGENDARY WASHTUB USED BY THE KURAMA TENGU.
IF THAT'S TRUE, THEN IT WOULD BE GOOD NEWS FOR ME TOO, BUT—
WAIT A MINUTE! THAT'S NOT THE ISSUE!

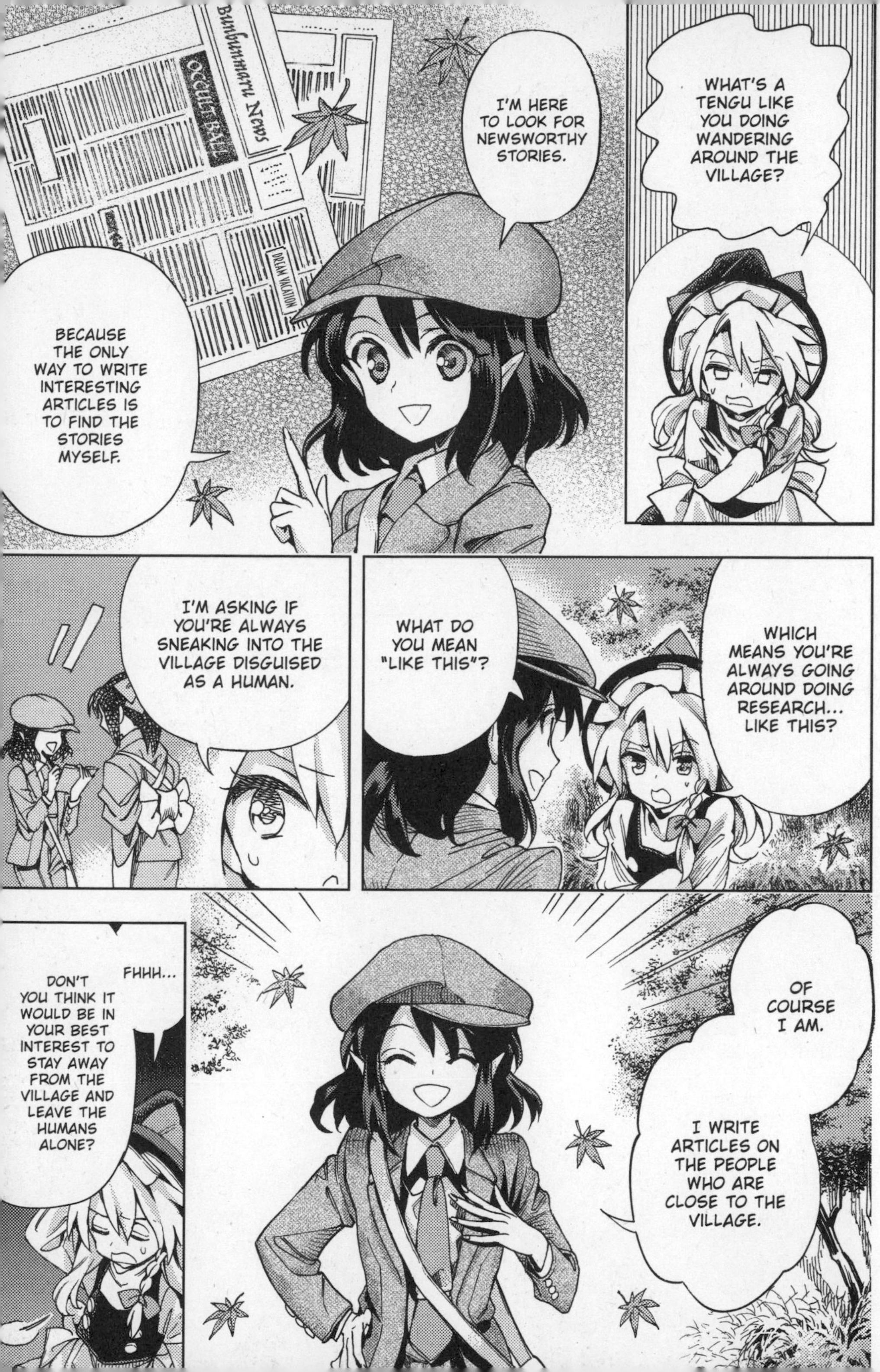
WHAT'S A TENGU LIKE YOU DOING WANDERING AROUND THE VILLAGE?
Bunbunmaru News
OCCULT BALL
DREAM VACATION
I'M HERE TO LOOK FOR NEWSWORTHY STORIES.
BECAUSE THE ONLY WAY TO WRITE INTERESTING ARTICLES IS TO FIND THE STORIES MYSELF.
WHICH MEANS YOU'RE ALWAYS GOING AROUND DOING RESEARCH... LIKE THIS?
WHAT DO YOU MEAN "LIKE THIS"?
I'M ASKING IF YOU'RE ALWAYS SNEAKING INTO THE VILLAGE DISGUISED AS A HUMAN.
OF COURSE I AM.
I WRITE ARTICLES ON THE PEOPLE WHO ARE CLOSE TO THE VILLAGE.
FHHH...
DON'T YOU THINK IT WOULD BE IN YOUR BEST INTEREST TO STAY AWAY FROM THE VILLAGE AND LEAVE THE HUMANS ALONE?

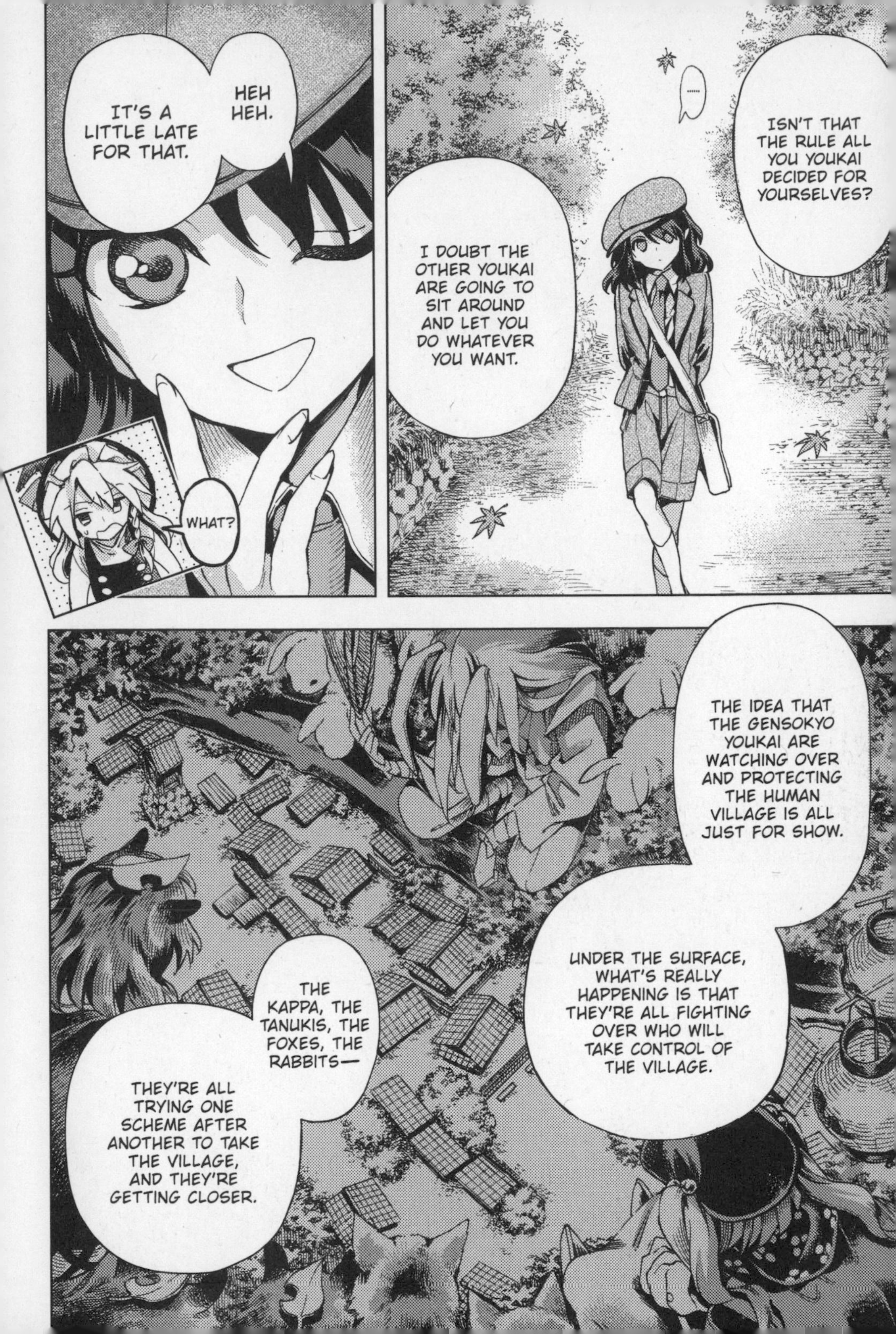
ISN'T THAT THE RULE ALL YOU YOUKAI DECIDED FOR YOURSELVES?
......
I DOUBT THE OTHER YOUKAI ARE GOING TO SIT AROUND AND LET YOU DO WHATEVER YOU WANT.
HEH HEH.
IT'S A LITTLE LATE FOR THAT.
WHAT?
THE IDEA THAT THE GENSOKYO YOUKAI ARE WATCHING OVER AND PROTECTING THE HUMAN VILLAGE IS ALL JUST FOR SHOW.
UNDER THE SURFACE, WHAT'S REALLY HAPPENING IS THAT THEY'RE ALL FIGHTING OVER WHO WILL TAKE CONTROL OF THE VILLAGE.
THE KAPPA, THE TANUKIS, THE FOXES, THE RABBITS—
THEY'RE ALL TRYING ONE SCHEME AFTER ANOTHER TO TAKE THE VILLAGE, AND THEY'RE GETTING CLOSER.

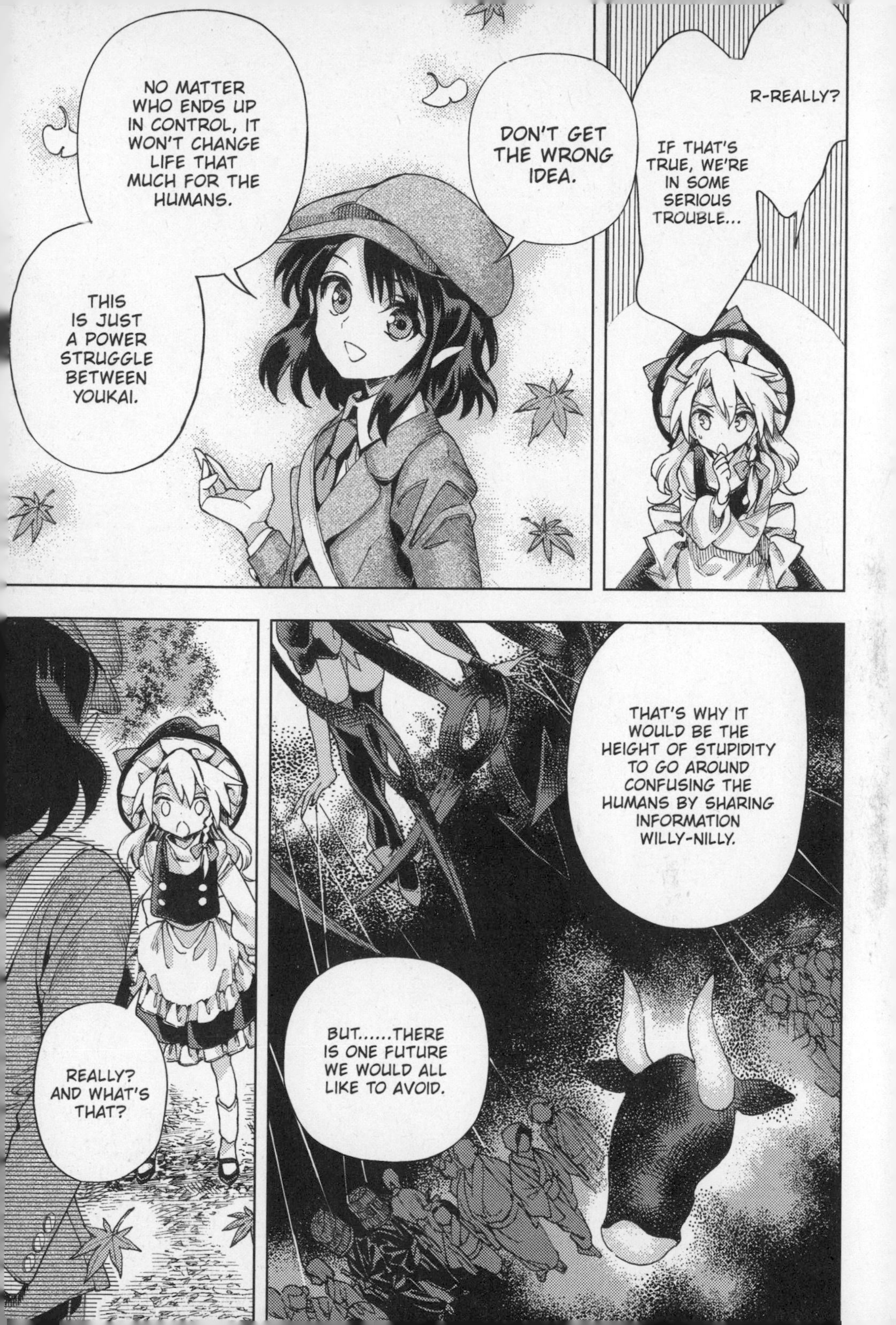
R-REALLY?
IF THAT'S TRUE, WE'RE IN SOME SERIOUS TROUBLE...
DON'T GET THE WRONG IDEA.
NO MATTER WHO ENDS UP IN CONTROL, IT WON'T CHANGE LIFE THAT MUCH FOR THE HUMANS.
THIS IS JUST A POWER STRUGGLE BETWEEN YOUKAI.
THAT'S WHY IT WOULD BE THE HEIGHT OF STUPIDITY TO GO AROUND CONFUSING THE HUMANS BY SHARING INFORMATION WILLY-NILLY.
BUT......THERE IS ONE FUTURE WE WOULD ALL LIKE TO AVOID.
REALLY? AND WHAT'S THAT?

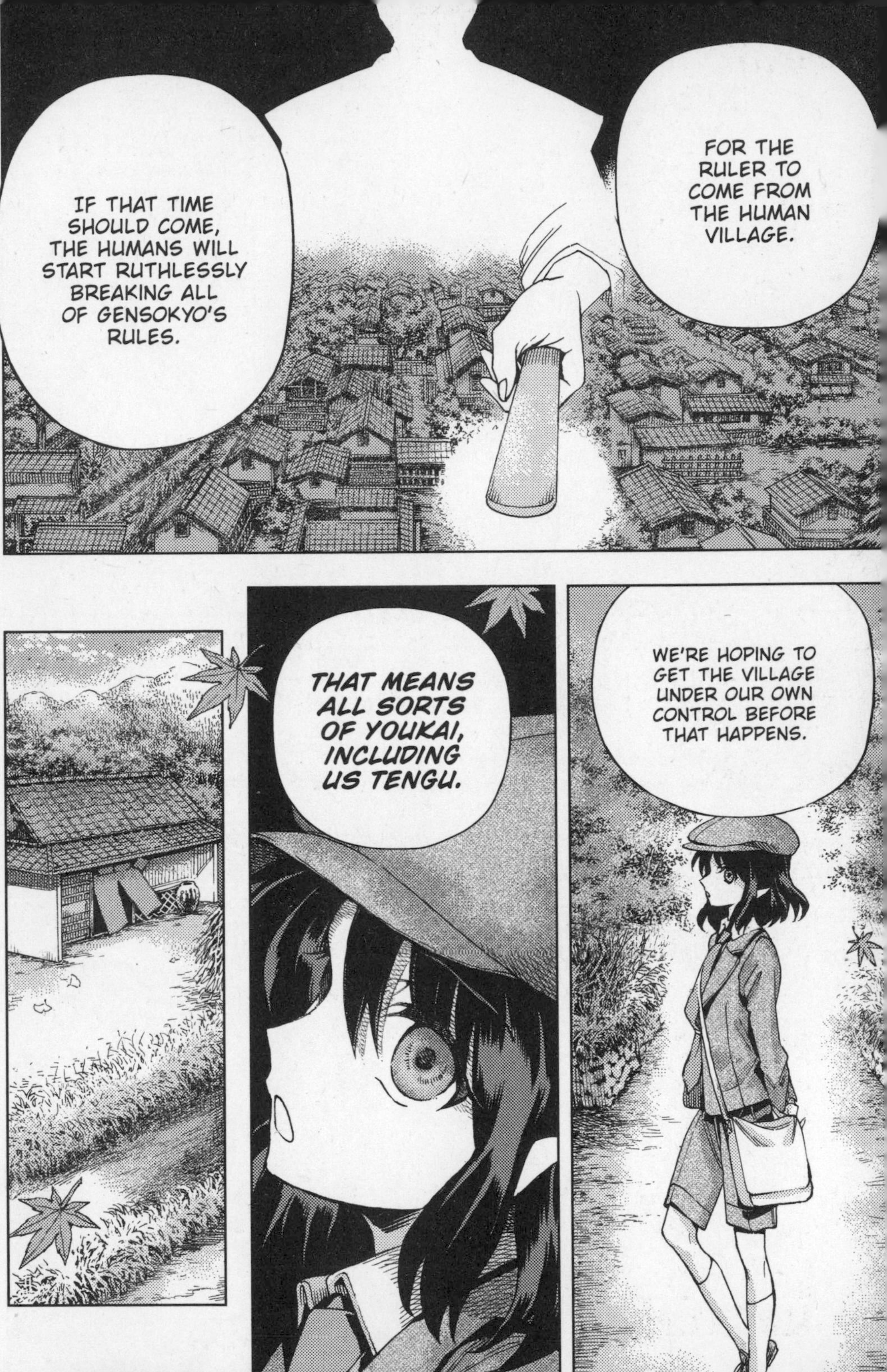
FOR THE RULER TO COME FROM THE HUMAN VILLAGE.
IF THAT TIME SHOULD COME, THE HUMANS WILL START RUTHLESSLY BREAKING ALL OF GENSOKYO'S RULES.
WE'RE HOPING TO GET THE VILLAGE UNDER OUR OWN CONTROL BEFORE THAT HAPPENS.
THAT MEANS ALL SORTS OF YOUKAI, INCLUDING US TENGU.

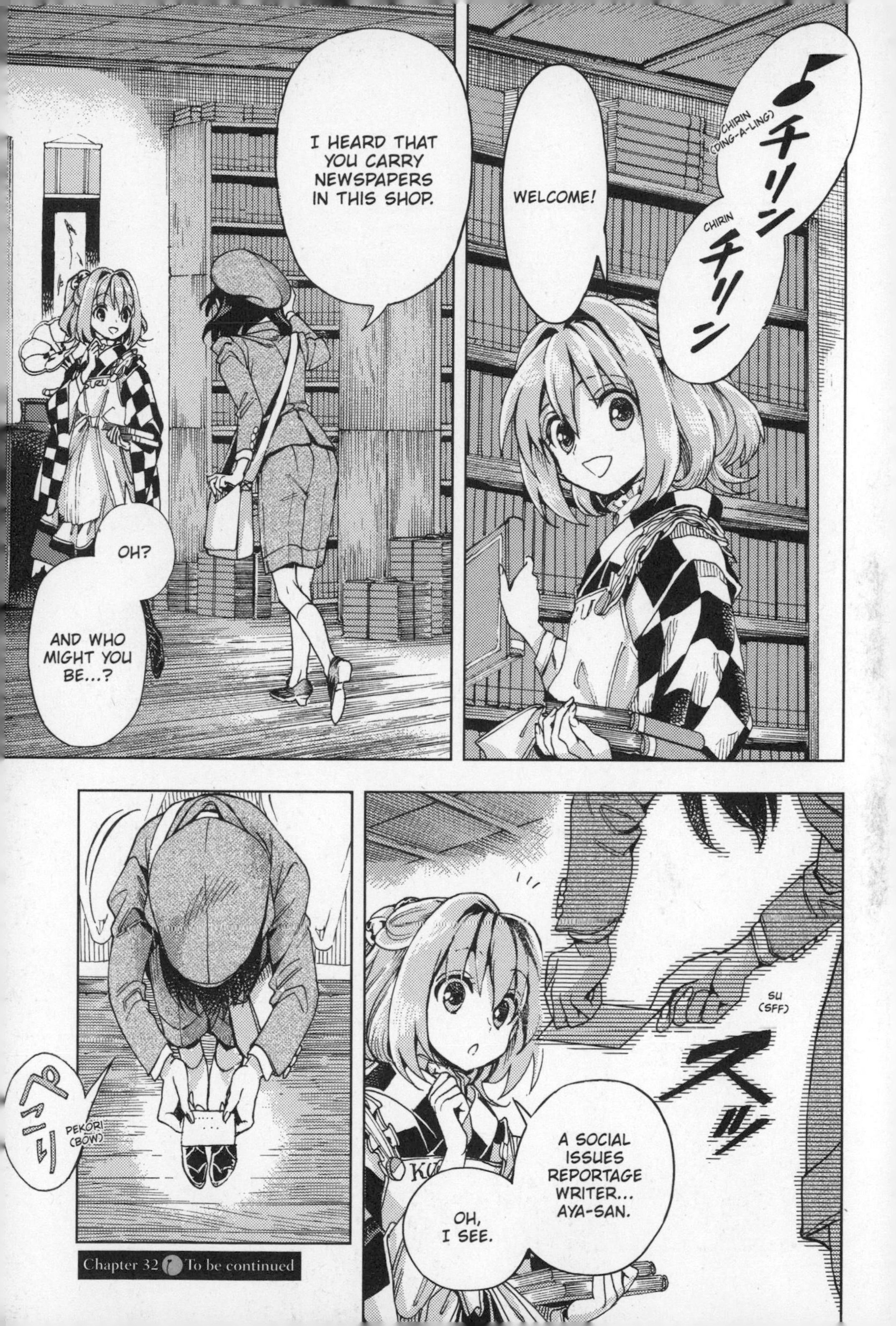
チリン
CHIRIN (DING-A-LING)
チリン
CHIRIN
WELCOME!
I HEARD THAT YOU CARRY NEWSPAPERS IN THIS SHOP.
OH?
AND WHO MIGHT YOU BE...?
スッ
SU (SFF)
A SOCIAL ISSUES REPORTAGE WRITER... AYA-SAN.
OH, I SEE.
ペコリ
PEKORI (BOW)

Chapter 32 To be continued

Forbidden Scrollery

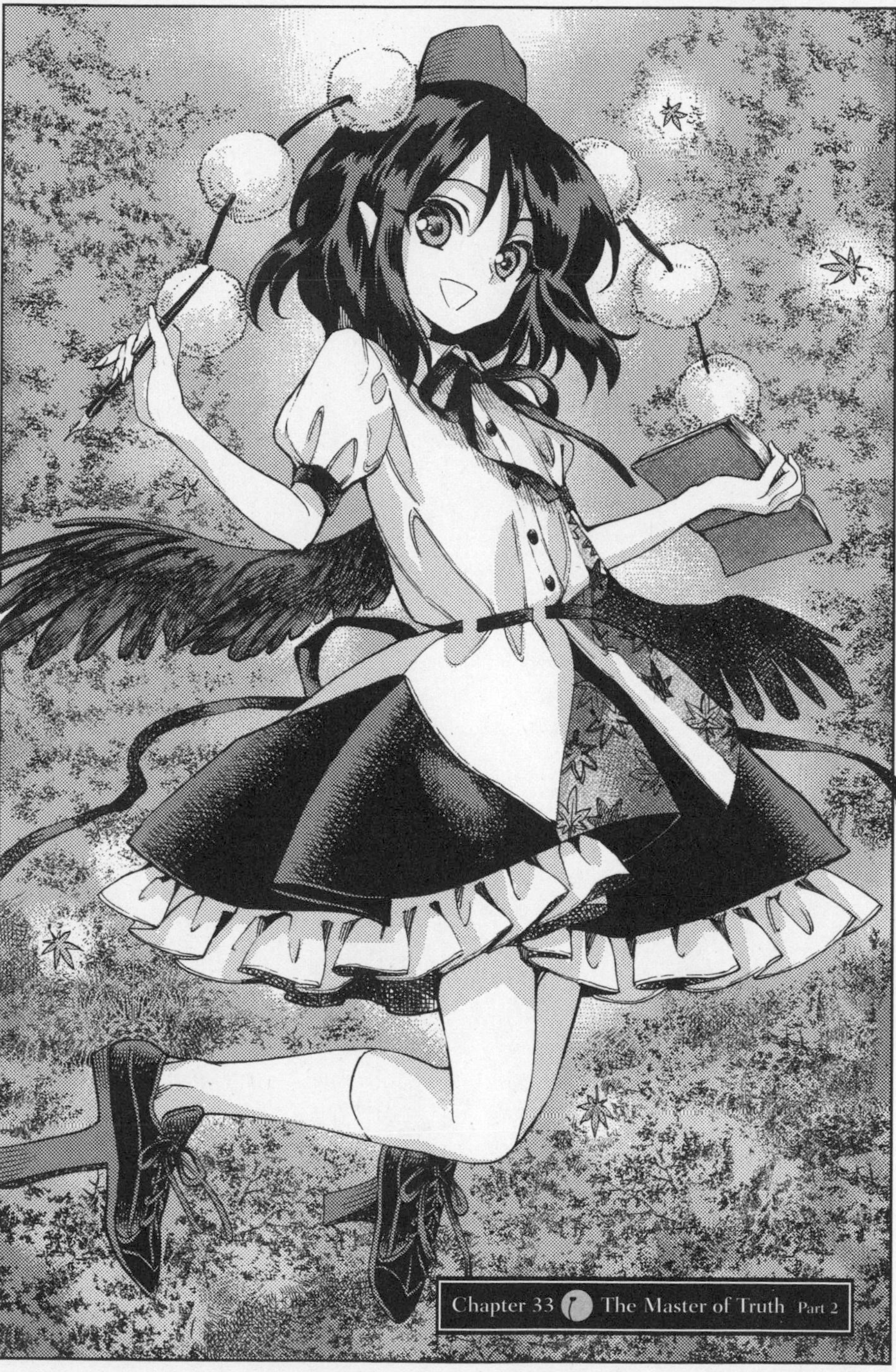

Chapter 33 The Master of Truth Part 2

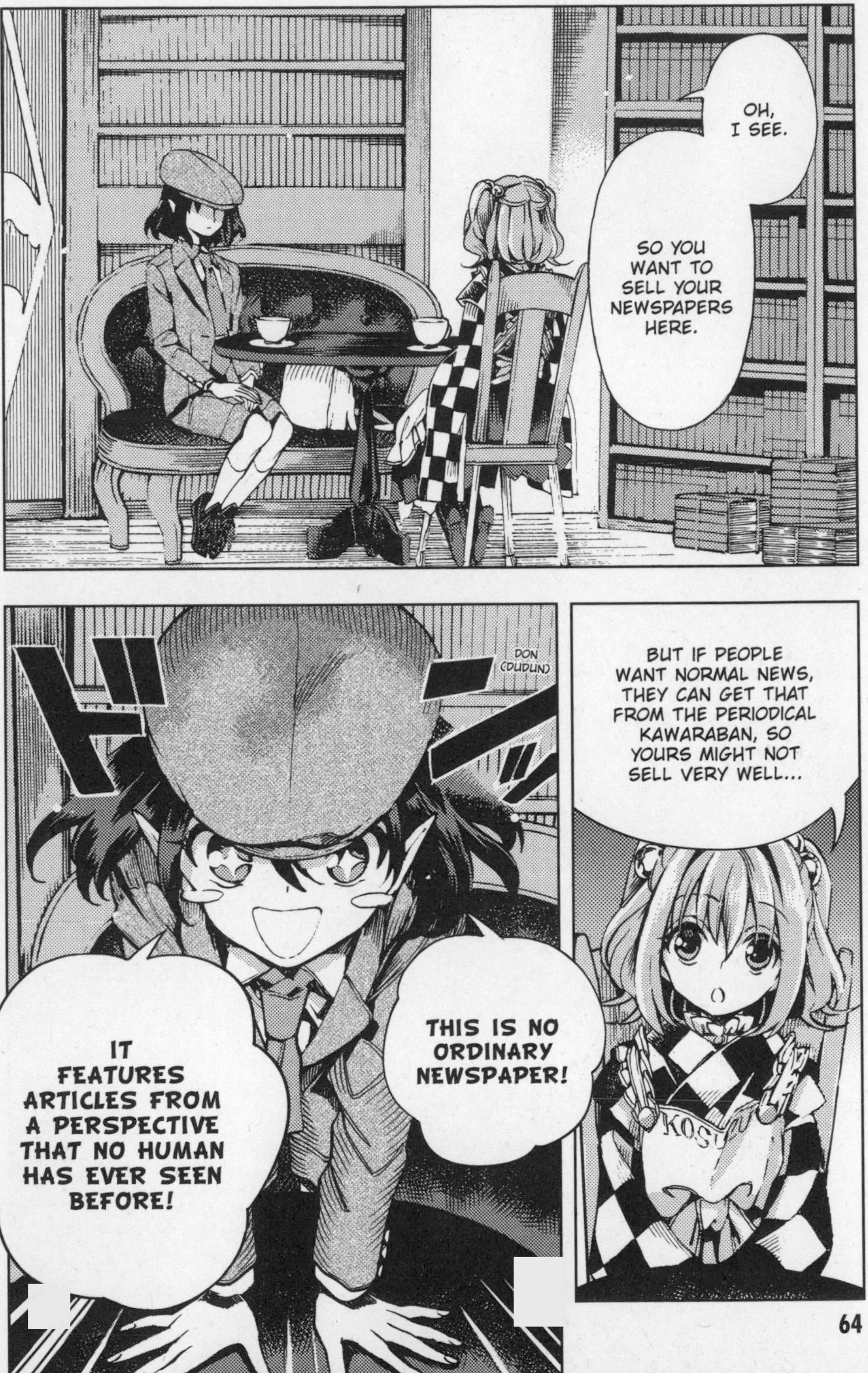
OH, I SEE.
SO YOU WANT TO SELL YOUR NEWSPAPERS HERE.
BUT IF PEOPLE WANT NORMAL NEWS, THEY CAN GET THAT FROM THE PERIODICAL KAWARABAN, SO YOURS MIGHT NOT SELL VERY WELL...
DON (DUDUN)
THIS IS NO ORDINARY NEWSPAPER!
IT FEATURES ARTICLES FROM A PERSPECTIVE THAT NO HUMAN HAS EVER SEEN BEFORE!

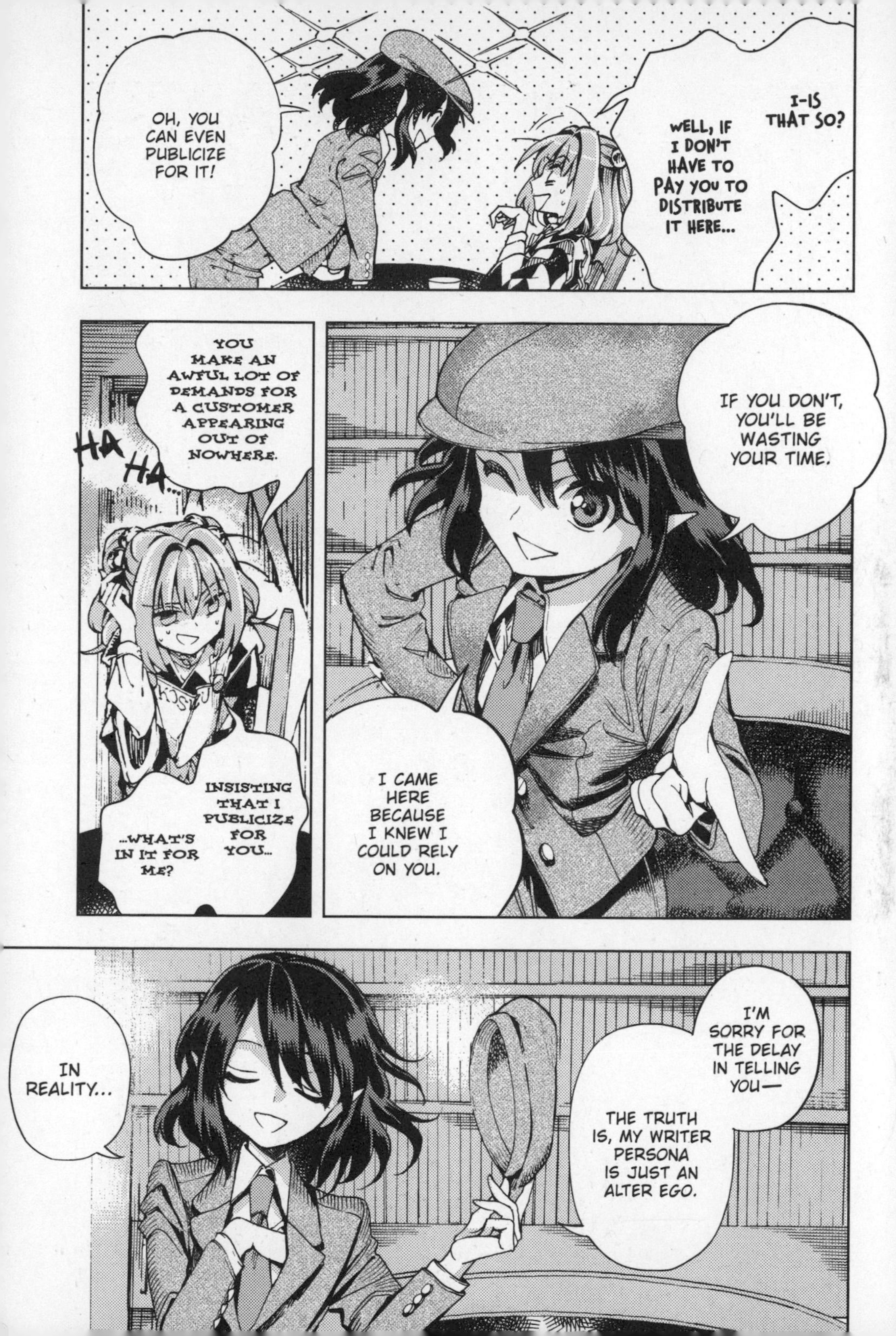
I-IS THAT SO?
WELL, IF I DON'T HAVE TO PAY YOU TO DISTRIBUTE IT HERE...
OH, YOU CAN EVEN PUBLICIZE FOR IT!
IF YOU DON'T, YOU'LL BE WASTING YOUR TIME.
I CAME HERE BECAUSE I KNEW I COULD RELY ON YOU.
YOU MAKE AN AWFUL LOT OF DEMANDS FOR A CUSTOMER APPEARING OUT OF NOWHERE.
HA HA...
INSISTING THAT I PUBLICIZE FOR YOU...
...WHAT'S IN IT FOR ME?
I'M SORRY FOR THE DELAY IN TELLING YOU—
THE TRUTH IS, MY WRITER PERSONA IS JUST AN ALTER EGO.
IN REALITY...

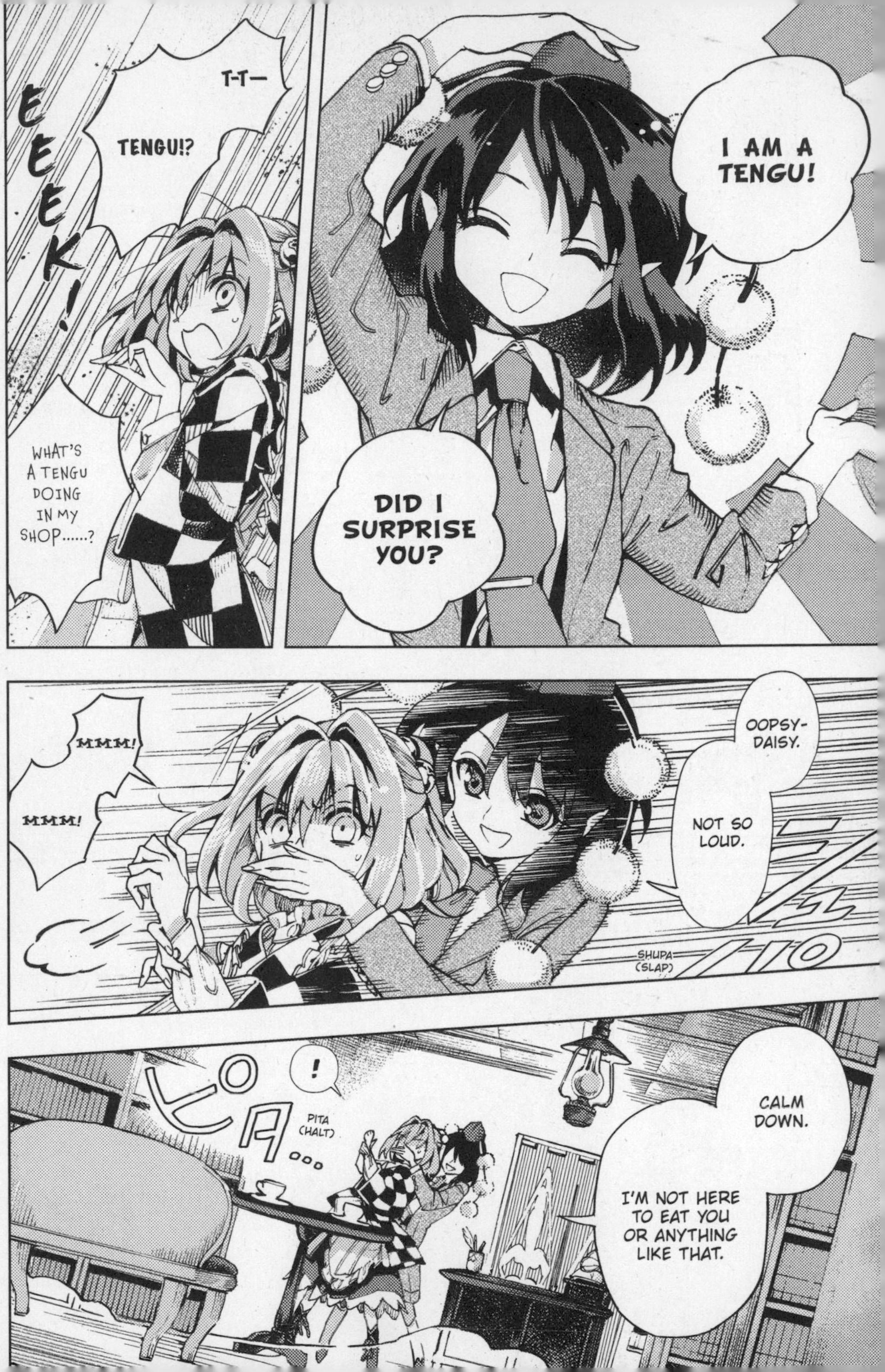
I AM A TENGU!
DID I SURPRISE YOU?
T-T—
TENGU!?
EEEK!
WHAT'S A TENGU DOING IN MY SHOP......?
OOPSY-DAISY.
NOT SO LOUD.
SHUPA (SLAP)
MMM!
MMM!
CALM DOWN.
I'M NOT HERE TO EAT YOU OR ANYTHING LIKE THAT.
!
PITA (HALT)

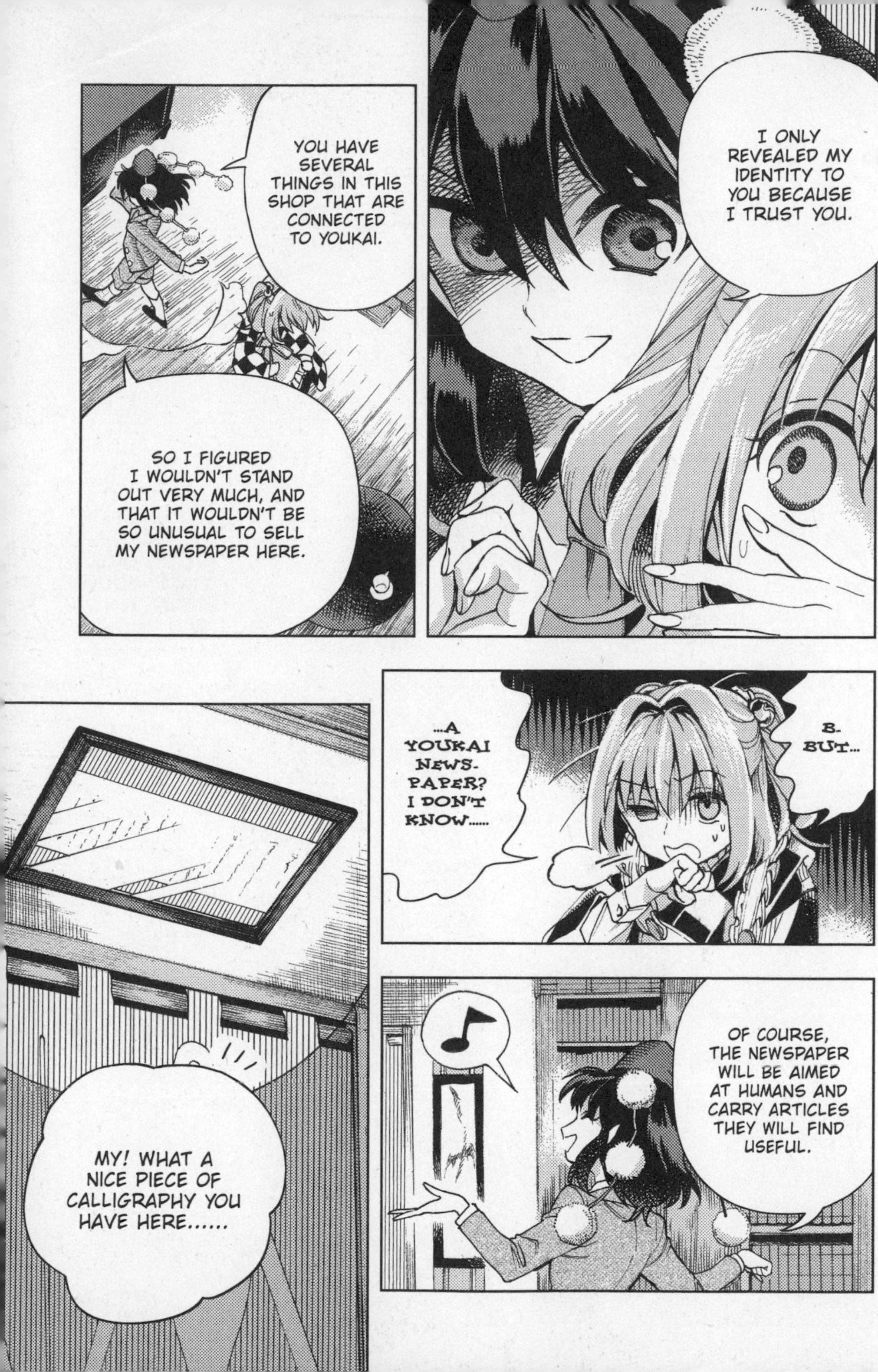
I ONLY REVEALED MY IDENTITY TO YOU BECAUSE I TRUST YOU.
YOU HAVE SEVERAL THINGS IN THIS SHOP THAT ARE CONNECTED TO YOUKAI.
SO I FIGURED I WOULDN'T STAND OUT VERY MUCH, AND THAT IT WOULDN'T BE SO UNUSUAL TO SELL MY NEWSPAPER HERE.
B-BUT...
...A YOUKAI NEWS-PAPER? I DON'T KNOW......
OF COURSE, THE NEWSPAPER WILL BE AIMED AT HUMANS AND CARRY ARTICLES THEY WILL FIND USEFUL.
MY! WHAT A NICE PIECE OF CALLIGRAPHY YOU HAVE HERE......

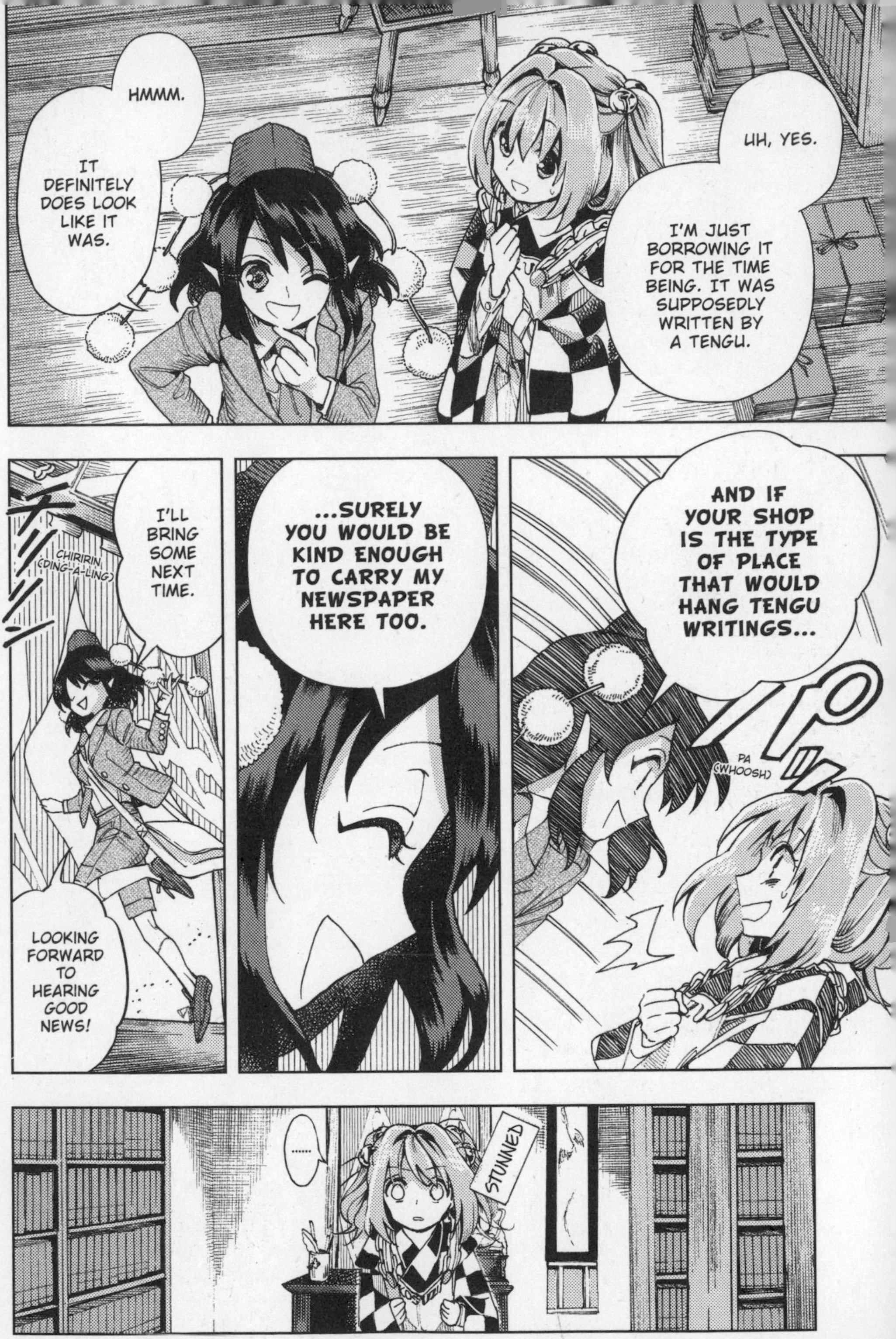
UH, YES.
I'M JUST BORROWING IT FOR THE TIME BEING. IT WAS SUPPOSEDLY WRITTEN BY A TENGU.
HMMM.
IT DEFINITELY DOES LOOK LIKE IT WAS.
AND IF YOUR SHOP IS THE TYPE OF PLACE THAT WOULD HANG TENGU WRITINGS...
PA (WHOOSH)
...SURELY YOU WOULD BE KIND ENOUGH TO CARRY MY NEWSPAPER HERE TOO.
I'LL BRING SOME NEXT TIME.
CHIRIRIN (DING-A-LING)
LOOKING FORWARD TO HEARING GOOD NEWS!
STUNNED
......

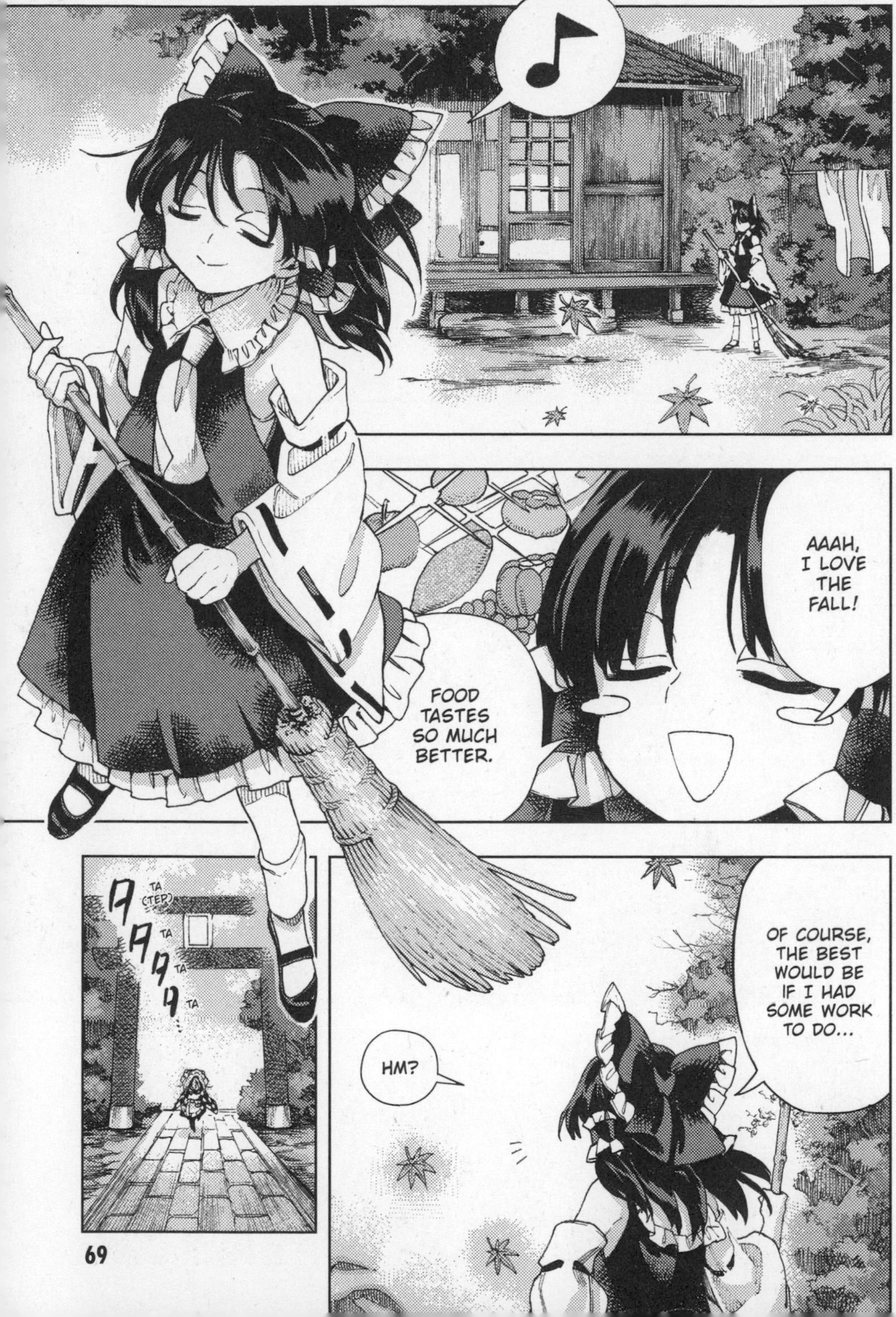
♪
AAAH, I LOVE THE FALL!
FOOD TASTES SO MUCH BETTER.
OF COURSE, THE BEST WOULD BE IF I HAD SOME WORK TO DO...
HM?
タ TA (STEP)
タ TA
タ TA
タ TA

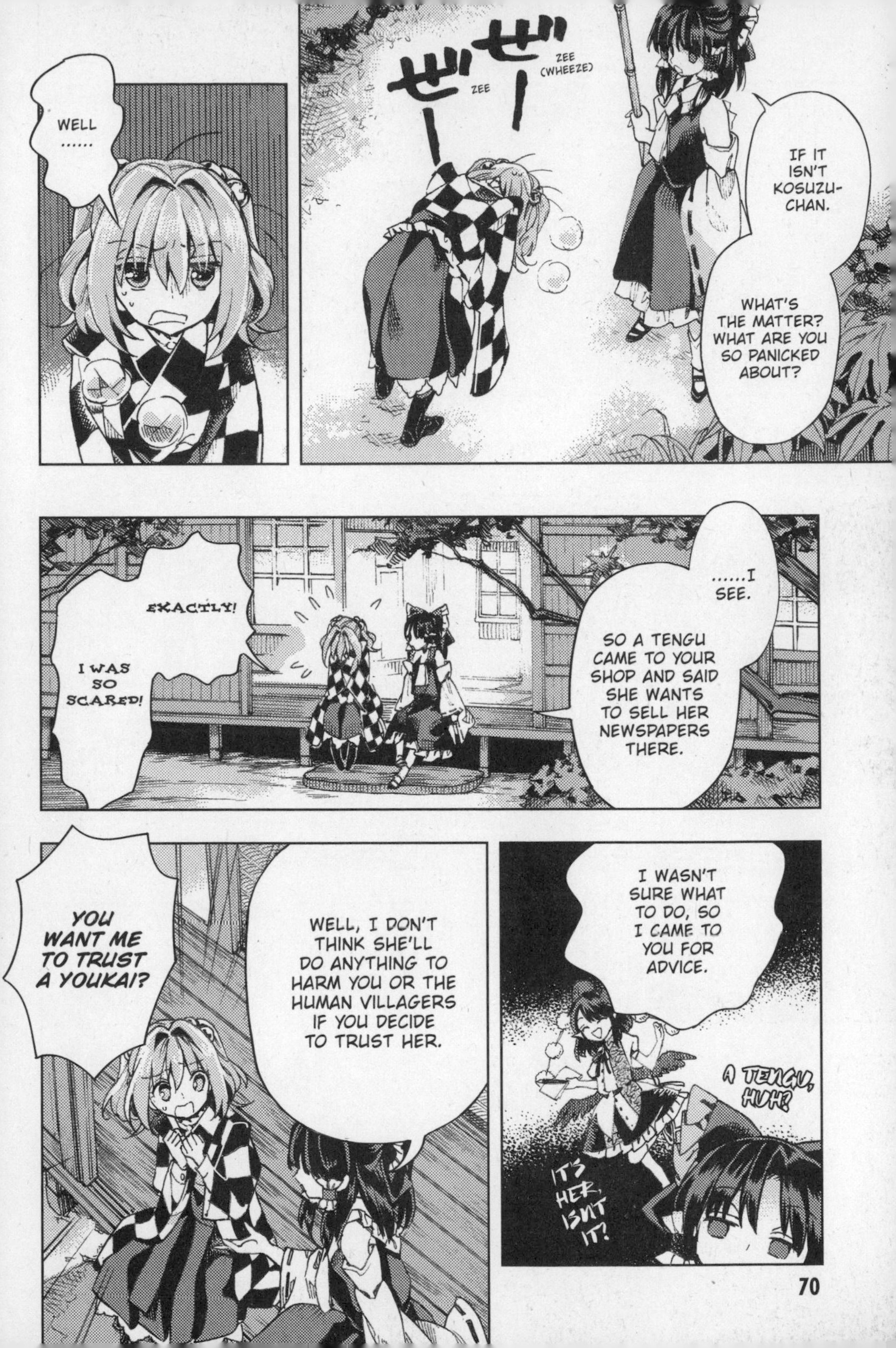
ゼー
ゼー
ZEE (WHEEZE)
ZEE
IF IT ISN'T KOSUZU-CHAN.
WHAT'S THE MATTER? WHAT ARE YOU SO PANICKED ABOUT?
WELL ......
......I SEE.
SO A TENGU CAME TO YOUR SHOP AND SAID SHE WANTS TO SELL HER NEWSPAPERS THERE.
EXACTLY!
I WAS SO SCARED!
I WASN'T SURE WHAT TO DO, SO I CAME TO YOU FOR ADVICE.
A TENGU, HUH?
IT'S HER, ISN'T IT?
WELL, I DON'T THINK SHE'LL DO ANYTHING TO HARM YOU OR THE HUMAN VILLAGERS IF YOU DECIDE TO TRUST HER.
YOU WANT ME TO TRUST A YOUKAI?

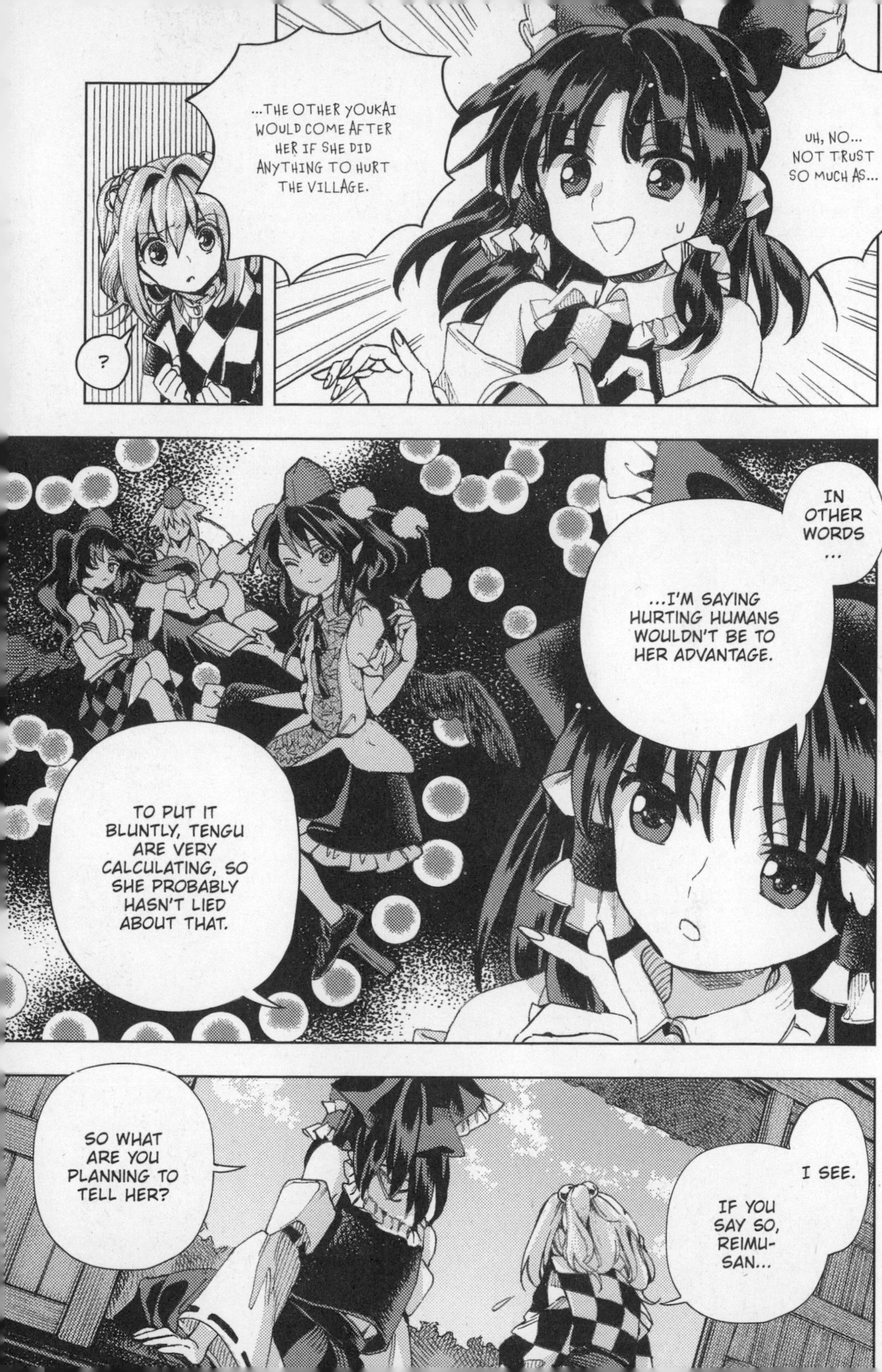
UH, NO... NOT TRUST SO MUCH AS...
...THE OTHER YOUKAI WOULD COME AFTER HER IF SHE DID ANYTHING TO HURT THE VILLAGE.
?
IN OTHER WORDS...
...I'M SAYING HURTING HUMANS WOULDN'T BE TO HER ADVANTAGE.
TO PUT IT BLUNTLY, TENGU ARE VERY CALCULATING, SO SHE PROBABLY HASN'T LIED ABOUT THAT.
I SEE.
IF YOU SAY SO, REIMU-SAN...
SO WHAT ARE YOU PLANNING TO TELL HER?

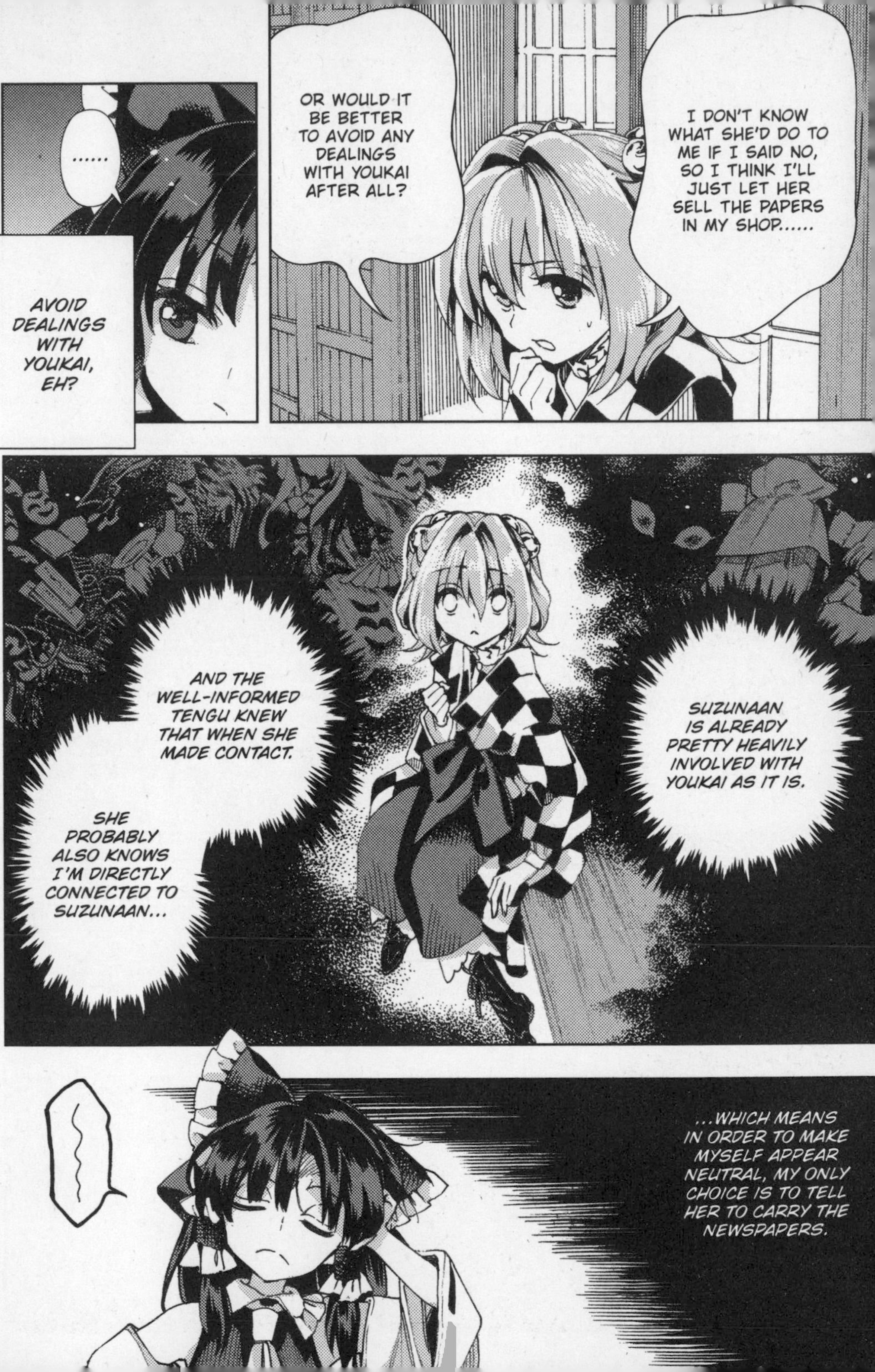
I DON'T KNOW WHAT SHE'D DO TO ME IF I SAID NO, SO I THINK I'LL JUST LET HER SELL THE PAPERS IN MY SHOP......
OR WOULD IT BE BETTER TO AVOID ANY DEALINGS WITH YOUKAI AFTER ALL?
......
AVOID DEALINGS WITH YOUKAI, EH?
SUZUNAAN IS ALREADY PRETTY HEAVILY INVOLVED WITH YOUKAI AS IT IS.
AND THE WELL-INFORMED TENGU KNEW THAT WHEN SHE MADE CONTACT.
SHE PROBABLY ALSO KNOWS I'M DIRECTLY CONNECTED TO SUZUNAAN...
...WHICH MEANS IN ORDER TO MAKE MYSELF APPEAR NEUTRAL, MY ONLY CHOICE IS TO TELL HER TO CARRY THE NEWSPAPERS.

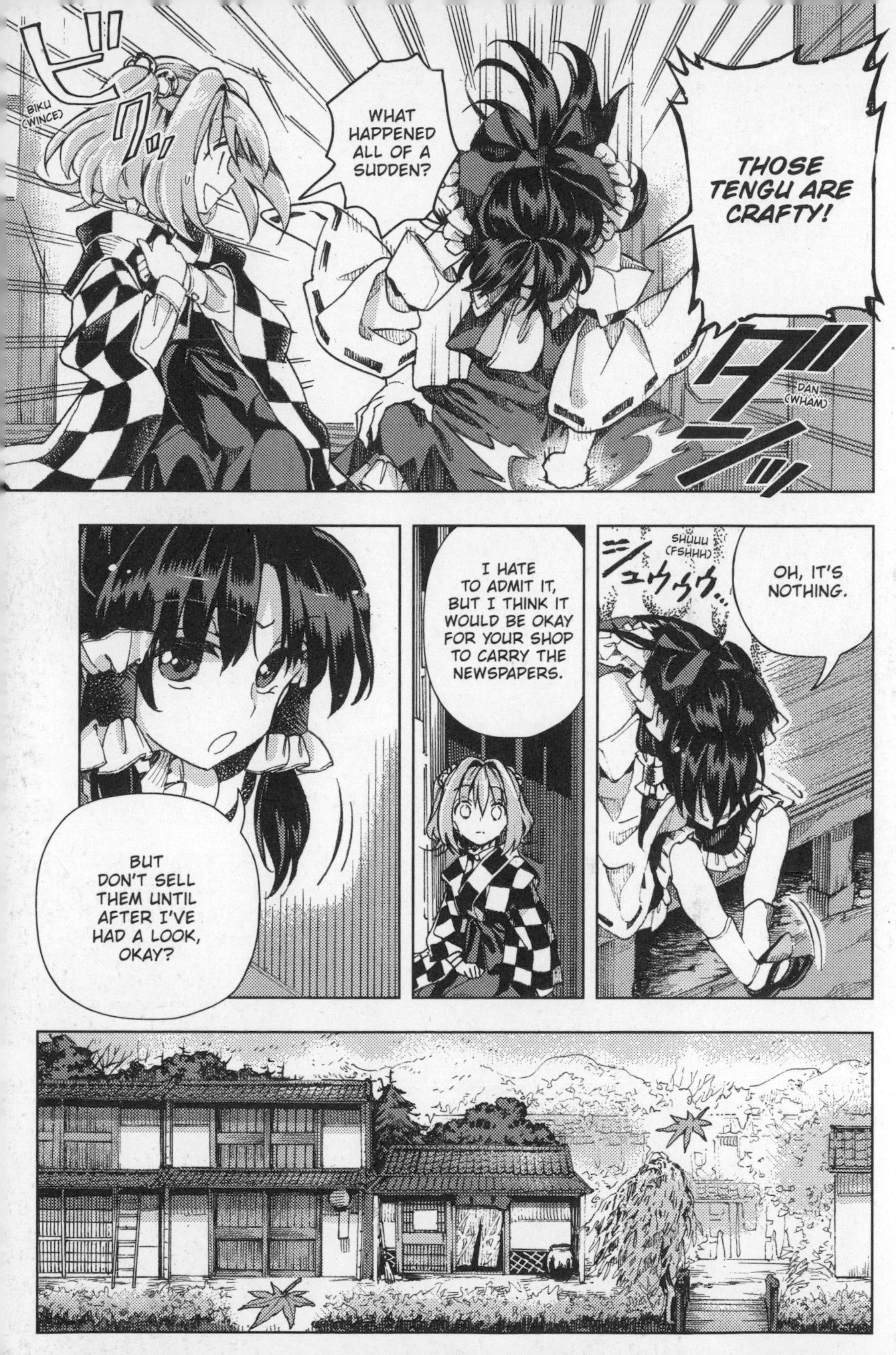
THOSE TENGU ARE CRAFTY!
DAN (WHAM)
WHAT HAPPENED ALL OF A SUDDEN?
BIKU (WINCE)
OH, IT'S NOTHING.
SHUUU (FSHHH)
I HATE TO ADMIT IT, BUT I THINK IT WOULD BE OKAY FOR YOUR SHOP TO CARRY THE NEWSPAPERS.
BUT DON'T SELL THEM UNTIL AFTER I'VE HAD A LOOK, OKAY?

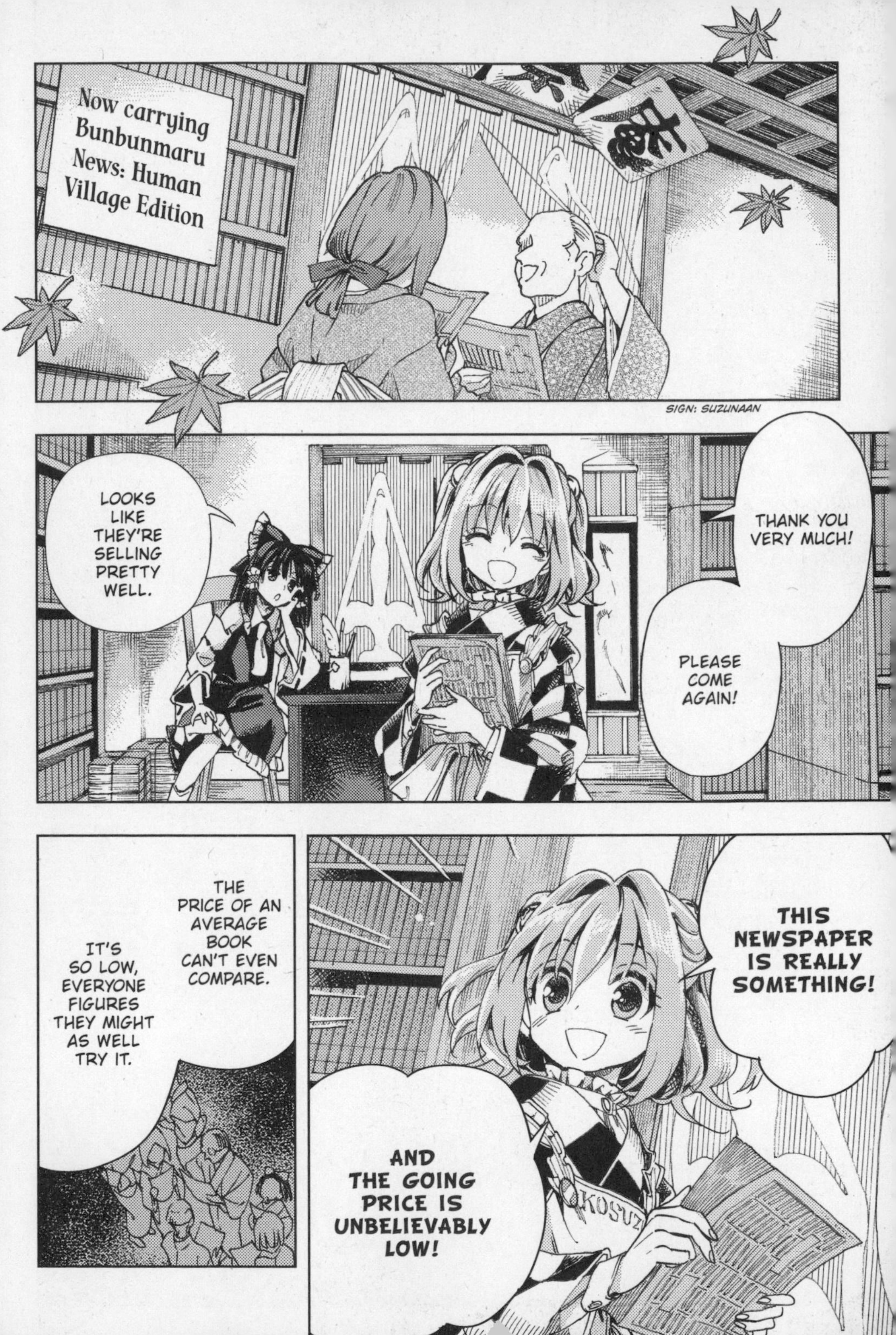
Now carrying Bunbunmaru News: Human Village Edition
SIGN: SUZUNAAN
THANK YOU VERY MUCH!
PLEASE COME AGAIN!
LOOKS LIKE THEY'RE SELLING PRETTY WELL.
THIS NEWSPAPER IS REALLY SOMETHING!
AND THE GOING PRICE IS UNBELIEVABLY LOW!
THE PRICE OF AN AVERAGE BOOK CAN'T EVEN COMPARE.
IT'S SO LOW, EVERYONE FIGURES THEY MIGHT AS WELL TRY IT.

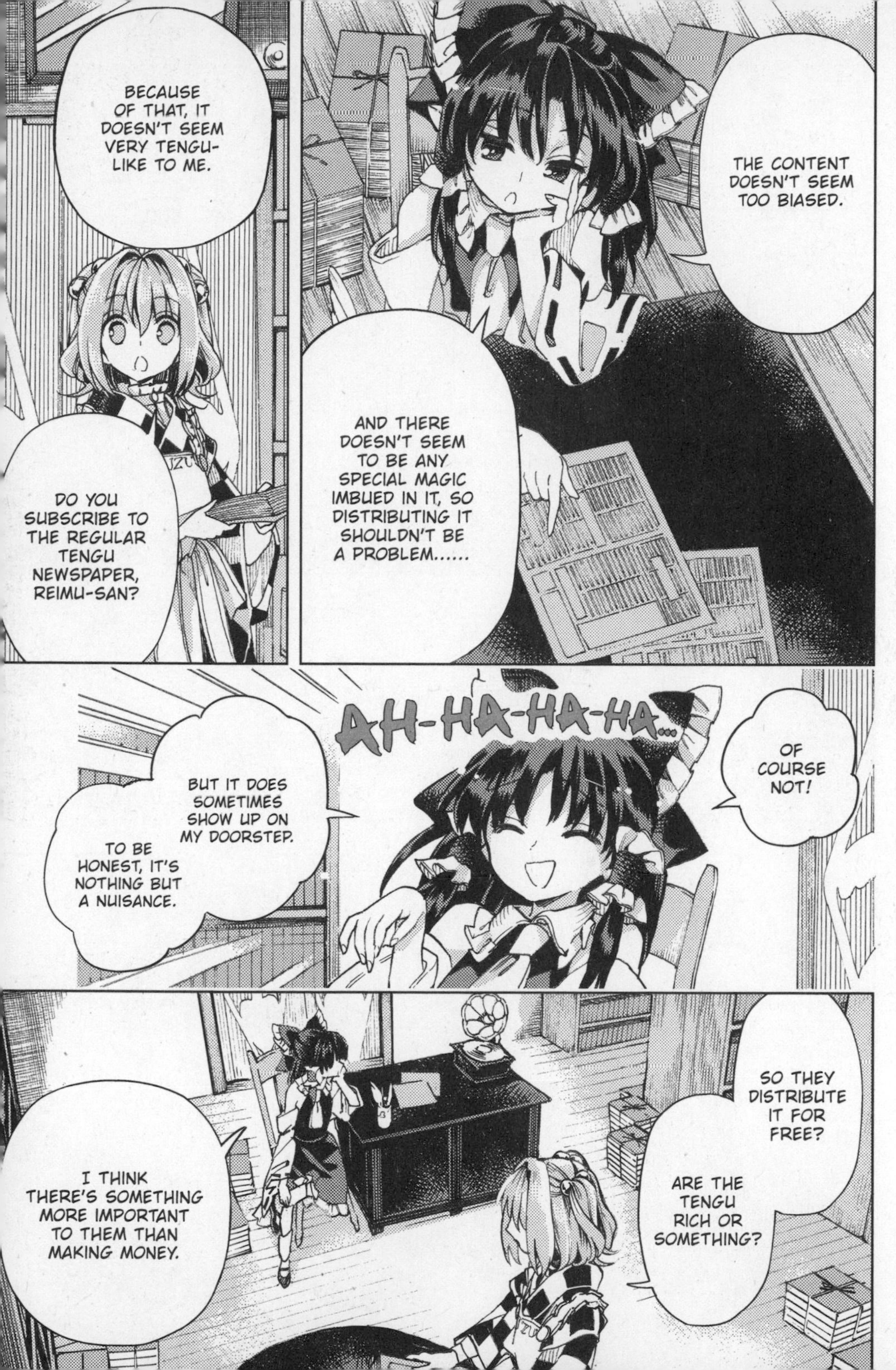
THE CONTENT DOESN'T SEEM TOO BIASED.
AND THERE DOESN'T SEEM TO BE ANY SPECIAL MAGIC IMBUED IN IT, SO DISTRIBUTING IT SHOULDN'T BE A PROBLEM......
BECAUSE OF THAT, IT DOESN'T SEEM VERY TENGU-LIKE TO ME.
DO YOU SUBSCRIBE TO THE REGULAR TENGU NEWSPAPER, REIMU-SAN?
AH-HA-HA-HA...
OF COURSE NOT!
BUT IT DOES SOMETIMES SHOW UP ON MY DOORSTEP.
TO BE HONEST, IT'S NOTHING BUT A NUISANCE.
SO THEY DISTRIBUTE IT FOR FREE?
ARE THE TENGU RICH OR SOMETHING?
I THINK THERE'S SOMETHING MORE IMPORTANT TO THEM THAN MAKING MONEY.

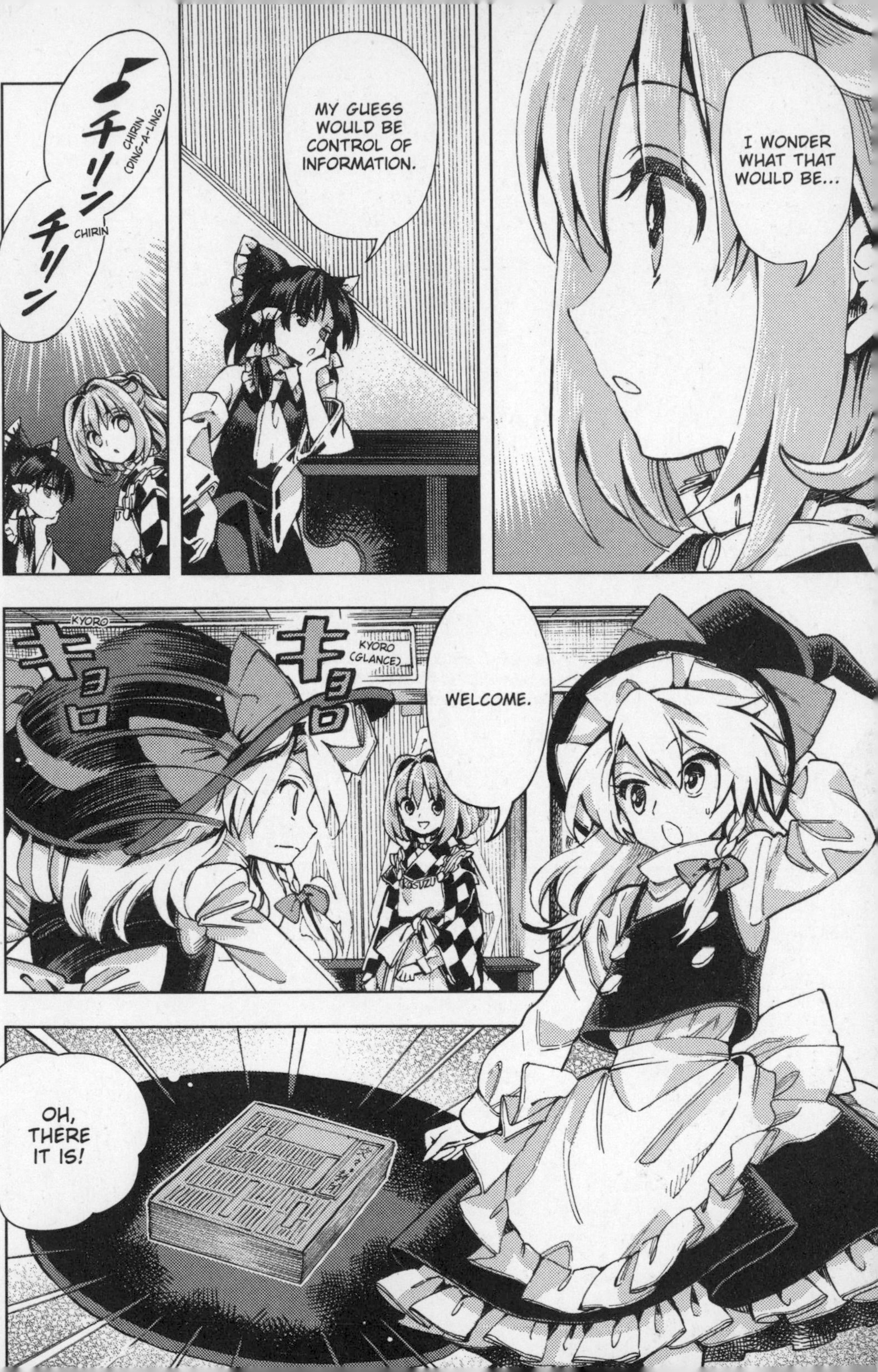
I WONDER WHAT THAT WOULD BE...
MY GUESS WOULD BE CONTROL OF INFORMATION.
♪ チリン
CHIRIN (DING-A-LING)
チリン
CHIRIN
WELCOME.
キョロ
KYORO (GLANCE)
キョロ
KYORO
OH, THERE IT IS!

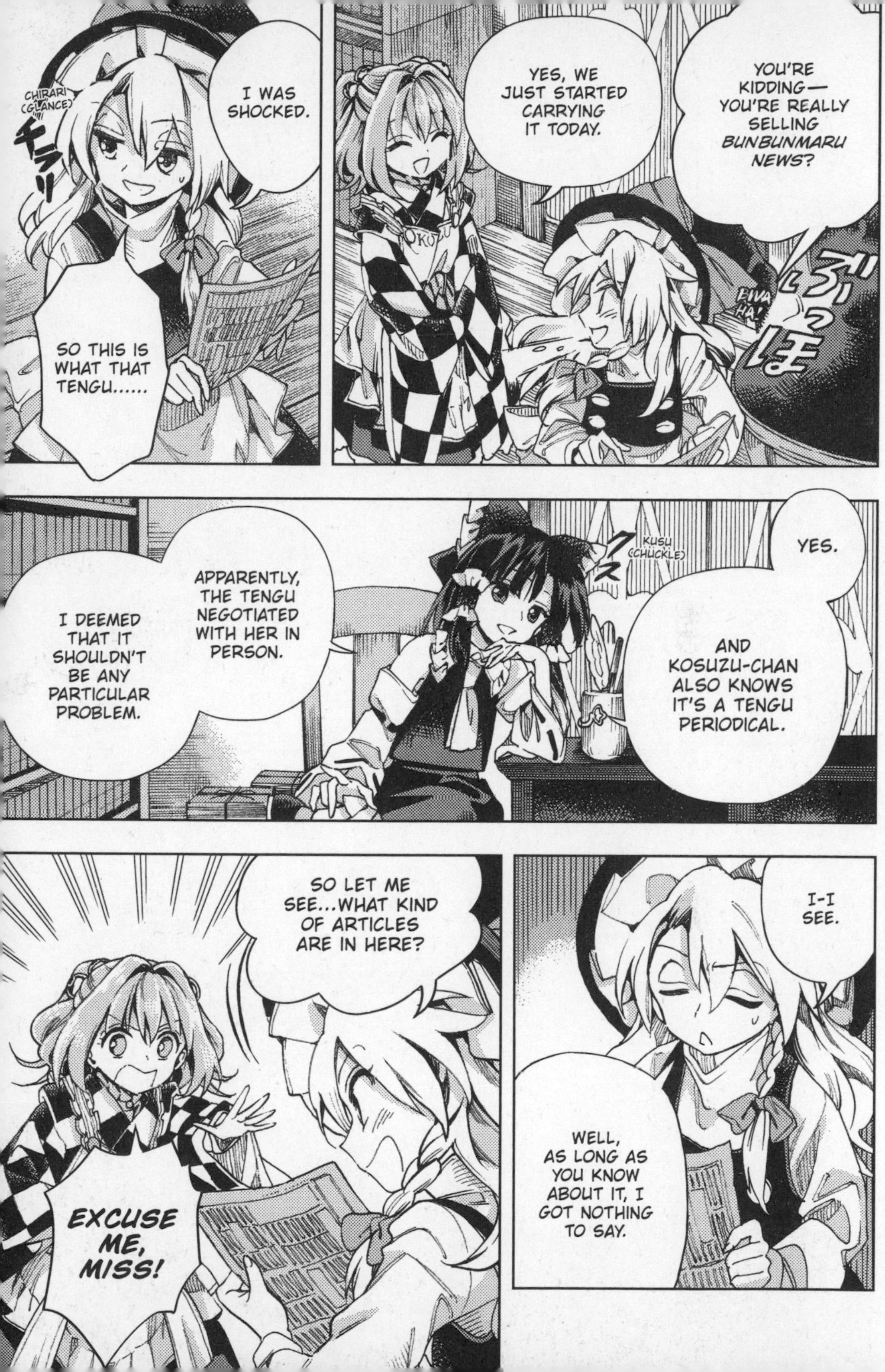
YOU'RE KIDDING— YOU'RE REALLY SELLING *BUNBUNMARU NEWS*?
BWAHA!
YES, WE JUST STARTED CARRYING IT TODAY.
I WAS SHOCKED.
CHIRARI (GLANCE)
SO THIS IS WHAT THAT TENGU......
YES.
AND KOSUZU-CHAN ALSO KNOWS IT'S A TENGU PERIODICAL.
KUSU (CHUCKLE)
APPARENTLY, THE TENGU NEGOTIATED WITH HER IN PERSON.
I DEEMED THAT IT SHOULDN'T BE ANY PARTICULAR PROBLEM.
I-I SEE.
WELL, AS LONG AS YOU KNOW ABOUT IT, I GOT NOTHING TO SAY.
SO LET ME SEE...WHAT KIND OF ARTICLES ARE IN HERE?
EXCUSE ME, MISS!

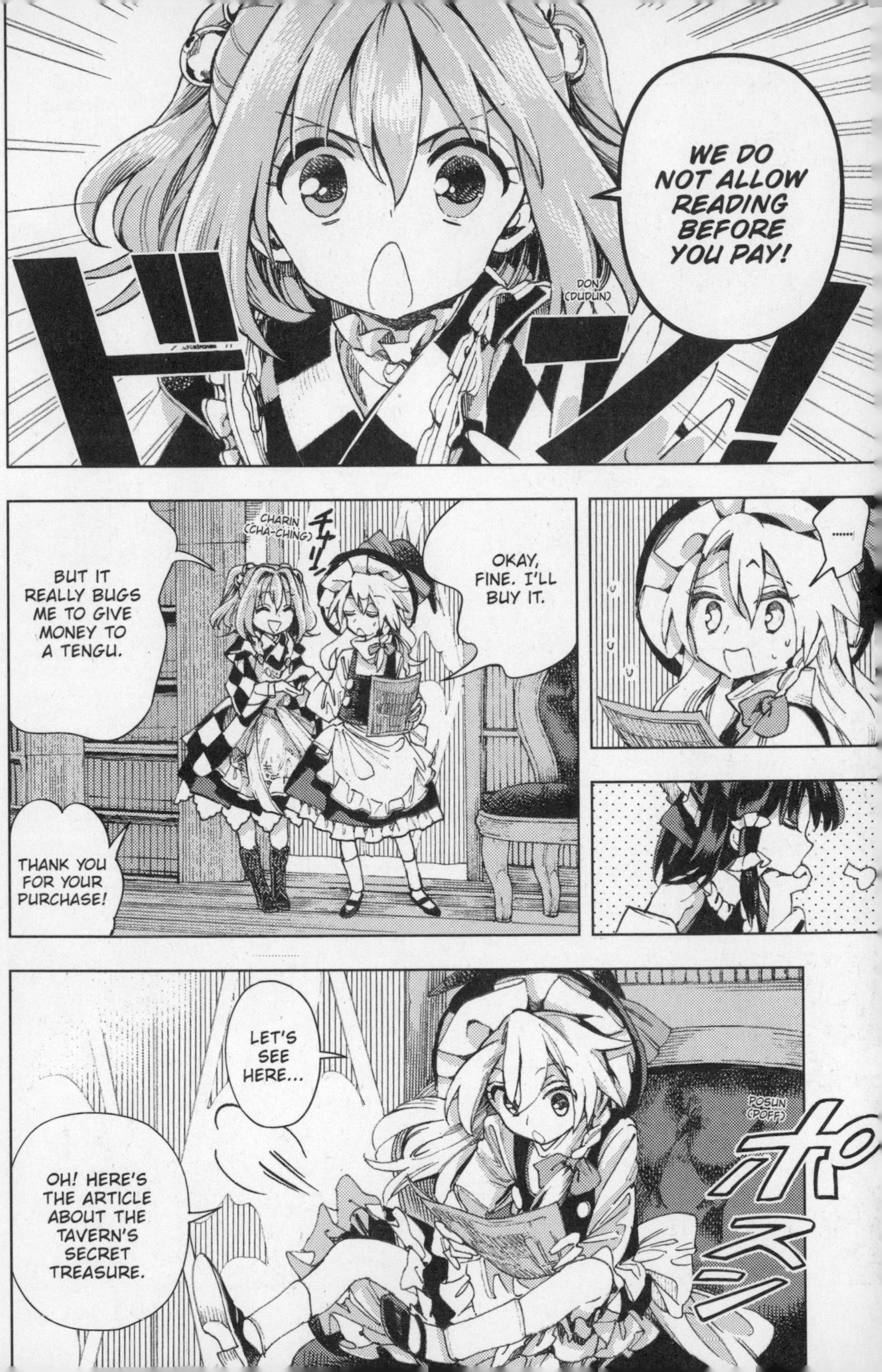
WE DO NOT ALLOW READING BEFORE YOU PAY!
DON (DUDUN)
......
OKAY, FINE. I'LL BUY IT.
CHARIN (CHA-CHING)
BUT IT REALLY BUGS ME TO GIVE MONEY TO A TENGU.
THANK YOU FOR YOUR PURCHASE!
POSUN (POFF)
LET'S SEE HERE...
OH! HERE'S THE ARTICLE ABOUT THE TAVERN'S SECRET TREASURE.

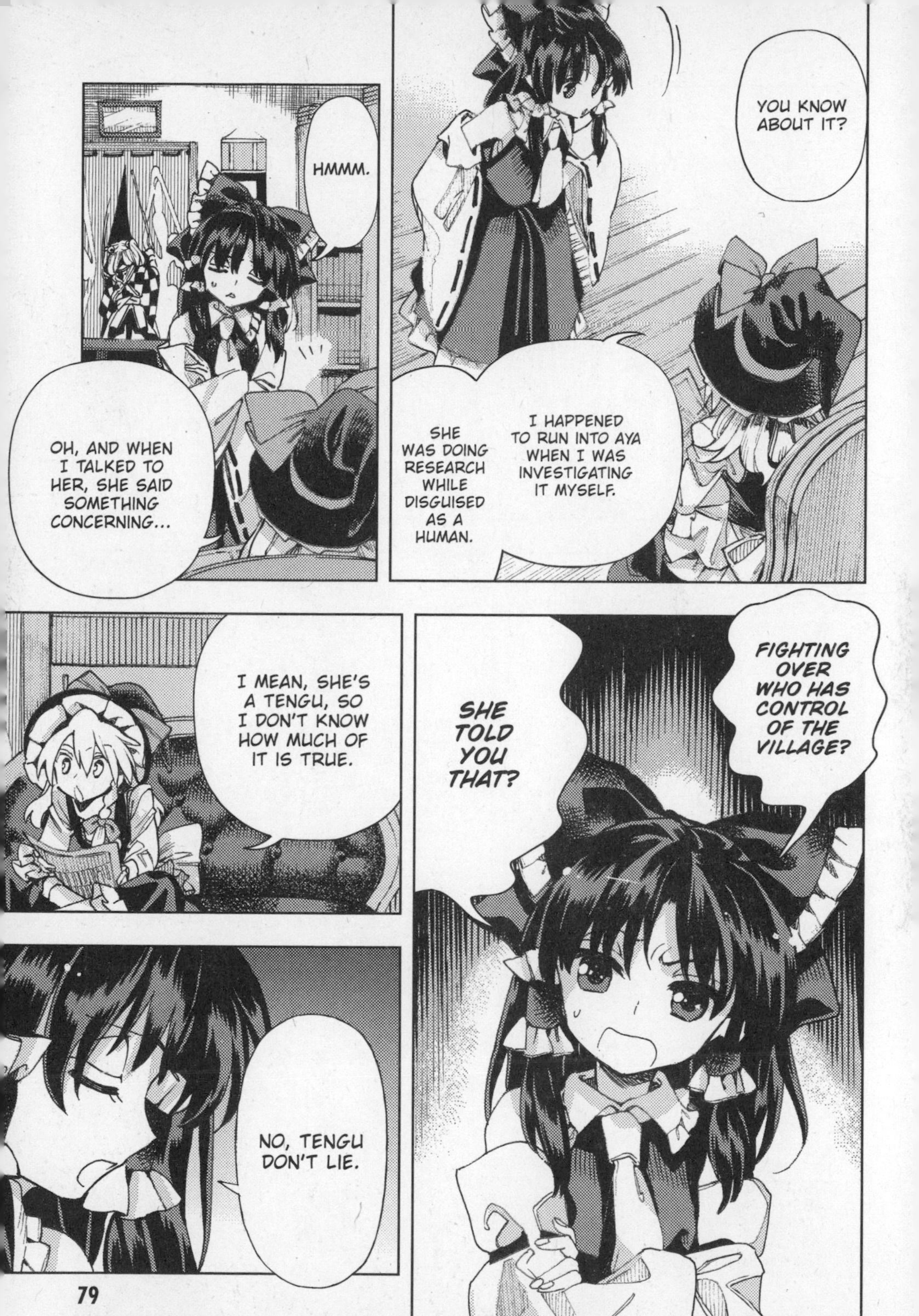
YOU KNOW ABOUT IT?
I HAPPENED TO RUN INTO AYA WHEN I WAS INVESTIGATING IT MYSELF.
SHE WAS DOING RESEARCH WHILE DISGUISED AS A HUMAN.
HMMM.
OH, AND WHEN I TALKED TO HER, SHE SAID SOMETHING CONCERNING...
FIGHTING OVER WHO HAS CONTROL OF THE VILLAGE?
SHE TOLD YOU THAT?
I MEAN, SHE'S A TENGU, SO I DON'T KNOW HOW MUCH OF IT IS TRUE.
NO, TENGU DON'T LIE.

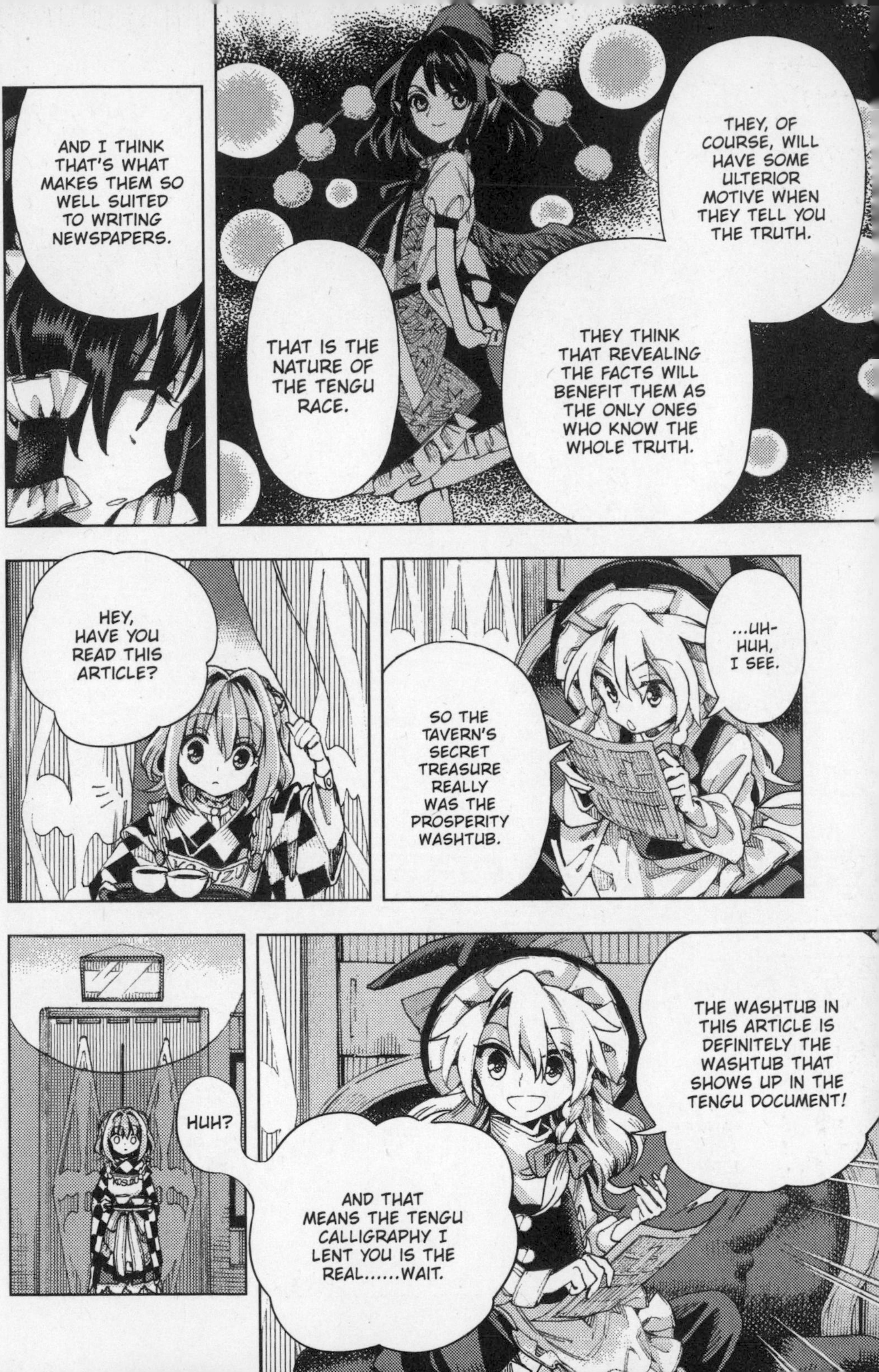
THEY, OF COURSE, WILL HAVE SOME ULTERIOR MOTIVE WHEN THEY TELL YOU THE TRUTH.
THEY THINK THAT REVEALING THE FACTS WILL BENEFIT THEM AS THE ONLY ONES WHO KNOW THE WHOLE TRUTH.
THAT IS THE NATURE OF THE TENGU RACE.
AND I THINK THAT'S WHAT MAKES THEM SO WELL SUITED TO WRITING NEWSPAPERS.
...UH-HUH, I SEE.
SO THE TAVERN'S SECRET TREASURE REALLY WAS THE PROSPERITY WASHTUB.
HEY, HAVE YOU READ THIS ARTICLE?
THE WASHTUB IN THIS ARTICLE IS DEFINITELY THE WASHTUB THAT SHOWS UP IN THE TENGU DOCUMENT!
AND THAT MEANS THE TENGU CALLIGRAPHY I LENT YOU IS THE REAL......WAIT.
HUH?

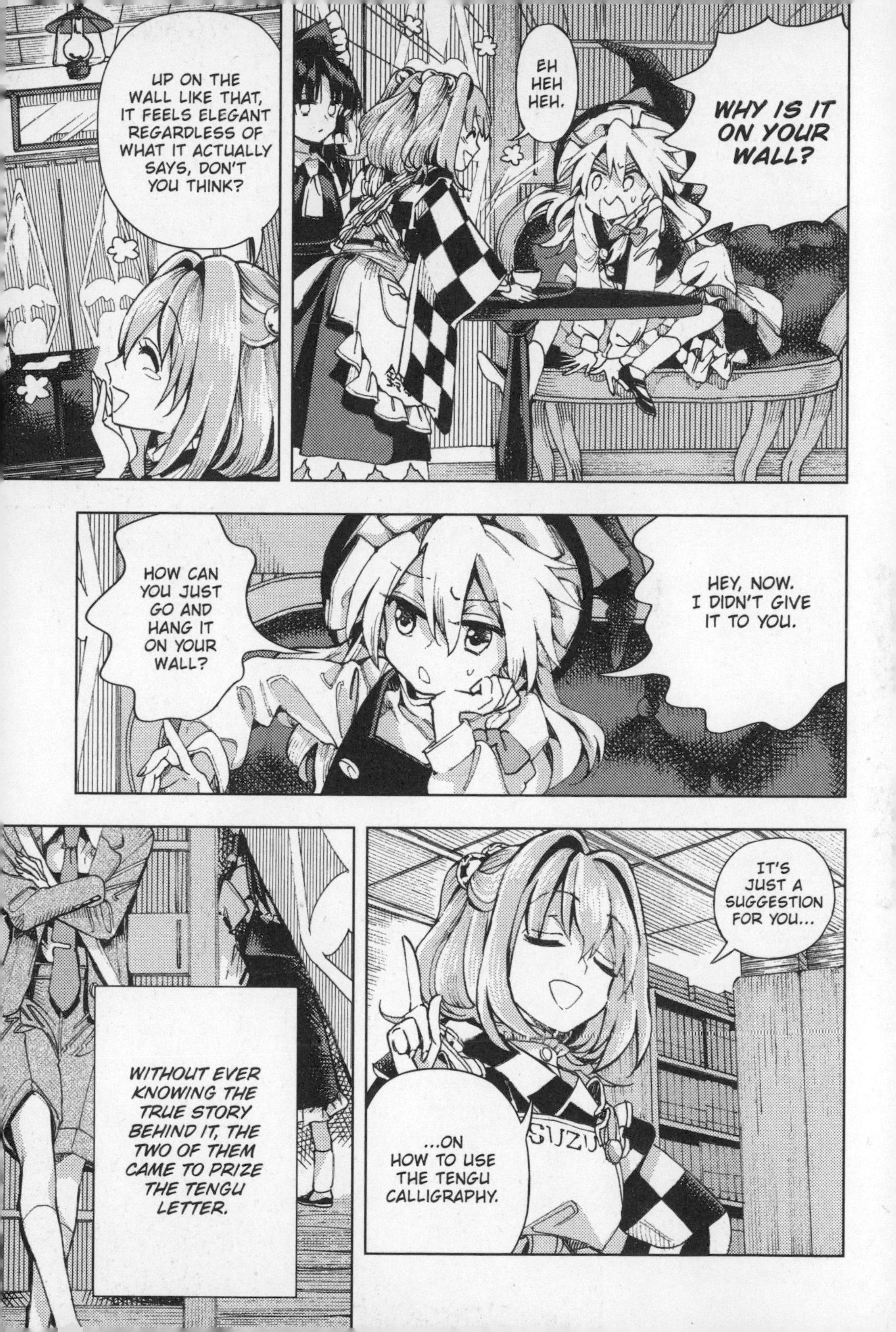
WHY IS IT ON YOUR WALL?
EH HEH HEH.
UP ON THE WALL LIKE THAT, IT FEELS ELEGANT REGARDLESS OF WHAT IT ACTUALLY SAYS, DON'T YOU THINK?
HEY, NOW. I DIDN'T GIVE IT TO YOU.
HOW CAN YOU JUST GO AND HANG IT ON YOUR WALL?
IT'S JUST A SUGGESTION FOR YOU...
...ON HOW TO USE THE TENGU CALLIGRAPHY.
SUZU
WITHOUT EVER KNOWING THE TRUE STORY BEHIND IT, THE TWO OF THEM CAME TO PRIZE THE TENGU LETTER.

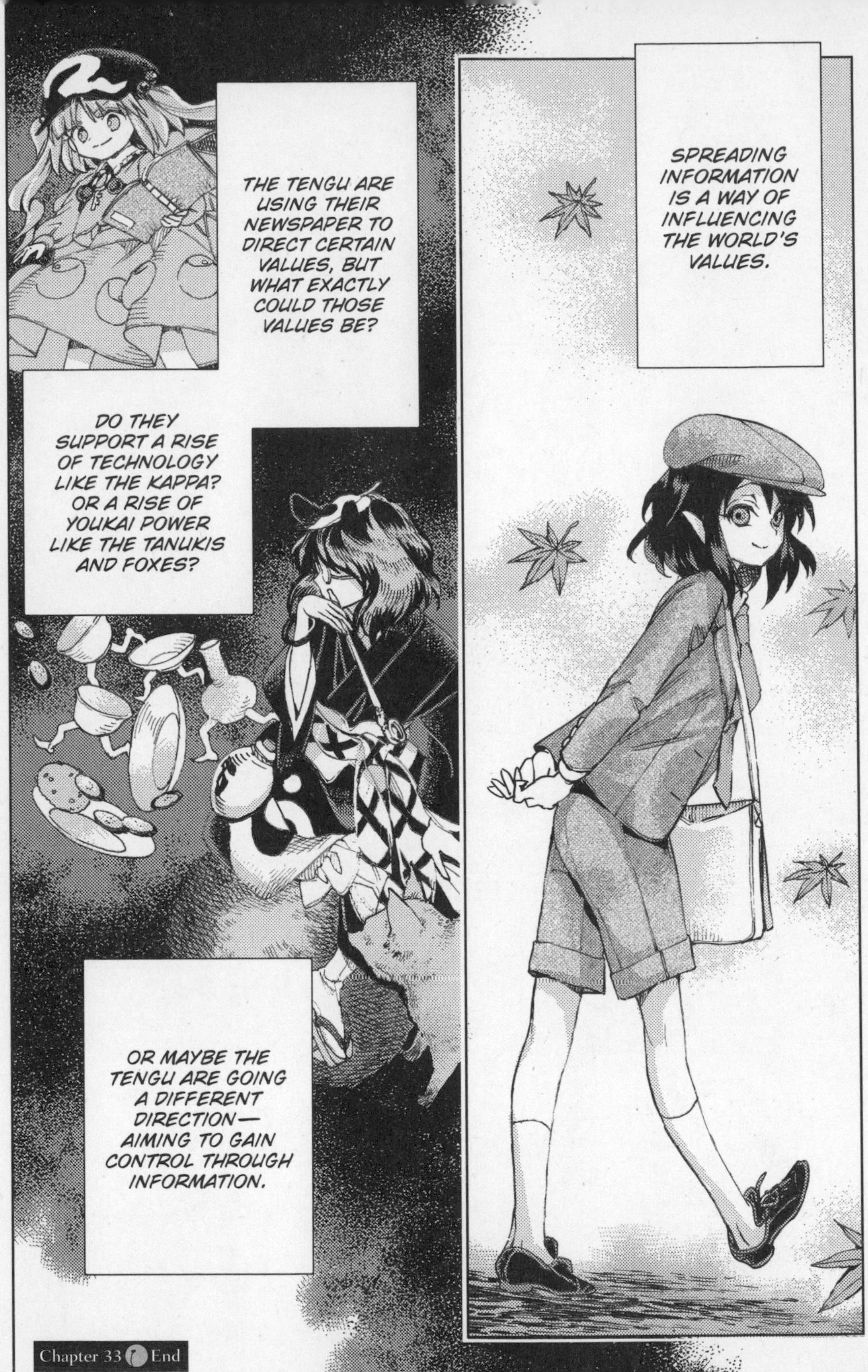
SPREADING INFORMATION IS A WAY OF INFLUENCING THE WORLD'S VALUES.
THE TENGU ARE USING THEIR NEWSPAPER TO DIRECT CERTAIN VALUES, BUT WHAT EXACTLY COULD THOSE VALUES BE?
DO THEY SUPPORT A RISE OF TECHNOLOGY LIKE THE KAPPA? OR A RISE OF YOUKAI POWER LIKE THE TANUKIS AND FOXES?
OR MAYBE THE TENGU ARE GOING A DIFFERENT DIRECTION—AIMING TO GAIN CONTROL THROUGH INFORMATION.

Chapter 33 End

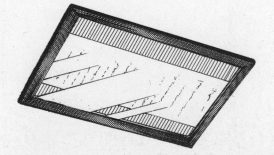

Forbidden Scrollery

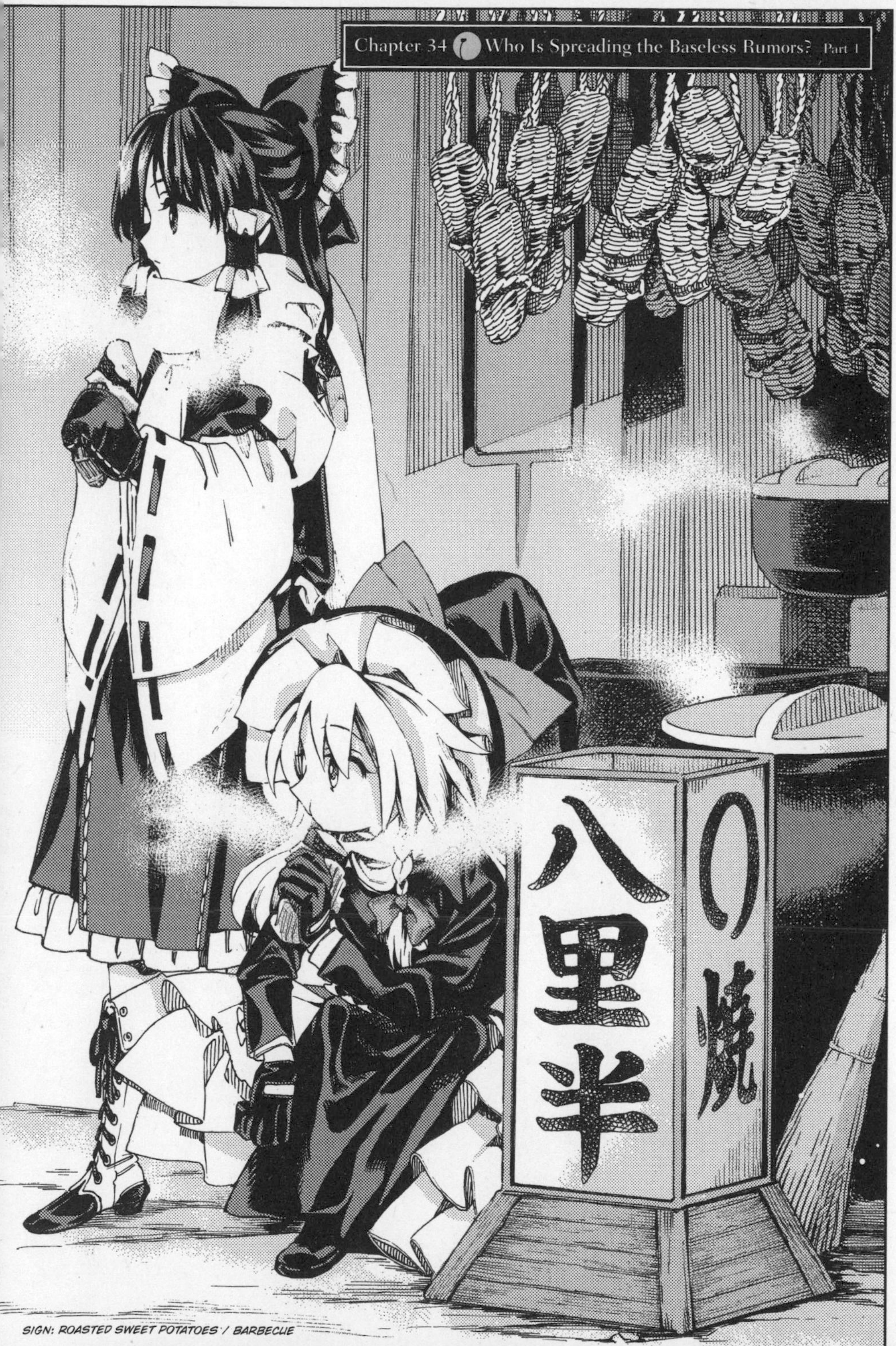
Chapter 34 Who Is Spreading the Baseless Rumors? Part 1
八里半
〇焼

SIGN: ROASTED SWEET POTATOES / BARBECUE

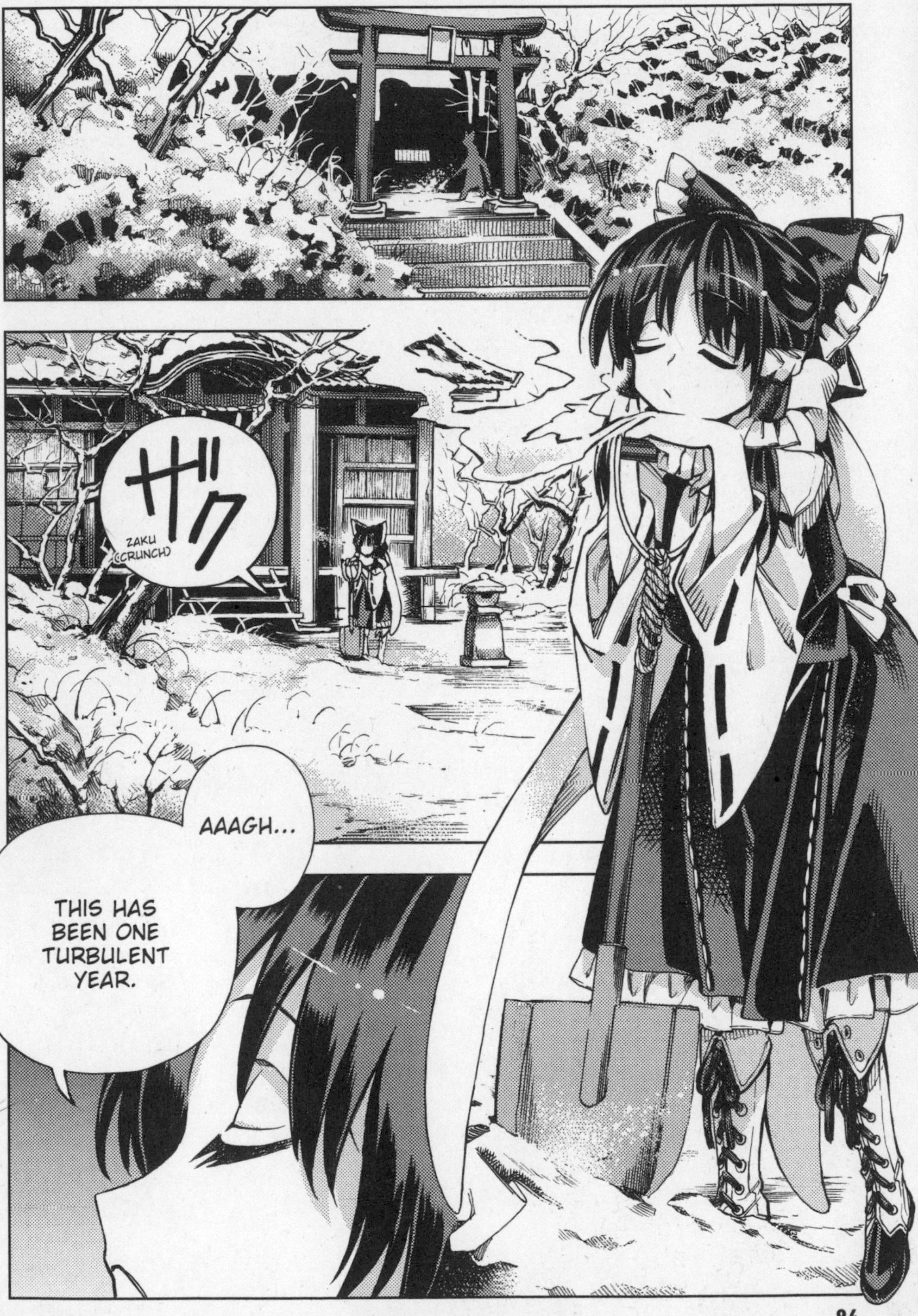
ザク
ZAKU (CRUNCH)
AAAGH...
THIS HAS BEEN ONE TURBULENT YEAR.

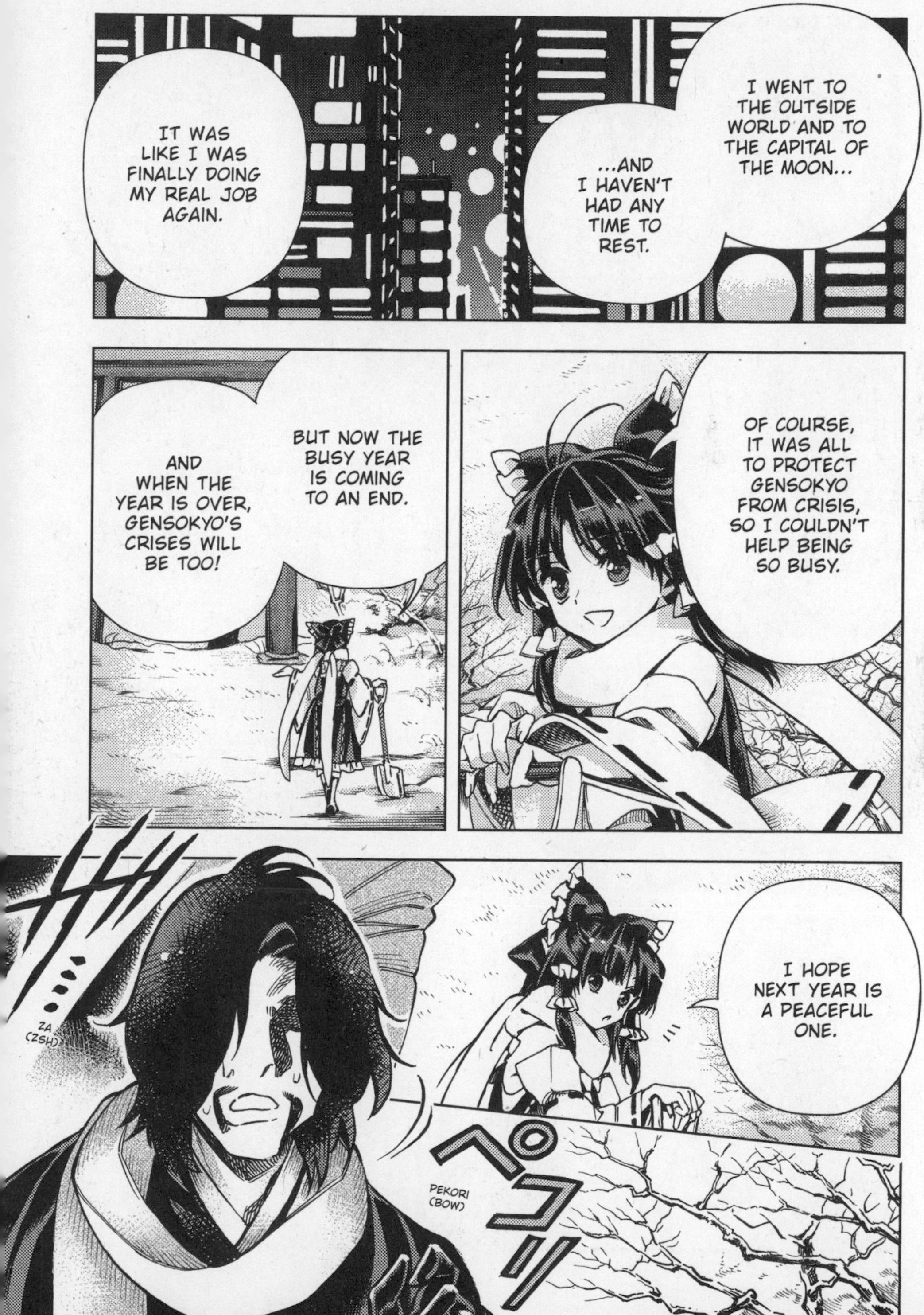
I WENT TO THE OUTSIDE WORLD AND TO THE CAPITAL OF THE MOON...
...AND I HAVEN'T HAD ANY TIME TO REST.
IT WAS LIKE I WAS FINALLY DOING MY REAL JOB AGAIN.
OF COURSE, IT WAS ALL TO PROTECT GENSOKYO FROM CRISIS, SO I COULDN'T HELP BEING SO BUSY.
BUT NOW THE BUSY YEAR IS COMING TO AN END.
AND WHEN THE YEAR IS OVER, GENSOKYO'S CRISES WILL BE TOO!
I HOPE NEXT YEAR IS A PEACEFUL ONE.
ペコリ
PEKORI (BOW)
...
ZA (ZSH)

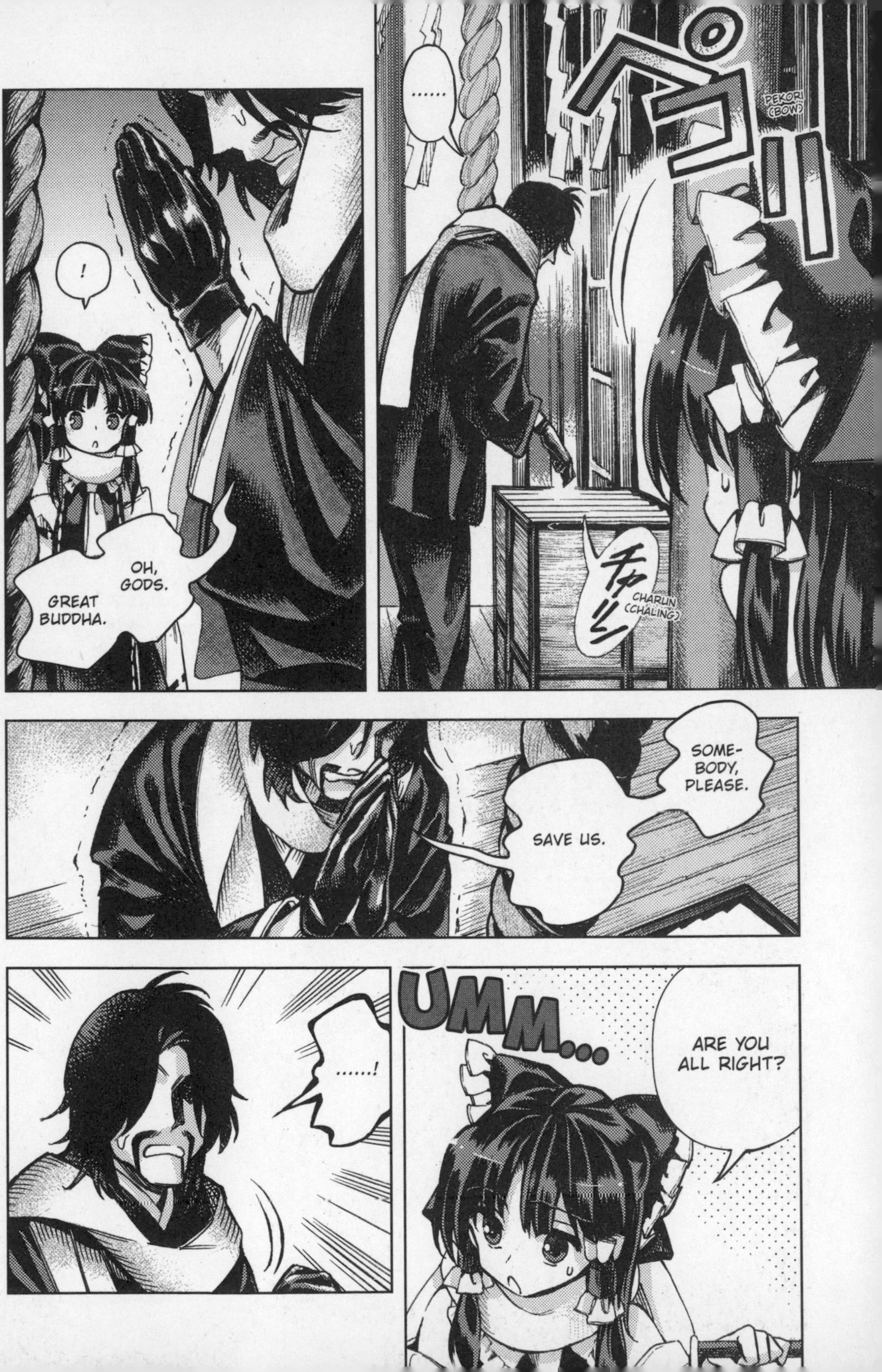
......
PEKORI (BOW)
CHARUN (CHALING)
!
OH, GODS.
GREAT BUDDHA.
SOME-BODY, PLEASE.
SAVE US.
UMM...
ARE YOU ALL RIGHT?
......!

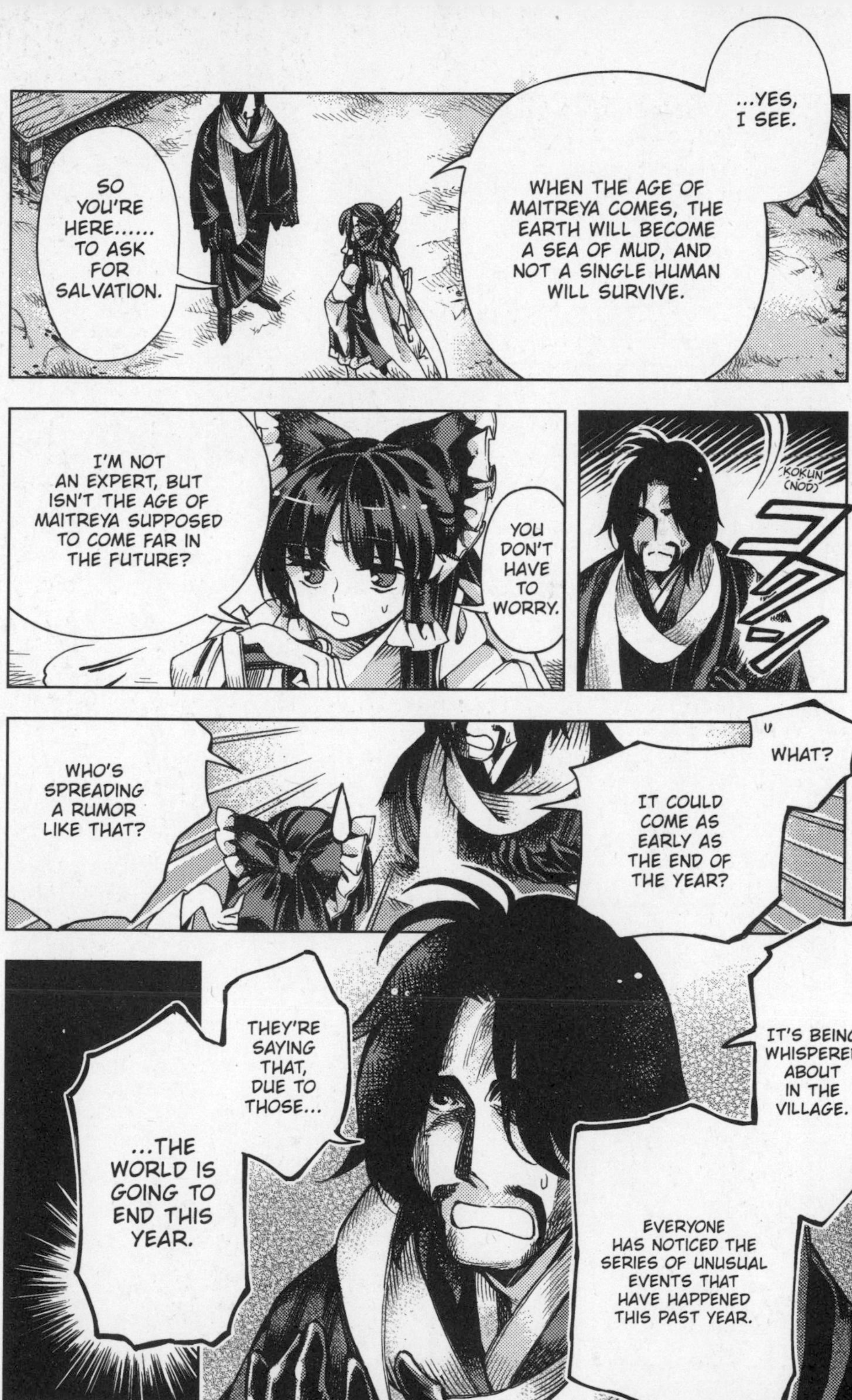
...YES, I SEE.
WHEN THE AGE OF MAITREYA COMES, THE EARTH WILL BECOME A SEA OF MUD, AND NOT A SINGLE HUMAN WILL SURVIVE.
SO YOU'RE HERE...... TO ASK FOR SALVATION.
KOKUN (NOD)
YOU DON'T HAVE TO WORRY.
I'M NOT AN EXPERT, BUT ISN'T THE AGE OF MAITREYA SUPPOSED TO COME FAR IN THE FUTURE?
WHAT?
IT COULD COME AS EARLY AS THE END OF THE YEAR?
WHO'S SPREADING A RUMOR LIKE THAT?
IT'S BEING WHISPERED ABOUT IN THE VILLAGE.
EVERYONE HAS NOTICED THE SERIES OF UNUSUAL EVENTS THAT HAVE HAPPENED THIS PAST YEAR.
THEY'RE SAYING THAT, DUE TO THOSE...
...THE WORLD IS GOING TO END THIS YEAR.

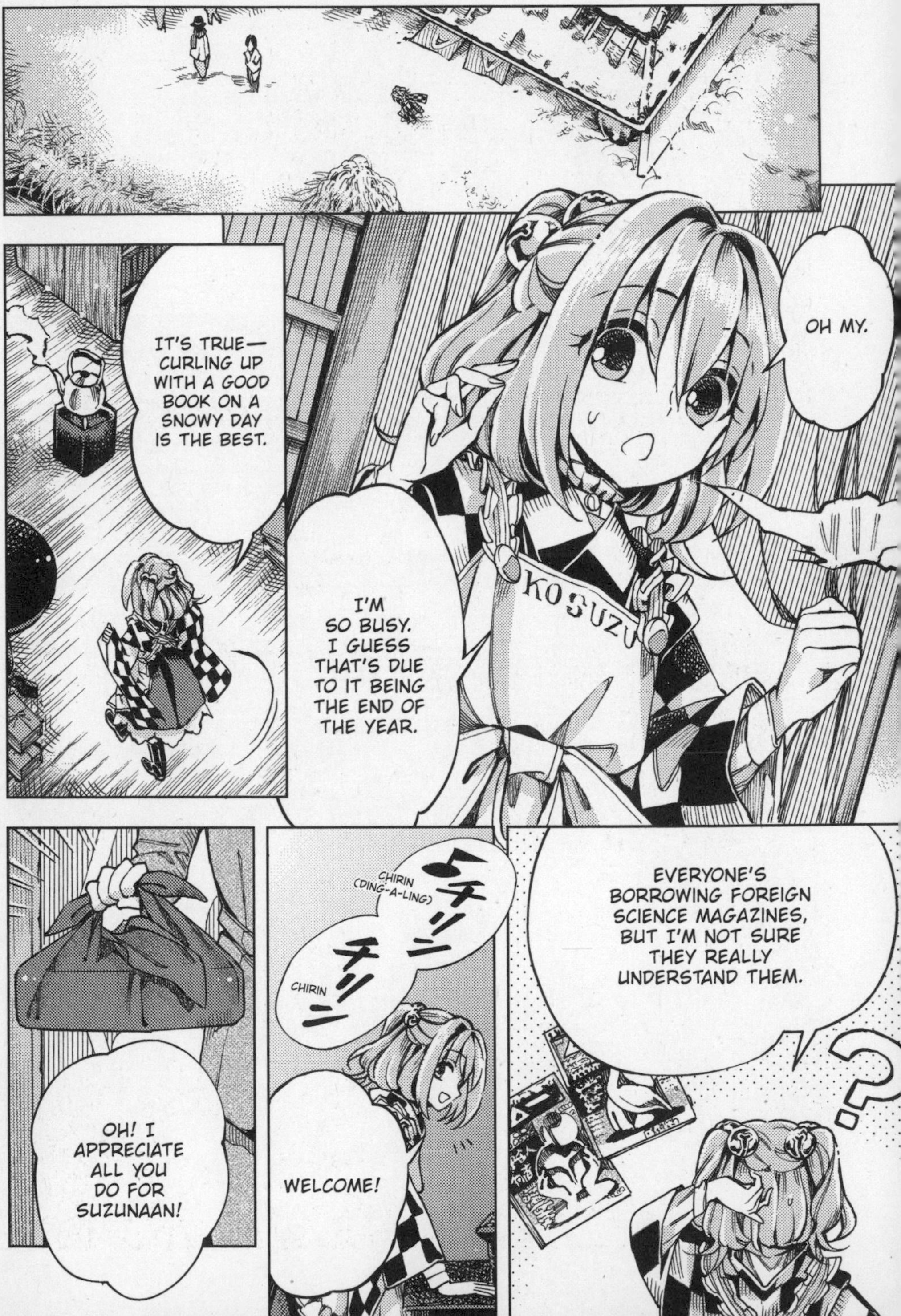
OH MY.
I'M SO BUSY. I GUESS THAT'S DUE TO IT BEING THE END OF THE YEAR.
IT'S TRUE—CURLING UP WITH A GOOD BOOK ON A SNOWY DAY IS THE BEST.
EVERYONE'S BORROWING FOREIGN SCIENCE MAGAZINES, BUT I'M NOT SURE THEY REALLY UNDERSTAND THEM.
チリン
CHIRIN (DING-A-LING)
チリン
CHIRIN
WELCOME!
OH! I APPRECIATE ALL YOU DO FOR SUZUNAAN!

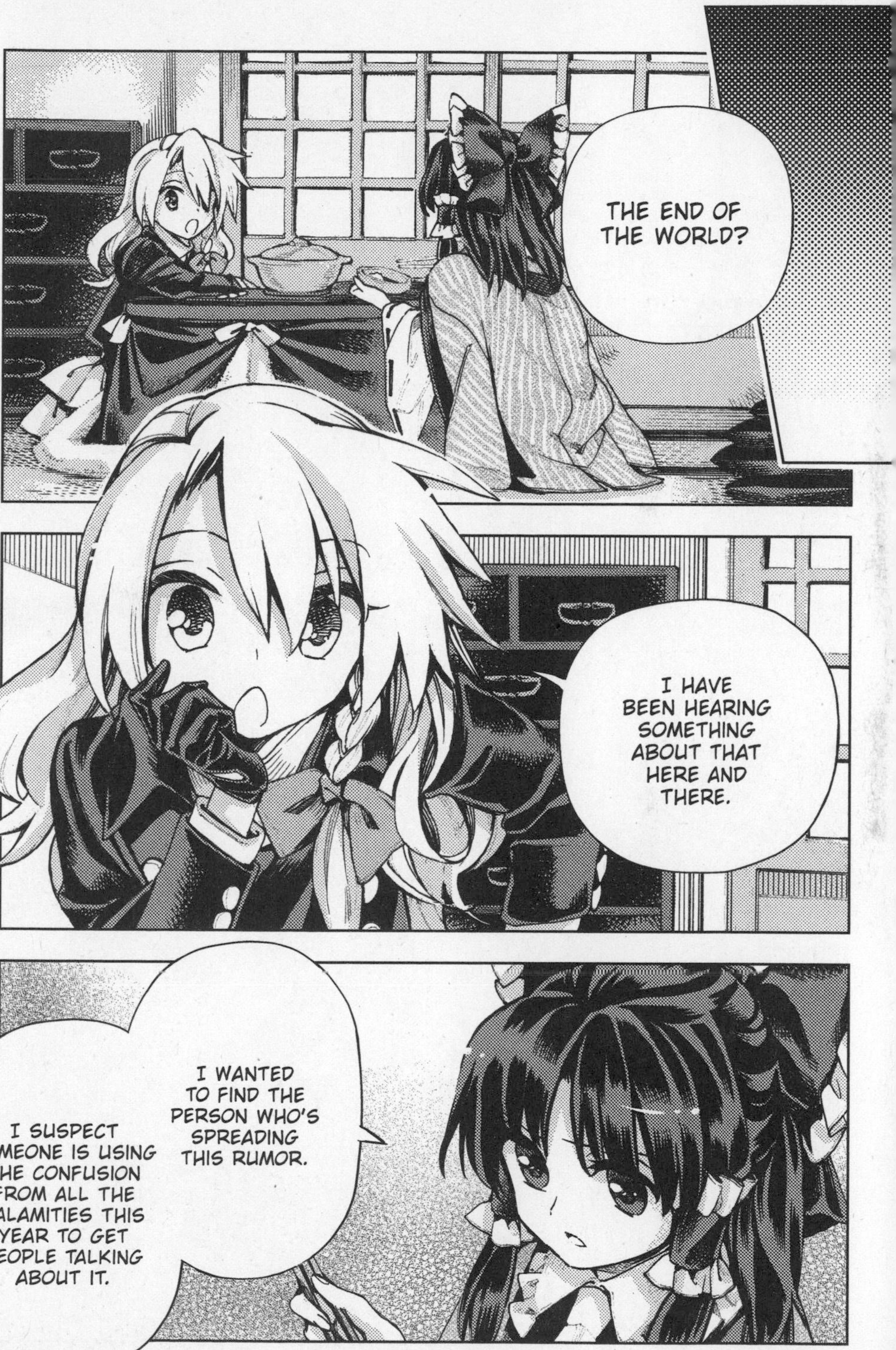
THE END OF THE WORLD?
I HAVE BEEN HEARING SOMETHING ABOUT THAT HERE AND THERE.
I WANTED TO FIND THE PERSON WHO'S SPREADING THIS RUMOR.
I SUSPECT SOMEONE IS USING THE CONFUSION FROM ALL THE CALAMITIES THIS YEAR TO GET PEOPLE TALKING ABOUT IT.

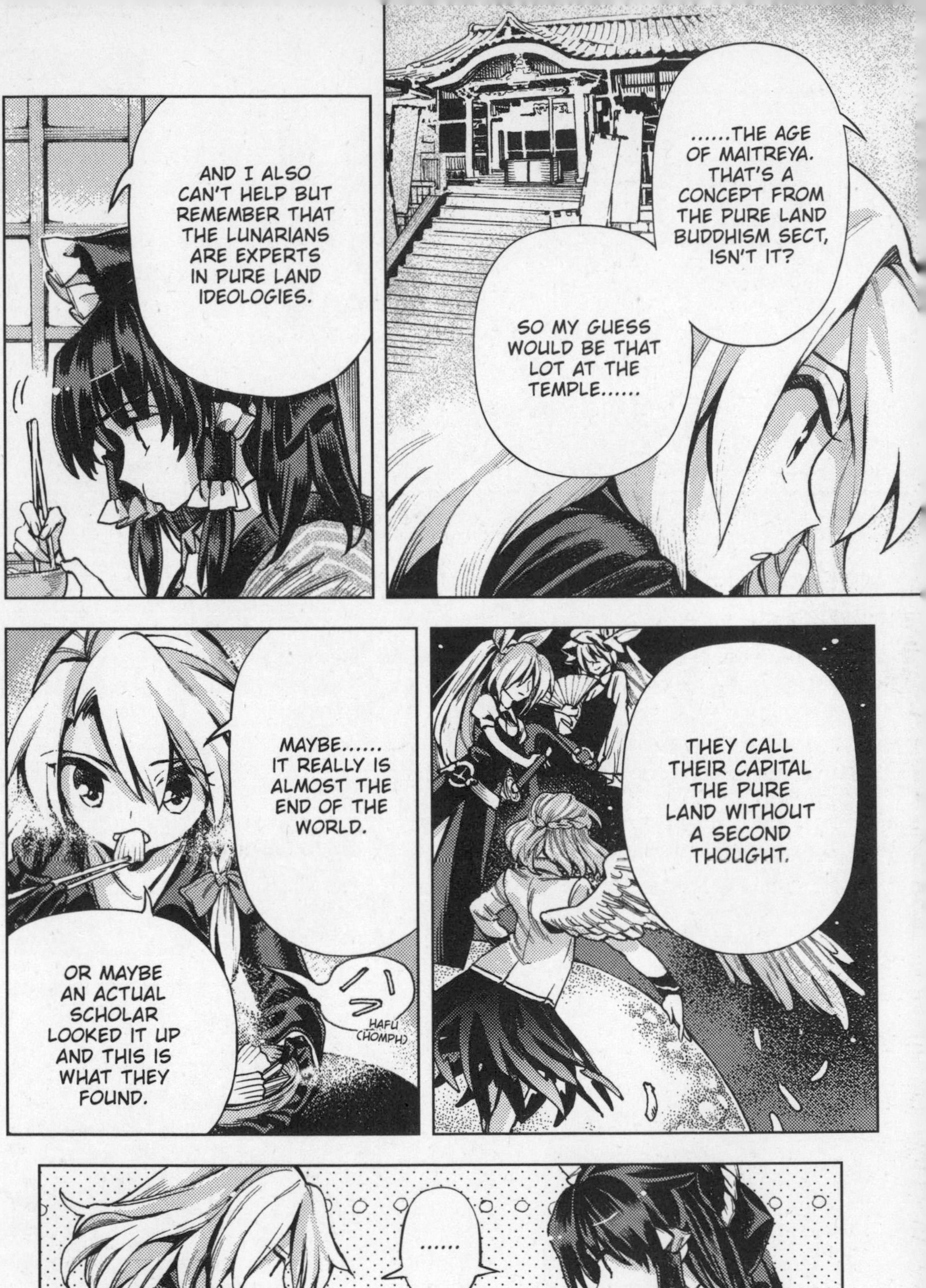
......THE AGE OF MAITREYA. THAT'S A CONCEPT FROM THE PURE LAND BUDDHISM SECT, ISN'T IT?
SO MY GUESS WOULD BE THAT LOT AT THE TEMPLE......
AND I ALSO CAN'T HELP BUT REMEMBER THAT THE LUNARIANS ARE EXPERTS IN PURE LAND IDEOLOGIES.
THEY CALL THEIR CAPITAL THE PURE LAND WITHOUT A SECOND THOUGHT.
MAYBE...... IT REALLY IS ALMOST THE END OF THE WORLD.
HAFU (HOMPH)
OR MAYBE AN ACTUAL SCHOLAR LOOKED IT UP AND THIS IS WHAT THEY FOUND.
......

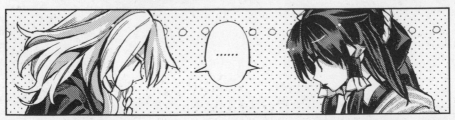

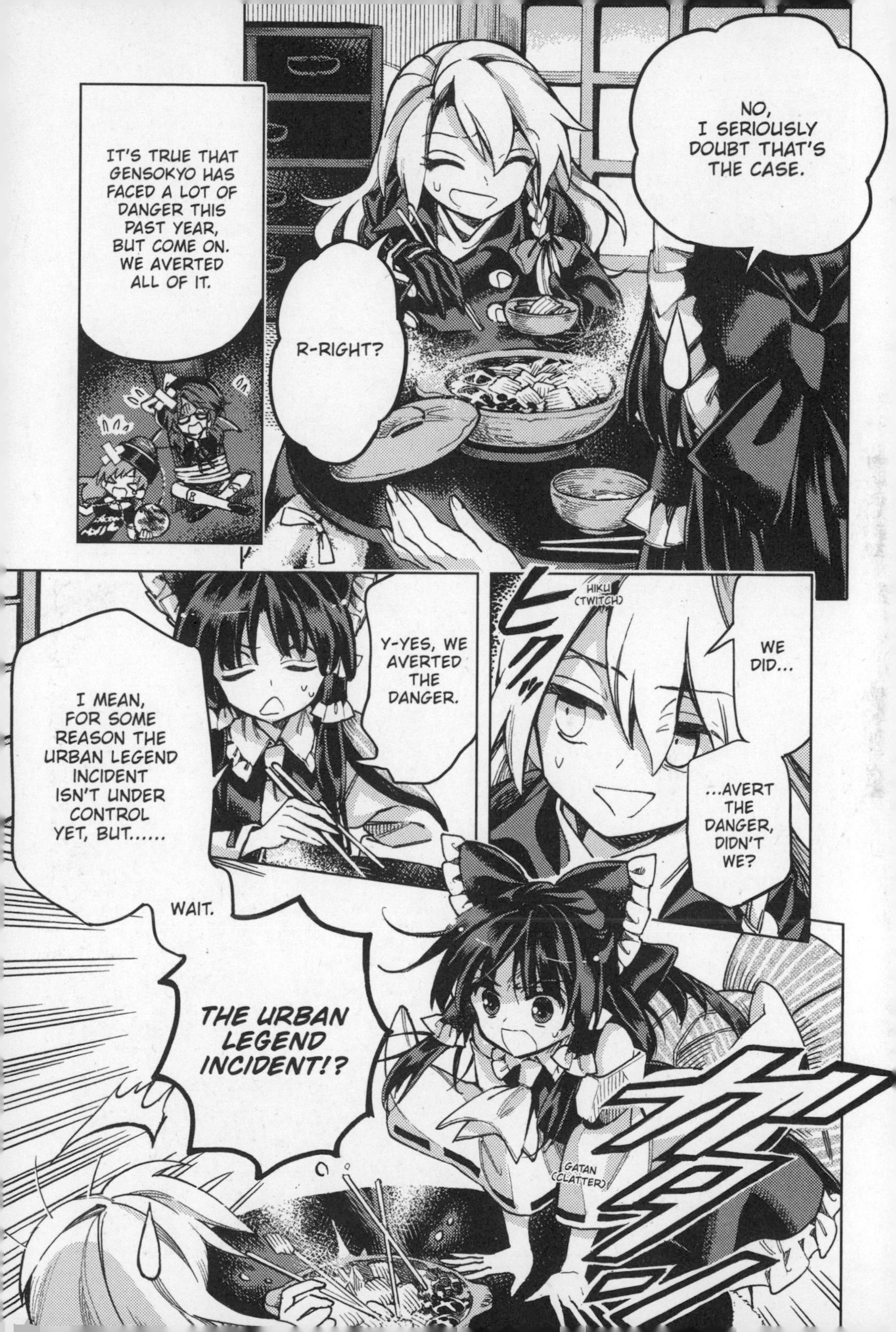
NO, I SERIOUSLY DOUBT THAT'S THE CASE.
IT'S TRUE THAT GENSOKYO HAS FACED A LOT OF DANGER THIS PAST YEAR, BUT COME ON. WE AVERTED ALL OF IT.
R-RIGHT?
HIKU (TWITCH)
WE DID...
...AVERT THE DANGER, DIDN'T WE?
Y-YES, WE AVERTED THE DANGER.
I MEAN, FOR SOME REASON THE URBAN LEGEND INCIDENT ISN'T UNDER CONTROL YET, BUT......
WAIT.
THE URBAN LEGEND INCIDENT!?
GATAN (CLATTER)

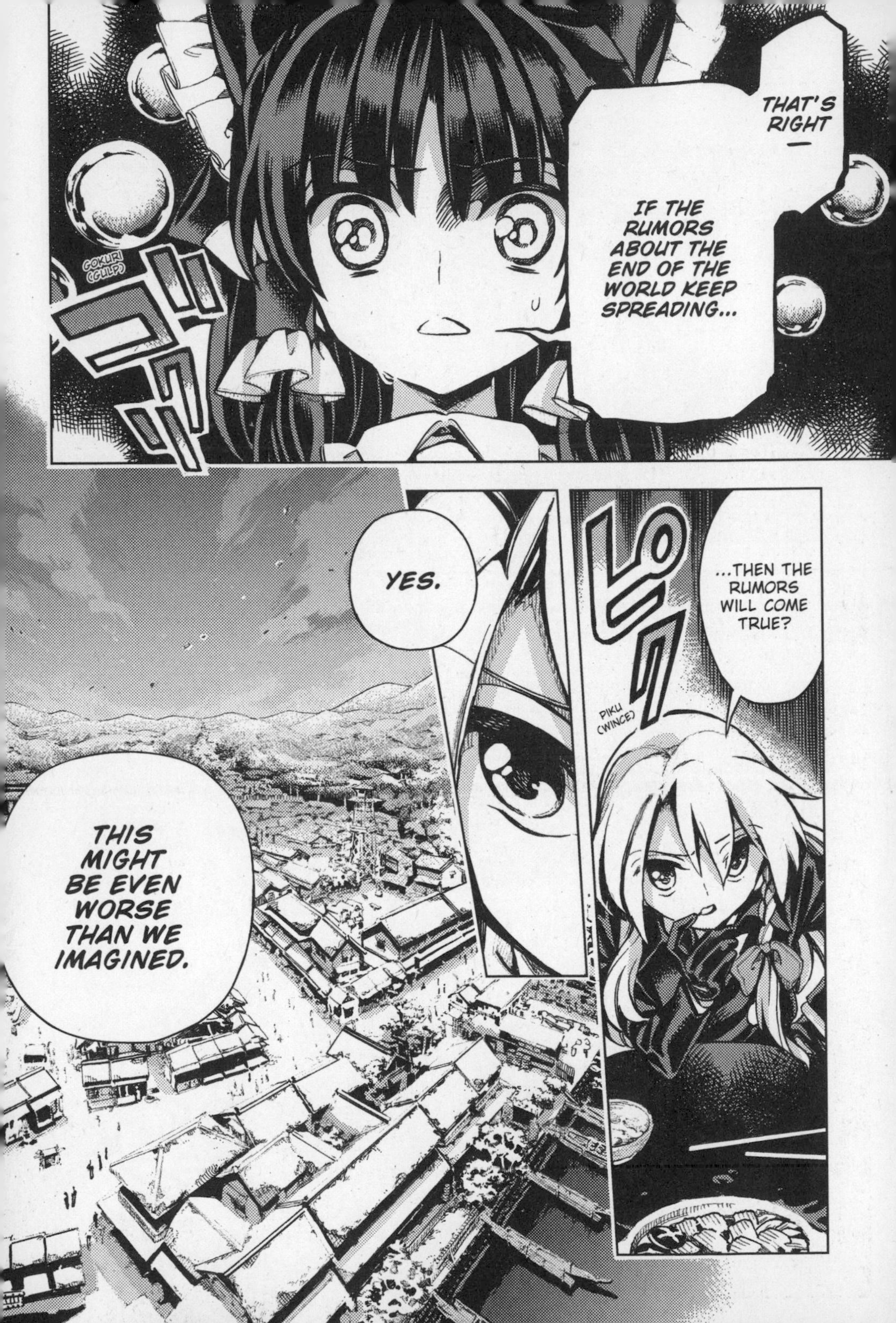
THAT'S RIGHT —
IF THE RUMORS ABOUT THE END OF THE WORLD KEEP SPREADING...
GOKURI (GULP)
...THEN THE RUMORS WILL COME TRUE?
PIKU (WINCE)
YES.
THIS MIGHT BE EVEN WORSE THAN WE IMAGINED.

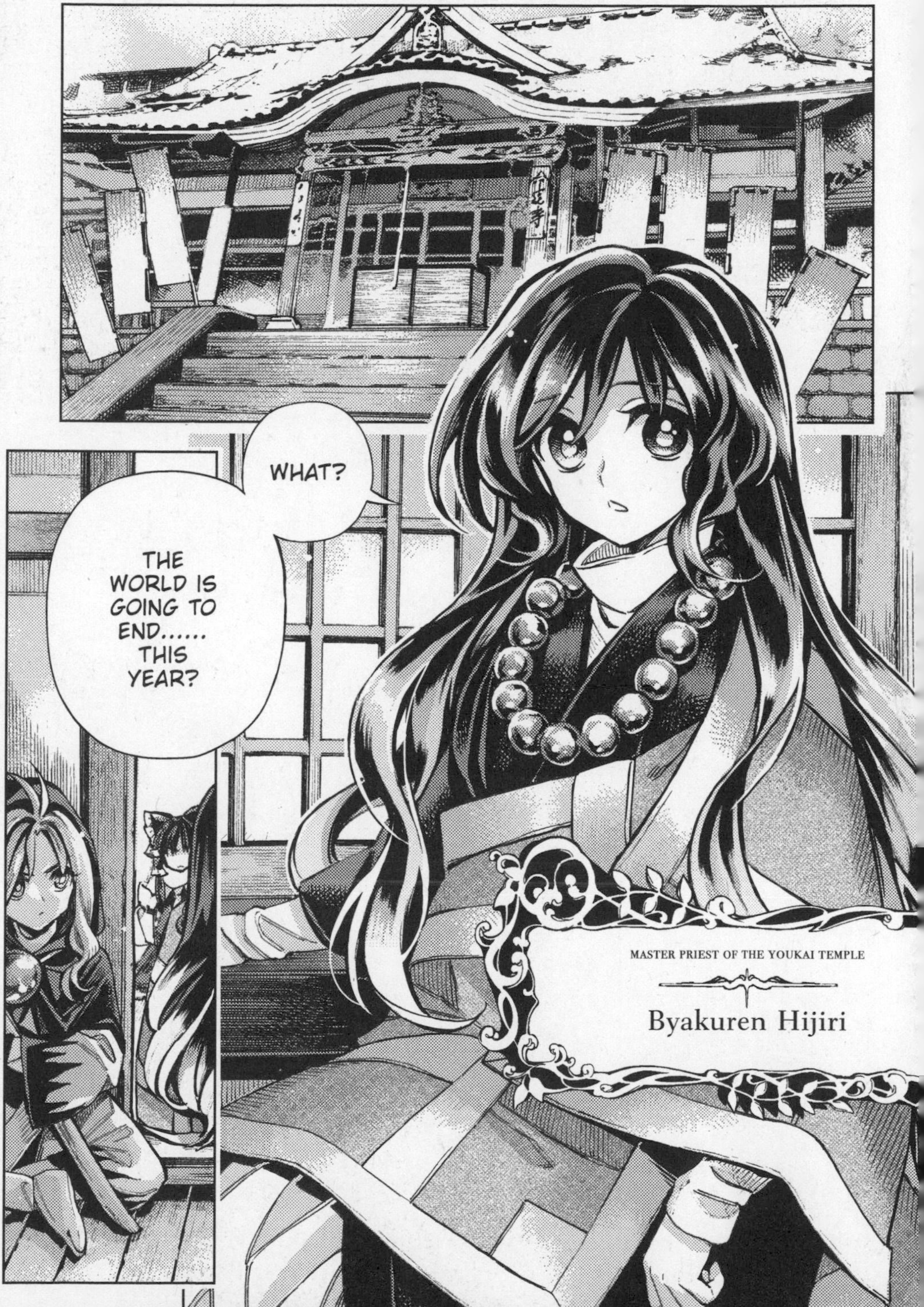
WHAT?
THE WORLD IS GOING TO END...... THIS YEAR?
MASTER PRIEST OF THE YOUKAI TEMPLE
Byakuren Hijiri

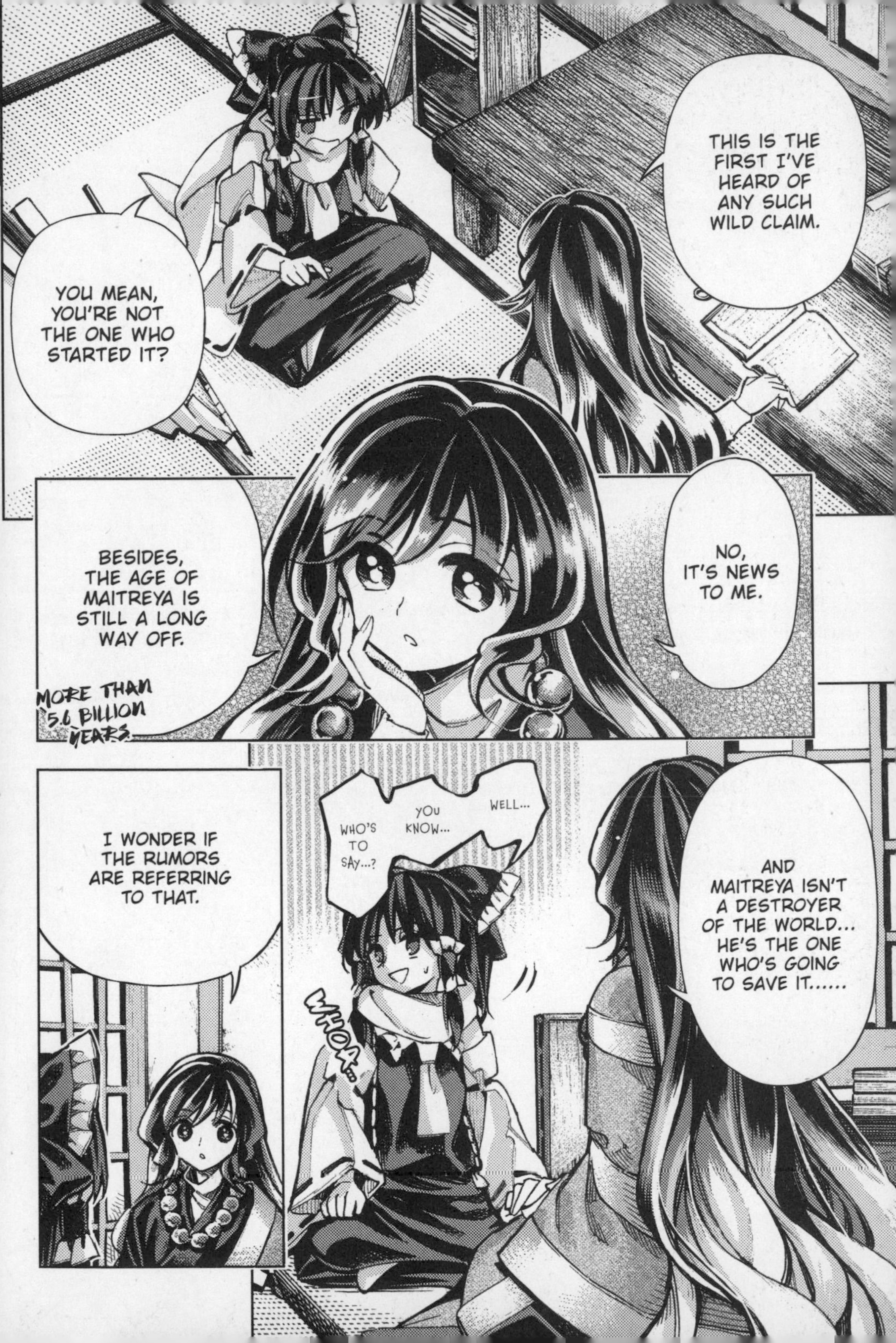
THIS IS THE FIRST I'VE HEARD OF ANY SUCH WILD CLAIM.
YOU MEAN, YOU'RE NOT THE ONE WHO STARTED IT?
NO, IT'S NEWS TO ME.
BESIDES, THE AGE OF MAITREYA IS STILL A LONG WAY OFF.
MORE THAN 5.6 BILLION YEARS.
AND MAITREYA ISN'T A DESTROYER OF THE WORLD... HE'S THE ONE WHO'S GOING TO SAVE IT......
WELL...
YOU KNOW...
WHO'S TO SAY...?
WHOA...
I WONDER IF THE RUMORS ARE REFERRING TO THAT.

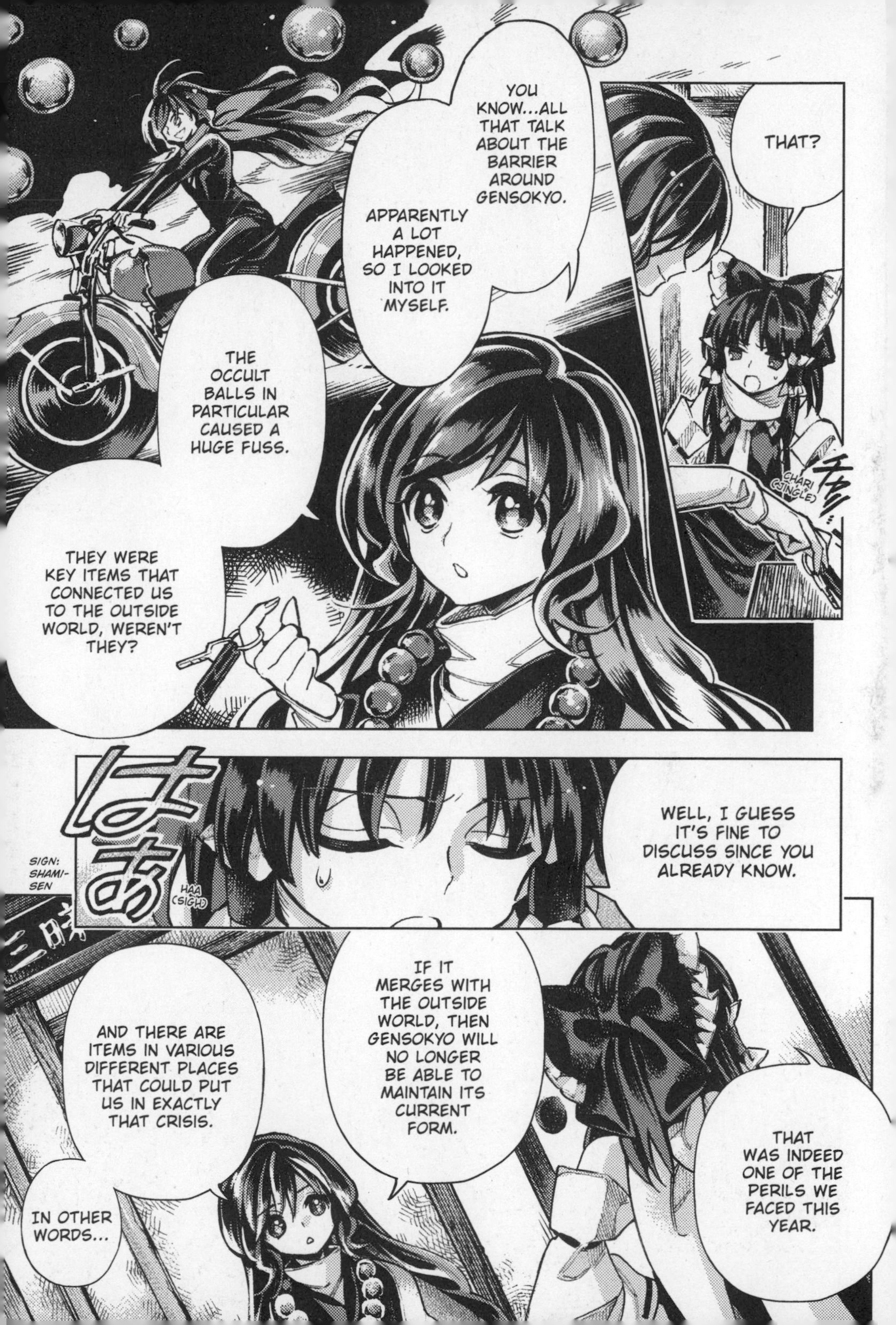
THAT?
CHARI (JINGLE)
YOU KNOW...ALL THAT TALK ABOUT THE BARRIER AROUND GENSOKYO.
APPARENTLY A LOT HAPPENED, SO I LOOKED INTO IT MYSELF.
THE OCCULT BALLS IN PARTICULAR CAUSED A HUGE FUSS.
THEY WERE KEY ITEMS THAT CONNECTED US TO THE OUTSIDE WORLD, WEREN'T THEY?
WELL, I GUESS IT'S FINE TO DISCUSS SINCE YOU ALREADY KNOW.
HAA (SIGH)
SIGN: SHAMISEN
THAT WAS INDEED ONE OF THE PERILS WE FACED THIS YEAR.
IF IT MERGES WITH THE OUTSIDE WORLD, THEN GENSOKYO WILL NO LONGER BE ABLE TO MAINTAIN ITS CURRENT FORM.
AND THERE ARE ITEMS IN VARIOUS DIFFERENT PLACES THAT COULD PUT US IN EXACTLY THAT CRISIS.
IN OTHER WORDS...

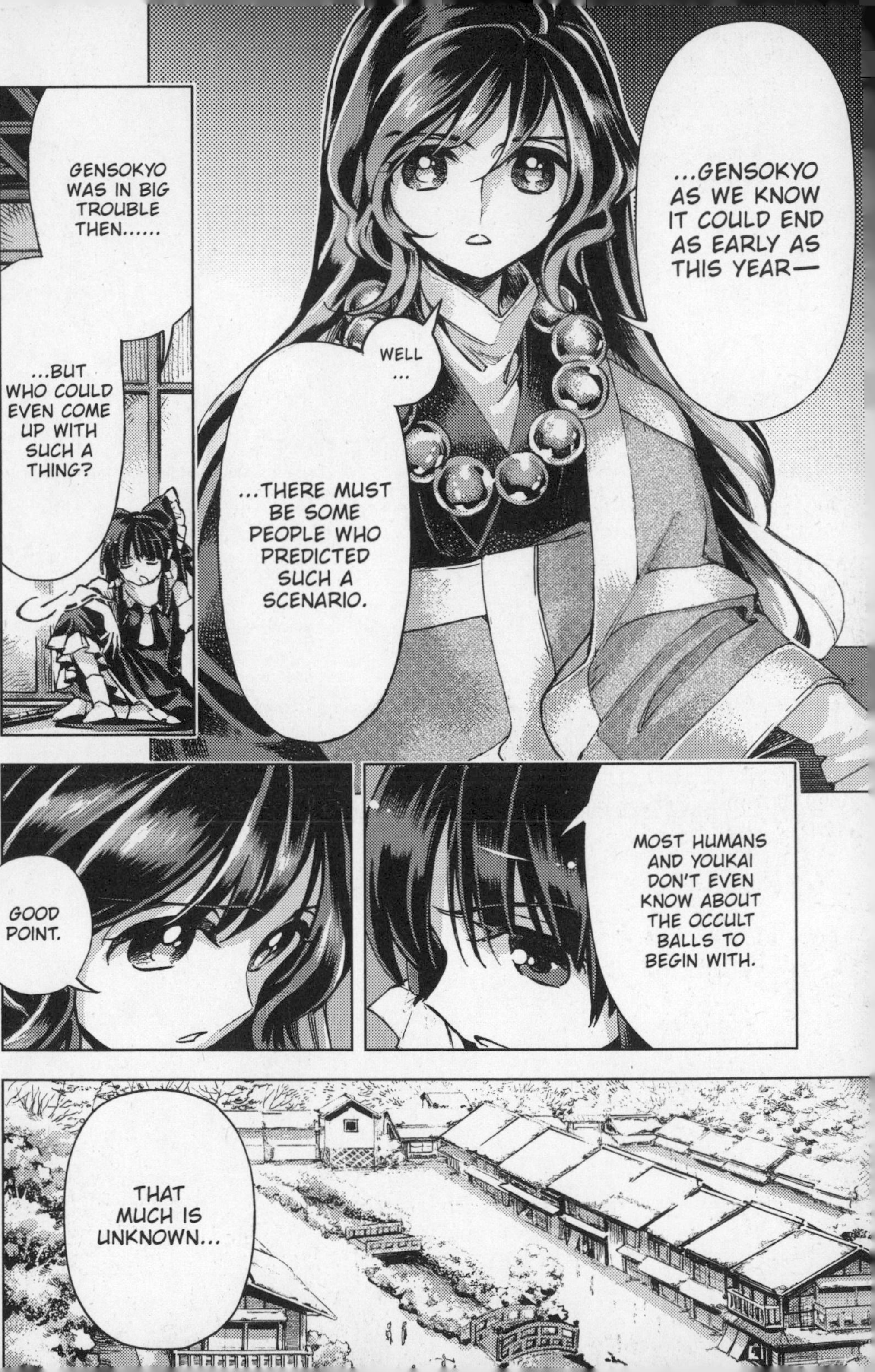
...GENSOKYO AS WE KNOW IT COULD END AS EARLY AS THIS YEAR—
GENSOKYO WAS IN BIG TROUBLE THEN......
...BUT WHO COULD EVEN COME UP WITH SUCH A THING?
WELL ...
...THERE MUST BE SOME PEOPLE WHO PREDICTED SUCH A SCENARIO.
MOST HUMANS AND YOUKAI DON'T EVEN KNOW ABOUT THE OCCULT BALLS TO BEGIN WITH.
GOOD POINT.
THAT MUCH IS UNKNOWN...

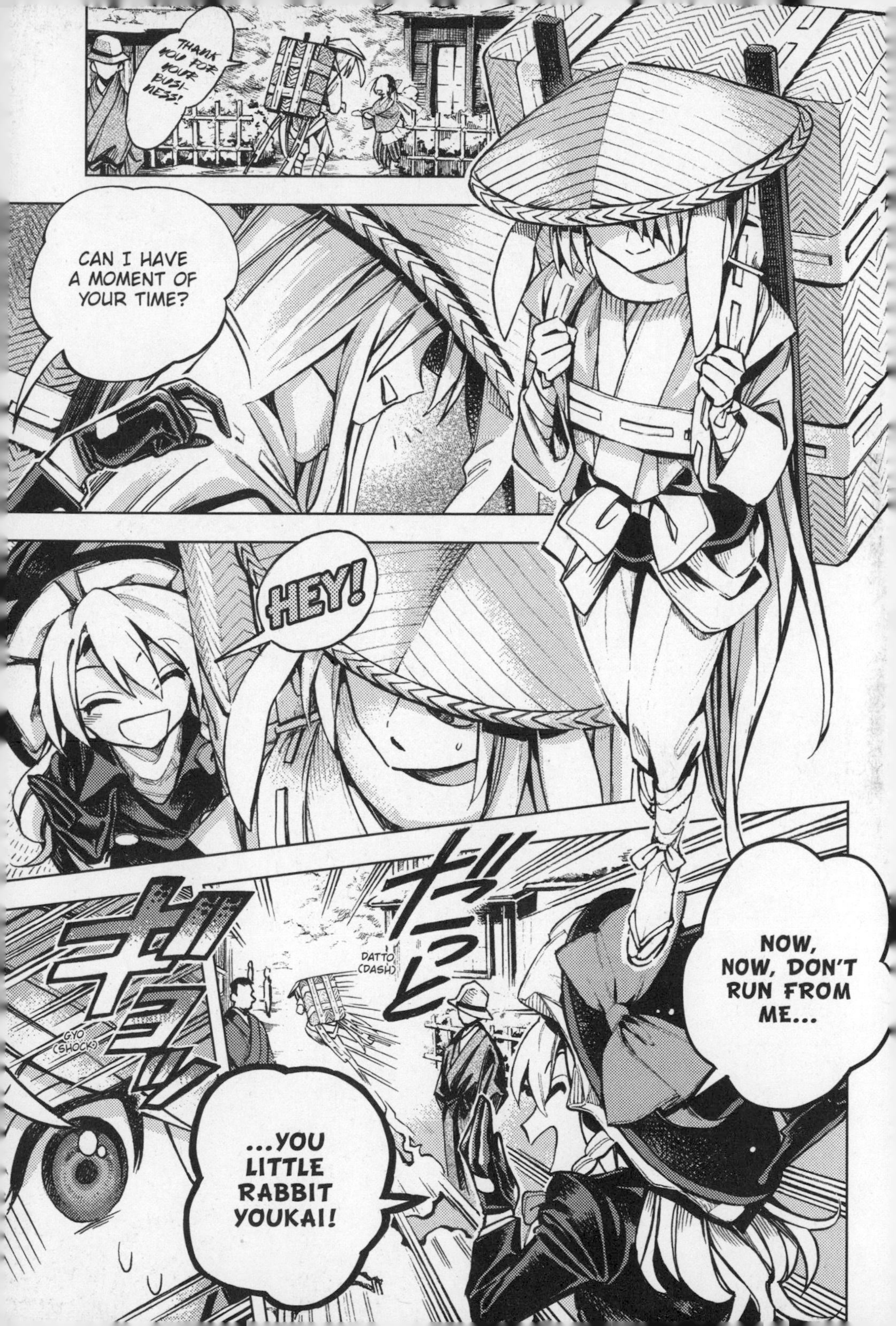
THANK YOU FOR YOUR BUSINESS!
CAN I HAVE A MOMENT OF YOUR TIME?
HEY!
NOW, NOW, DON'T RUN FROM ME...
DATTO (DASH)
GYO (SHOCK)
...YOU LITTLE RABBIT YOUKAI!

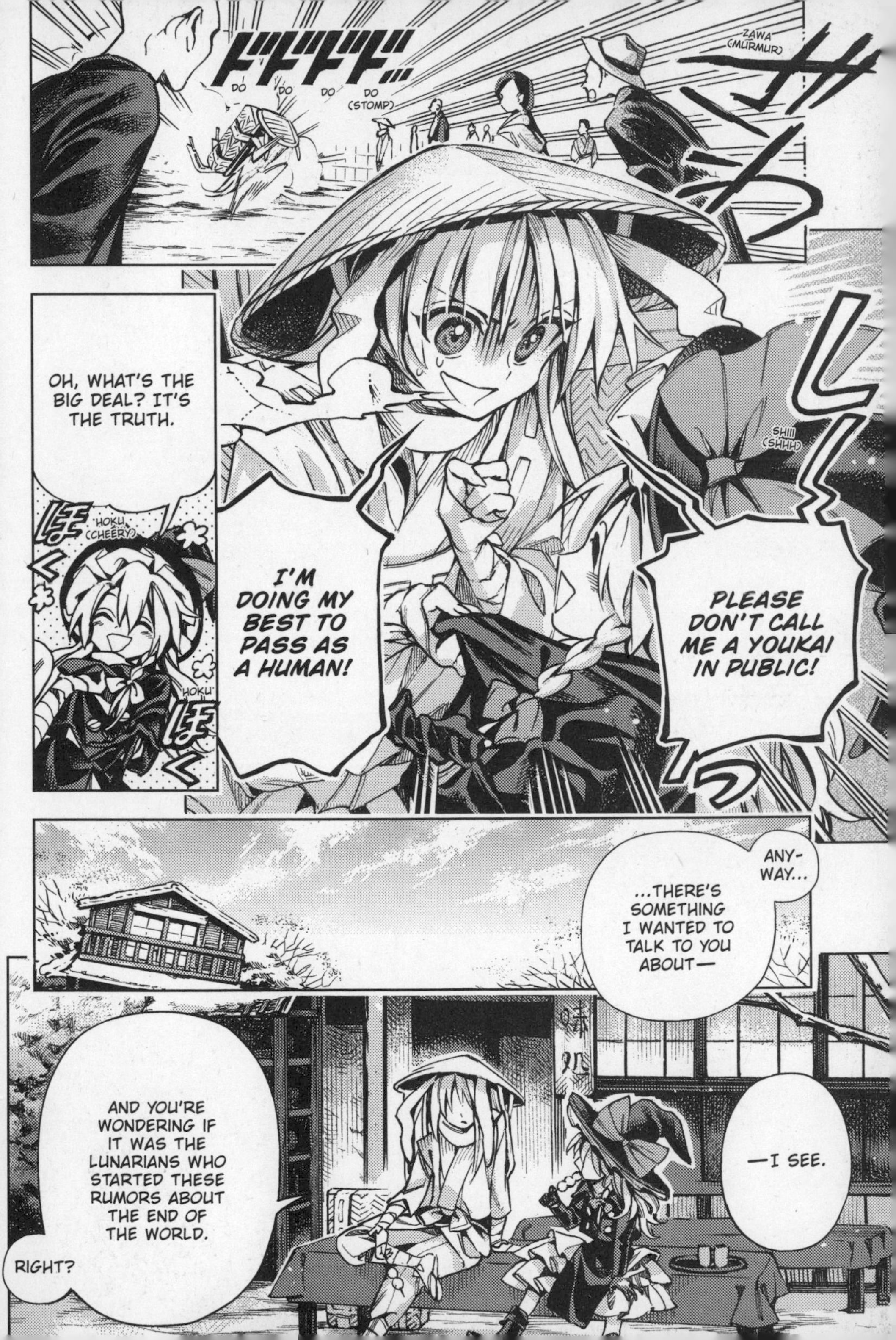
ZAWA (MURMUR)
DO DO DO DO (STOMP)
SHIII (SHHH)
PLEASE DON'T CALL ME A YOUKAI IN PUBLIC!
I'M DOING MY BEST TO PASS AS A HUMAN!
OH, WHAT'S THE BIG DEAL? IT'S THE TRUTH.
HOKU (CHEERY)
HOKU
ANY-WAY...
...THERE'S SOMETHING I WANTED TO TALK TO YOU ABOUT—
—I SEE.
AND YOU'RE WONDERING IF IT WAS THE LUNARIANS WHO STARTED THESE RUMORS ABOUT THE END OF THE WORLD.
RIGHT?

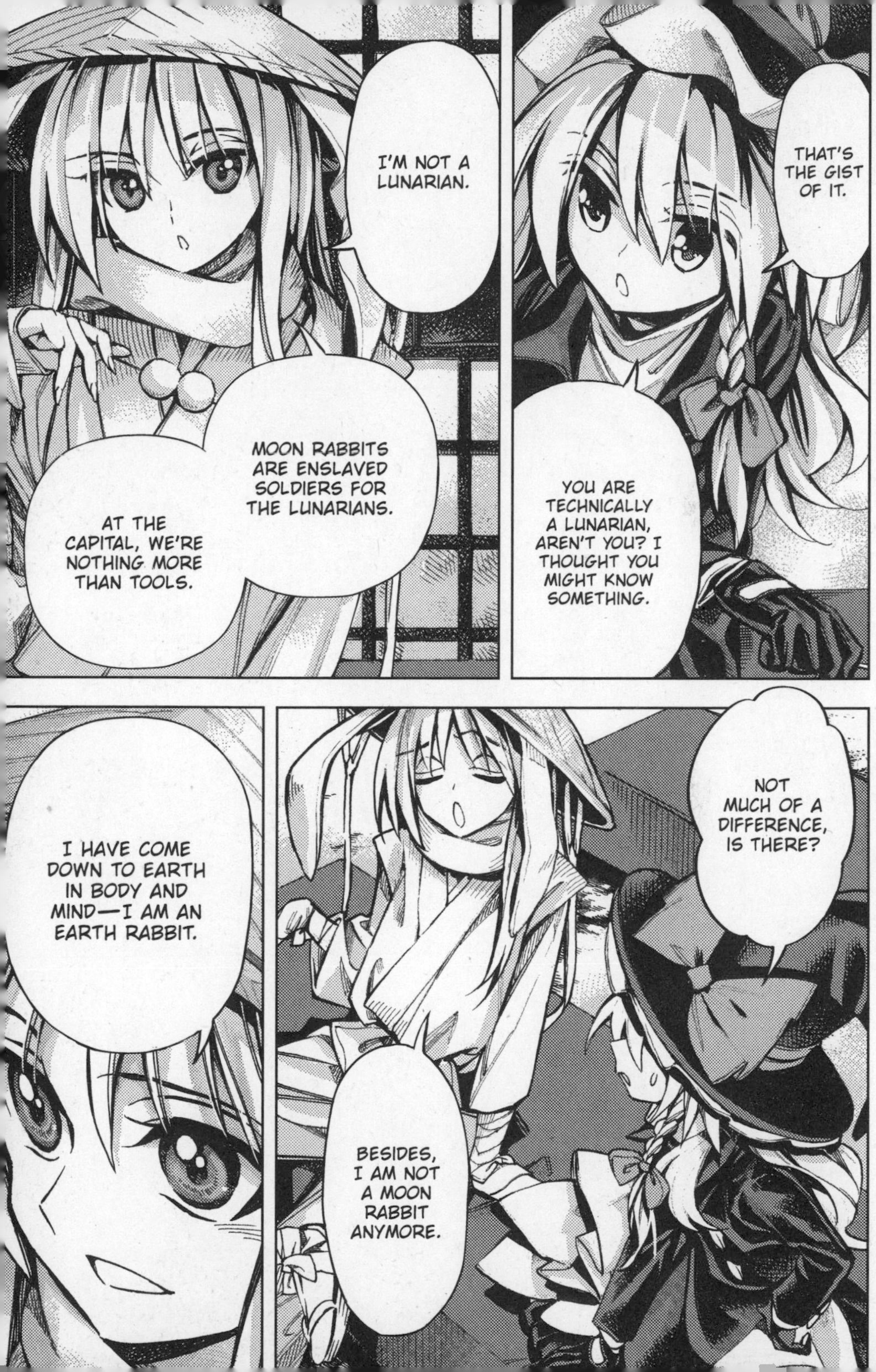
THAT'S THE GIST OF IT.
YOU ARE TECHNICALLY A LUNARIAN, AREN'T YOU? I THOUGHT YOU MIGHT KNOW SOMETHING.
I'M NOT A LUNARIAN.
MOON RABBITS ARE ENSLAVED SOLDIERS FOR THE LUNARIANS.
AT THE CAPITAL, WE'RE NOTHING MORE THAN TOOLS.
NOT MUCH OF A DIFFERENCE, IS THERE?
BESIDES, I AM NOT A MOON RABBIT ANYMORE.
I HAVE COME DOWN TO EARTH IN BODY AND MIND—I AM AN EARTH RABBIT.

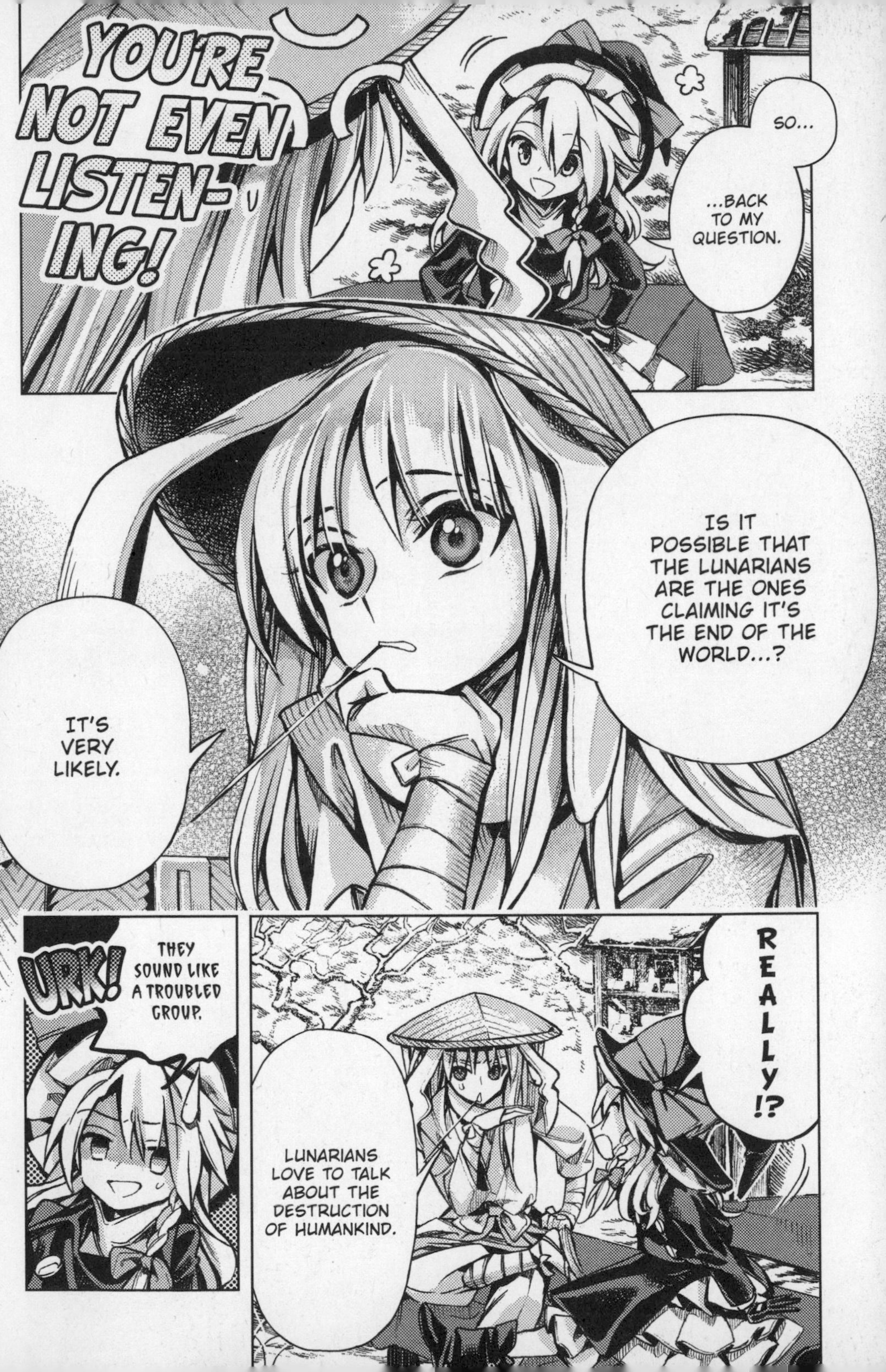
SO...
...BACK TO MY QUESTION.
YOU'RE NOT EVEN LISTEN-ING!
IS IT POSSIBLE THAT THE LUNARIANS ARE THE ONES CLAIMING IT'S THE END OF THE WORLD...?
IT'S VERY LIKELY.
REALLY!?
LUNARIANS LOVE TO TALK ABOUT THE DESTRUCTION OF HUMANKIND.
URK!
THEY SOUND LIKE A TROUBLED GROUP.

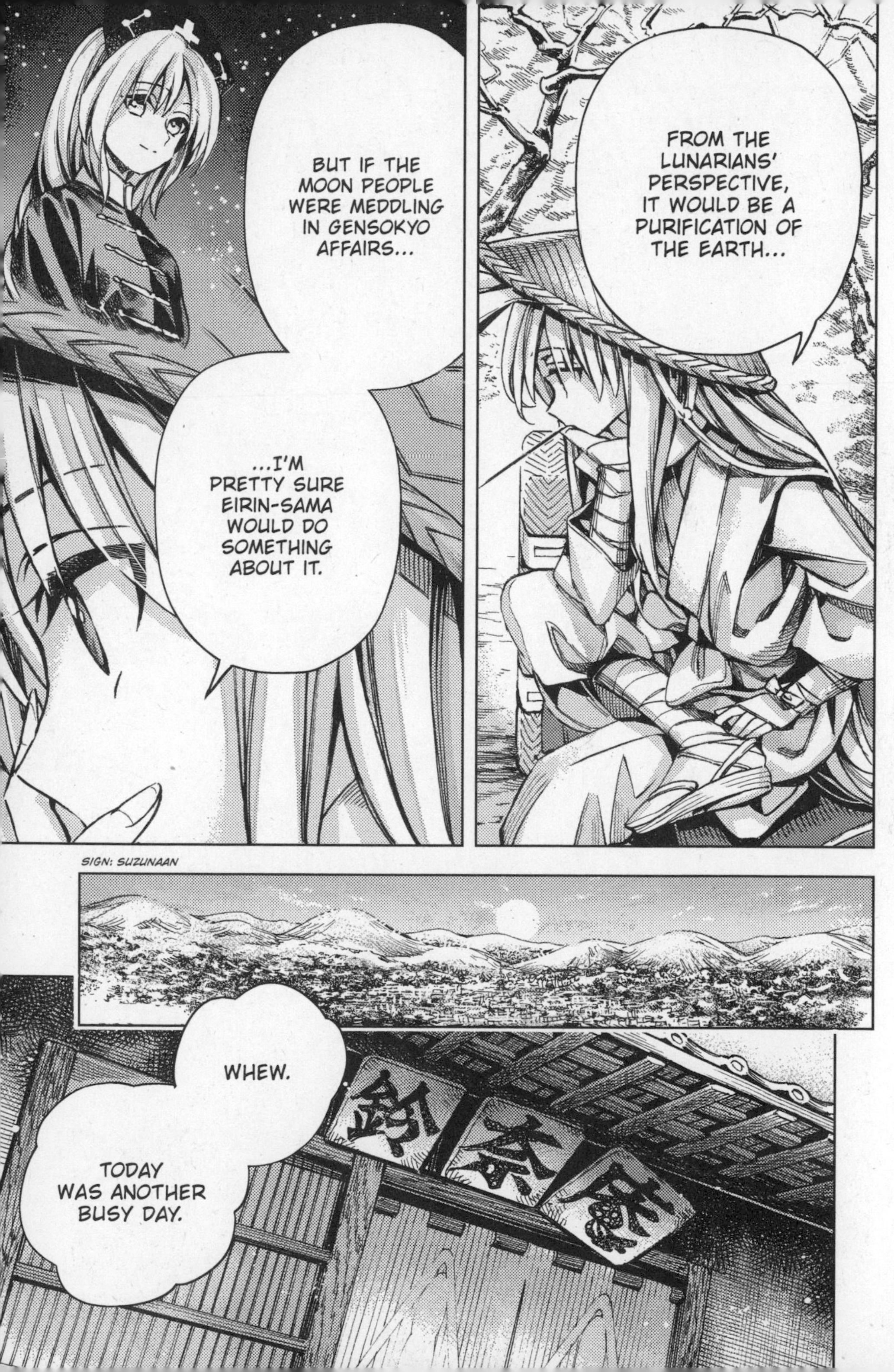

FROM THE LUNARIANS' PERSPECTIVE, IT WOULD BE A PURIFICATION OF THE EARTH...
BUT IF THE MOON PEOPLE WERE MEDDLING IN GENSOKYO AFFAIRS...
...I'M PRETTY SURE EIRIN-SAMA WOULD DO SOMETHING ABOUT IT.
SIGN: SUZUNAAN
WHEW.
TODAY WAS ANOTHER BUSY DAY.

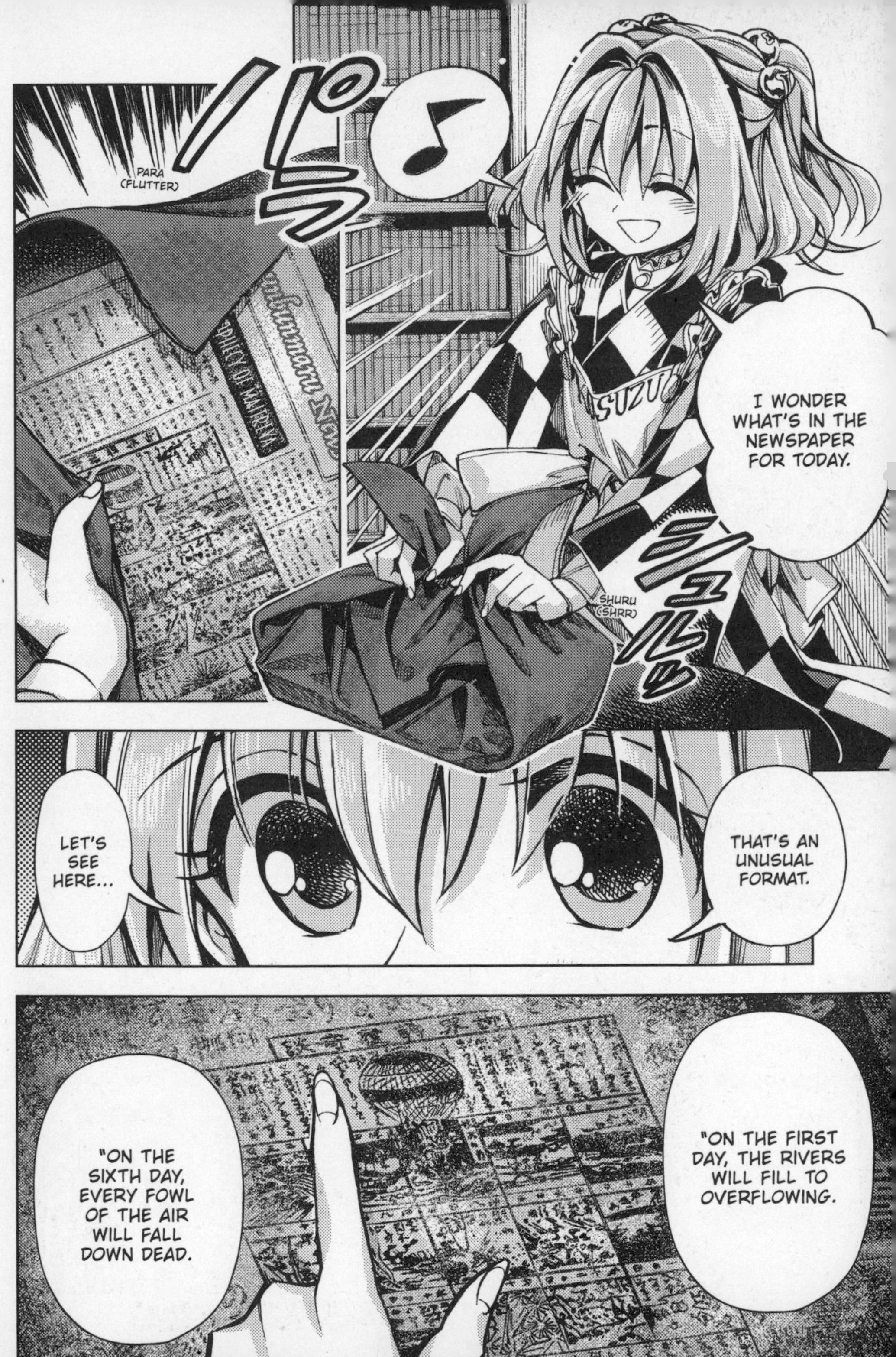
♪
I WONDER WHAT'S IN THE NEWSPAPER FOR TODAY.
SHURU (SHRR)
PARA (FLUTTER)
THAT'S AN UNUSUAL FORMAT.
LET'S SEE HERE...
"ON THE FIRST DAY, THE RIVERS WILL FILL TO OVERFLOWING.
"ON THE SIXTH DAY, EVERY FOWL OF THE AIR WILL FALL DOWN DEAD.

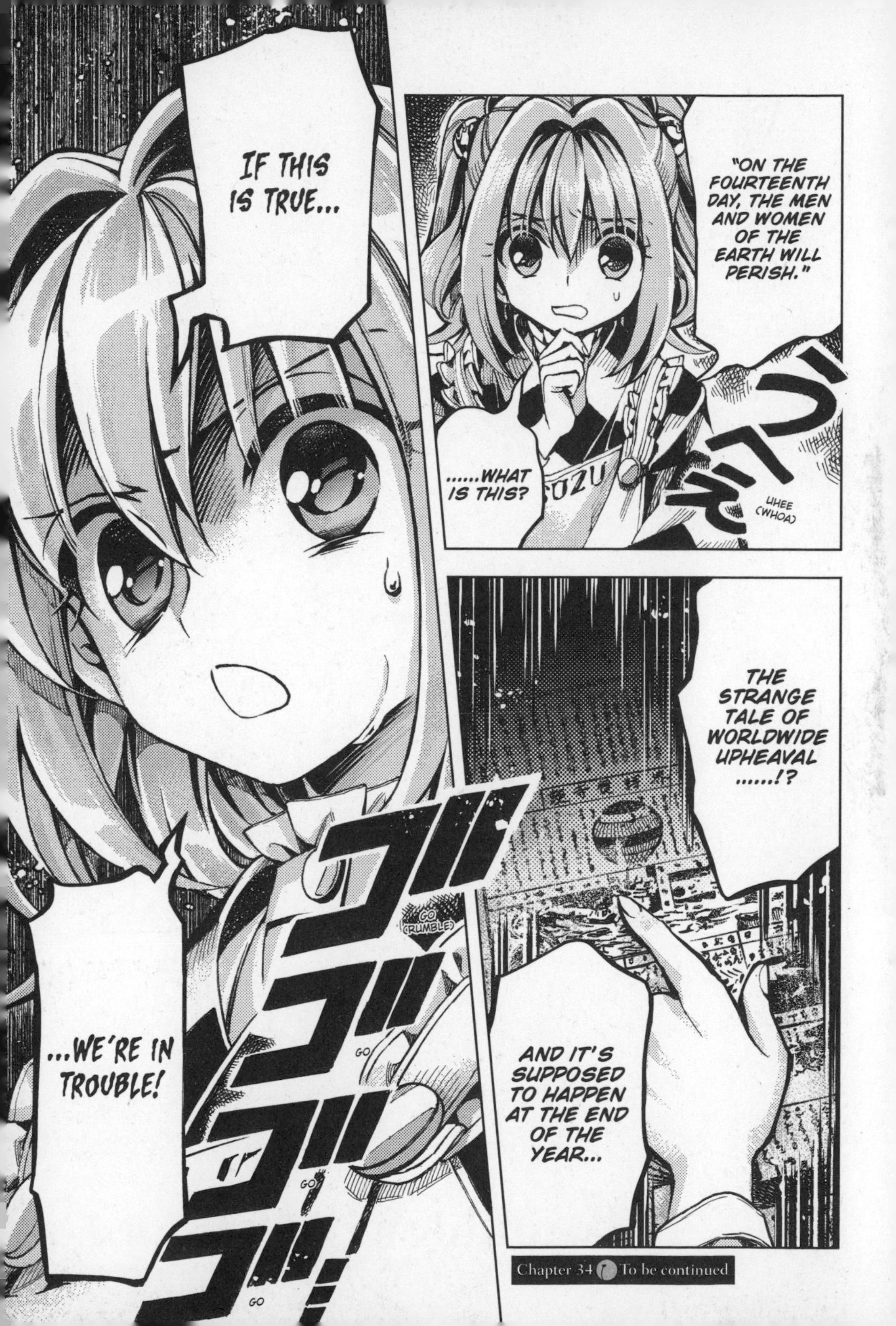
"ON THE FOURTEENTH DAY, THE MEN AND WOMEN OF THE EARTH WILL PERISH."
......WHAT IS THIS?
UHEE (WHOA)
THE STRANGE TALE OF WORLDWIDE UPHEAVAL ......!?
AND IT'S SUPPOSED TO HAPPEN AT THE END OF THE YEAR...
IF THIS IS TRUE...
GO (RUMBLE)
...WE'RE IN TROUBLE!
GO
GO
GO

Chapter 34 To be continued

Forbidden Scrollery

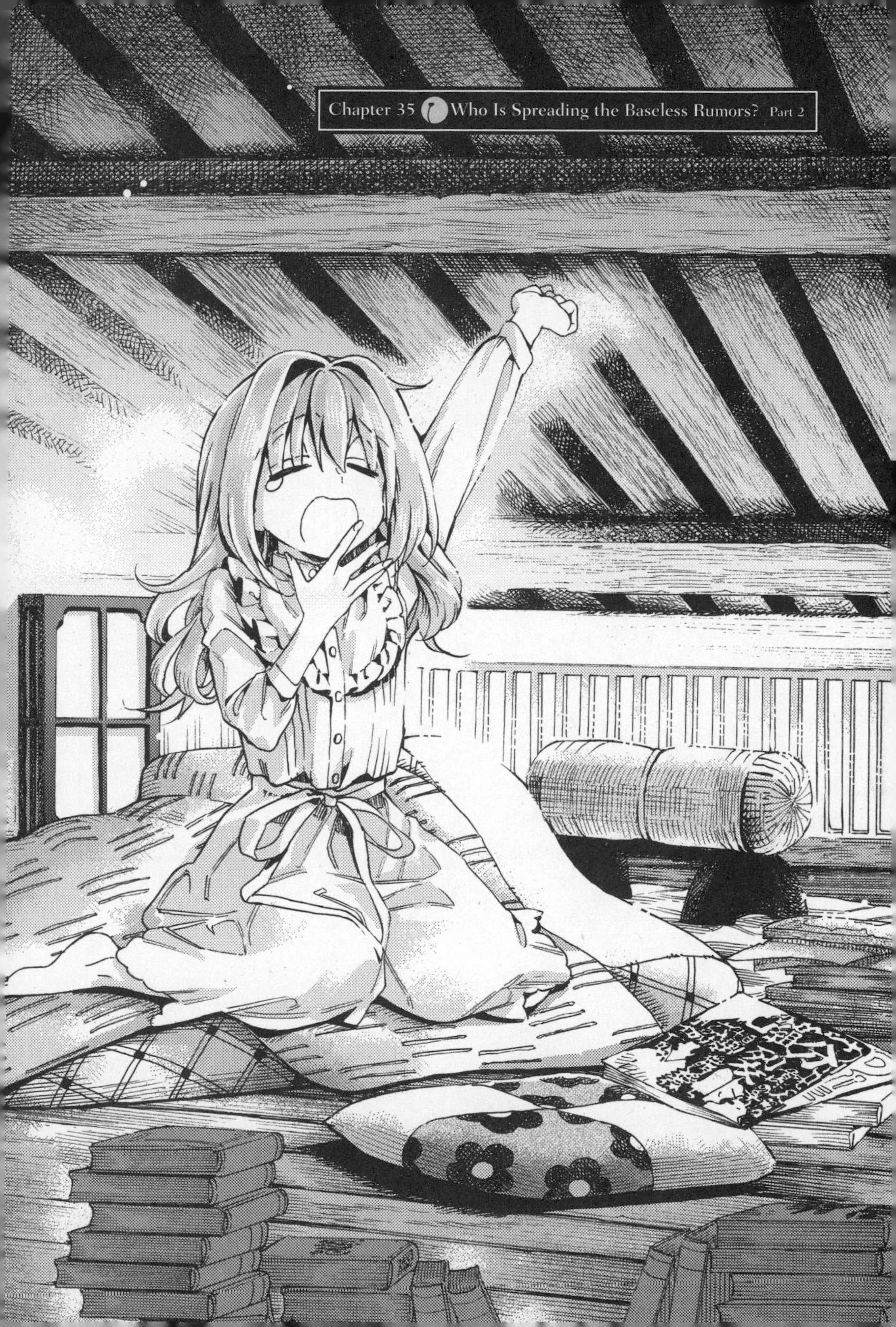
Chapter 35 Who Is Spreading the Baseless Rumors? Part 2

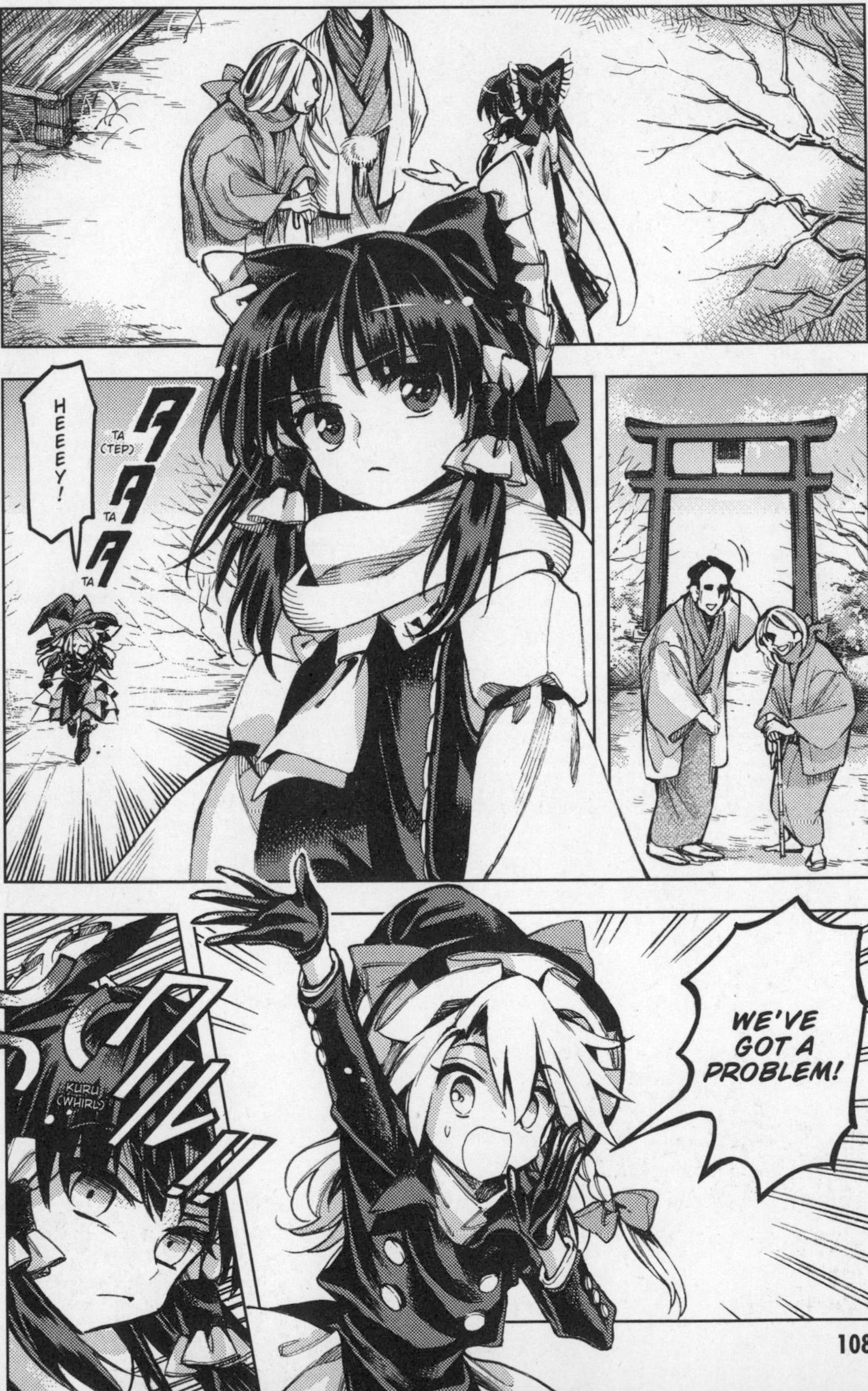
HEEEY!
TA (TEP)
TA
TA
WE'VE GOT A PROBLEM!
KURU (WHIRL)

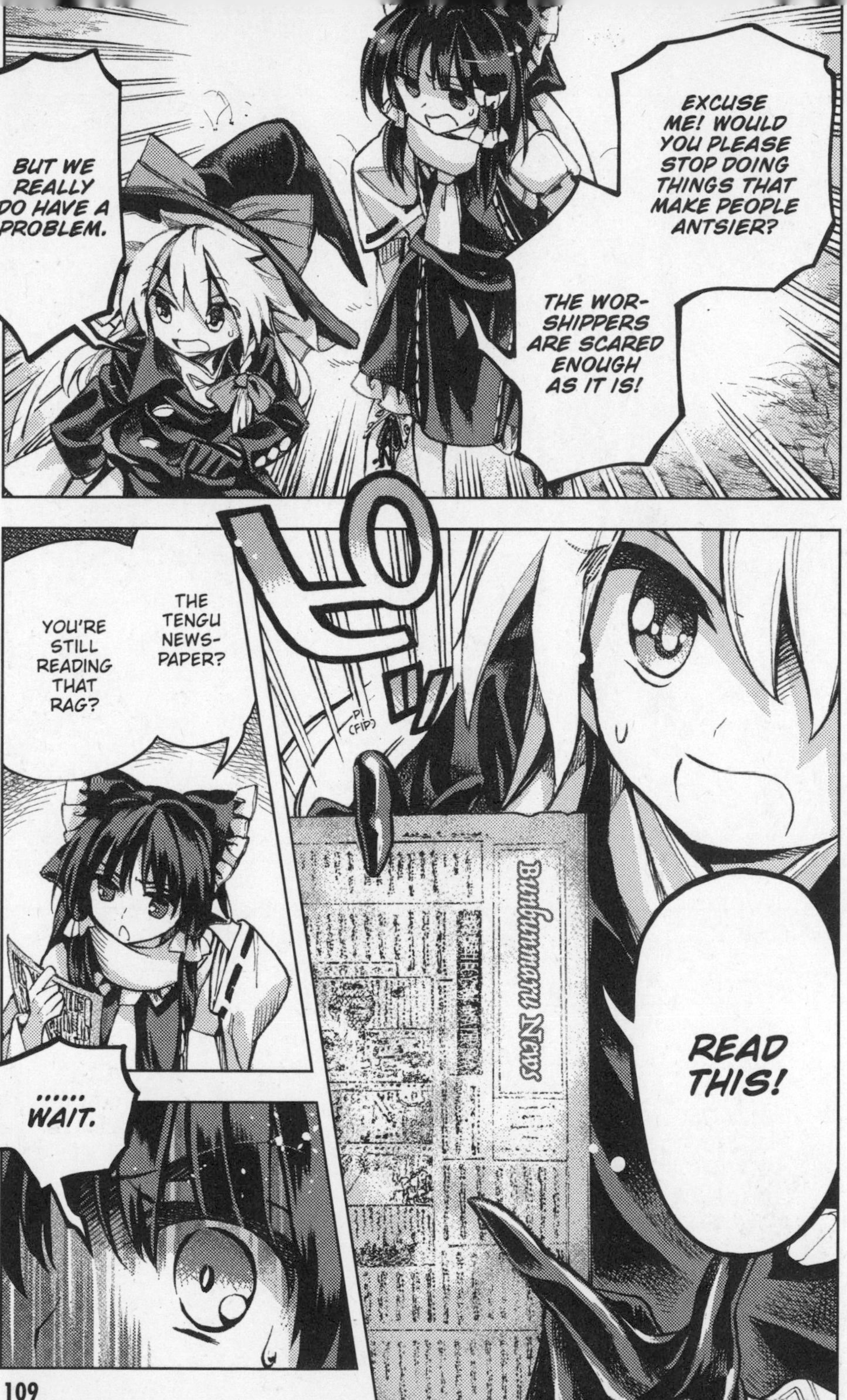
EXCUSE ME! WOULD YOU PLEASE STOP DOING THINGS THAT MAKE PEOPLE ANTSIER?
THE WOR-SHIPPERS ARE SCARED ENOUGH AS IT IS!
BUT WE REALLY DO HAVE A PROBLEM.
PI (FIP)
READ THIS!
Bunbunmaru News
THE TENGU NEWS-PAPER?
YOU'RE STILL READING THAT RAG?
......WAIT.

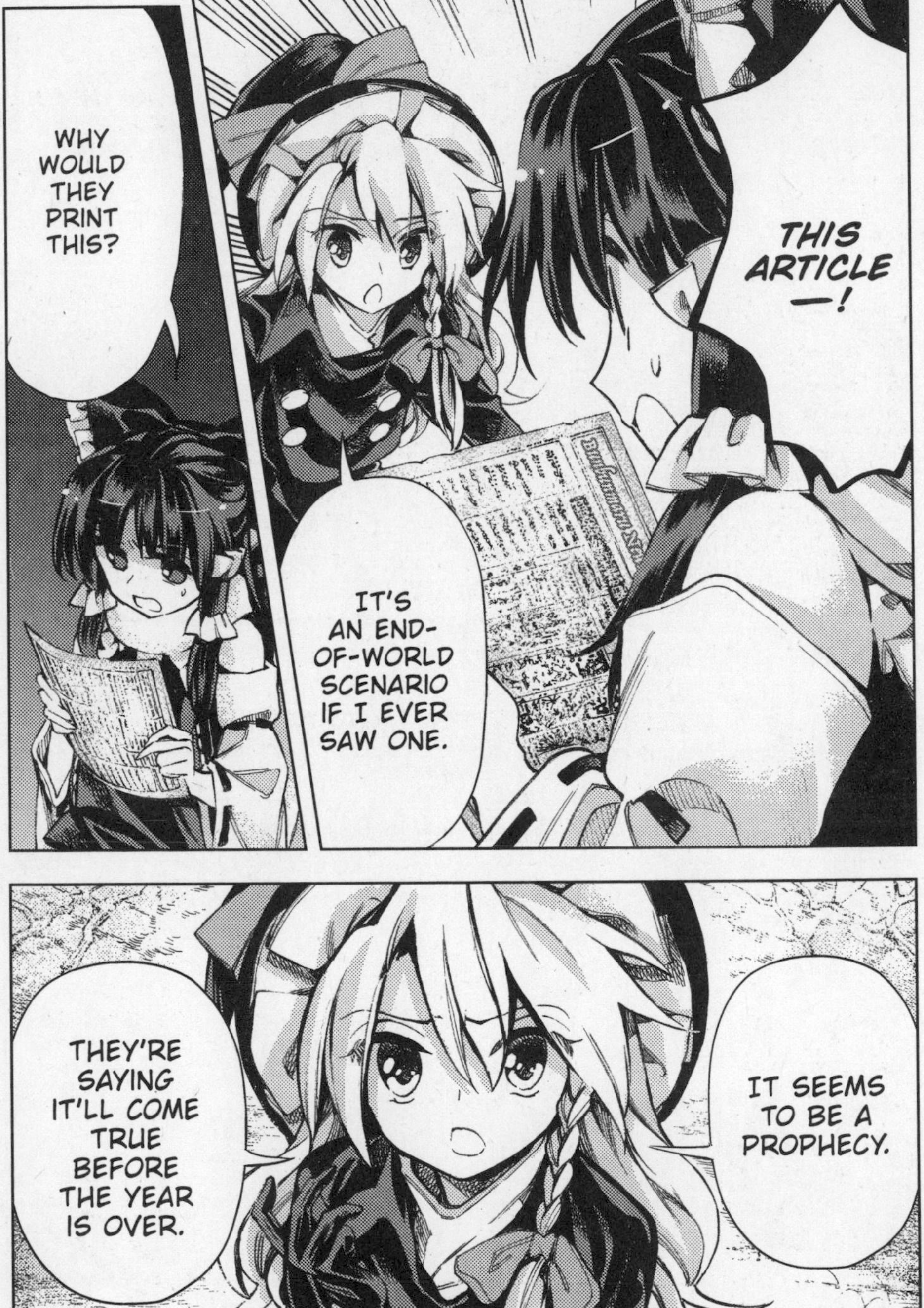
THIS ARTICLE—!
WHY WOULD THEY PRINT THIS?
IT'S AN END-OF-WORLD SCENARIO IF I EVER SAW ONE.
IT SEEMS TO BE A PROPHECY.
THEY'RE SAYING IT'LL COME TRUE BEFORE THE YEAR IS OVER.

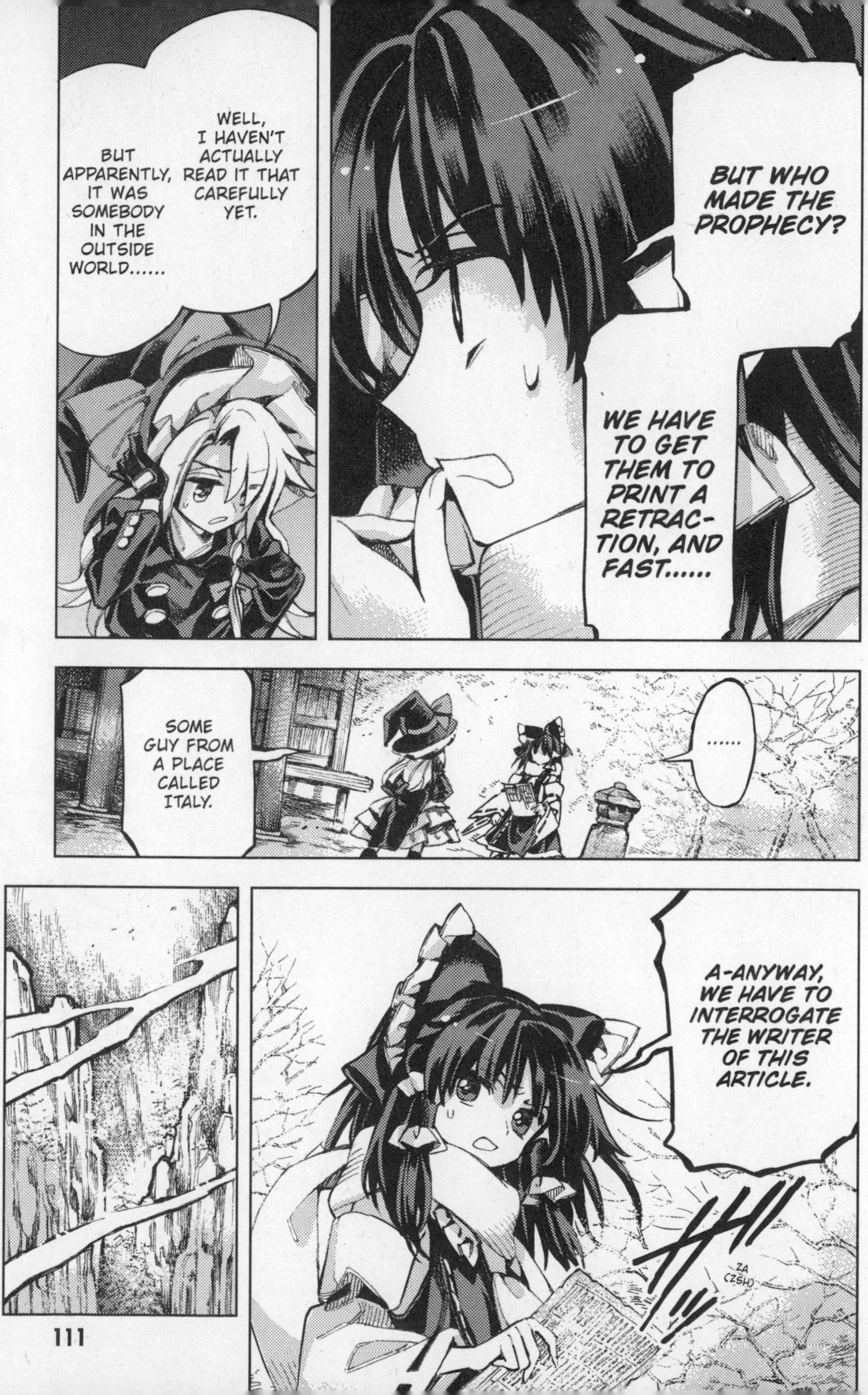
BUT WHO MADE THE PROPHECY?
WE HAVE TO GET THEM TO PRINT A RETRAC-TION, AND FAST......
WELL, I HAVEN'T ACTUALLY READ IT THAT CAREFULLY YET.
BUT APPARENTLY, IT WAS SOMEBODY IN THE OUTSIDE WORLD......
......
SOME GUY FROM A PLACE CALLED ITALY.
A-ANYWAY, WE HAVE TO INTERROGATE THE WRITER OF THIS ARTICLE.
ZA (ZSH)

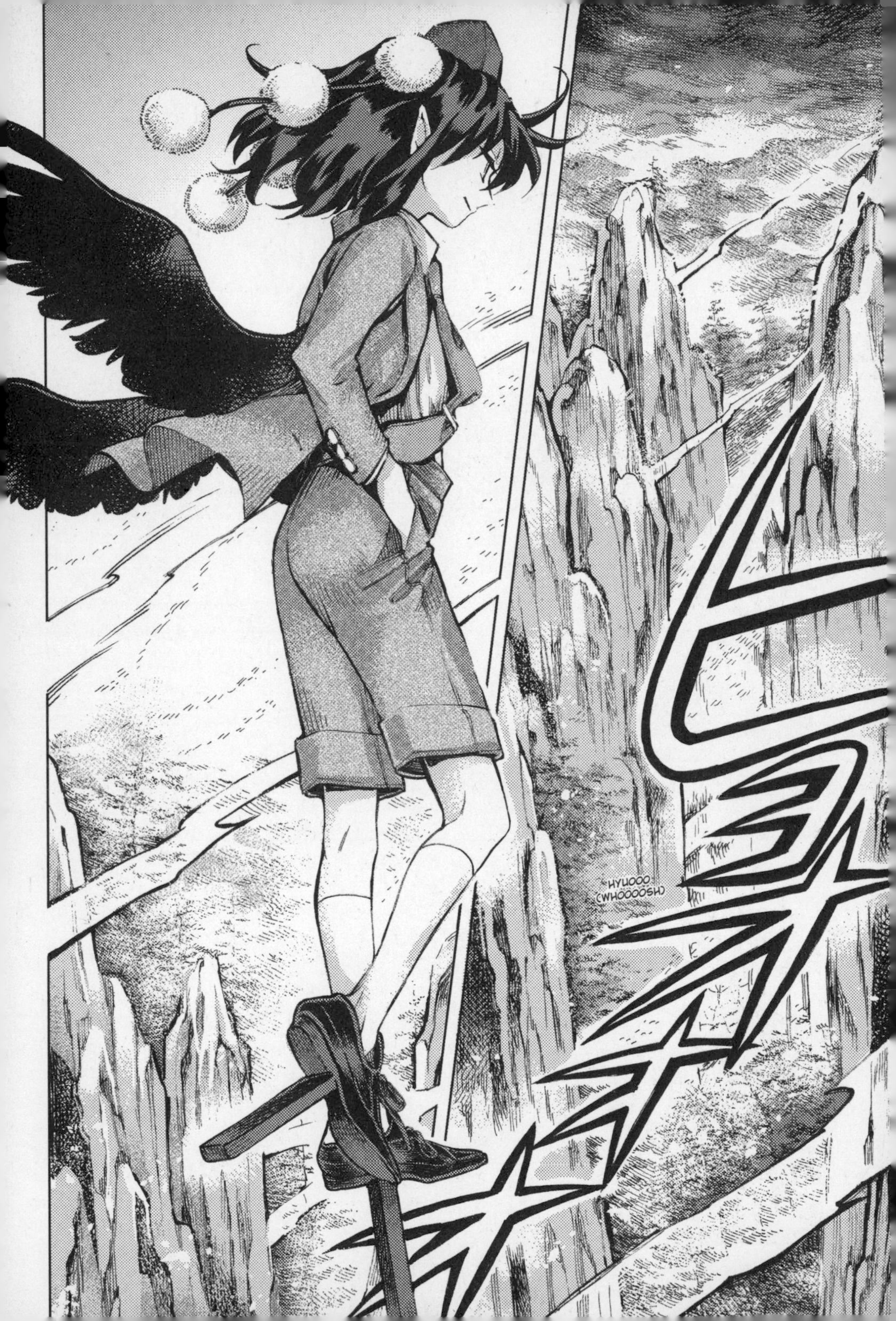
HYUOOO
(WHOOOOSH)

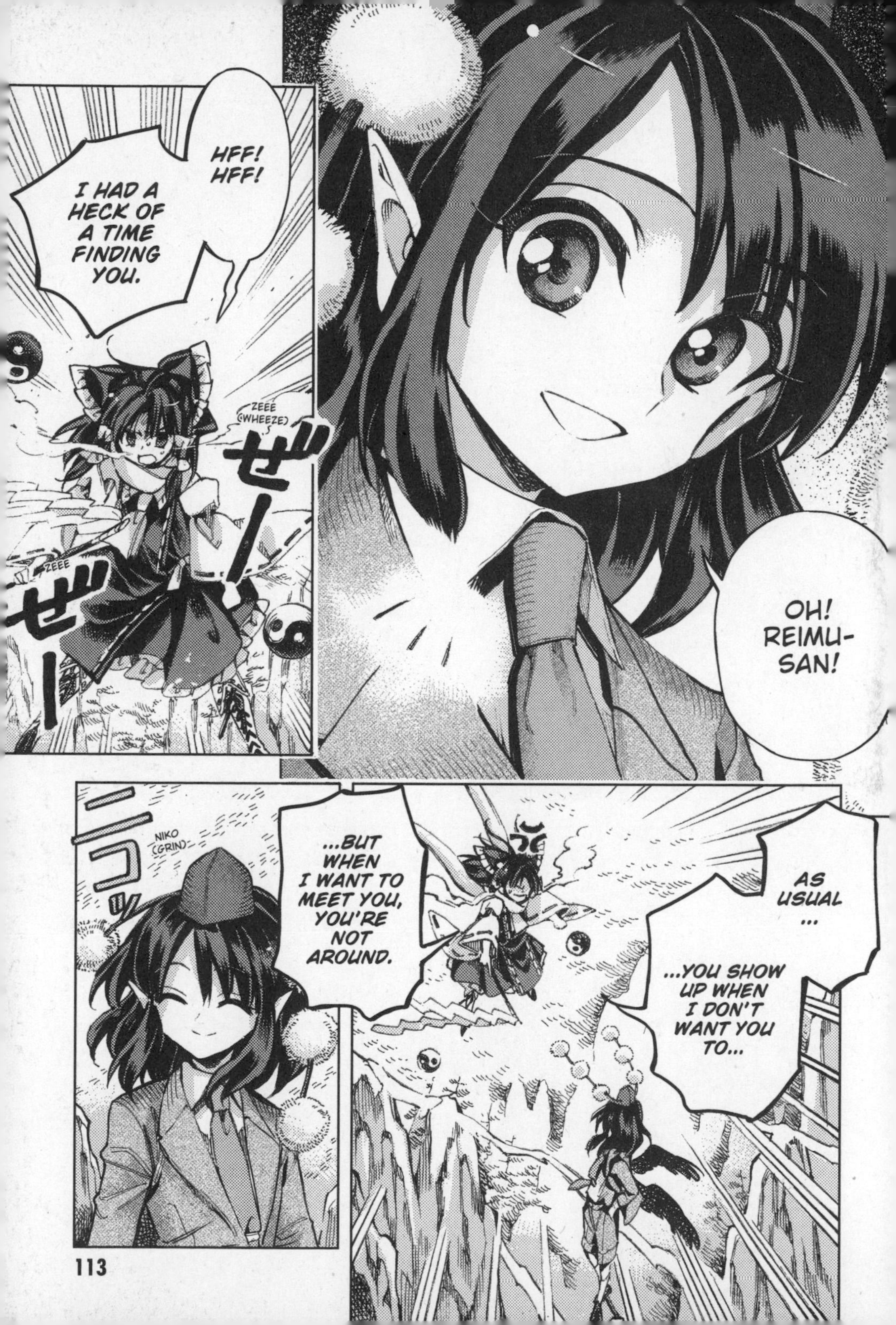
OH! REIMU-SAN!
HFF! HFF!
I HAD A HECK OF A TIME FINDING YOU.
ZEEE (WHEEZE)
ゼー
ZEEE
ゼー
AS USUAL...
...YOU SHOW UP WHEN I DON'T WANT YOU TO...
...BUT WHEN I WANT TO MEET YOU, YOU'RE NOT AROUND.
NIKO (GRIN)
ニコッ

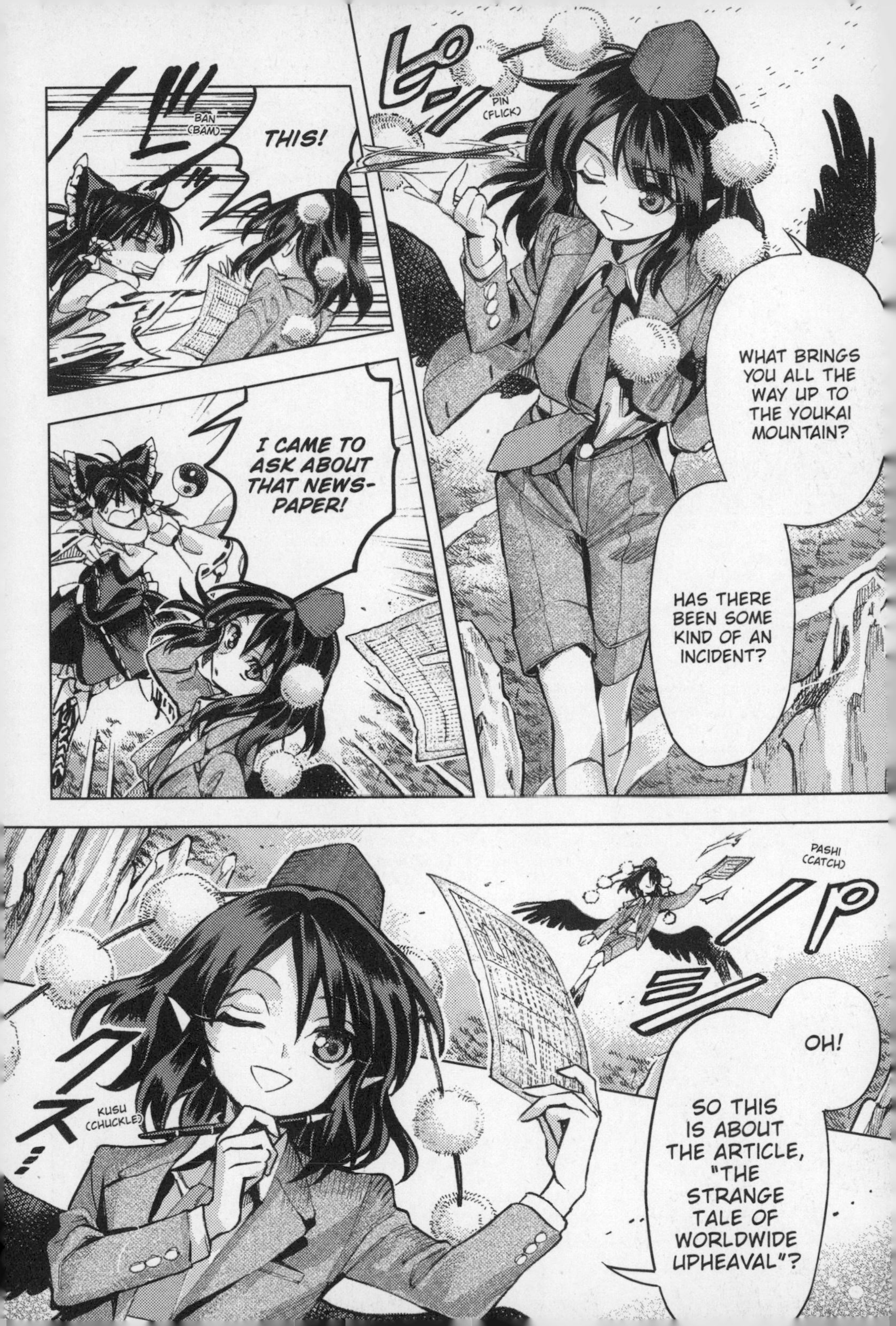
PIN (FLICK)
WHAT BRINGS YOU ALL THE WAY UP TO THE YOUKAI MOUNTAIN?
HAS THERE BEEN SOME KIND OF AN INCIDENT?
BAN (BAM)
THIS!
I CAME TO ASK ABOUT THAT NEWS-PAPER!
PASHI (CATCH)
OH!
SO THIS IS ABOUT THE ARTICLE, "THE STRANGE TALE OF WORLDWIDE UPHEAVAL"?
KUSU (CHUCKLE)

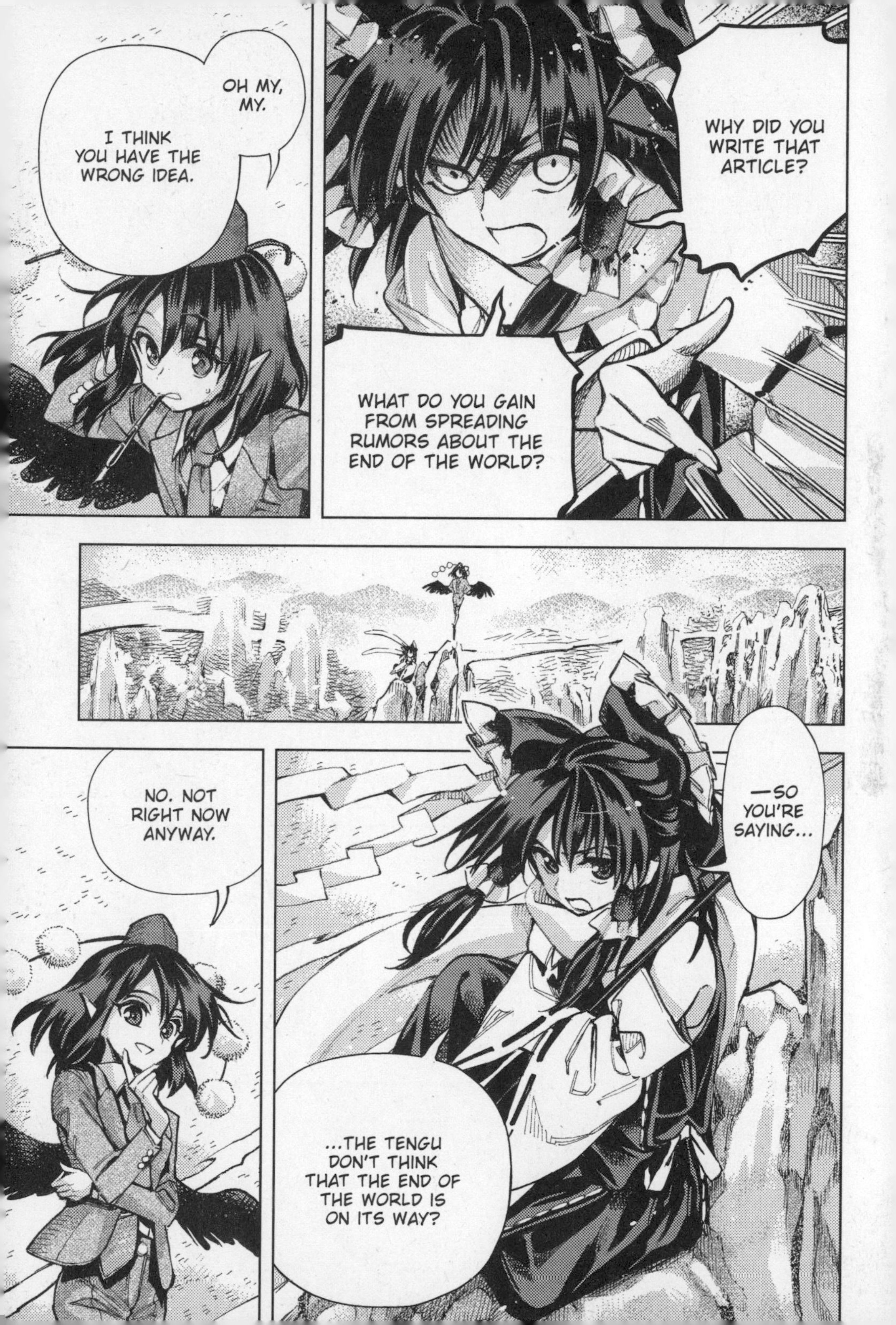
WHY DID YOU WRITE THAT ARTICLE?
WHAT DO YOU GAIN FROM SPREADING RUMORS ABOUT THE END OF THE WORLD?
OH MY, MY.
I THINK YOU HAVE THE WRONG IDEA.
—SO YOU'RE SAYING...
...THE TENGU DON'T THINK THAT THE END OF THE WORLD IS ON ITS WAY?
NO. NOT RIGHT NOW ANYWAY.

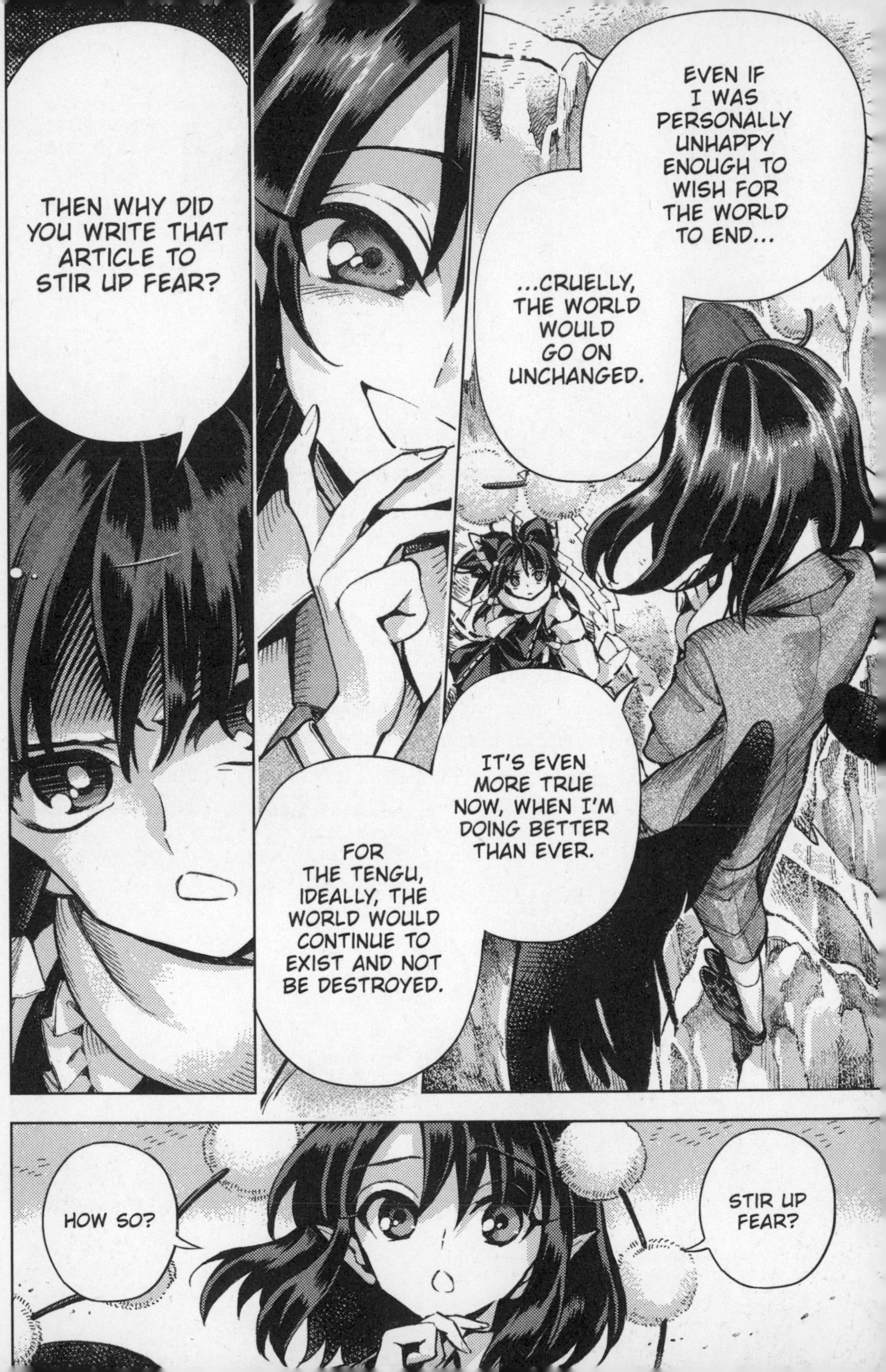
EVEN IF I WAS PERSONALLY UNHAPPY ENOUGH TO WISH FOR THE WORLD TO END...
...CRUELLY, THE WORLD WOULD GO ON UNCHANGED.
IT'S EVEN MORE TRUE NOW, WHEN I'M DOING BETTER THAN EVER.
FOR THE TENGU, IDEALLY, THE WORLD WOULD CONTINUE TO EXIST AND NOT BE DESTROYED.
THEN WHY DID YOU WRITE THAT ARTICLE TO STIR UP FEAR?
STIR UP FEAR?
HOW SO?

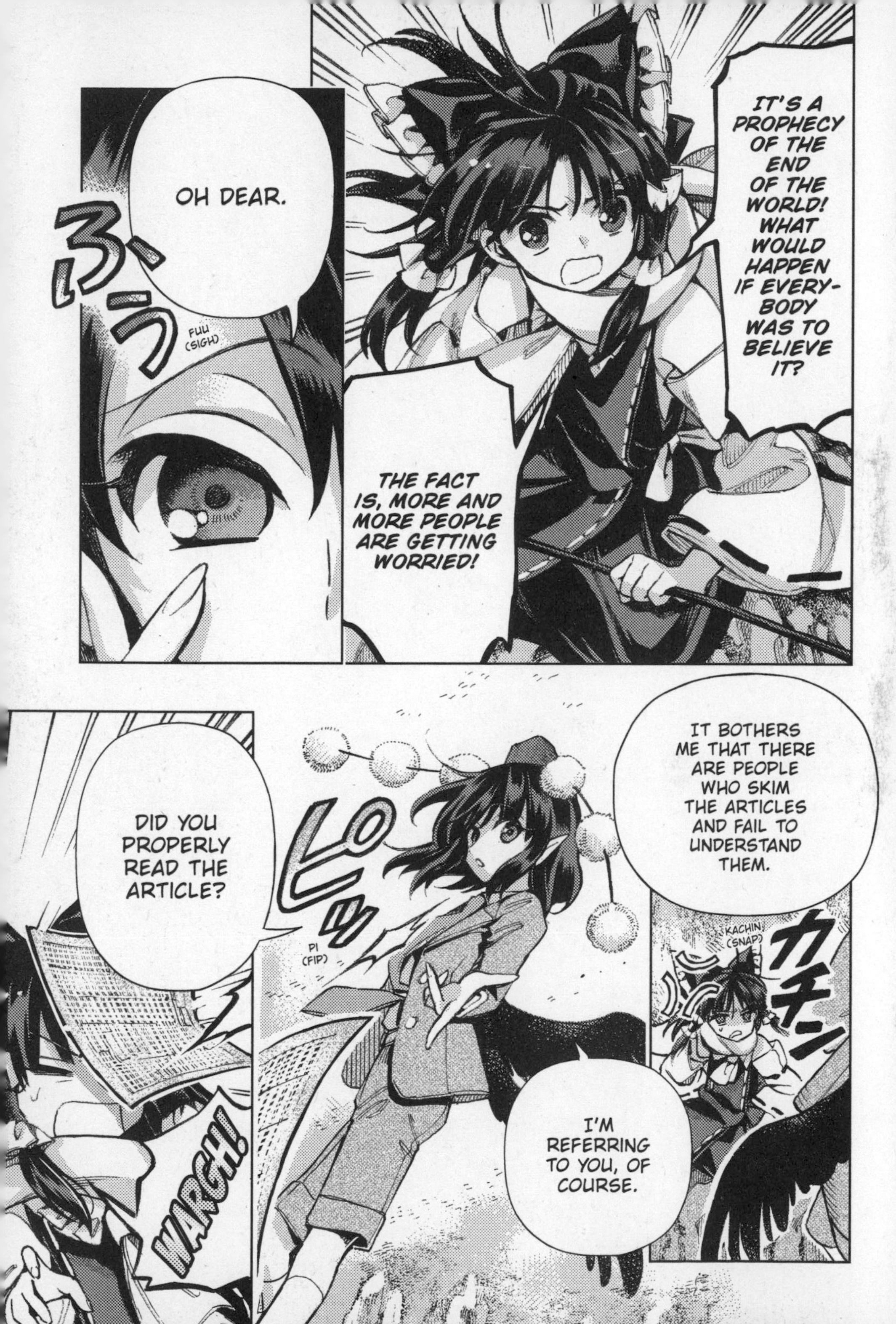
IT'S A PROPHECY OF THE END OF THE WORLD! WHAT WOULD HAPPEN IF EVERY-BODY WAS TO BELIEVE IT?
THE FACT IS, MORE AND MORE PEOPLE ARE GETTING WORRIED!
OH DEAR.
ふう
FUU (SIGH)
DID YOU PROPERLY READ THE ARTICLE?
ピッ
PI (FIP)
IT BOTHERS ME THAT THERE ARE PEOPLE WHO SKIM THE ARTICLES AND FAIL TO UNDERSTAND THEM.
カチン
KACHIN (SNAP)
I'M REFERRING TO YOU, OF COURSE.
WARGH!

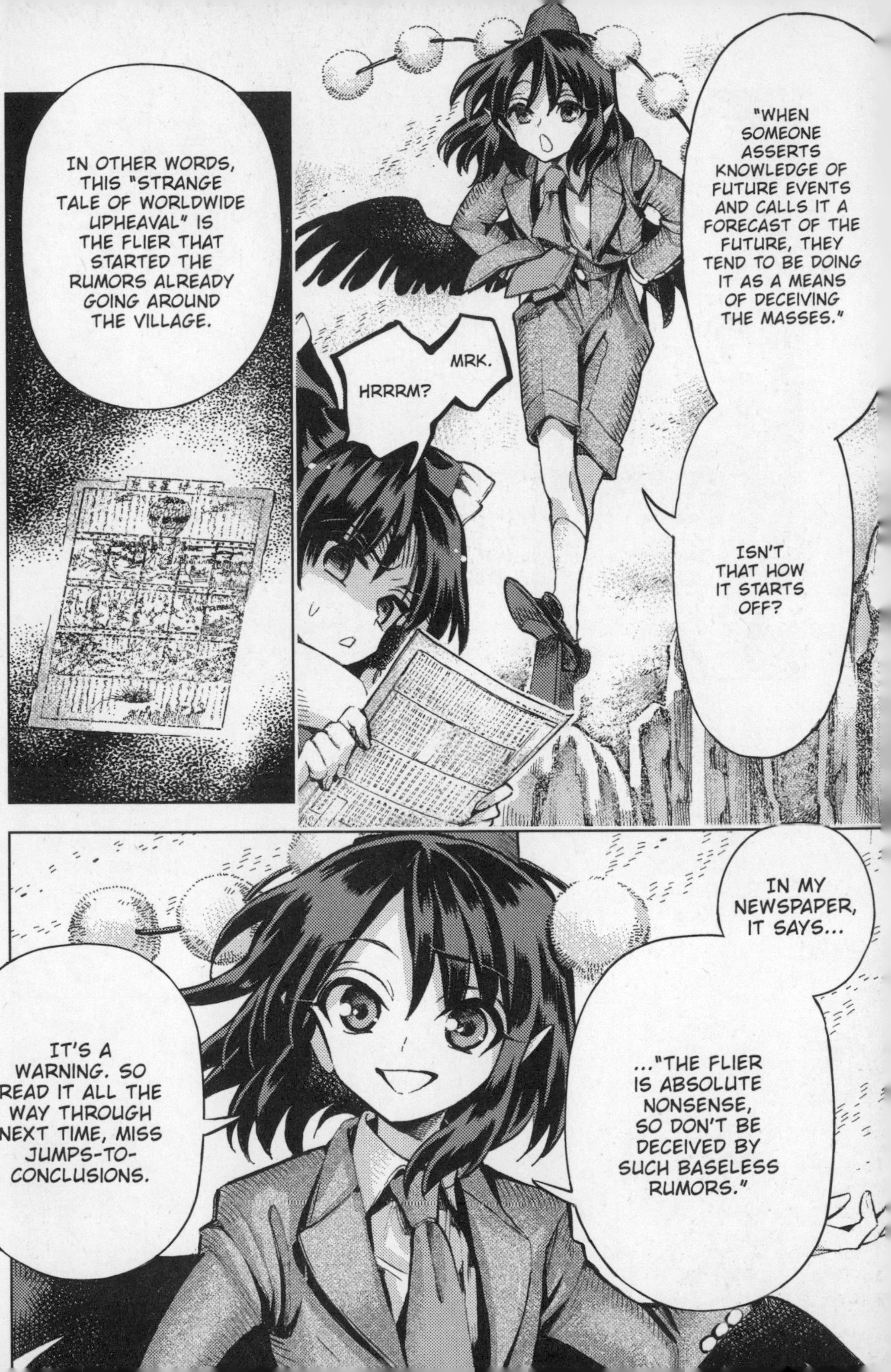
"WHEN SOMEONE ASSERTS KNOWLEDGE OF FUTURE EVENTS AND CALLS IT A FORECAST OF THE FUTURE, THEY TEND TO BE DOING IT AS A MEANS OF DECEIVING THE MASSES."
ISN'T THAT HOW IT STARTS OFF?
MRK.
HRRRM?
IN OTHER WORDS, THIS "STRANGE TALE OF WORLDWIDE UPHEAVAL" IS THE FLIER THAT STARTED THE RUMORS ALREADY GOING AROUND THE VILLAGE.
IN MY NEWSPAPER, IT SAYS...
..."THE FLIER IS ABSOLUTE NONSENSE, SO DON'T BE DECEIVED BY SUCH BASELESS RUMORS."
IT'S A WARNING. SO READ IT ALL THE WAY THROUGH NEXT TIME, MISS JUMPS-TO-CONCLUSIONS.

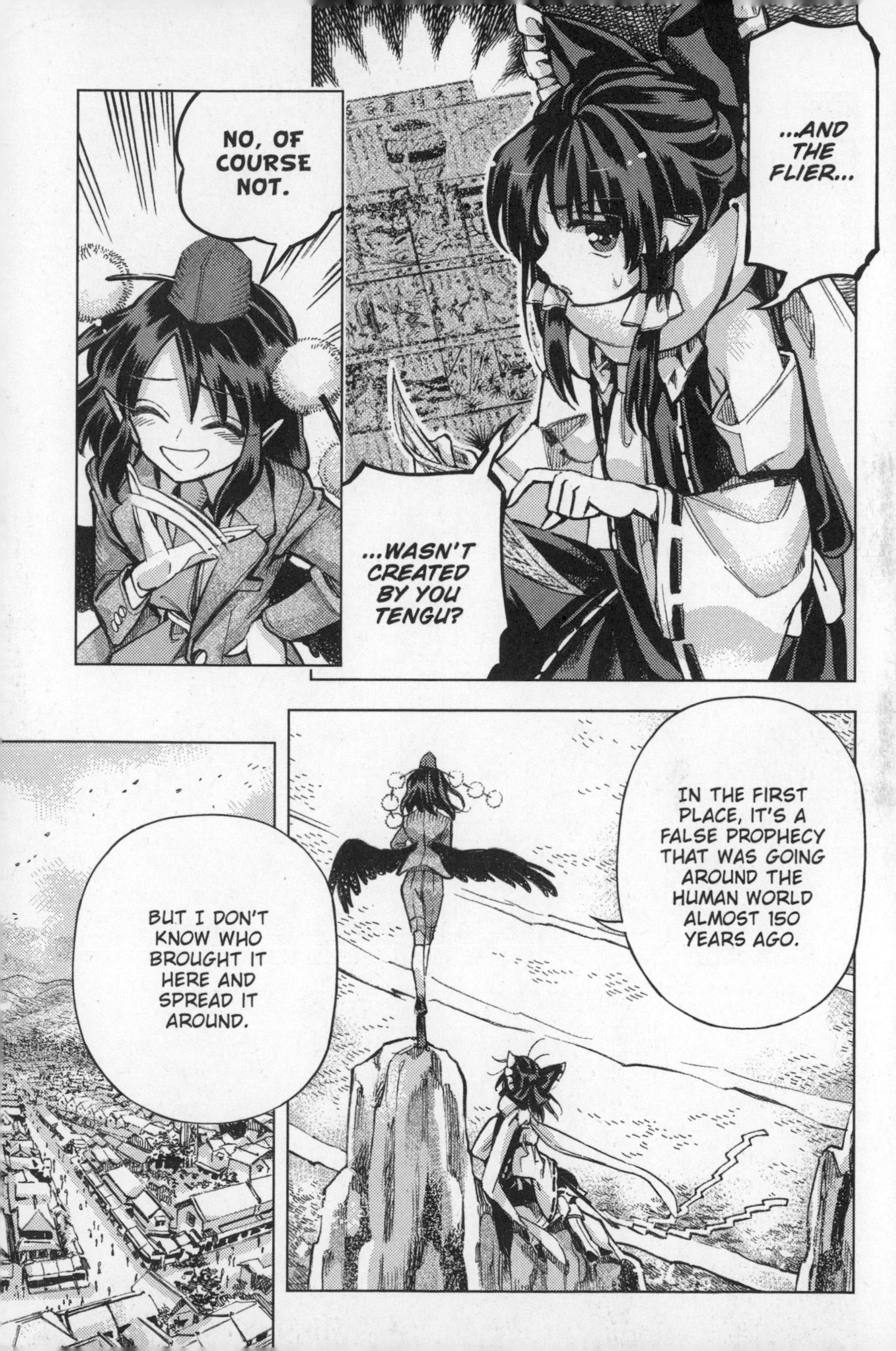
...AND THE FLIER...
...WASN'T CREATED BY YOU TENGU?
NO, OF COURSE NOT.
IN THE FIRST PLACE, IT'S A FALSE PROPHECY THAT WAS GOING AROUND THE HUMAN WORLD ALMOST 150 YEARS AGO.
BUT I DON'T KNOW WHO BROUGHT IT HERE AND SPREAD IT AROUND.

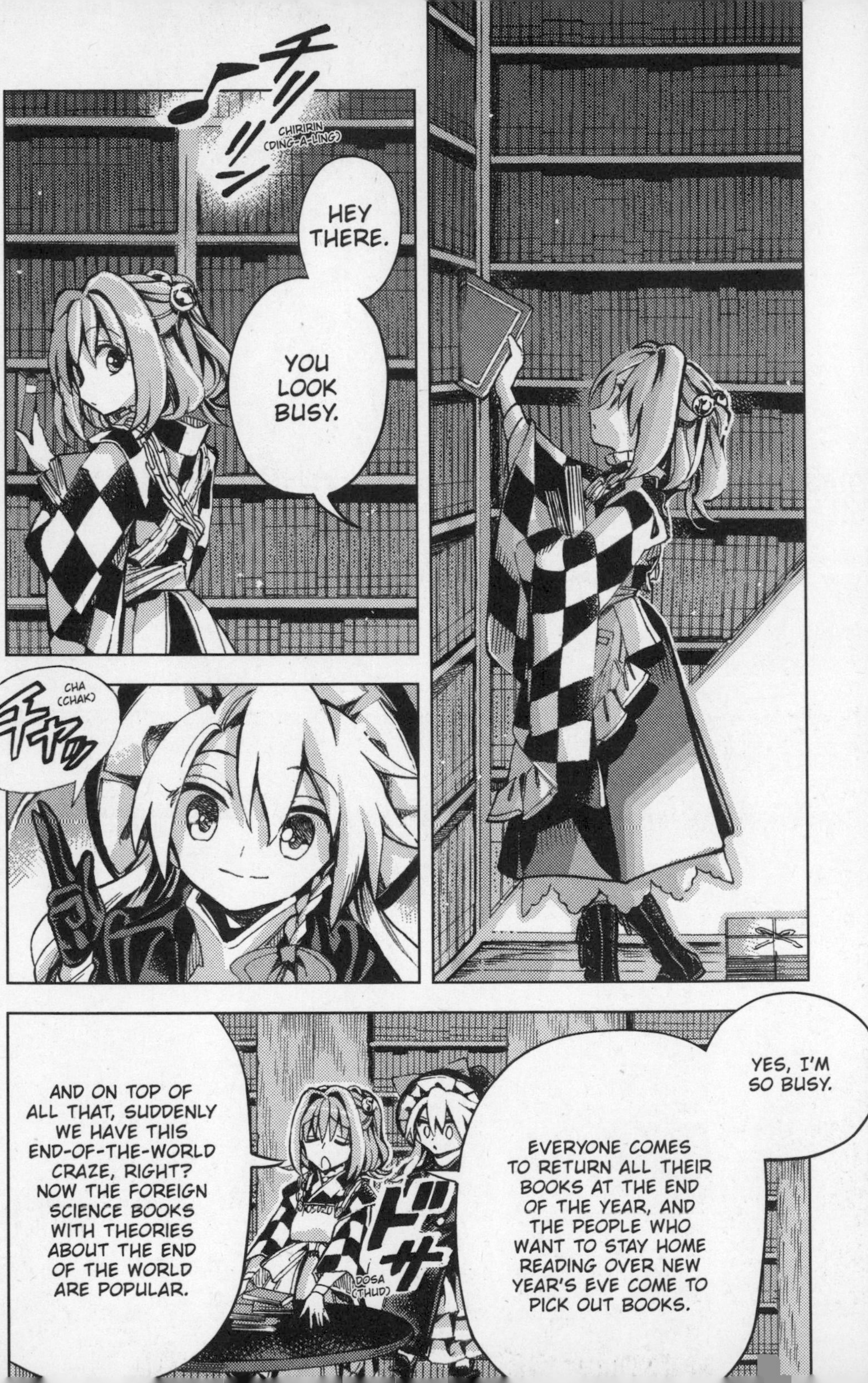

チリリン
CHIRIRIN (DING-A-LING)
HEY THERE.
YOU LOOK BUSY.
チャッ
CHA (CHAK)
YES, I'M SO BUSY.
EVERYONE COMES TO RETURN ALL THEIR BOOKS AT THE END OF THE YEAR, AND THE PEOPLE WHO WANT TO STAY HOME READING OVER NEW YEAR'S EVE COME TO PICK OUT BOOKS.
ドサ
DOSA (THUD)
AND ON TOP OF ALL THAT, SUDDENLY WE HAVE THIS END-OF-THE-WORLD CRAZE, RIGHT? NOW THE FOREIGN SCIENCE BOOKS WITH THEORIES ABOUT THE END OF THE WORLD ARE POPULAR.

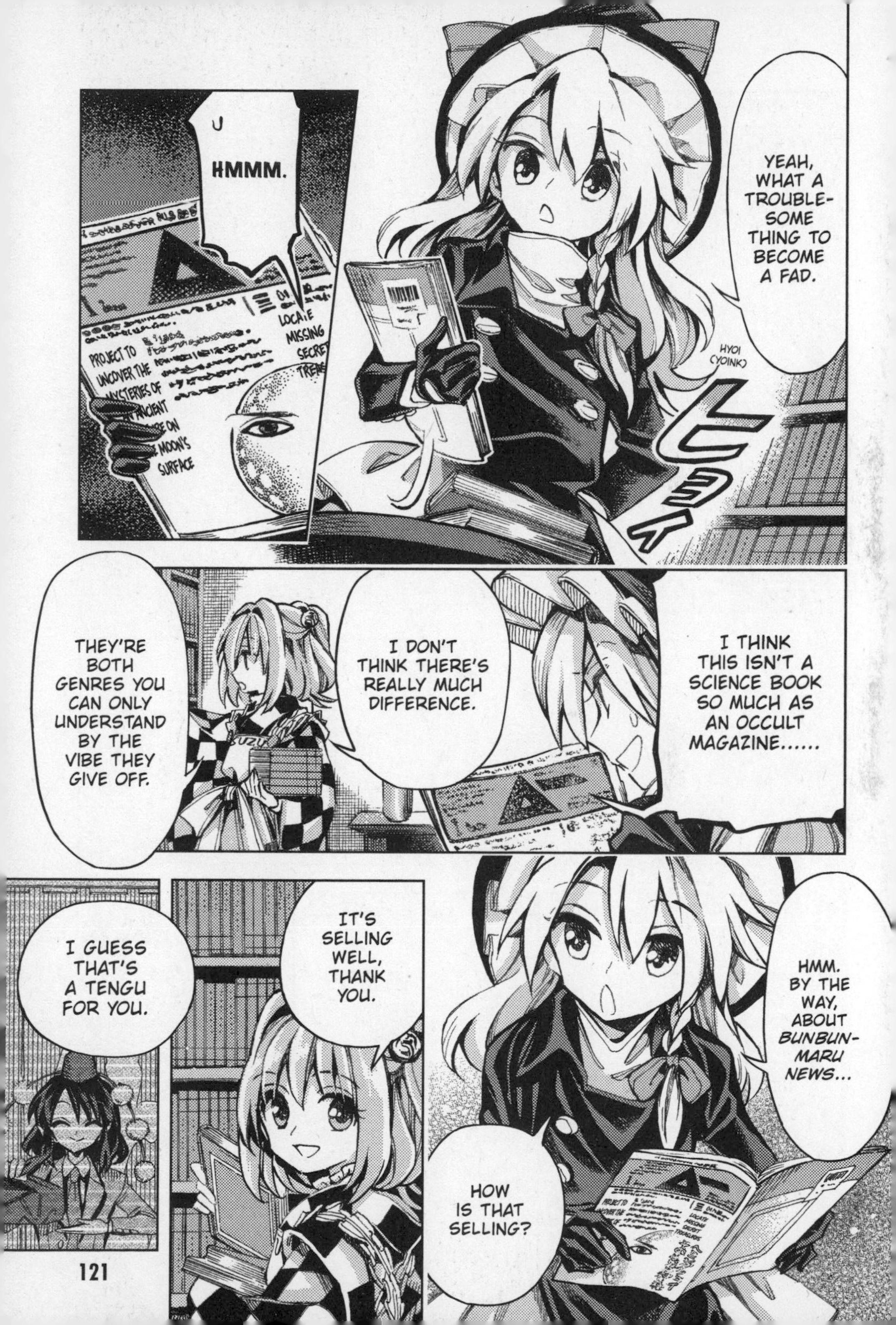
YEAH, WHAT A TROUBLESOME THING TO BECOME A FAD.
HYOI (YOINK)
HMMM.
I THINK THIS ISN'T A SCIENCE BOOK SO MUCH AS AN OCCULT MAGAZINE......
I DON'T THINK THERE'S REALLY MUCH DIFFERENCE.
THEY'RE BOTH GENRES YOU CAN ONLY UNDERSTAND BY THE VIBE THEY GIVE OFF.
HMM. BY THE WAY, ABOUT BUNBUNMARU NEWS...
HOW IS THAT SELLING?
IT'S SELLING WELL, THANK YOU.
I GUESS THAT'S A TENGU FOR YOU.

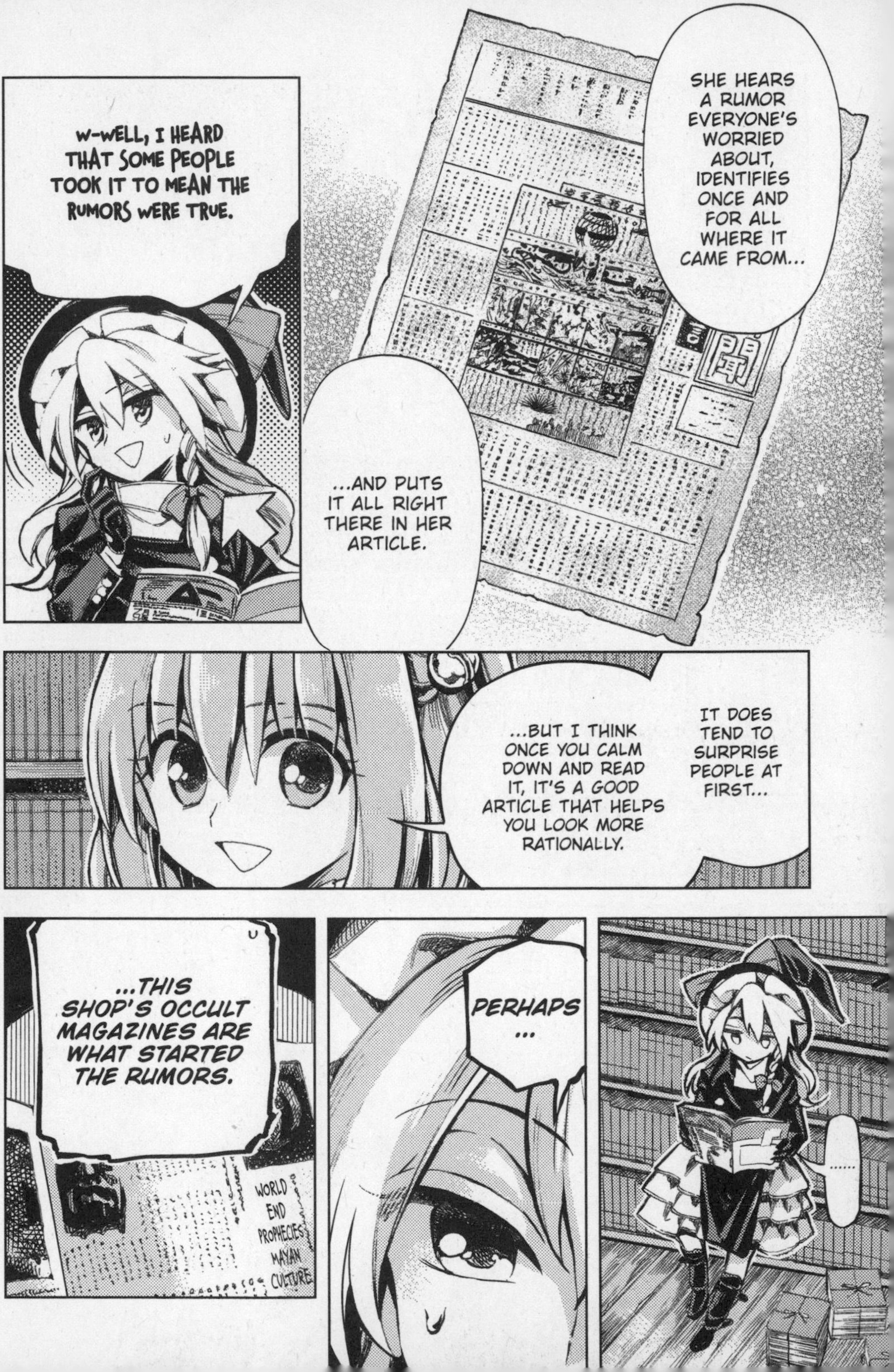
SHE HEARS A RUMOR EVERYONE'S WORRIED ABOUT, IDENTIFIES ONCE AND FOR ALL WHERE IT CAME FROM...
...AND PUTS IT ALL RIGHT THERE IN HER ARTICLE.
W-WELL, I HEARD THAT SOME PEOPLE TOOK IT TO MEAN THE RUMORS WERE TRUE.
IT DOES TEND TO SURPRISE PEOPLE AT FIRST...
...BUT I THINK ONCE YOU CALM DOWN AND READ IT, IT'S A GOOD ARTICLE THAT HELPS YOU LOOK MORE RATIONALLY.
......
PERHAPS ...
...THIS SHOP'S OCCULT MAGAZINES ARE WHAT STARTED THE RUMORS.
WORLD END PROPHECIES
MAYAN CULTURE

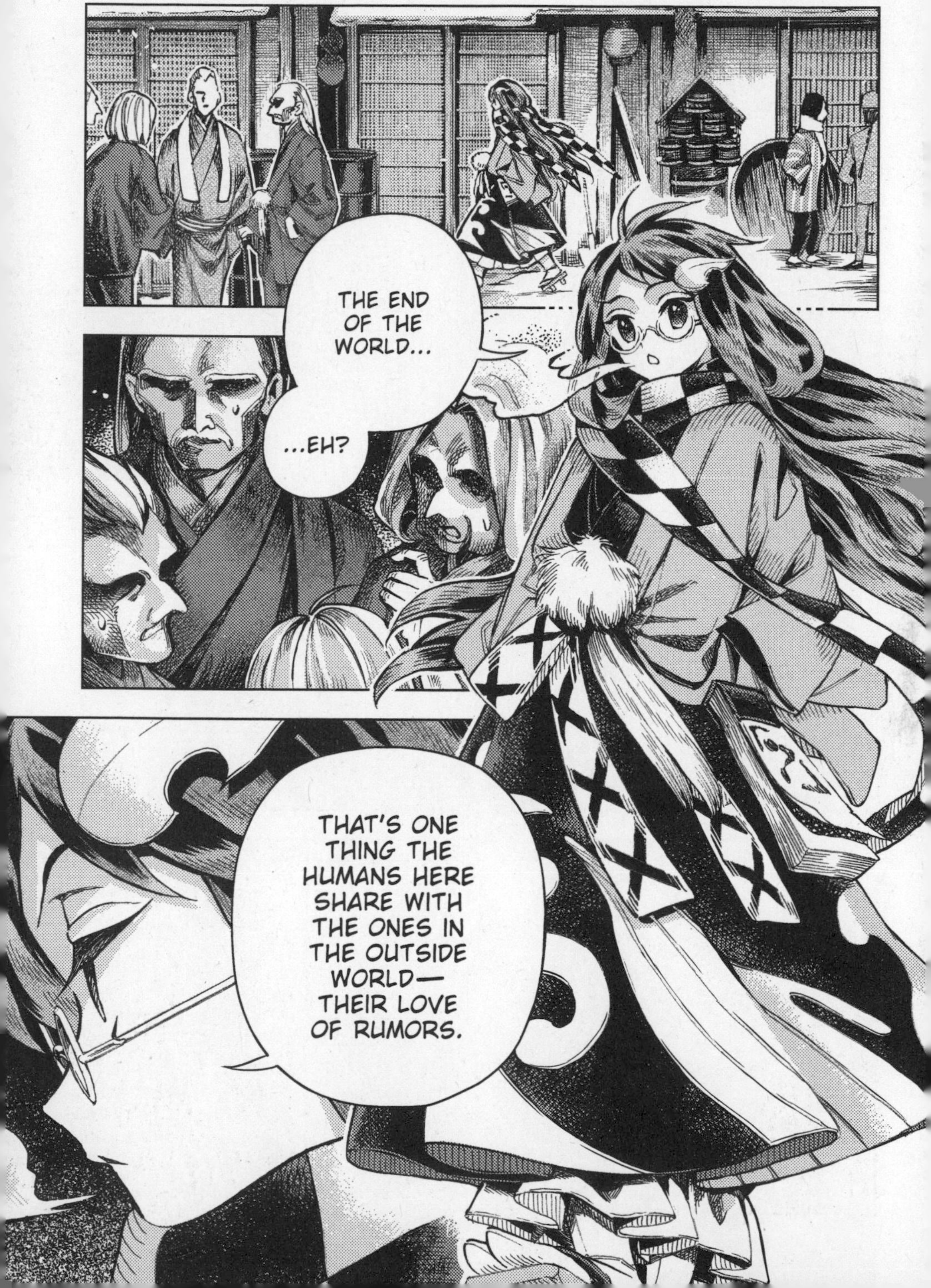
THE END OF THE WORLD...
...EH?
THAT'S ONE THING THE HUMANS HERE SHARE WITH THE ONES IN THE OUTSIDE WORLD—THEIR LOVE OF RUMORS.

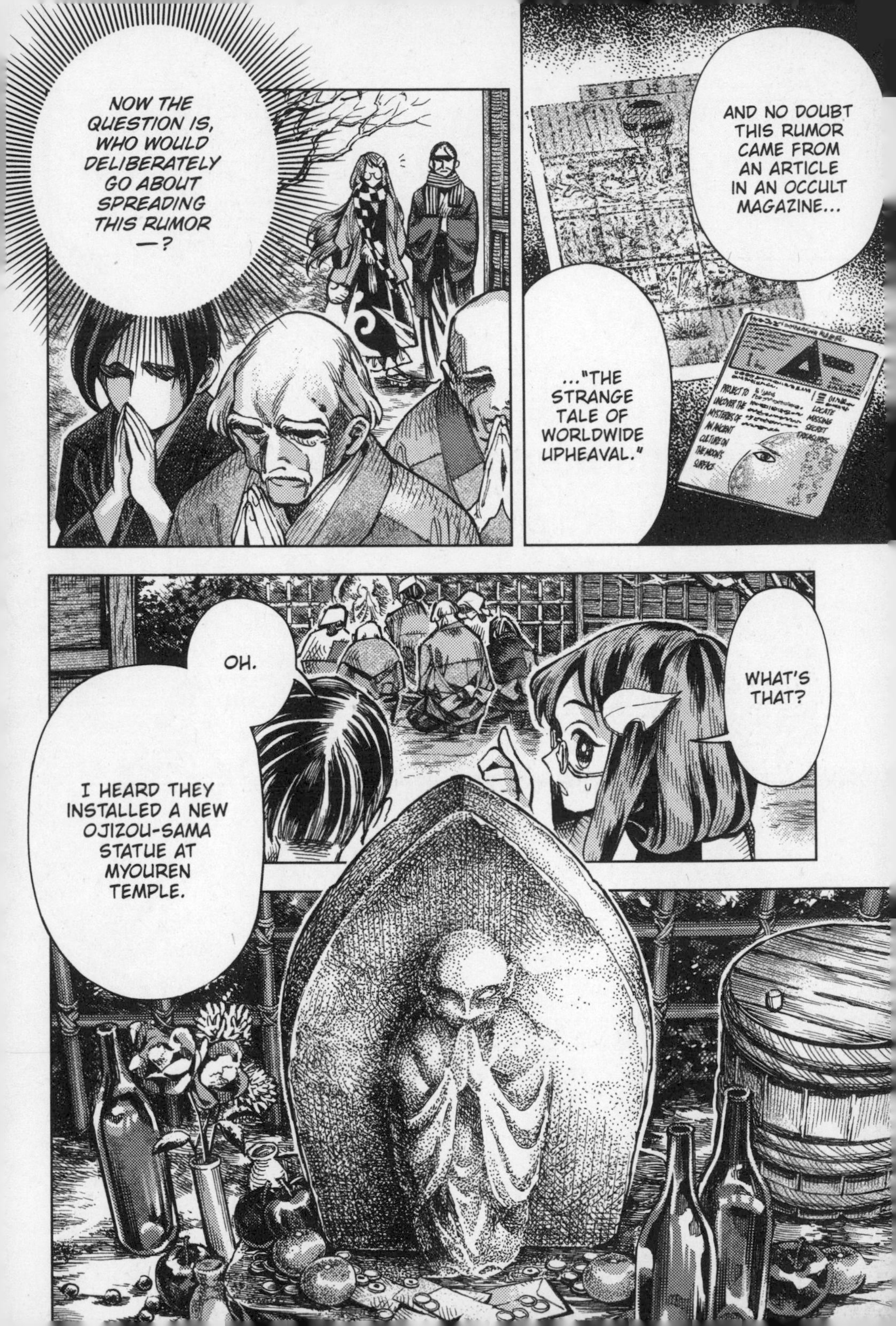
AND NO DOUBT THIS RUMOR CAME FROM AN ARTICLE IN AN OCCULT MAGAZINE...
..."THE STRANGE TALE OF WORLDWIDE UPHEAVAL."
PROJECT TO UNCOVER THE MYSTERIES OF AN ANCIENT CULTURE ON THE MOON'S SURFACE
LOCATE MISSING SECRET TREASURES
NOW THE QUESTION IS, WHO WOULD DELIBERATELY GO ABOUT SPREADING THIS RUMOR —?
WHAT'S THAT?
OH.
I HEARD THEY INSTALLED A NEW OJIZOU-SAMA STATUE AT MYOUREN TEMPLE.

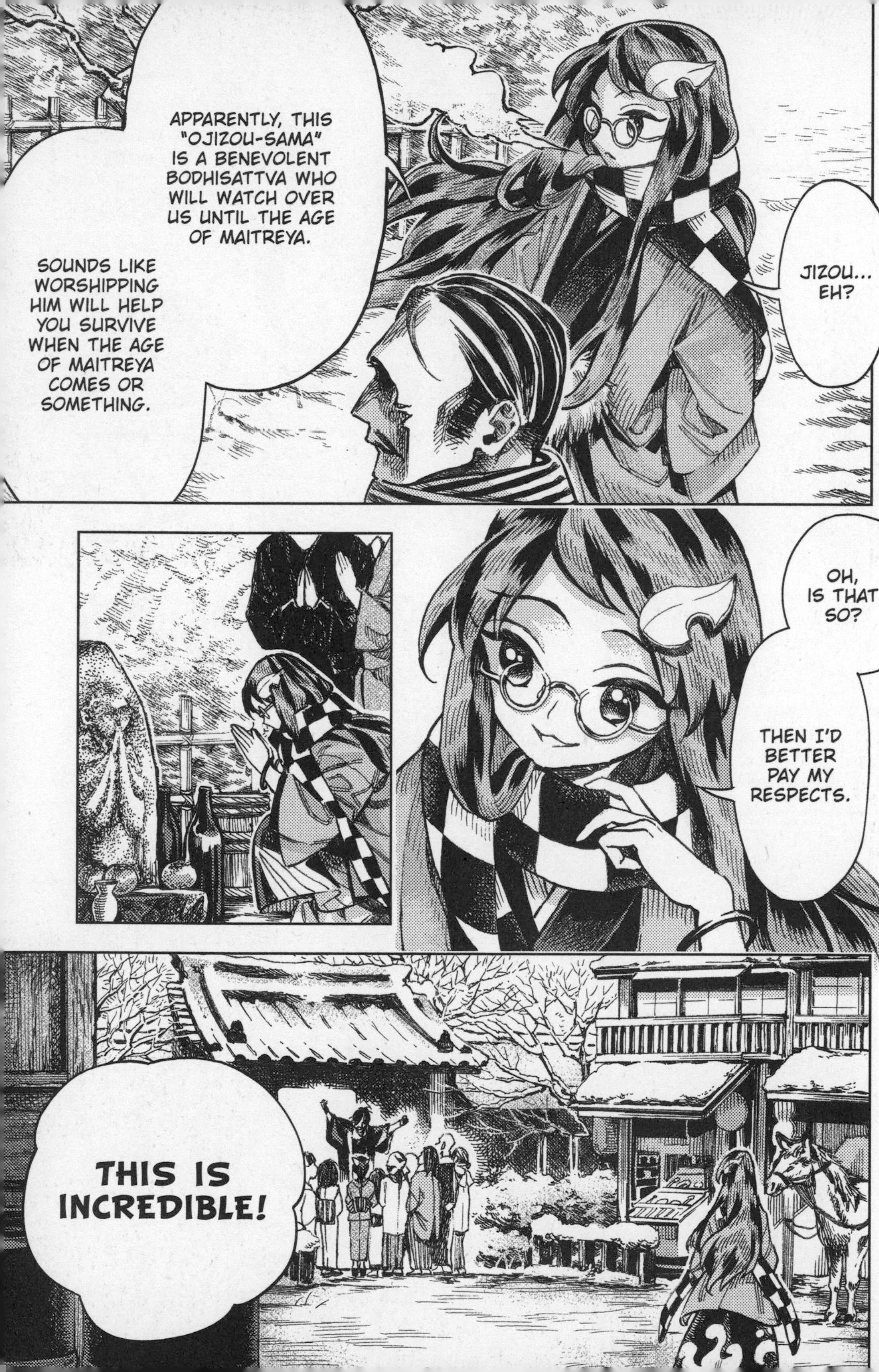
JIZOU... EH?
APPARENTLY, THIS "OJIZOU-SAMA" IS A BENEVOLENT BODHISATTVA WHO WILL WATCH OVER US UNTIL THE AGE OF MAITREYA.
SOUNDS LIKE WORSHIPPING HIM WILL HELP YOU SURVIVE WHEN THE AGE OF MAITREYA COMES OR SOMETHING.
OH, IS THAT SO?
THEN I'D BETTER PAY MY RESPECTS.
THIS IS INCREDIBLE!

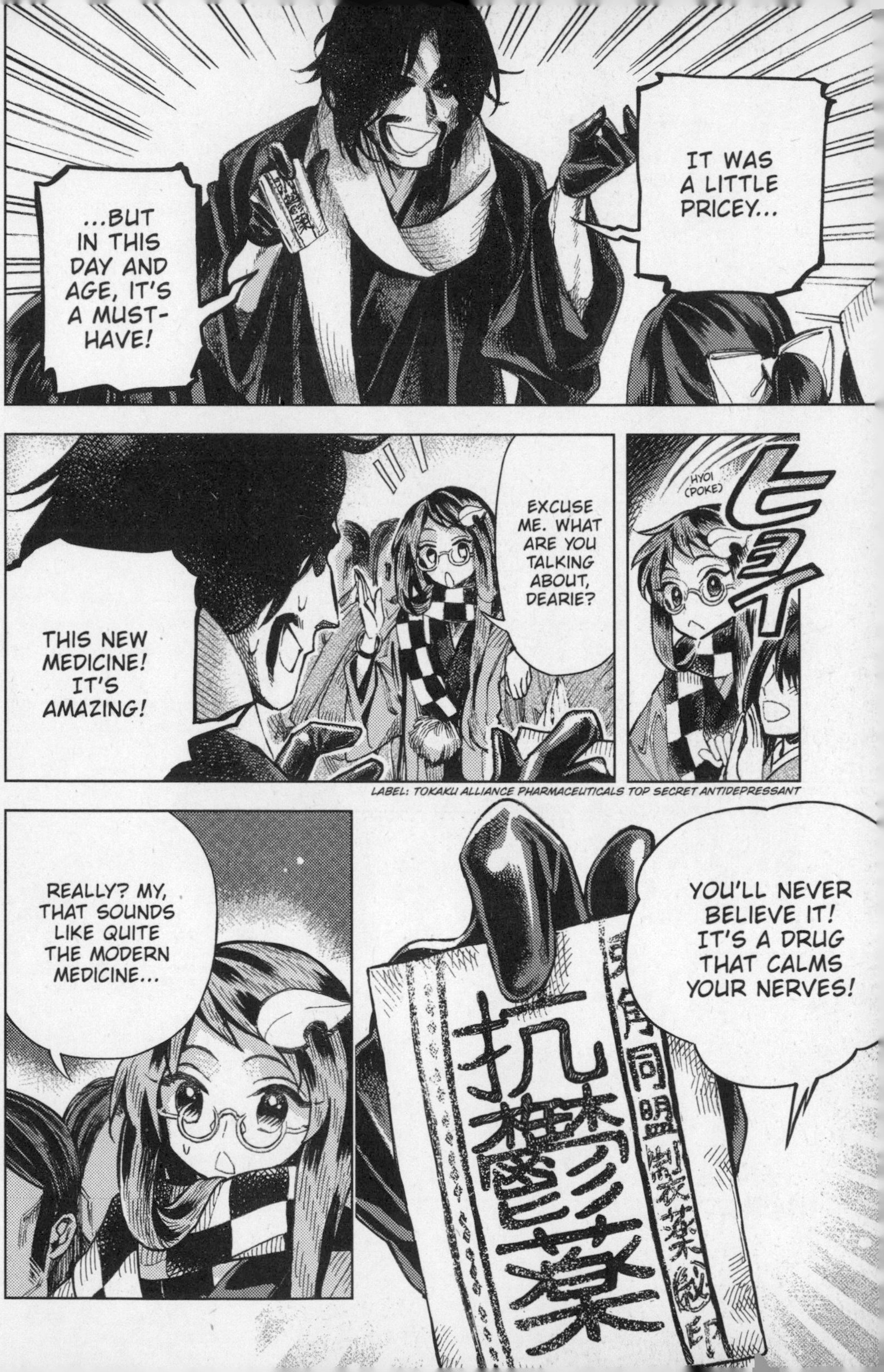
IT WAS A LITTLE PRICEY...
...BUT IN THIS DAY AND AGE, IT'S A MUST-HAVE!
ヒョイ
HYOI (POKE)
EXCUSE ME. WHAT ARE YOU TALKING ABOUT, DEARIE?
THIS NEW MEDICINE! IT'S AMAZING!
LABEL: TOKAKU ALLIANCE PHARMACEUTICALS TOP SECRET ANTIDEPRESSANT
YOU'LL NEVER BELIEVE IT! IT'S A DRUG THAT CALMS YOUR NERVES!
抗鬱薬
REALLY? MY, THAT SOUNDS LIKE QUITE THE MODERN MEDICINE...

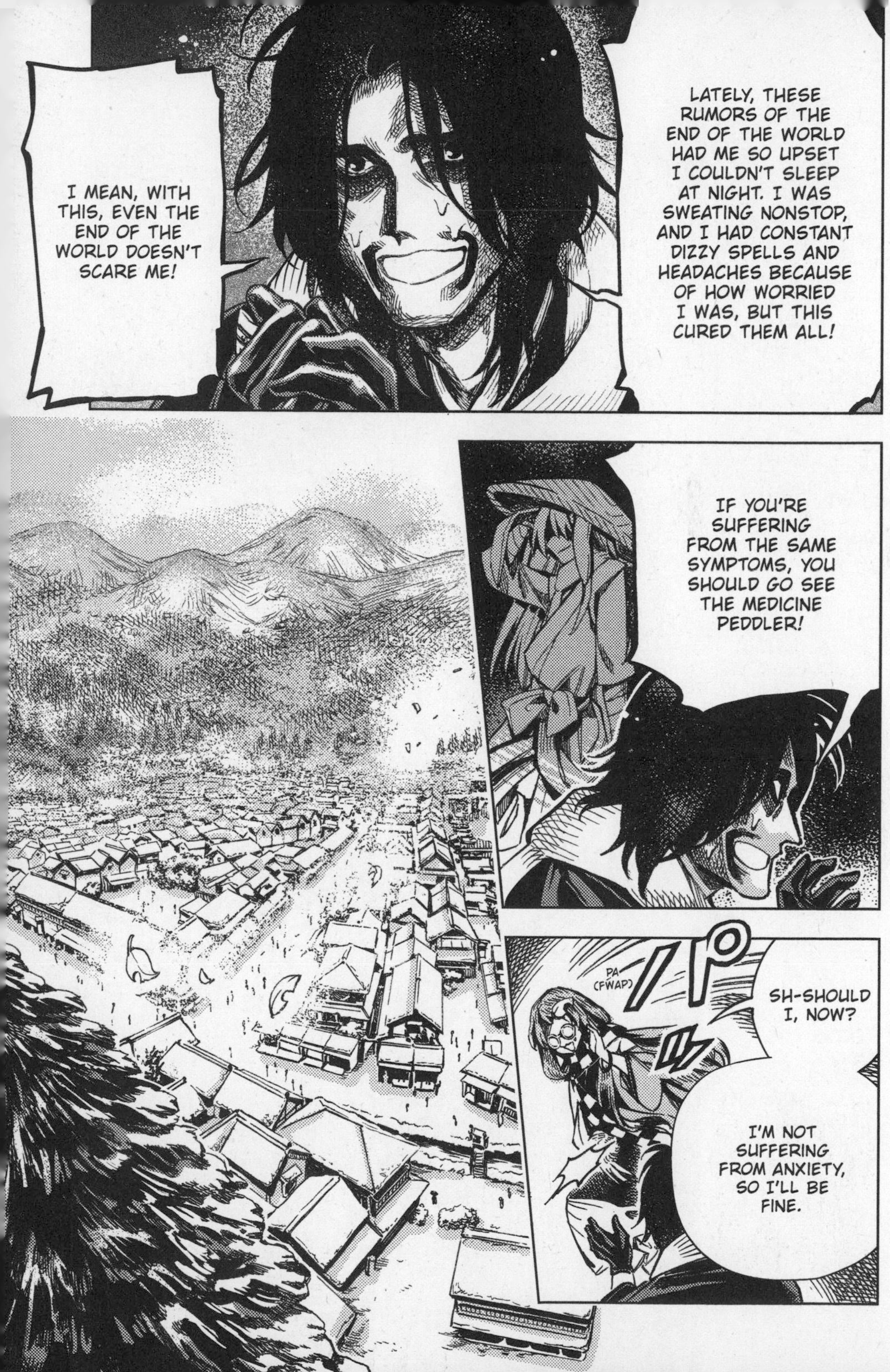
LATELY, THESE RUMORS OF THE END OF THE WORLD HAD ME SO UPSET I COULDN'T SLEEP AT NIGHT. I WAS SWEATING NONSTOP, AND I HAD CONSTANT DIZZY SPELLS AND HEADACHES BECAUSE OF HOW WORRIED I WAS, BUT THIS CURED THEM ALL!
I MEAN, WITH THIS, EVEN THE END OF THE WORLD DOESN'T SCARE ME!
IF YOU'RE SUFFERING FROM THE SAME SYMPTOMS, YOU SHOULD GO SEE THE MEDICINE PEDDLER!
SH-SHOULD I, NOW?
PA (FWAP)
I'M NOT SUFFERING FROM ANXIETY, SO I'LL BE FINE.

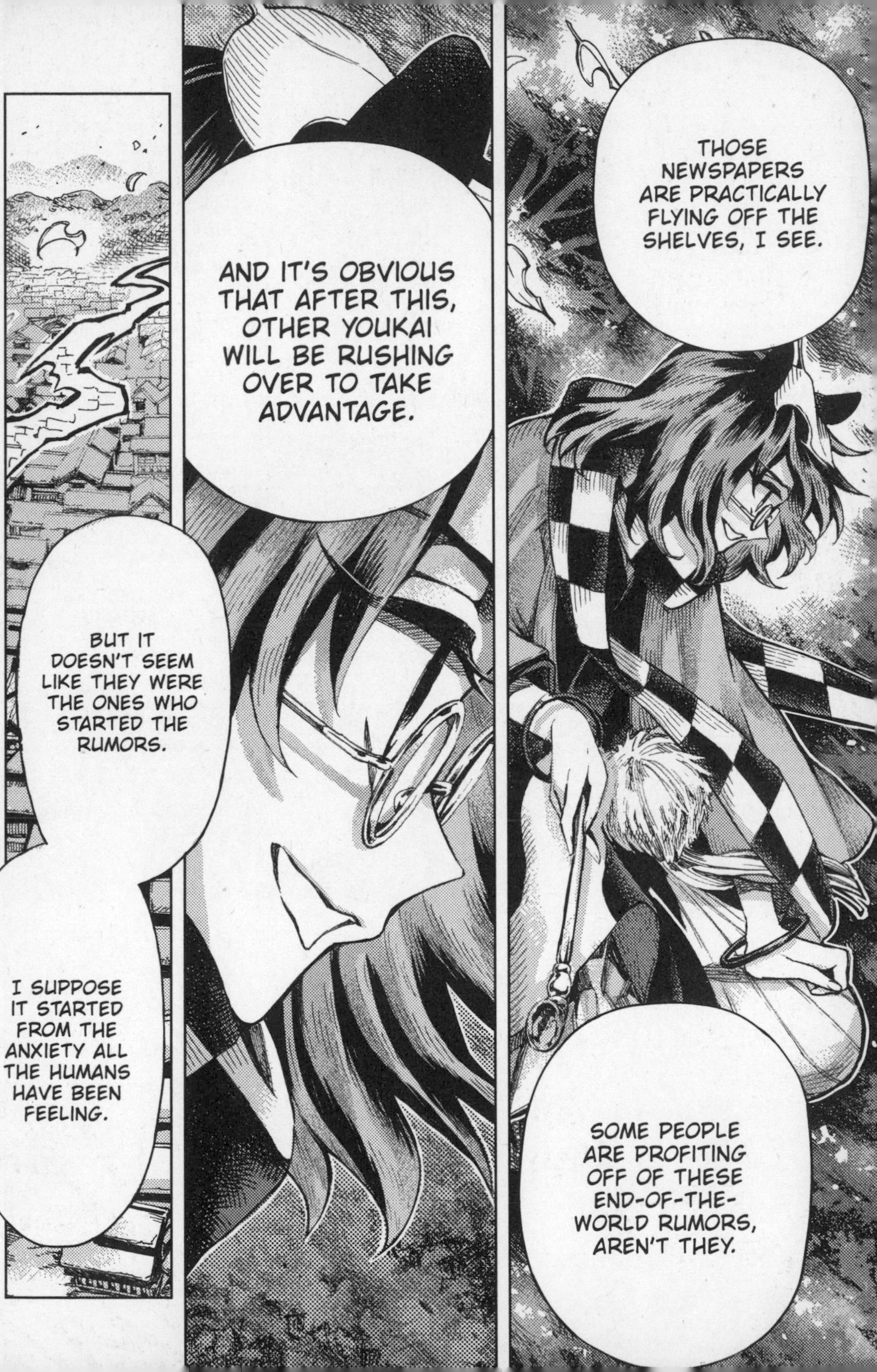
THOSE NEWSPAPERS ARE PRACTICALLY FLYING OFF THE SHELVES, I SEE.
SOME PEOPLE ARE PROFITING OFF OF THESE END-OF-THE-WORLD RUMORS, AREN'T THEY.
AND IT'S OBVIOUS THAT AFTER THIS, OTHER YOUKAI WILL BE RUSHING OVER TO TAKE ADVANTAGE.
BUT IT DOESN'T SEEM LIKE THEY WERE THE ONES WHO STARTED THE RUMORS.
I SUPPOSE IT STARTED FROM THE ANXIETY ALL THE HUMANS HAVE BEEN FEELING.

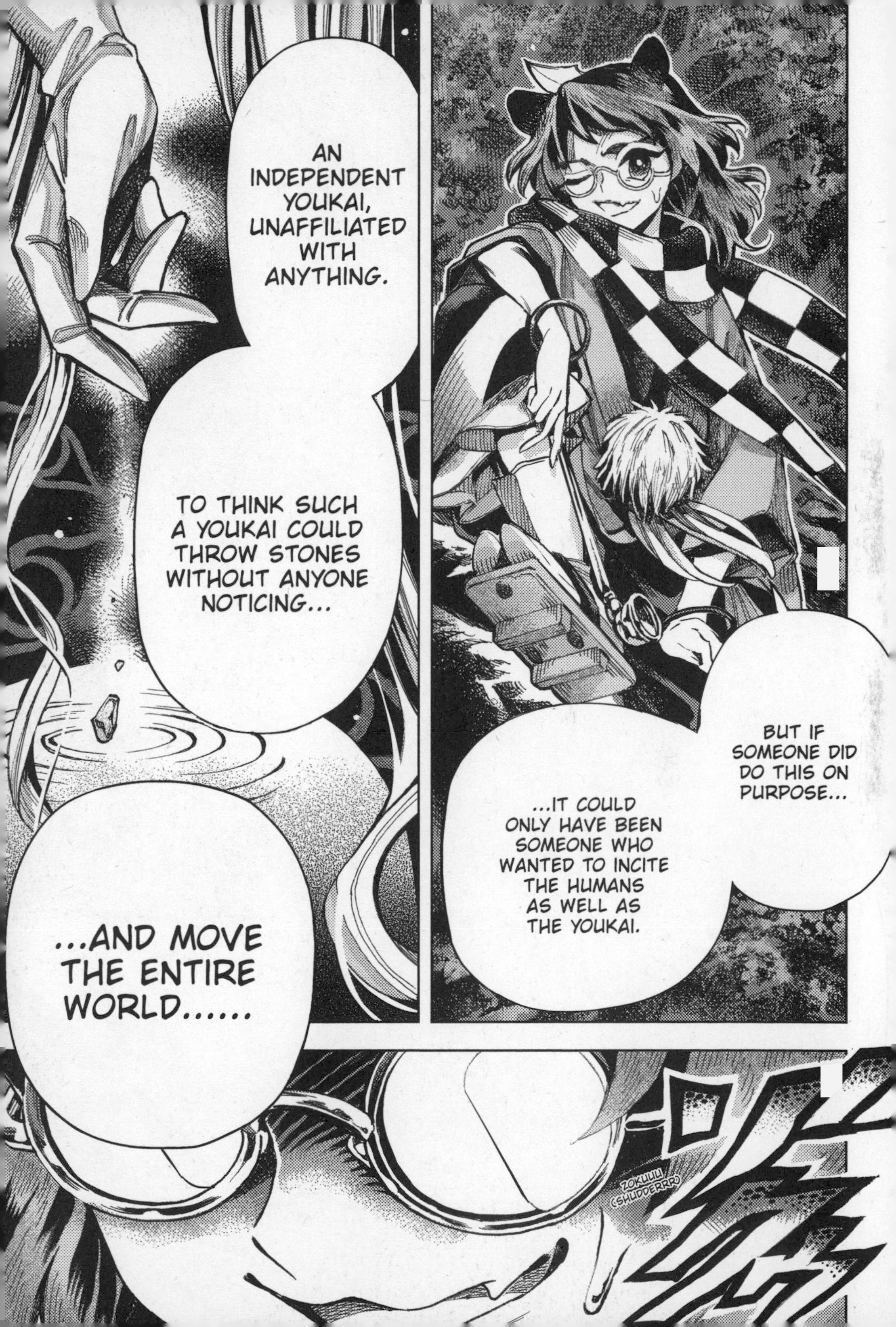
BUT IF SOMEONE DID DO THIS ON PURPOSE...
...IT COULD ONLY HAVE BEEN SOMEONE WHO WANTED TO INCITE THE HUMANS AS WELL AS THE YOUKAI.
AN INDEPENDENT YOUKAI, UNAFFILIATED WITH ANYTHING.
TO THINK SUCH A YOUKAI COULD THROW STONES WITHOUT ANYONE NOTICING...
...AND MOVE THE ENTIRE WORLD......
ZOKUUUU (SHUDDERRR)

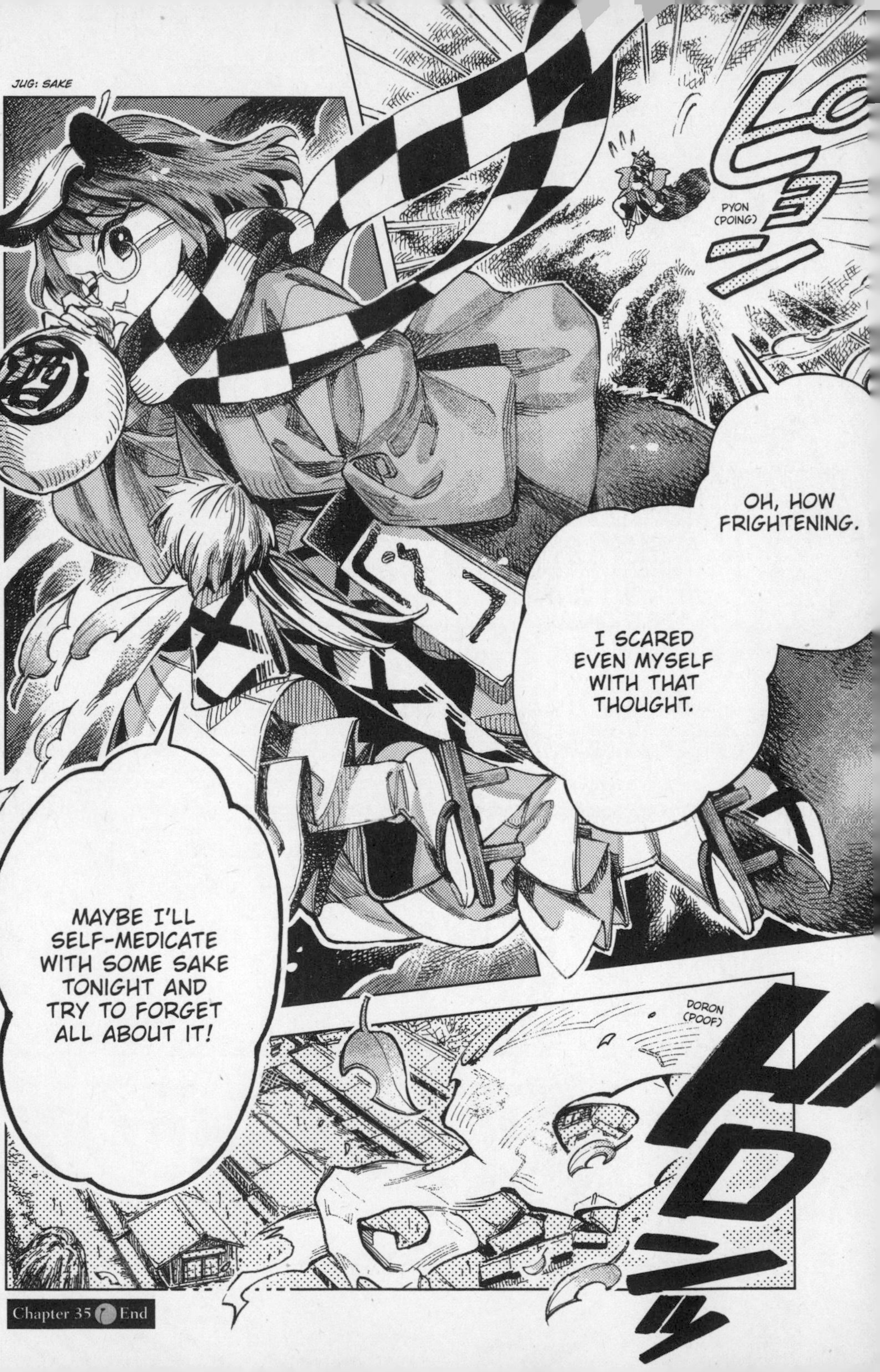
JUG: SAKE
PYON (POING)
OH, HOW FRIGHTENING.
I SCARED EVEN MYSELF WITH THAT THOUGHT.
MAYBE I'LL SELF-MEDICATE WITH SOME SAKE TONIGHT AND TRY TO FORGET ALL ABOUT IT!
DORON (POOF)

Chapter 35 End

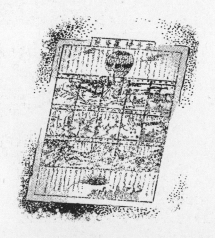

Forbidden Scrollery

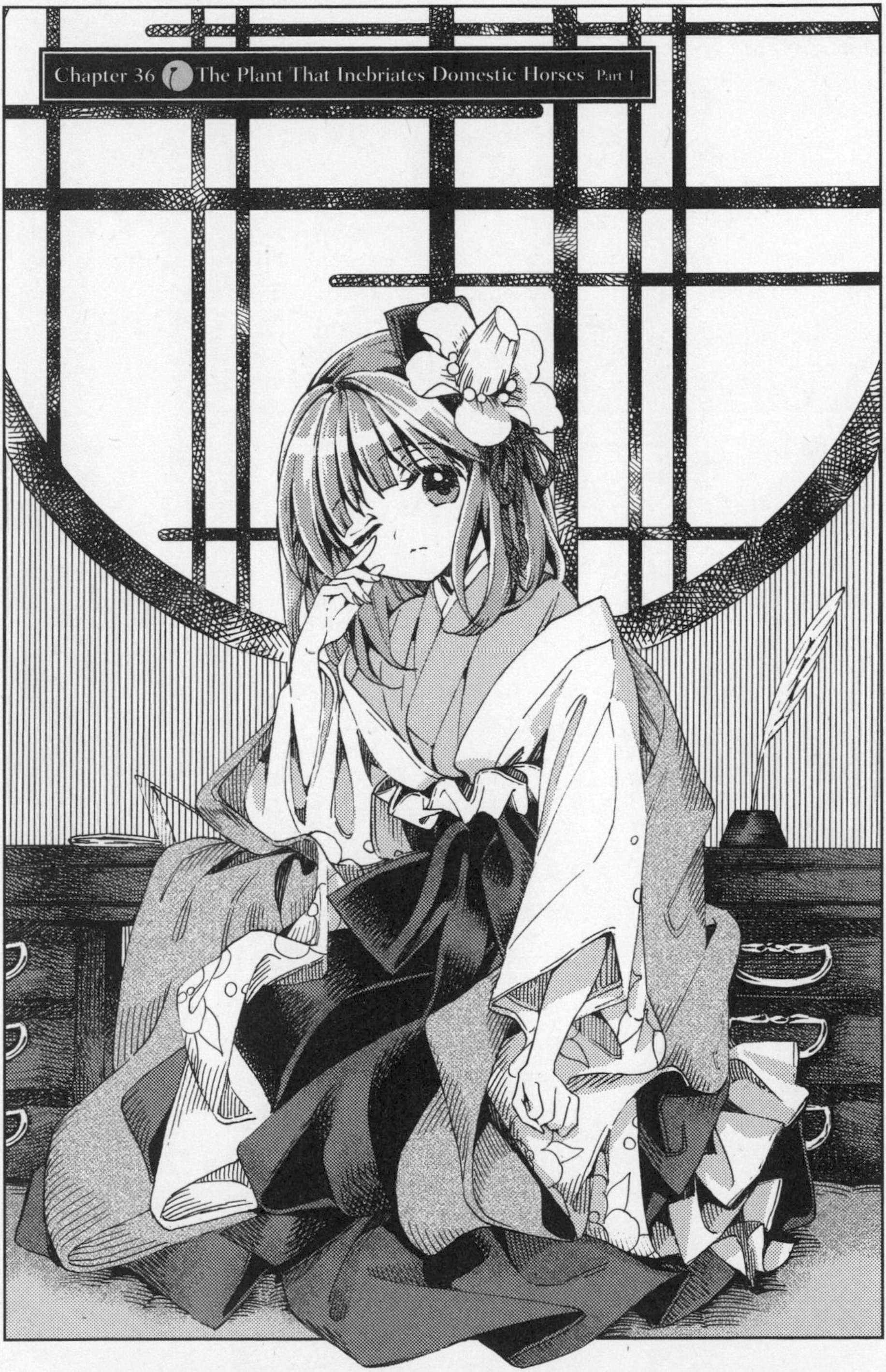
Chapter 36 The Plant That Inebriates Domestic Horses Part 1

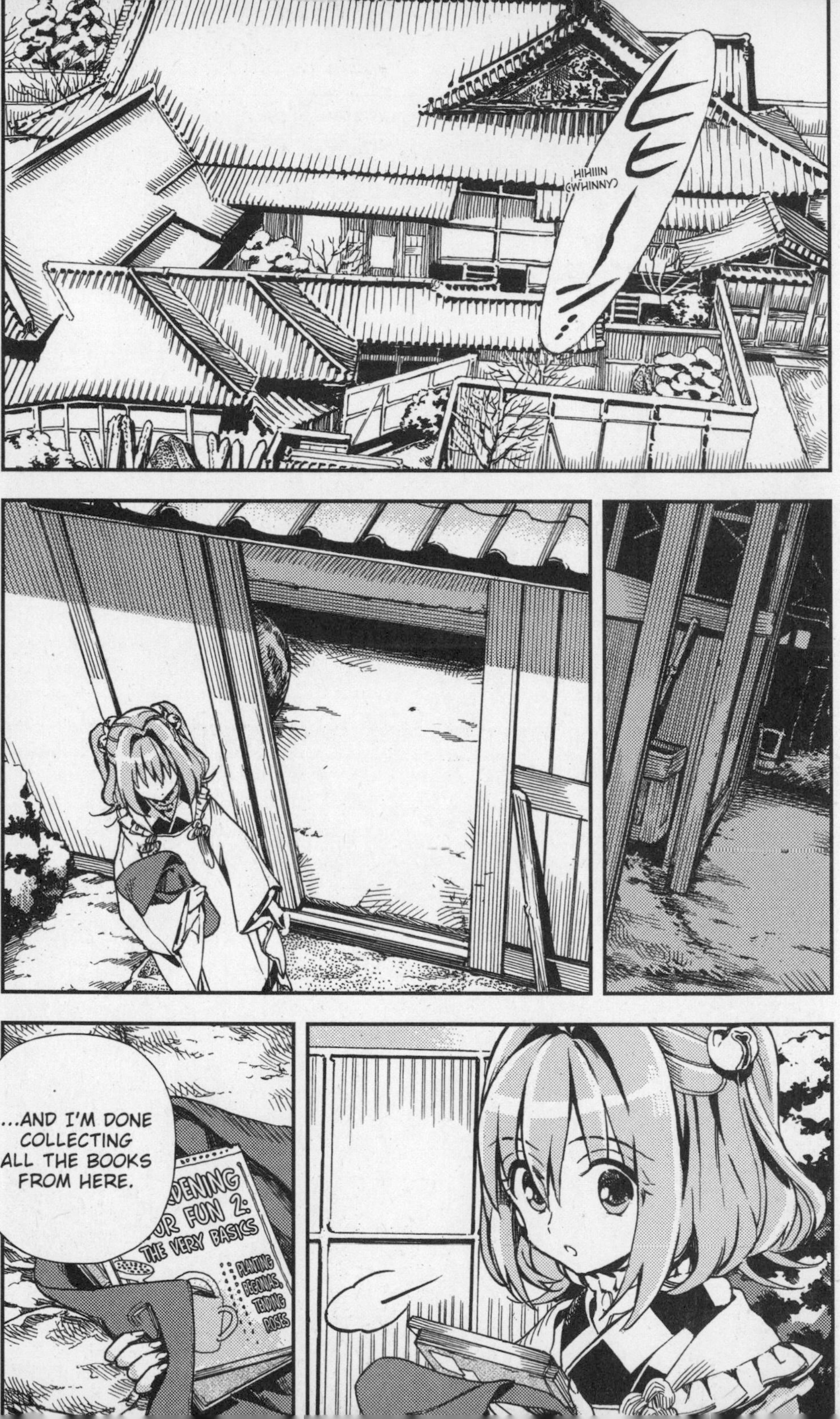
HIHIIIN (WHINNY)
...AND I'M DONE COLLECTING ALL THE BOOKS FROM HERE.
FUN 2: THE VERY BASICS
PLANTING BEGONIAS, TENDING ROSES

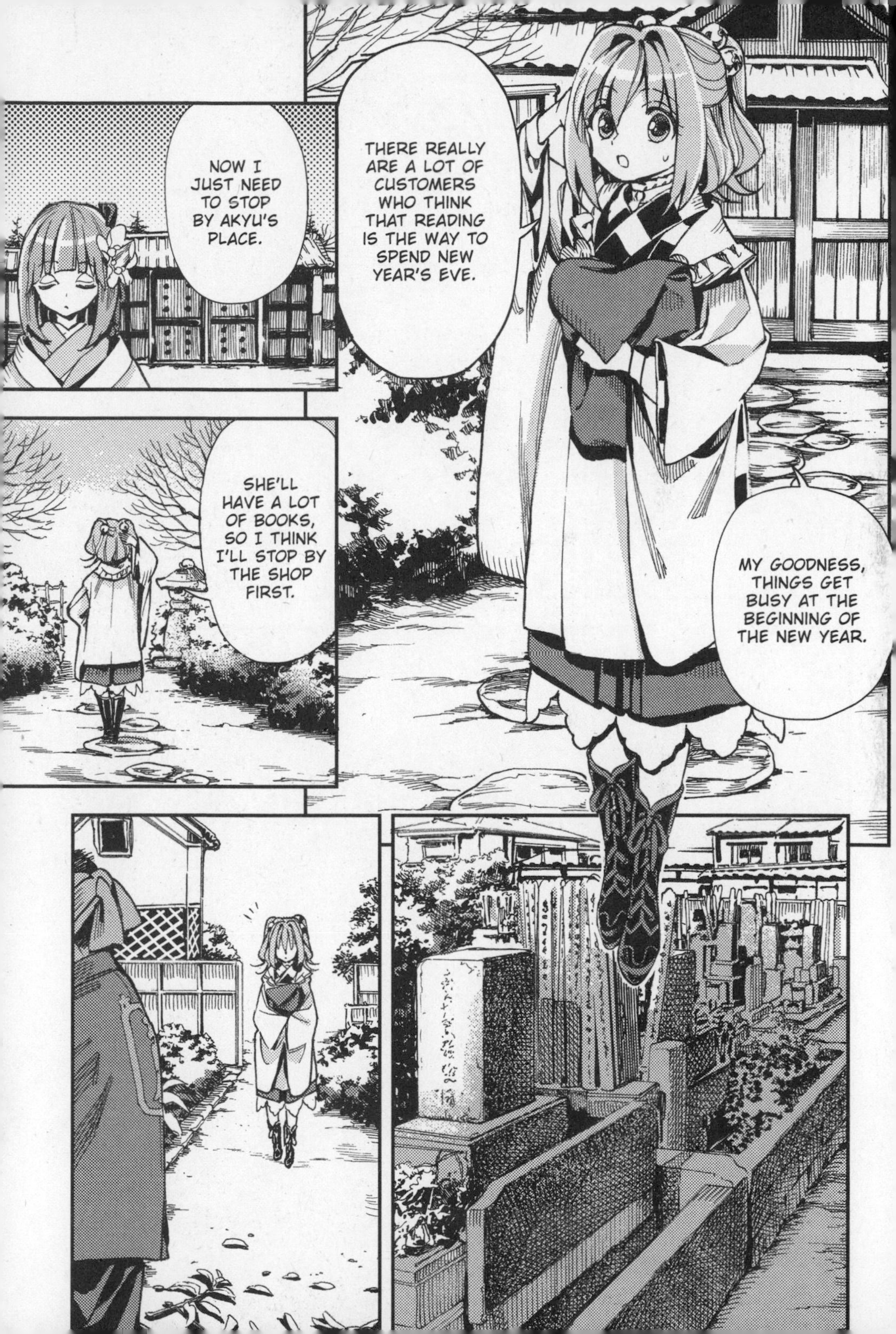
THERE REALLY ARE A LOT OF CUSTOMERS WHO THINK THAT READING IS THE WAY TO SPEND NEW YEAR'S EVE.
MY GOODNESS, THINGS GET BUSY AT THE BEGINNING OF THE NEW YEAR.
NOW I JUST NEED TO STOP BY AKYU'S PLACE.
SHE'LL HAVE A LOT OF BOOKS, SO I THINK I'LL STOP BY THE SHOP FIRST.

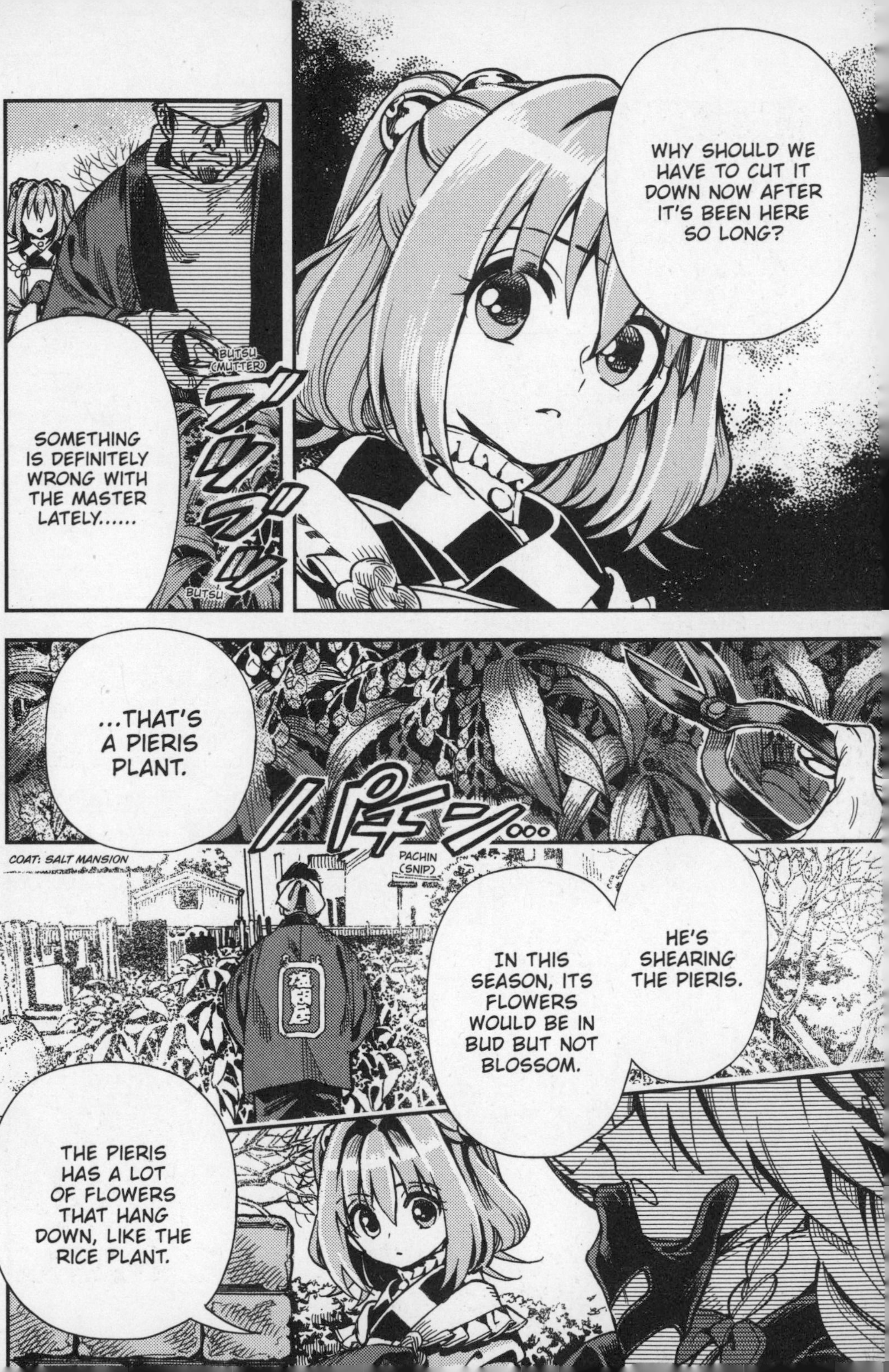
WHY SHOULD WE HAVE TO CUT IT DOWN NOW AFTER IT'S BEEN HERE SO LONG?
BUTSU (MUTTER)
SOMETHING IS DEFINITELY WRONG WITH THE MASTER LATELY......
BUTSU
...THAT'S A PIERIS PLANT.
PACHIN (SNIP)
COAT: SALT MANSION
HE'S SHEARING THE PIERIS.
IN THIS SEASON, ITS FLOWERS WOULD BE IN BUD BUT NOT BLOSSOM.
THE PIERIS HAS A LOT OF FLOWERS THAT HANG DOWN, LIKE THE RICE PLANT.

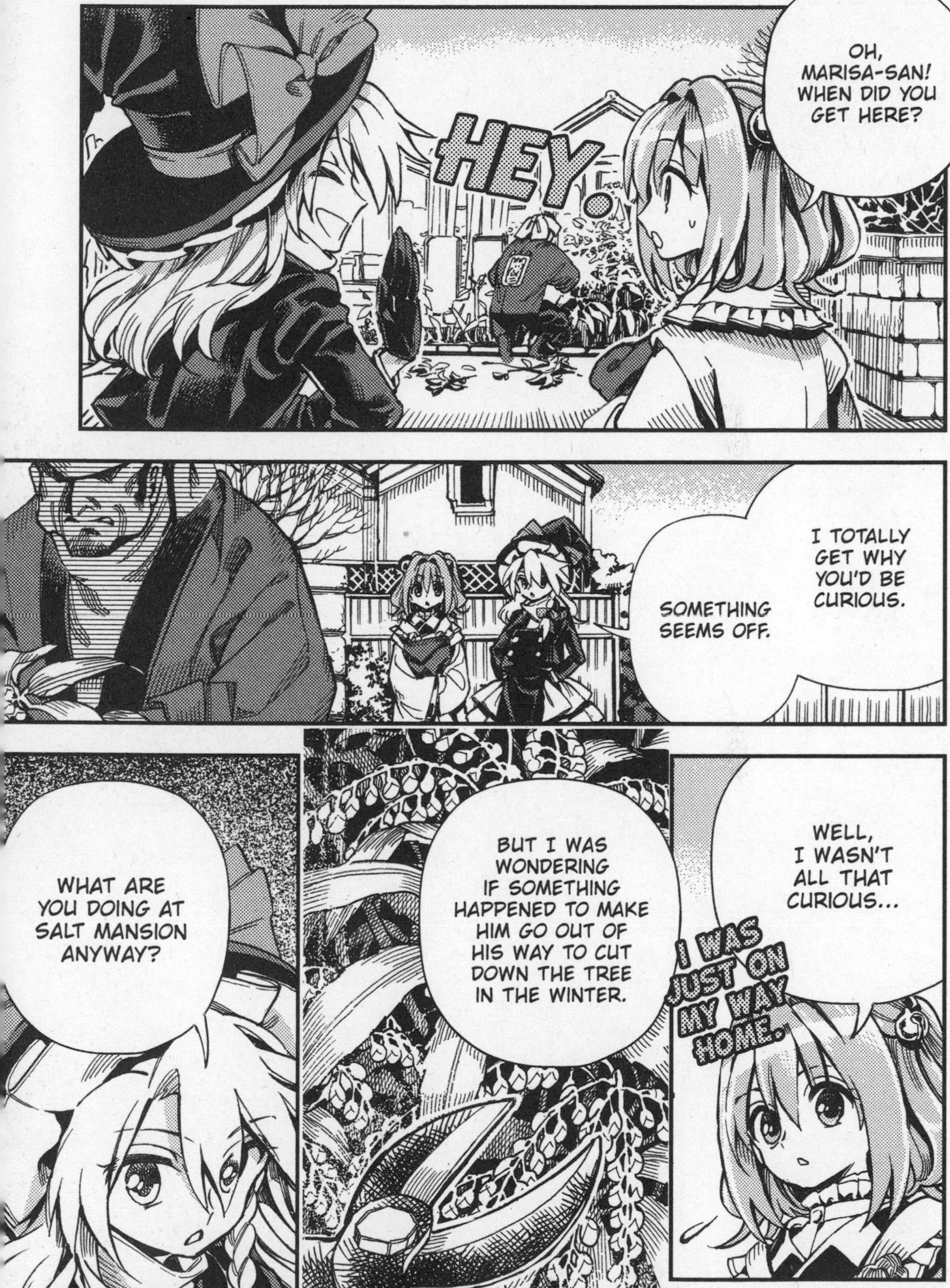
OH, MARISA-SAN! WHEN DID YOU GET HERE?
HEY.
I TOTALLY GET WHY YOU'D BE CURIOUS.
SOMETHING SEEMS OFF.
WELL, I WASN'T ALL THAT CURIOUS...
I WAS JUST ON MY WAY HOME.
BUT I WAS WONDERING IF SOMETHING HAPPENED TO MAKE HIM GO OUT OF HIS WAY TO CUT DOWN THE TREE IN THE WINTER.
WHAT ARE YOU DOING AT SALT MANSION ANYWAY?

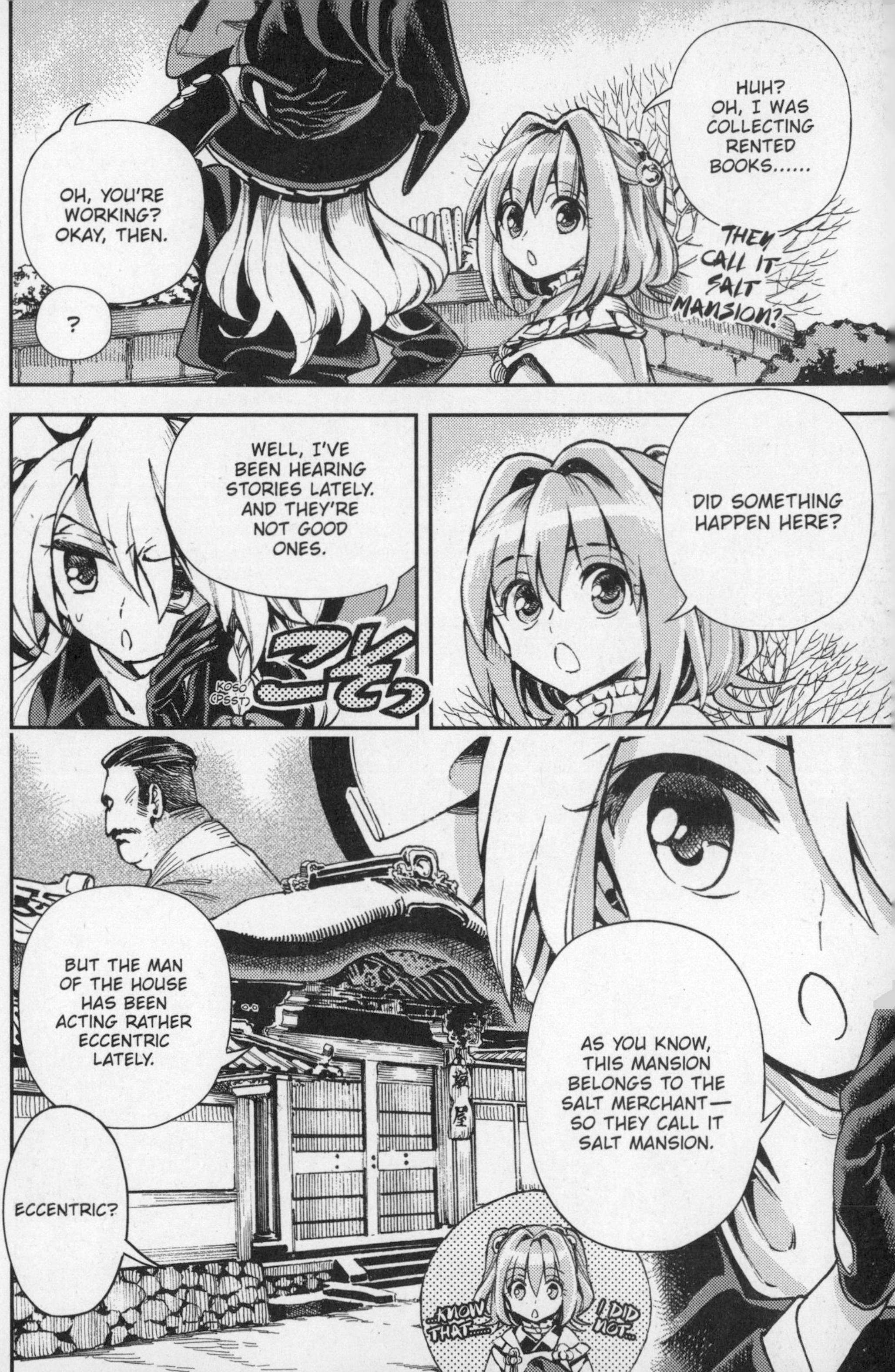
HUH? OH, I WAS COLLECTING RENTED BOOKS......
THEY CALL IT SALT MANSION?
OH, YOU'RE WORKING? OKAY, THEN.
?
DID SOMETHING HAPPEN HERE?
WELL, I'VE BEEN HEARING STORIES LATELY. AND THEY'RE NOT GOOD ONES.
KOSO (PSST)
AS YOU KNOW, THIS MANSION BELONGS TO THE SALT MERCHANT— SO THEY CALL IT SALT MANSION.
I DID NOT...
...KNOW THAT......
BUT THE MAN OF THE HOUSE HAS BEEN ACTING RATHER ECCENTRIC LATELY.
ECCENTRIC?

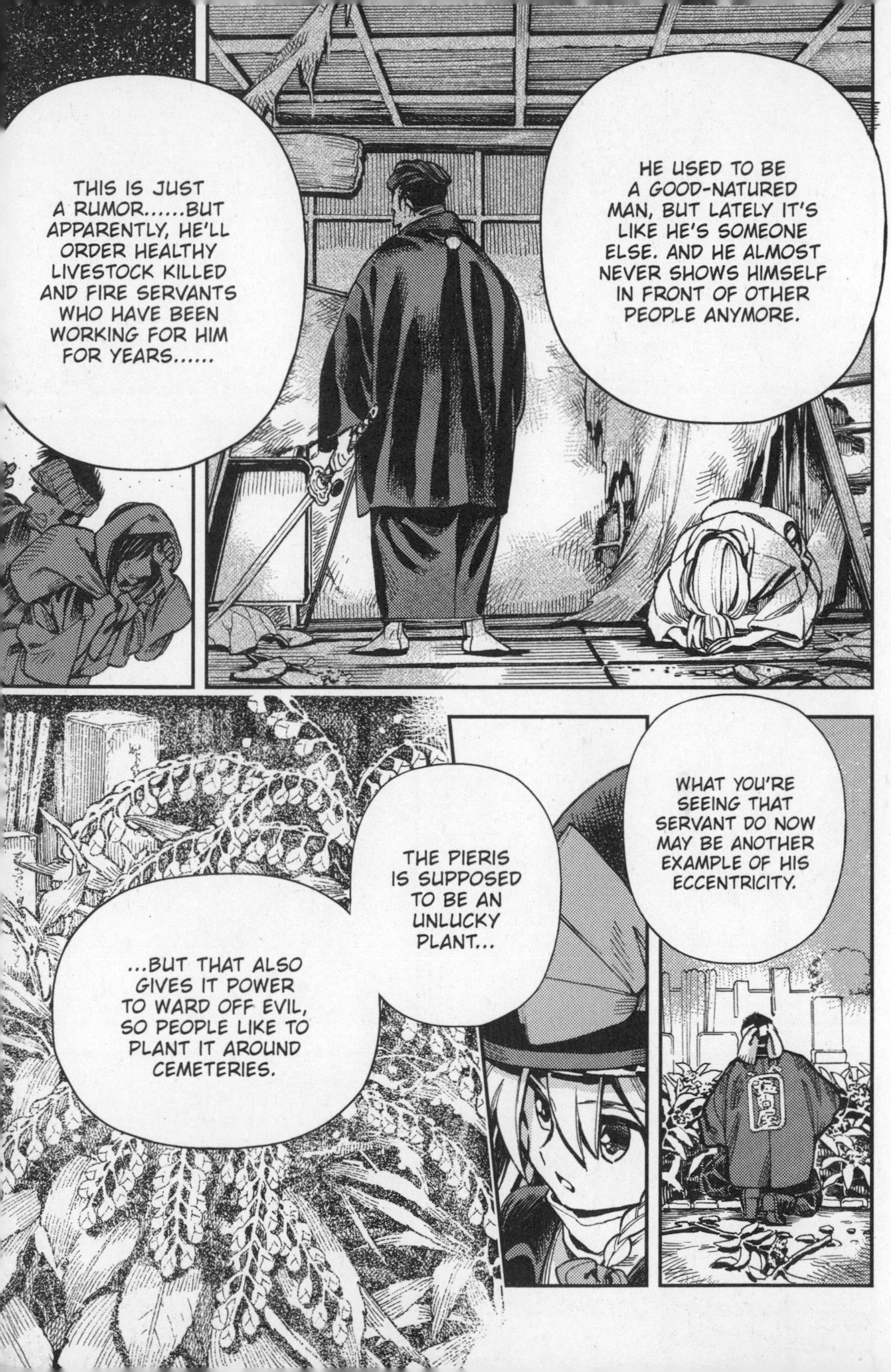
HE USED TO BE A GOOD-NATURED MAN, BUT LATELY IT'S LIKE HE'S SOMEONE ELSE. AND HE ALMOST NEVER SHOWS HIMSELF IN FRONT OF OTHER PEOPLE ANYMORE.
THIS IS JUST A RUMOR......BUT APPARENTLY, HE'LL ORDER HEALTHY LIVESTOCK KILLED AND FIRE SERVANTS WHO HAVE BEEN WORKING FOR HIM FOR YEARS......
WHAT YOU'RE SEEING THAT SERVANT DO NOW MAY BE ANOTHER EXAMPLE OF HIS ECCENTRICITY.
THE PIERIS IS SUPPOSED TO BE AN UNLUCKY PLANT...
...BUT THAT ALSO GIVES IT POWER TO WARD OFF EVIL, SO PEOPLE LIKE TO PLANT IT AROUND CEMETERIES.

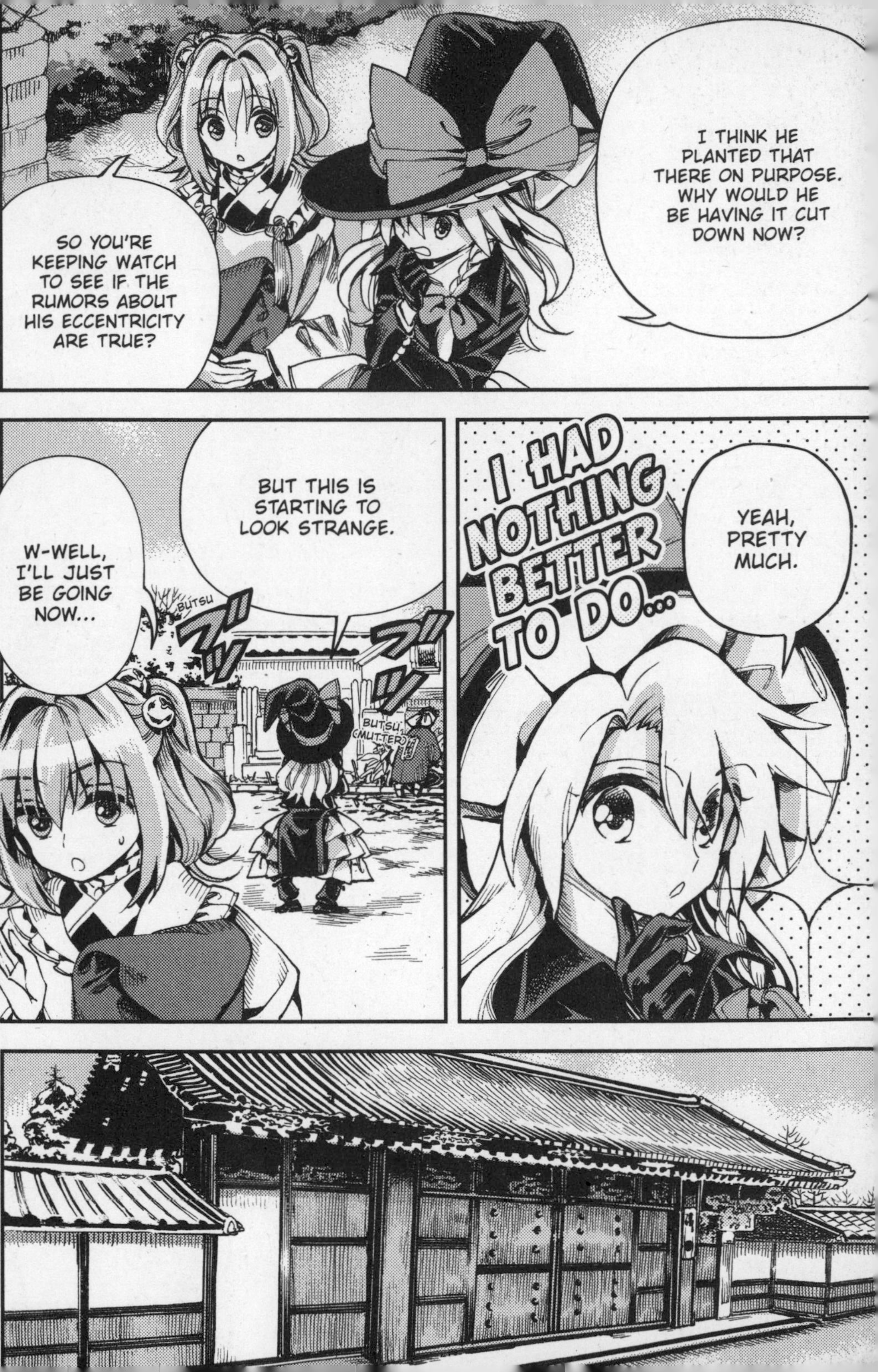
I THINK HE PLANTED THAT THERE ON PURPOSE. WHY WOULD HE BE HAVING IT CUT DOWN NOW?
SO YOU'RE KEEPING WATCH TO SEE IF THE RUMORS ABOUT HIS ECCENTRICITY ARE TRUE?
YEAH, PRETTY MUCH.
I HAD NOTHING BETTER TO DO...
BUT THIS IS STARTING TO LOOK STRANGE.
BUTSU
BUTSU (MUTTER)
W-WELL, I'LL JUST BE GOING NOW...

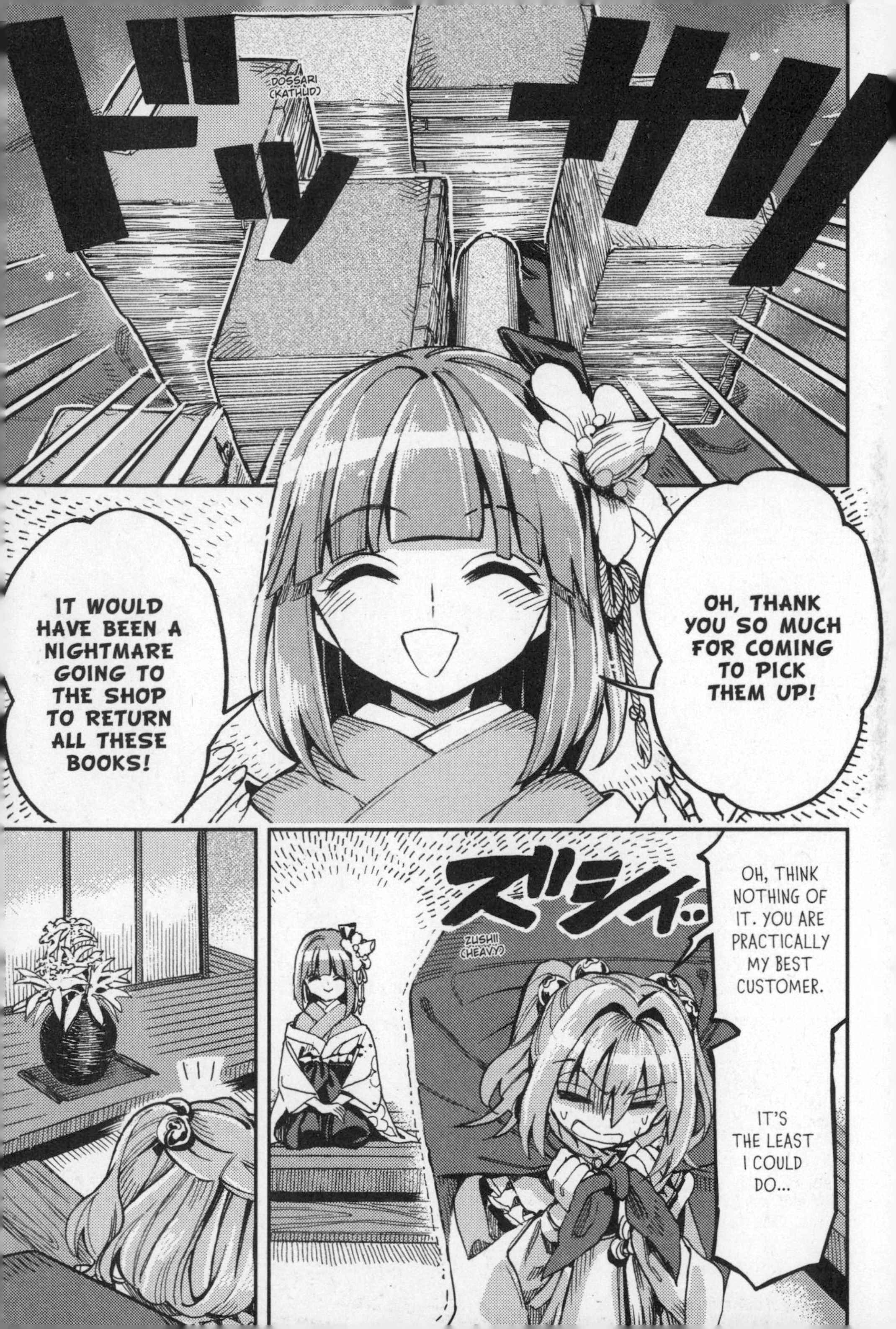
ドッサリ
DOSSARI (KATHUD)
OH, THANK YOU SO MUCH FOR COMING TO PICK THEM UP!
IT WOULD HAVE BEEN A NIGHTMARE GOING TO THE SHOP TO RETURN ALL THESE BOOKS!
ズシィ..
ZUSHII (HEAVY)
OH, THINK NOTHING OF IT. YOU ARE PRACTICALLY MY BEST CUSTOMER.
IT'S THE LEAST I COULD DO...

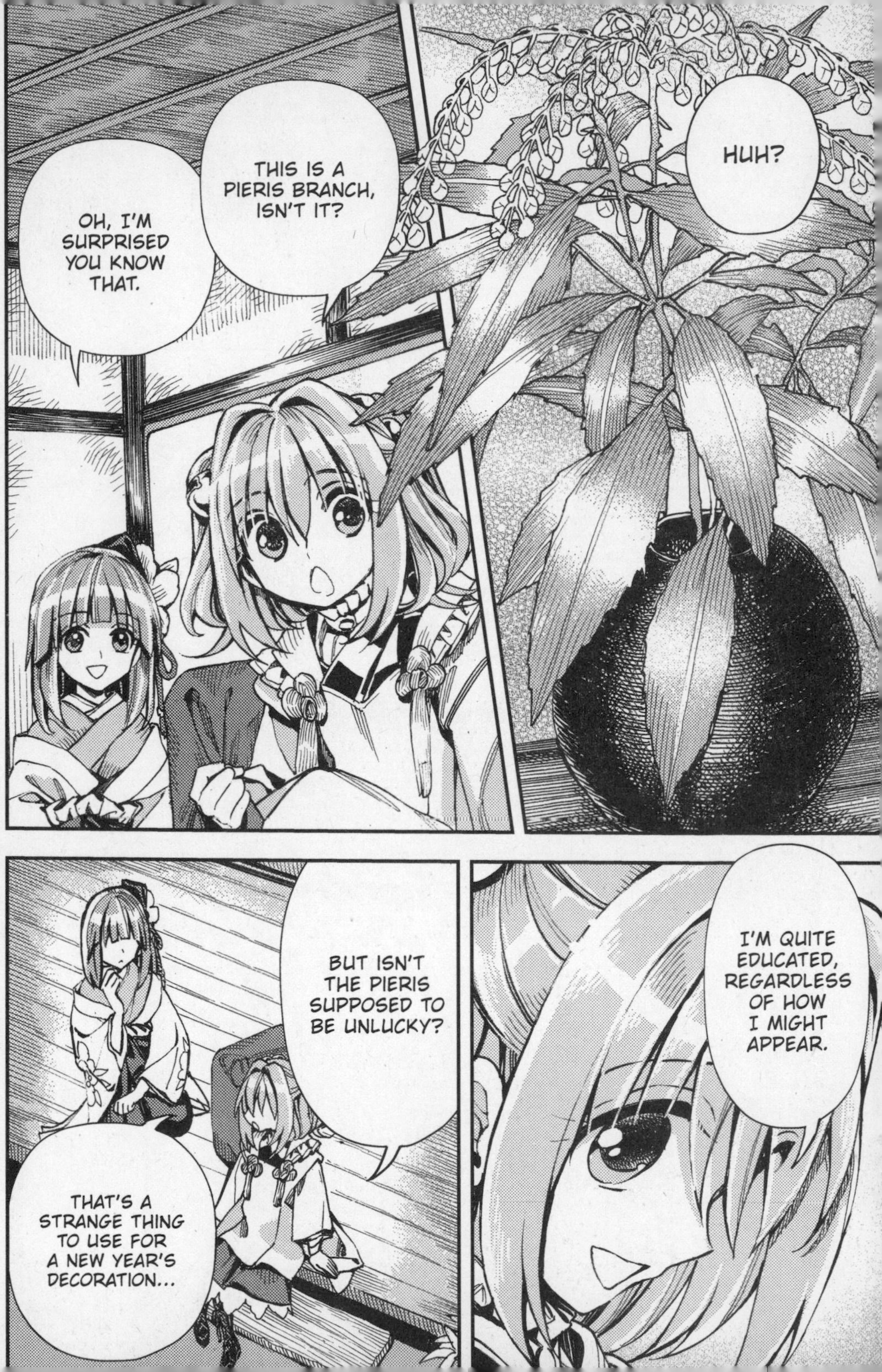
HUH?
THIS IS A PIERIS BRANCH, ISN'T IT?
OH, I'M SURPRISED YOU KNOW THAT.
I'M QUITE EDUCATED, REGARDLESS OF HOW I MIGHT APPEAR.
BUT ISN'T THE PIERIS SUPPOSED TO BE UNLUCKY?
THAT'S A STRANGE THING TO USE FOR A NEW YEAR'S DECORATION...

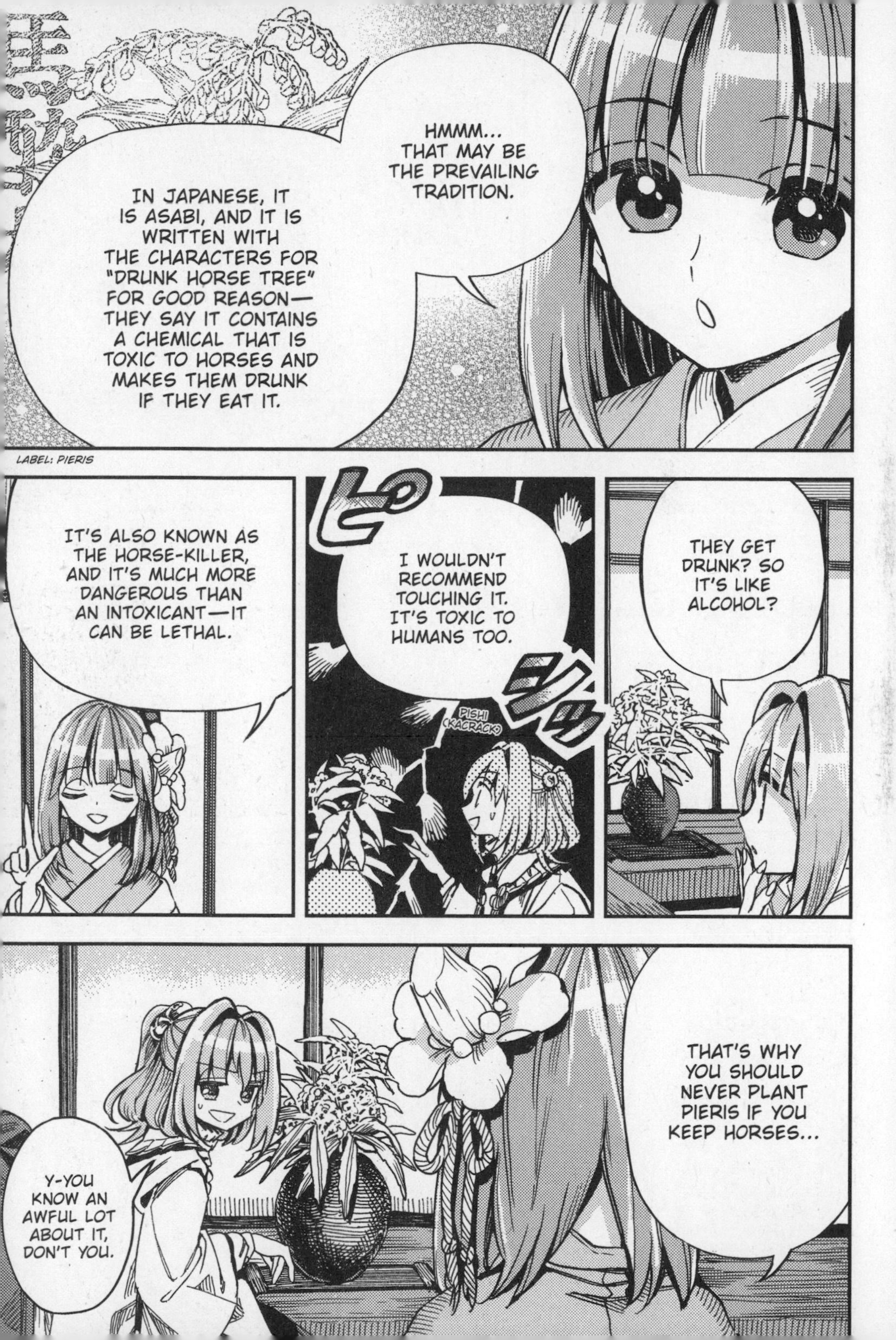
HMMM... THAT MAY BE THE PREVAILING TRADITION.
IN JAPANESE, IT IS ASABI, AND IT IS WRITTEN WITH THE CHARACTERS FOR "DRUNK HORSE TREE" FOR GOOD REASON—THEY SAY IT CONTAINS A CHEMICAL THAT IS TOXIC TO HORSES AND MAKES THEM DRUNK IF THEY EAT IT.
LABEL: PIERIS
THEY GET DRUNK? SO IT'S LIKE ALCOHOL?
I WOULDN'T RECOMMEND TOUCHING IT. IT'S TOXIC TO HUMANS TOO.
PISHI (KACRACK)
IT'S ALSO KNOWN AS THE HORSE-KILLER, AND IT'S MUCH MORE DANGEROUS THAN AN INTOXICANT—IT CAN BE LETHAL.
THAT'S WHY YOU SHOULD NEVER PLANT PIERIS IF YOU KEEP HORSES...
Y-YOU KNOW AN AWFUL LOT ABOUT IT, DON'T YOU.

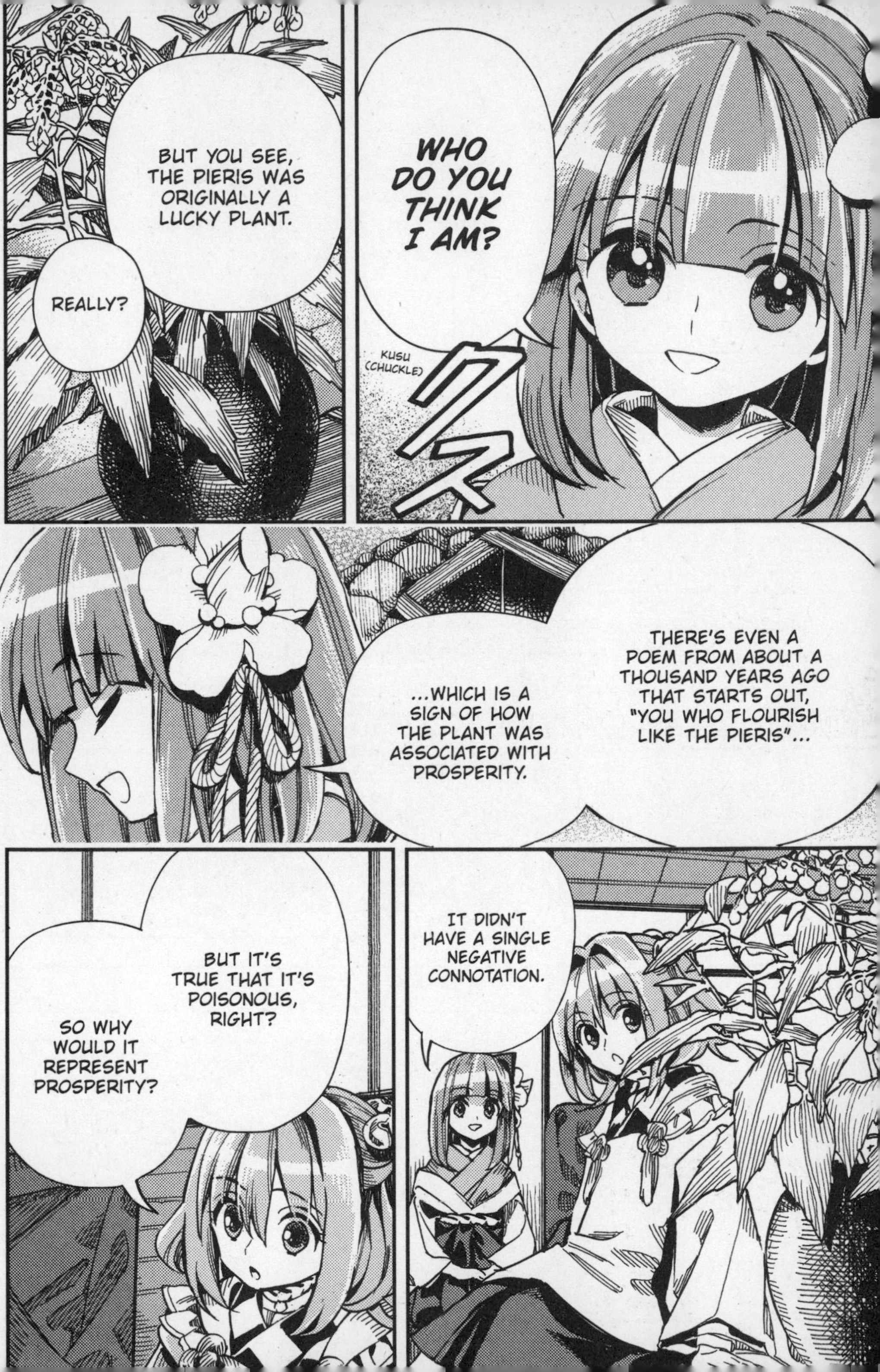
WHO DO YOU THINK I AM?
KUSU (CHUCKLE)
BUT YOU SEE, THE PIERIS WAS ORIGINALLY A LUCKY PLANT.
REALLY?
THERE'S EVEN A POEM FROM ABOUT A THOUSAND YEARS AGO THAT STARTS OUT, "YOU WHO FLOURISH LIKE THE PIERIS"...
...WHICH IS A SIGN OF HOW THE PLANT WAS ASSOCIATED WITH PROSPERITY.
IT DIDN'T HAVE A SINGLE NEGATIVE CONNOTATION.
BUT IT'S TRUE THAT IT'S POISONOUS, RIGHT?
SO WHY WOULD IT REPRESENT PROSPERITY?

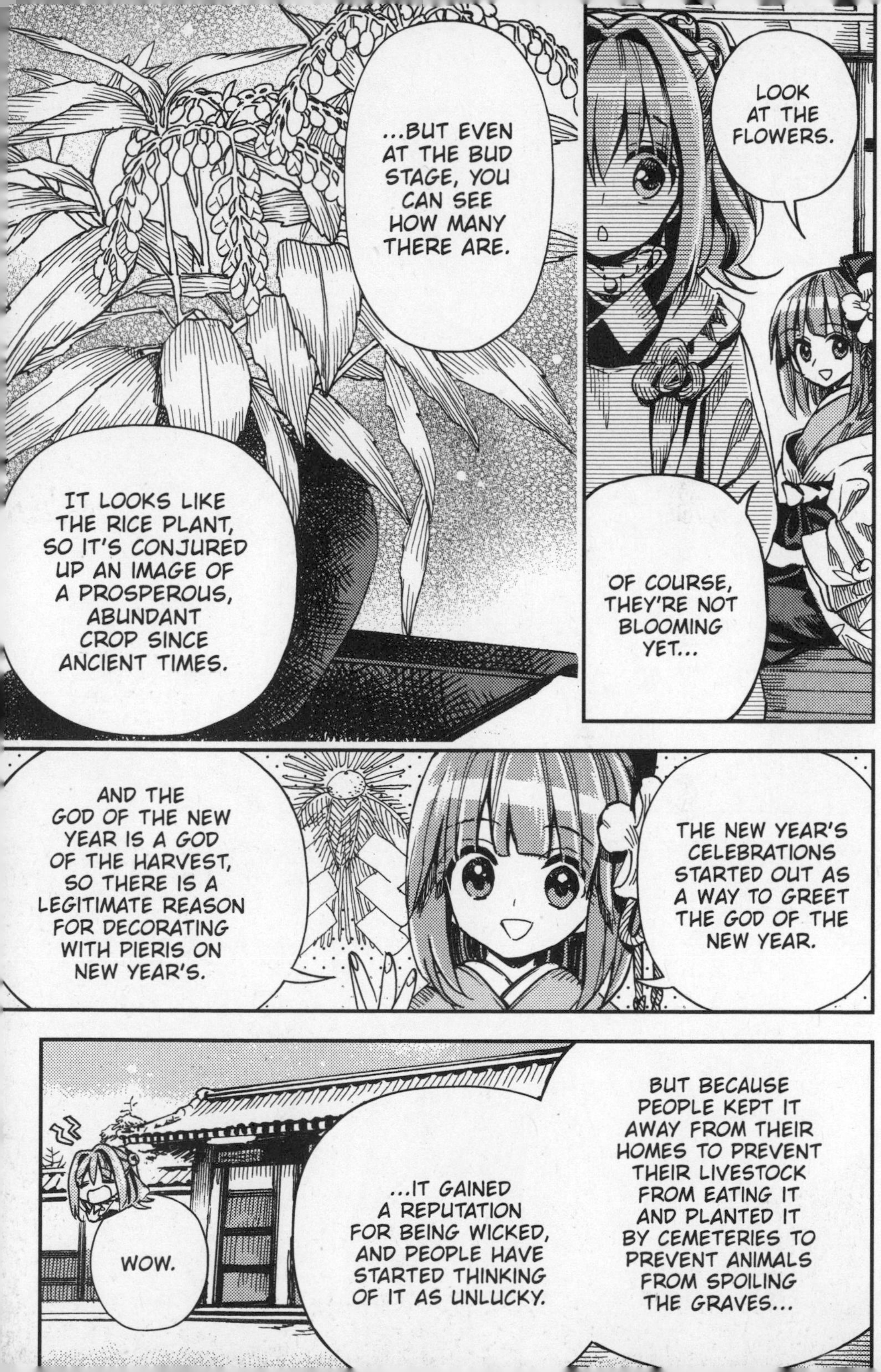
LOOK AT THE FLOWERS.
OF COURSE, THEY'RE NOT BLOOMING YET...
...BUT EVEN AT THE BUD STAGE, YOU CAN SEE HOW MANY THERE ARE.
IT LOOKS LIKE THE RICE PLANT, SO IT'S CONJURED UP AN IMAGE OF A PROSPEROUS, ABUNDANT CROP SINCE ANCIENT TIMES.
THE NEW YEAR'S CELEBRATIONS STARTED OUT AS A WAY TO GREET THE GOD OF THE NEW YEAR.
AND THE GOD OF THE NEW YEAR IS A GOD OF THE HARVEST, SO THERE IS A LEGITIMATE REASON FOR DECORATING WITH PIERIS ON NEW YEAR'S.
BUT BECAUSE PEOPLE KEPT IT AWAY FROM THEIR HOMES TO PREVENT THEIR LIVESTOCK FROM EATING IT AND PLANTED IT BY CEMETERIES TO PREVENT ANIMALS FROM SPOILING THE GRAVES...
...IT GAINED A REPUTATION FOR BEING WICKED, AND PEOPLE HAVE STARTED THINKING OF IT AS UNLUCKY.
WOW.

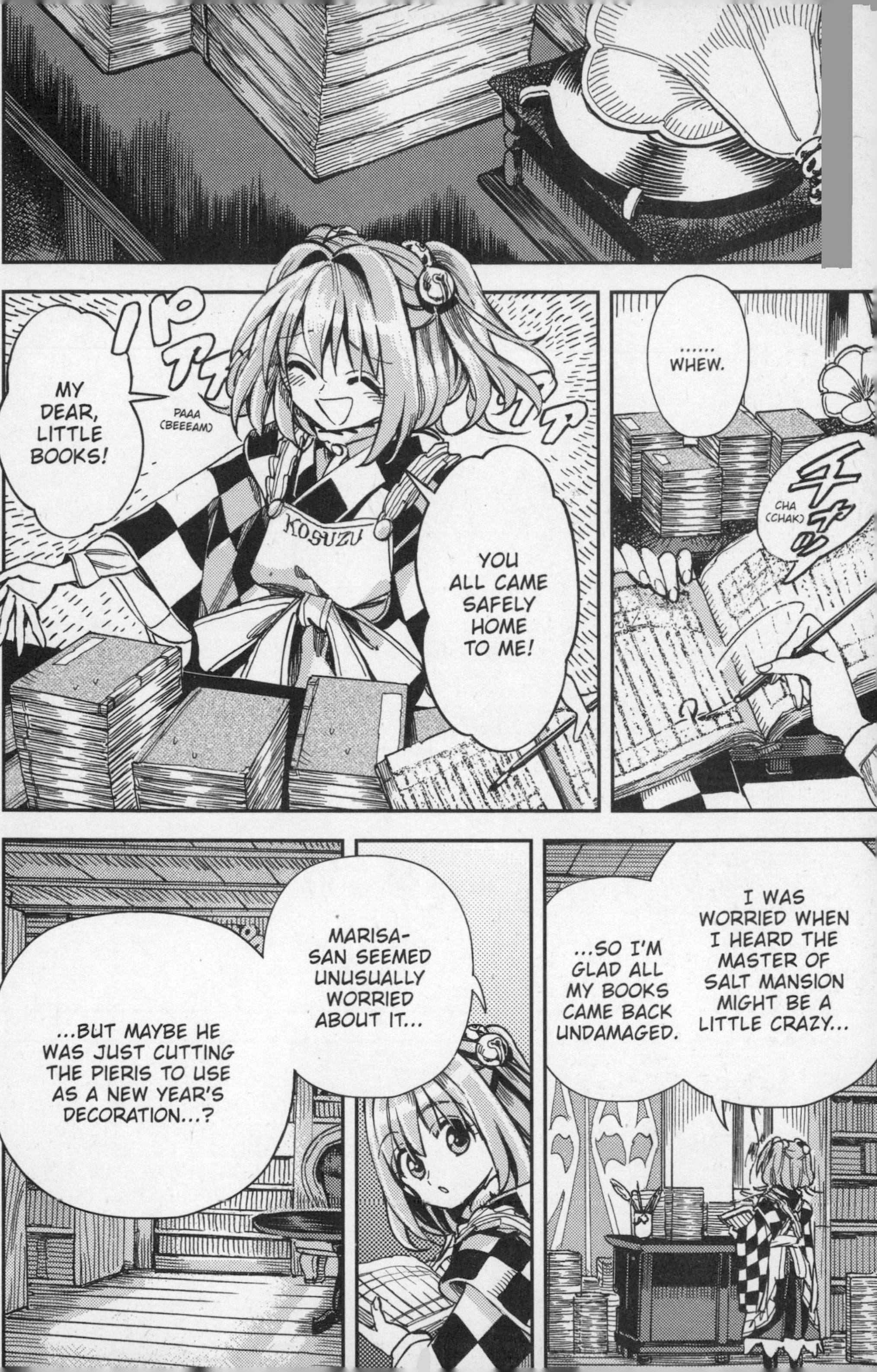
......WHEW.
CHA (CHAK)
MY DEAR, LITTLE BOOKS!
PAAA (BEEEAM)
YOU ALL CAME SAFELY HOME TO ME!
I WAS WORRIED WHEN I HEARD THE MASTER OF SALT MANSION MIGHT BE A LITTLE CRAZY...
...SO I'M GLAD ALL MY BOOKS CAME BACK UNDAMAGED.
MARISA-SAN SEEMED UNUSUALLY WORRIED ABOUT IT...
...BUT MAYBE HE WAS JUST CUTTING THE PIERIS TO USE AS A NEW YEAR'S DECORATION...?

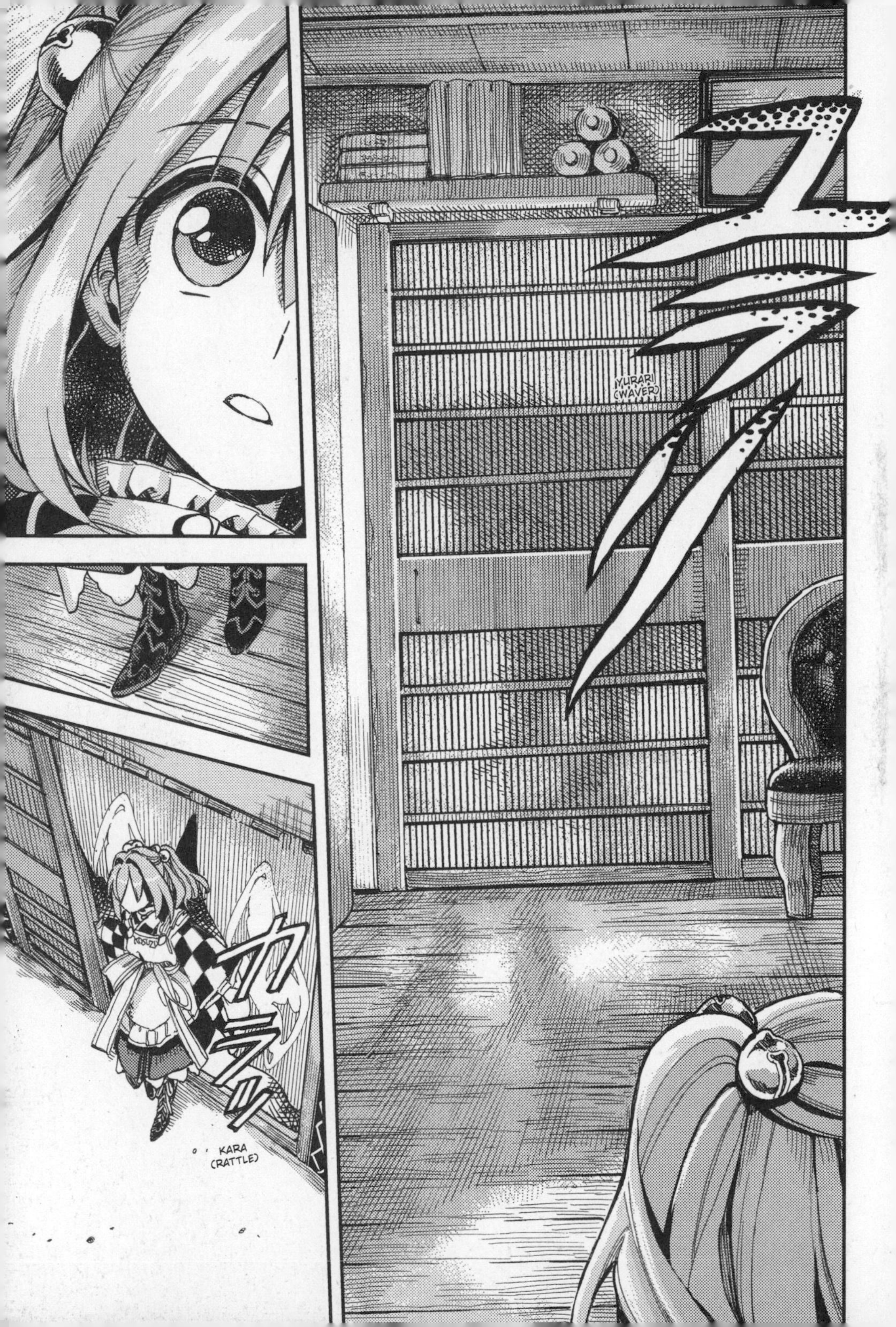
YURARI
(WAVER)
KARA
(RATTLE)

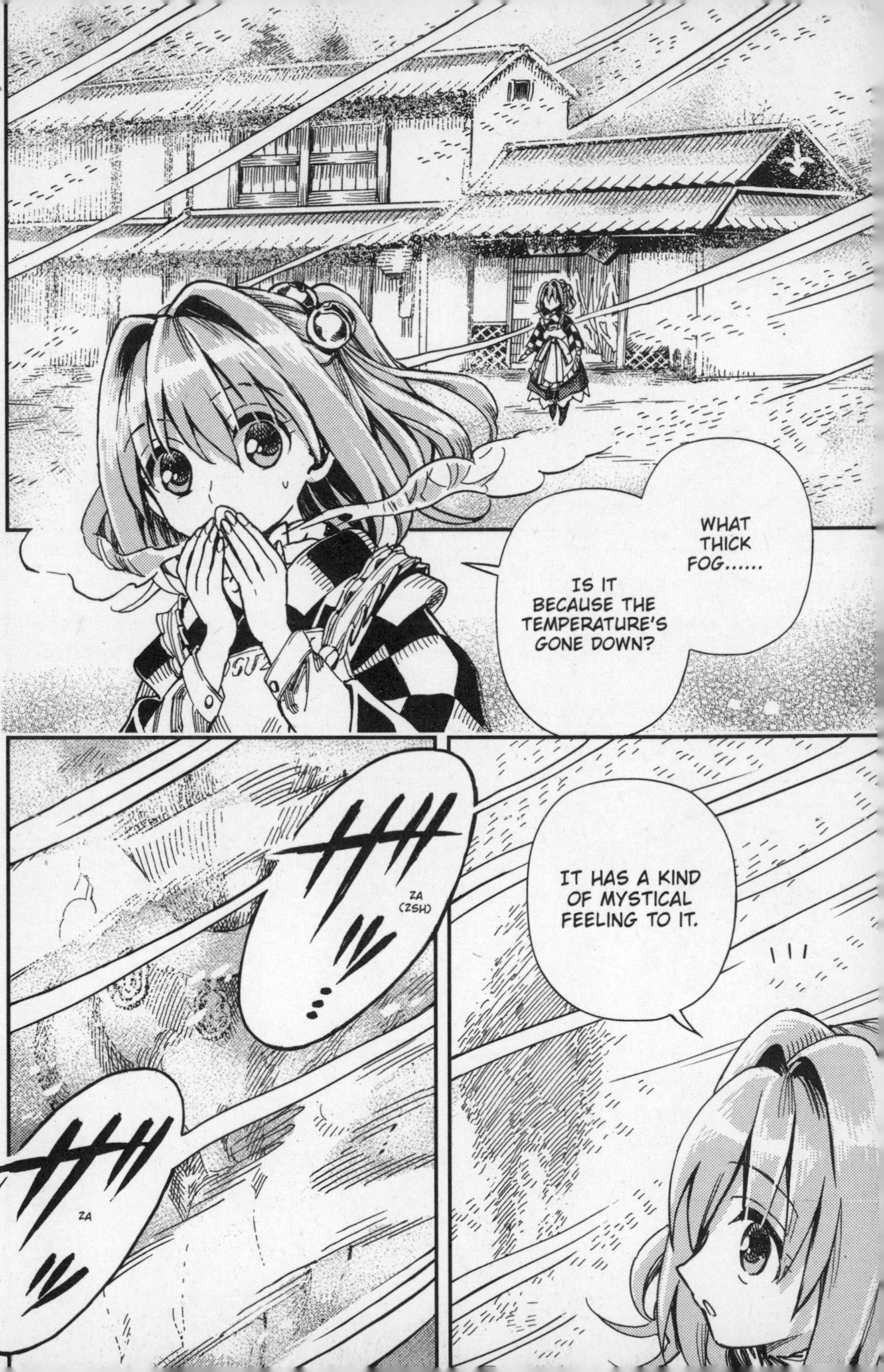
WHAT THICK FOG......
IS IT BECAUSE THE TEMPERATURE'S GONE DOWN?
IT HAS A KIND OF MYSTICAL FEELING TO IT.
ZA (ZSH)
ZA

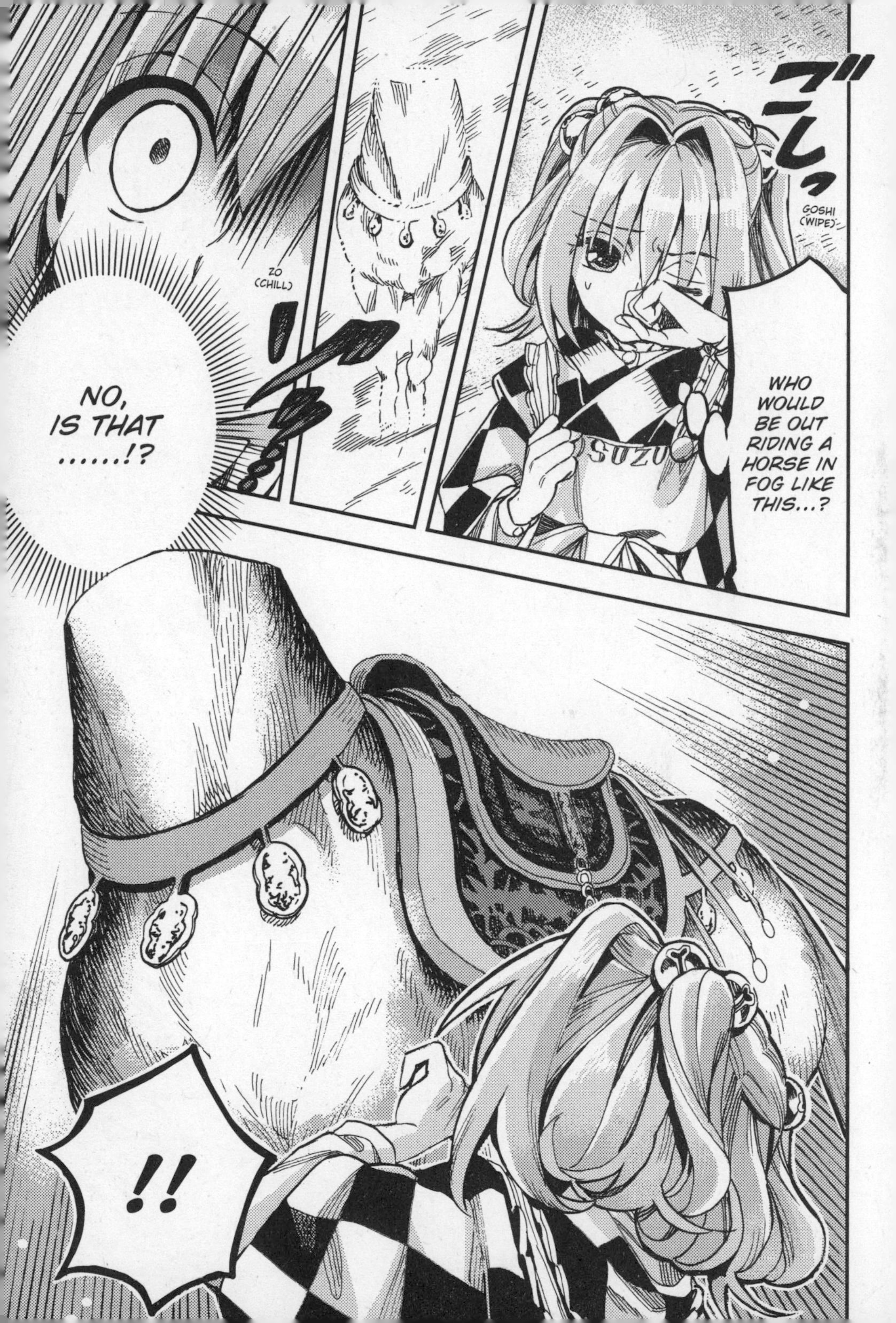
GOSHI (WIPE)
SUZU
WHO WOULD BE OUT RIDING A HORSE IN FOG LIKE THIS...?
ZO (CHILL)
NO, IS THAT ......!?
!!

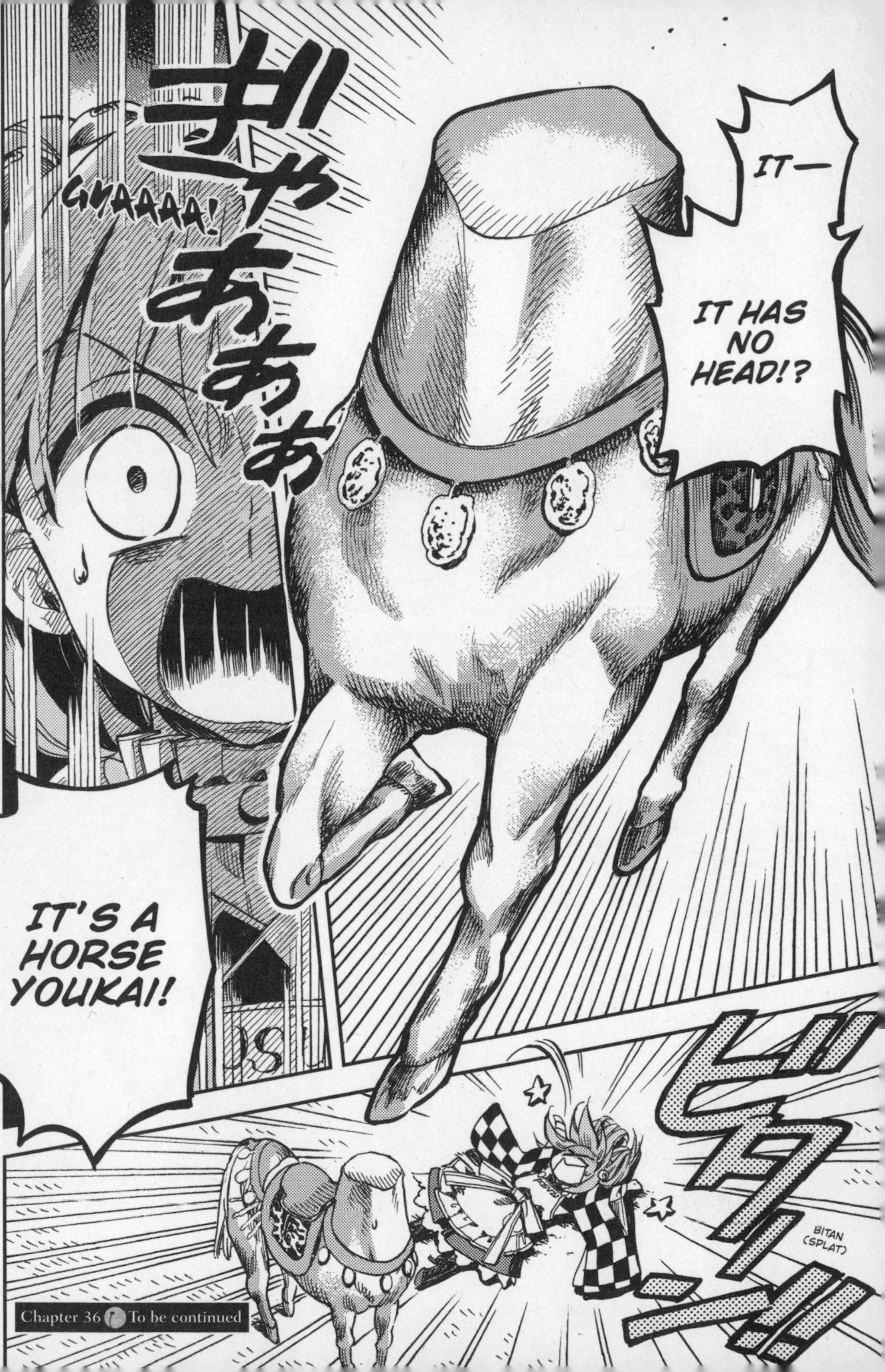
IT—
IT HAS NO HEAD!?
ギャあああ
GYAAAAA!
IT'S A HORSE YOUKAI!
BITAN (SPLAT)
Chapter 36 To be continued

Forbidden Scrollery

Chapter 37 The Plant That Inebriates Domestic Horses Part 2

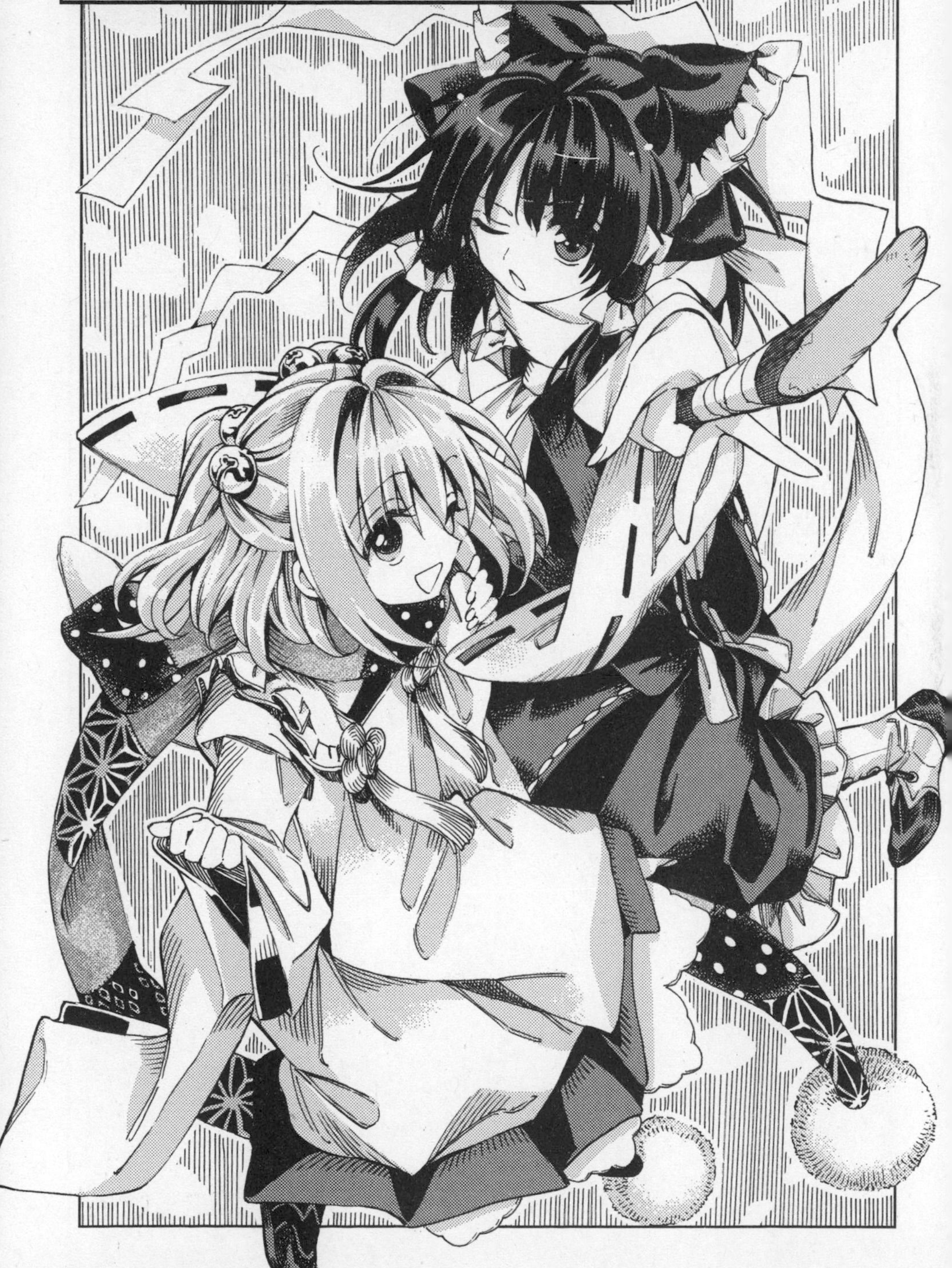

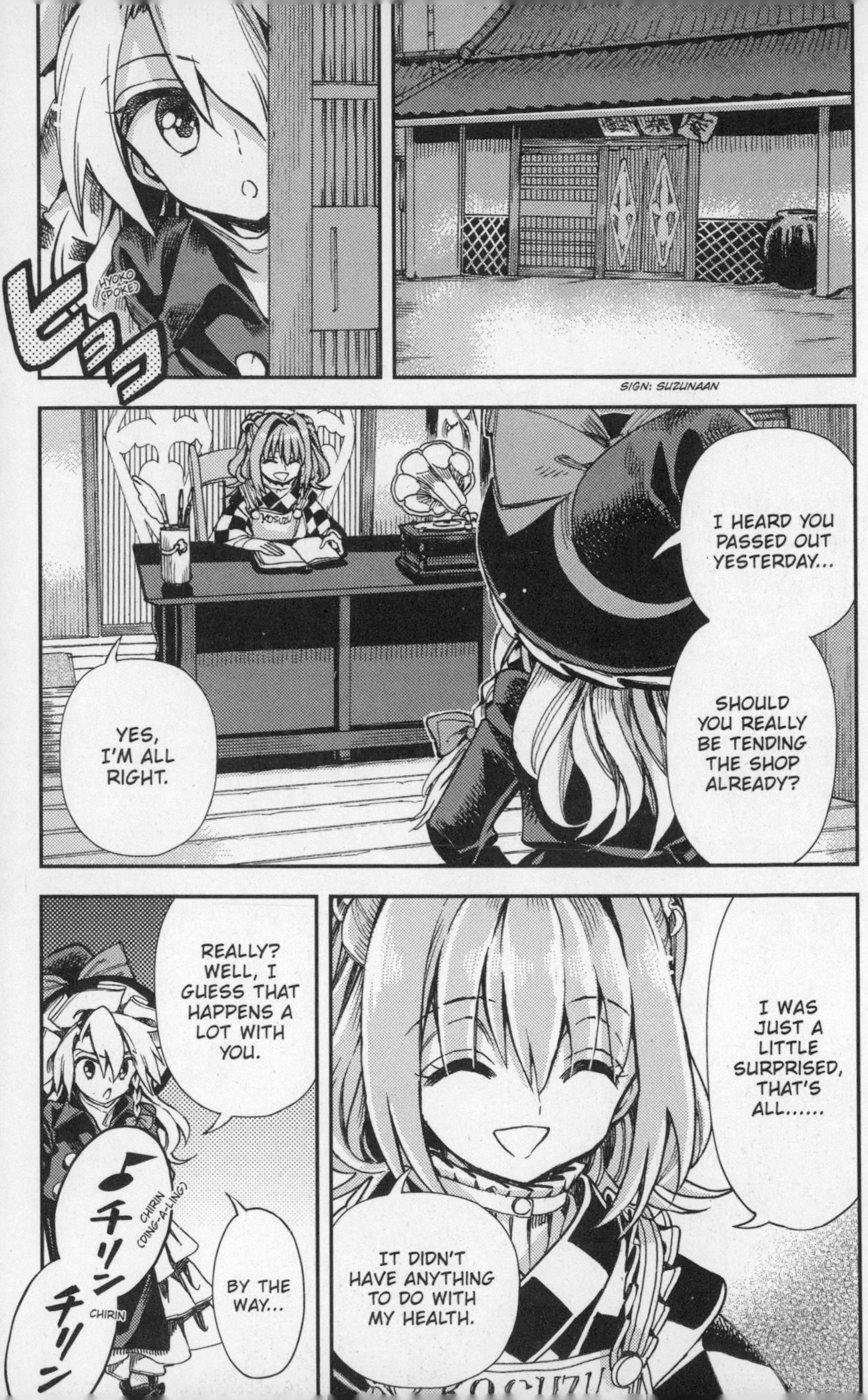
SIGN: SUZUNAAN
ヒョコ
HYOKO (POKE)
I HEARD YOU PASSED OUT YESTERDAY...
SHOULD YOU REALLY BE TENDING THE SHOP ALREADY?
YES, I'M ALL RIGHT.
I WAS JUST A LITTLE SURPRISED, THAT'S ALL......
IT DIDN'T HAVE ANYTHING TO DO WITH MY HEALTH.
REALLY? WELL, I GUESS THAT HAPPENS A LOT WITH YOU.
BY THE WAY...
♪チリン
CHIRIN (DING-A-LING)
チリン
CHIRIN

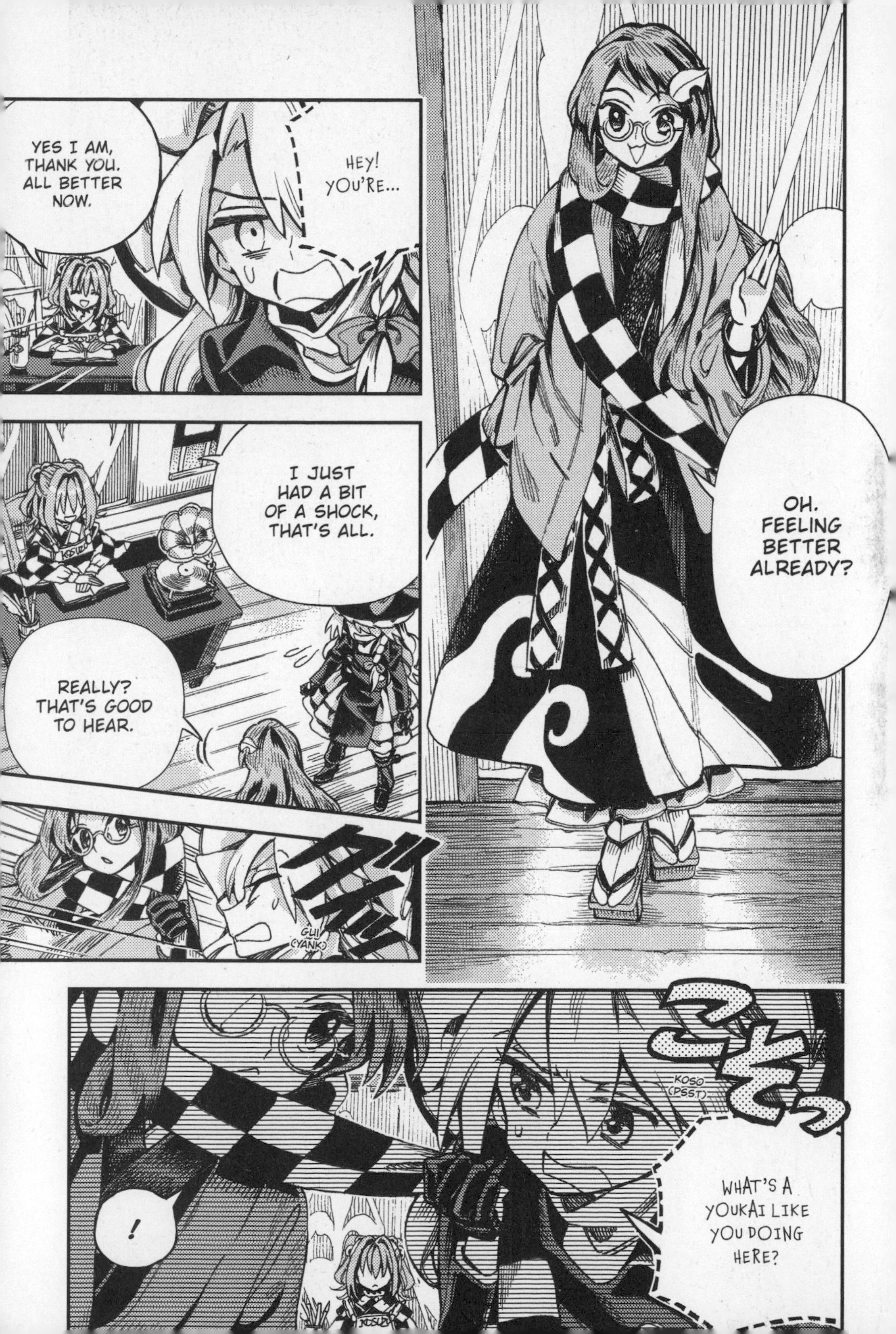
OH. FEELING BETTER ALREADY?
HEY! YOU'RE...
YES I AM, THANK YOU. ALL BETTER NOW.
I JUST HAD A BIT OF A SHOCK, THAT'S ALL.
REALLY? THAT'S GOOD TO HEAR.
GUI (YANK)
KOSO (PSST)
WHAT'S A YOUKAI LIKE YOU DOING HERE?
!

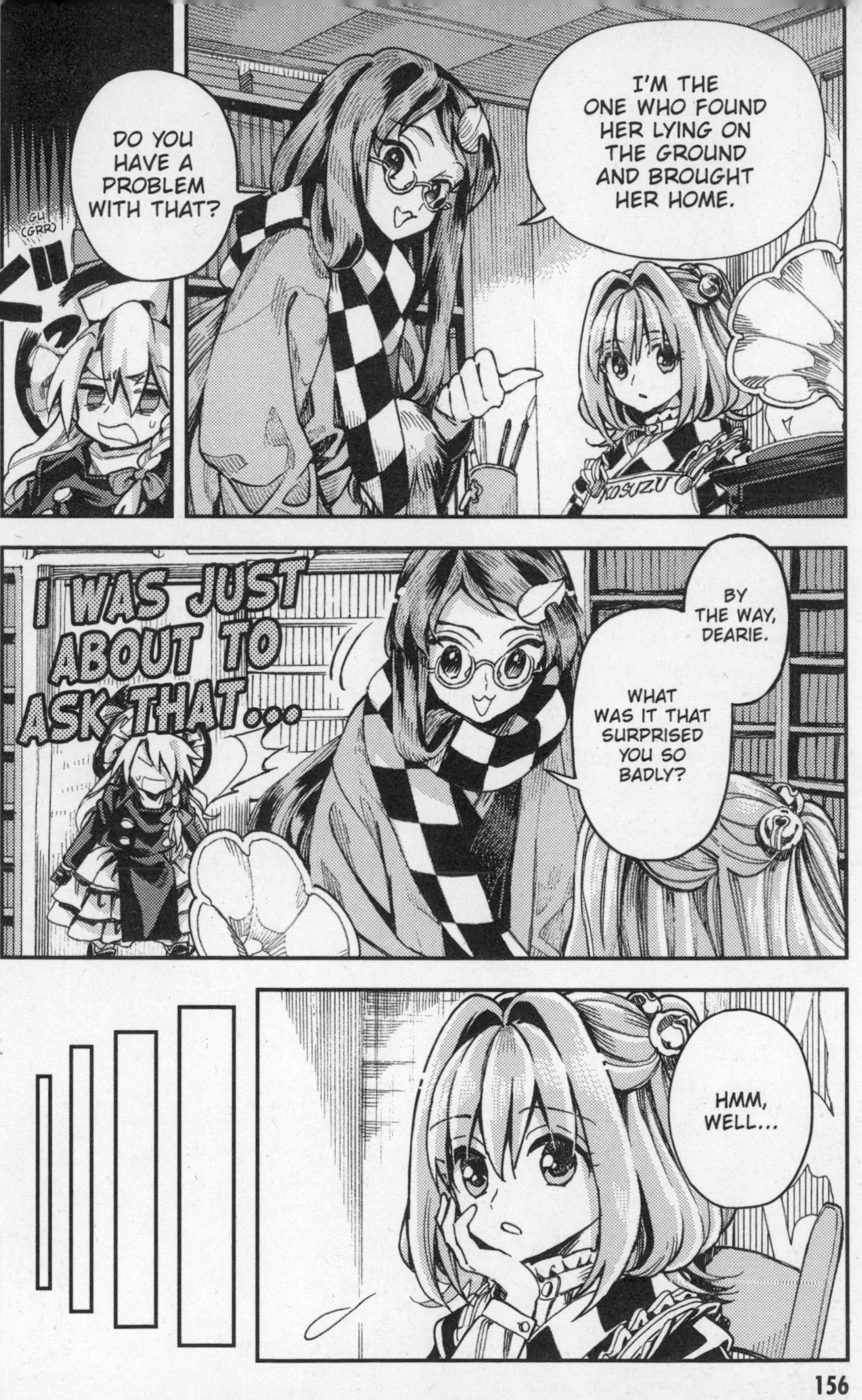
I'M THE ONE WHO FOUND HER LYING ON THE GROUND AND BROUGHT HER HOME.
DO YOU HAVE A PROBLEM WITH THAT?
GU (GRR)
BY THE WAY, DEARIE.
WHAT WAS IT THAT SURPRISED YOU SO BADLY?
I WAS JUST ABOUT TO ASK THAT...
HMM, WELL...

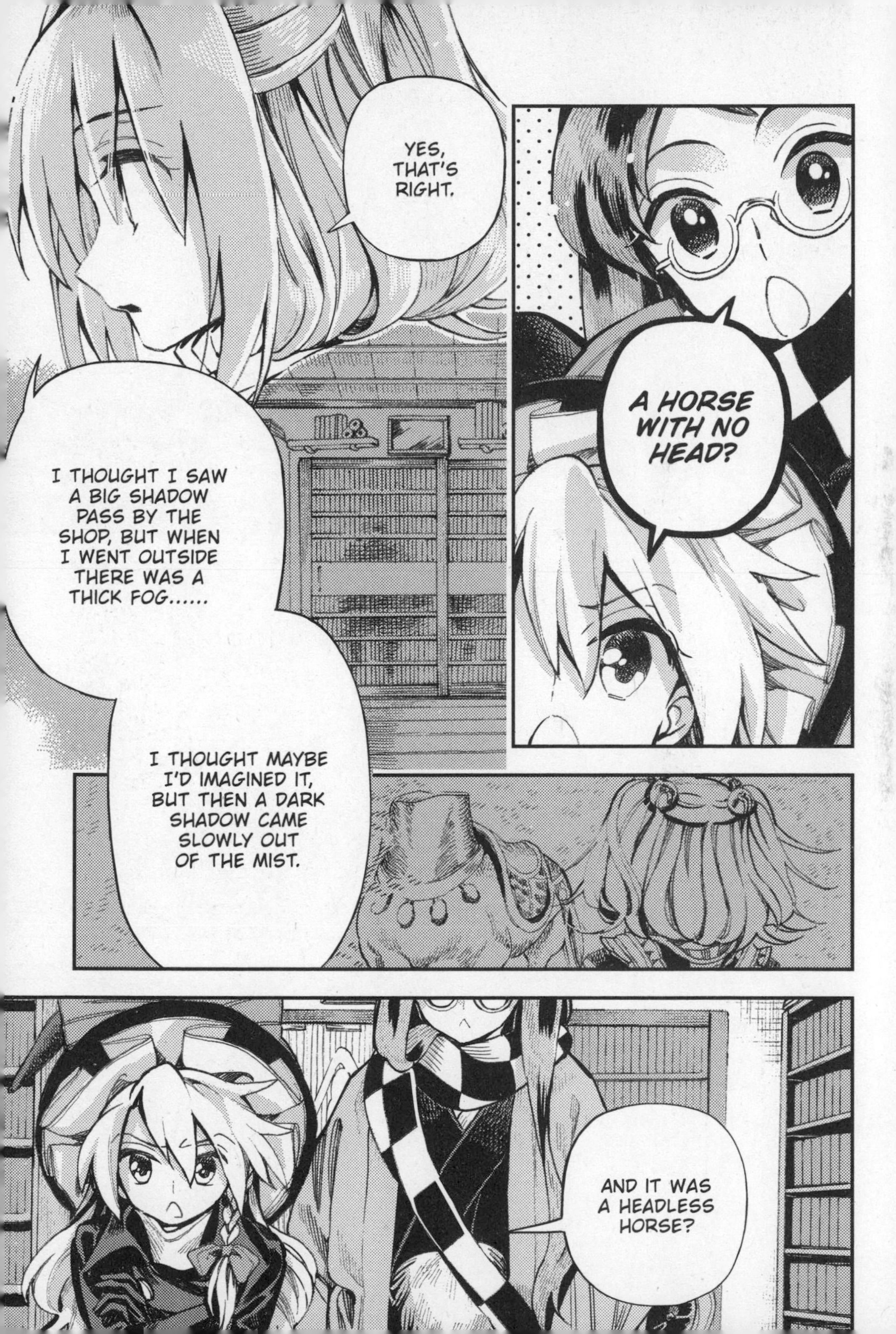
A HORSE WITH NO HEAD?
YES, THAT'S RIGHT.
I THOUGHT I SAW A BIG SHADOW PASS BY THE SHOP, BUT WHEN I WENT OUTSIDE THERE WAS A THICK FOG......
I THOUGHT MAYBE I'D IMAGINED IT, BUT THEN A DARK SHADOW CAME SLOWLY OUT OF THE MIST.
AND IT WAS A HEADLESS HORSE?

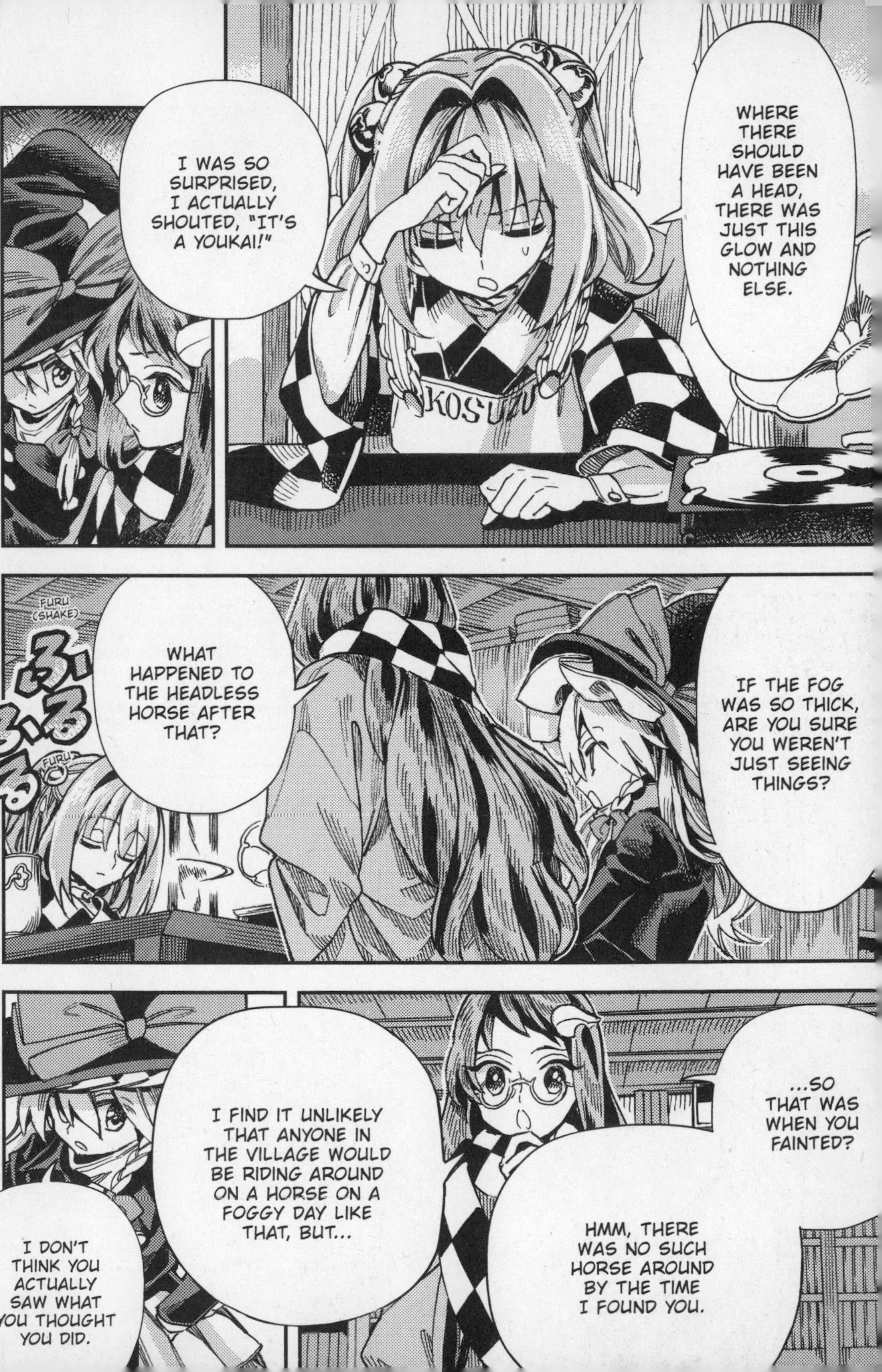
WHERE THERE SHOULD HAVE BEEN A HEAD, THERE WAS JUST THIS GLOW AND NOTHING ELSE.
I WAS SO SURPRISED, I ACTUALLY SHOUTED, "IT'S A YOUKAI!"
KOSUZU
IF THE FOG WAS SO THICK, ARE YOU SURE YOU WEREN'T JUST SEEING THINGS?
WHAT HAPPENED TO THE HEADLESS HORSE AFTER THAT?
FURU (SHAKE)
ふる、ふる、ふる
FURU
...SO THAT WAS WHEN YOU FAINTED?
HMM, THERE WAS NO SUCH HORSE AROUND BY THE TIME I FOUND YOU.
I FIND IT UNLIKELY THAT ANYONE IN THE VILLAGE WOULD BE RIDING AROUND ON A HORSE ON A FOGGY DAY LIKE THAT, BUT...
I DON'T THINK YOU ACTUALLY SAW WHAT YOU THOUGHT YOU DID.

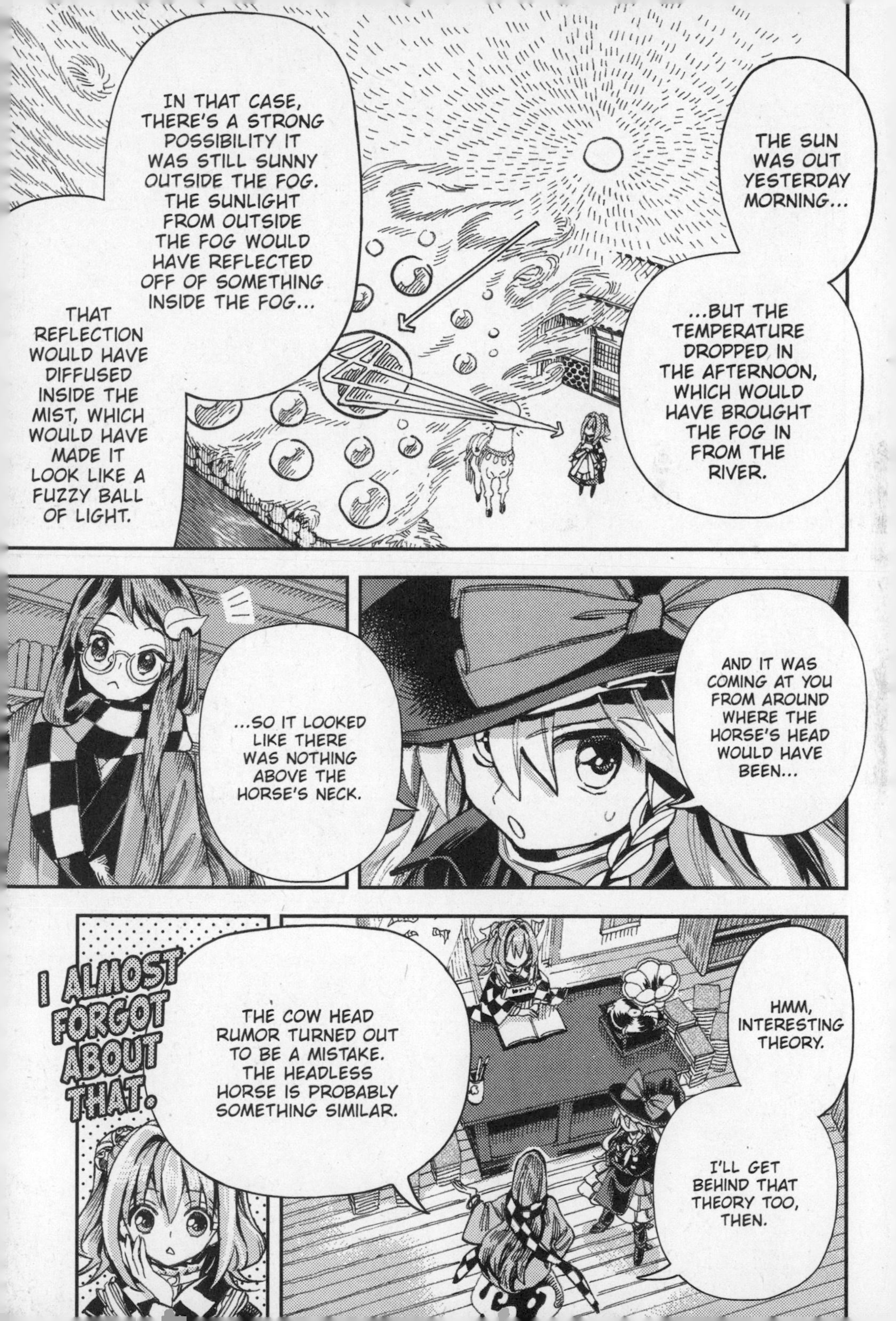
THE SUN WAS OUT YESTERDAY MORNING...
...BUT THE TEMPERATURE DROPPED IN THE AFTERNOON, WHICH WOULD HAVE BROUGHT THE FOG IN FROM THE RIVER.
IN THAT CASE, THERE'S A STRONG POSSIBILITY IT WAS STILL SUNNY OUTSIDE THE FOG. THE SUNLIGHT FROM OUTSIDE THE FOG WOULD HAVE REFLECTED OFF OF SOMETHING INSIDE THE FOG...
THAT REFLECTION WOULD HAVE DIFFUSED INSIDE THE MIST, WHICH WOULD HAVE MADE IT LOOK LIKE A FUZZY BALL OF LIGHT.
AND IT WAS COMING AT YOU FROM AROUND WHERE THE HORSE'S HEAD WOULD HAVE BEEN...
...SO IT LOOKED LIKE THERE WAS NOTHING ABOVE THE HORSE'S NECK.
HMM, INTERESTING THEORY.
I'LL GET BEHIND THAT THEORY TOO, THEN.
THE COW HEAD RUMOR TURNED OUT TO BE A MISTAKE. THE HEADLESS HORSE IS PROBABLY SOMETHING SIMILAR.
I ALMOST FORGOT ABOUT THAT.

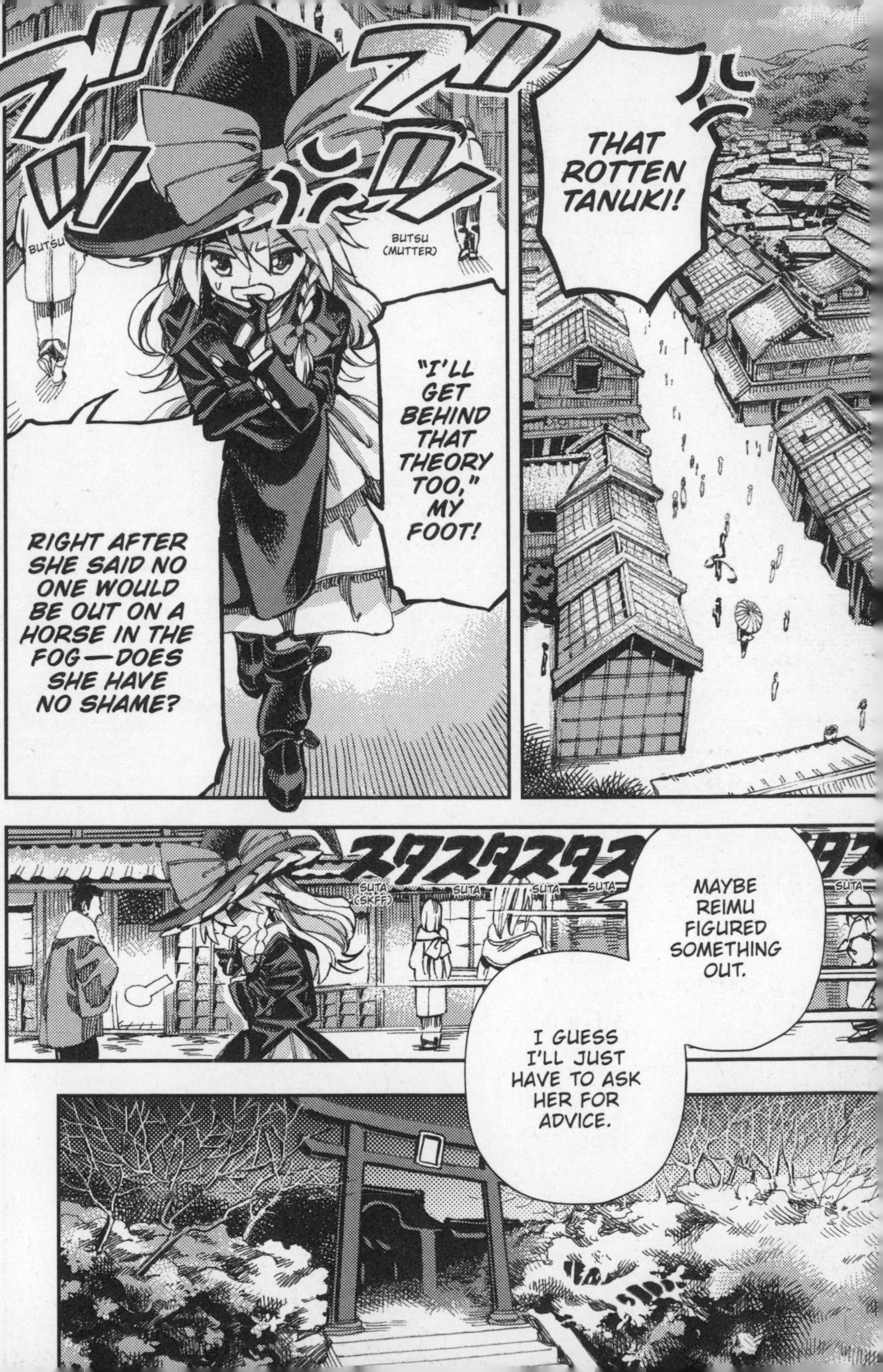
THAT ROTTEN TANUKI!
BUTSU (MUTTER)
"I'LL GET BEHIND THAT THEORY TOO," MY FOOT!
BUTSU
RIGHT AFTER SHE SAID NO ONE WOULD BE OUT ON A HORSE IN THE FOG—DOES SHE HAVE NO SHAME?
スタスタスタ
SUTA
SUTA
SUTA
SUTA
SUTA (SKFF)
MAYBE REIMU FIGURED SOMETHING OUT.
I GUESS I'LL JUST HAVE TO ASK HER FOR ADVICE.

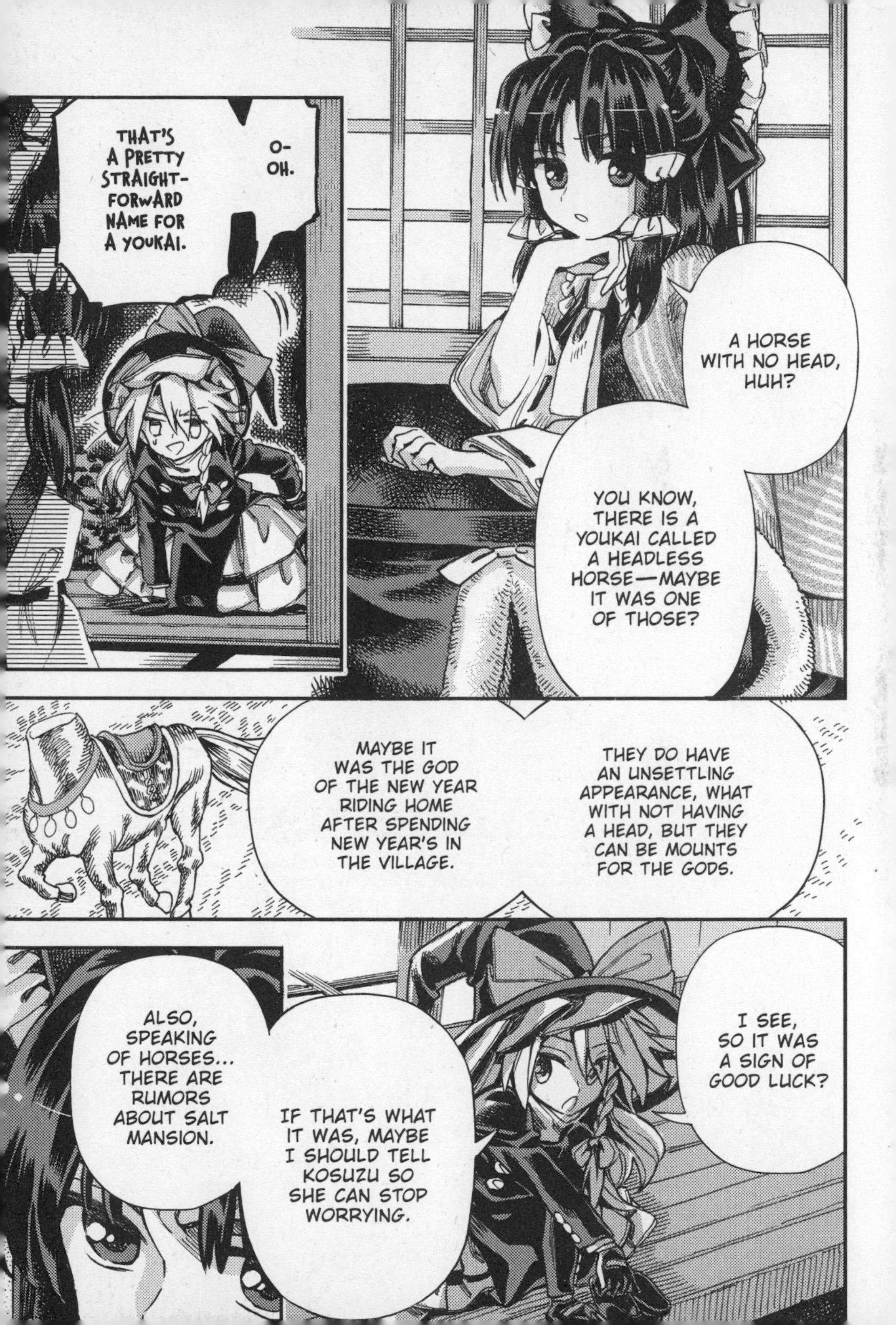
A HORSE WITH NO HEAD, HUH?
YOU KNOW, THERE IS A YOUKAI CALLED A HEADLESS HORSE—MAYBE IT WAS ONE OF THOSE?
O-OH.
THAT'S A PRETTY STRAIGHT-FORWARD NAME FOR A YOUKAI.
THEY DO HAVE AN UNSETTLING APPEARANCE, WHAT WITH NOT HAVING A HEAD, BUT THEY CAN BE MOUNTS FOR THE GODS.
MAYBE IT WAS THE GOD OF THE NEW YEAR RIDING HOME AFTER SPENDING NEW YEAR'S IN THE VILLAGE.
I SEE, SO IT WAS A SIGN OF GOOD LUCK?
IF THAT'S WHAT IT WAS, MAYBE I SHOULD TELL KOSUZU SO SHE CAN STOP WORRYING.
ALSO, SPEAKING OF HORSES... THERE ARE RUMORS ABOUT SALT MANSION.

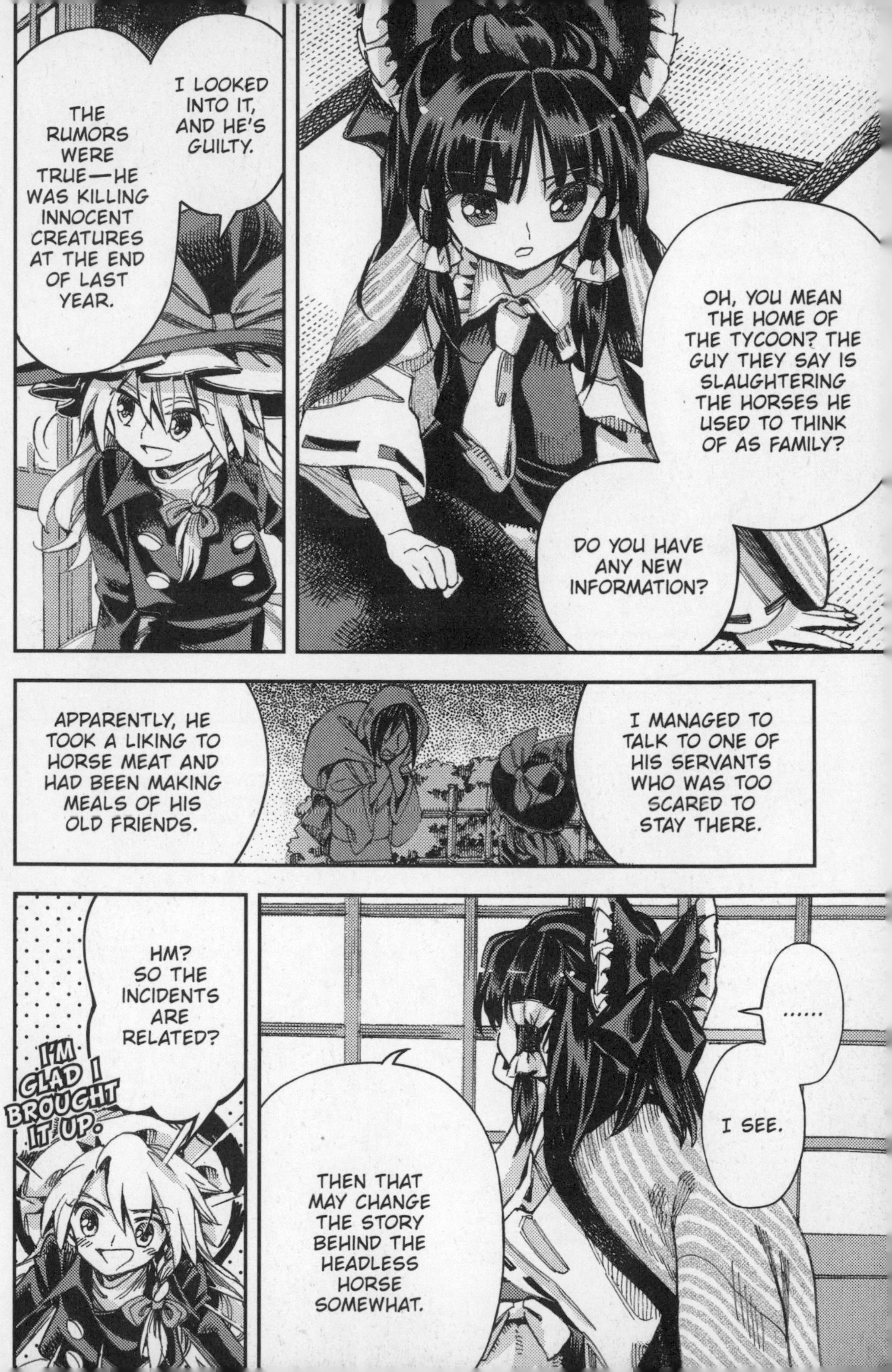
OH, YOU MEAN THE HOME OF THE TYCOON? THE GUY THEY SAY IS SLAUGHTERING THE HORSES HE USED TO THINK OF AS FAMILY?
DO YOU HAVE ANY NEW INFORMATION?
I LOOKED INTO IT, AND HE'S GUILTY.
THE RUMORS WERE TRUE—HE WAS KILLING INNOCENT CREATURES AT THE END OF LAST YEAR.
I MANAGED TO TALK TO ONE OF HIS SERVANTS WHO WAS TOO SCARED TO STAY THERE.
APPARENTLY, HE TOOK A LIKING TO HORSE MEAT AND HAD BEEN MAKING MEALS OF HIS OLD FRIENDS.
......
I SEE.
THEN THAT MAY CHANGE THE STORY BEHIND THE HEADLESS HORSE SOMEWHAT.
HM? SO THE INCIDENTS ARE RELATED?
I'M GLAD I BROUGHT IT UP.

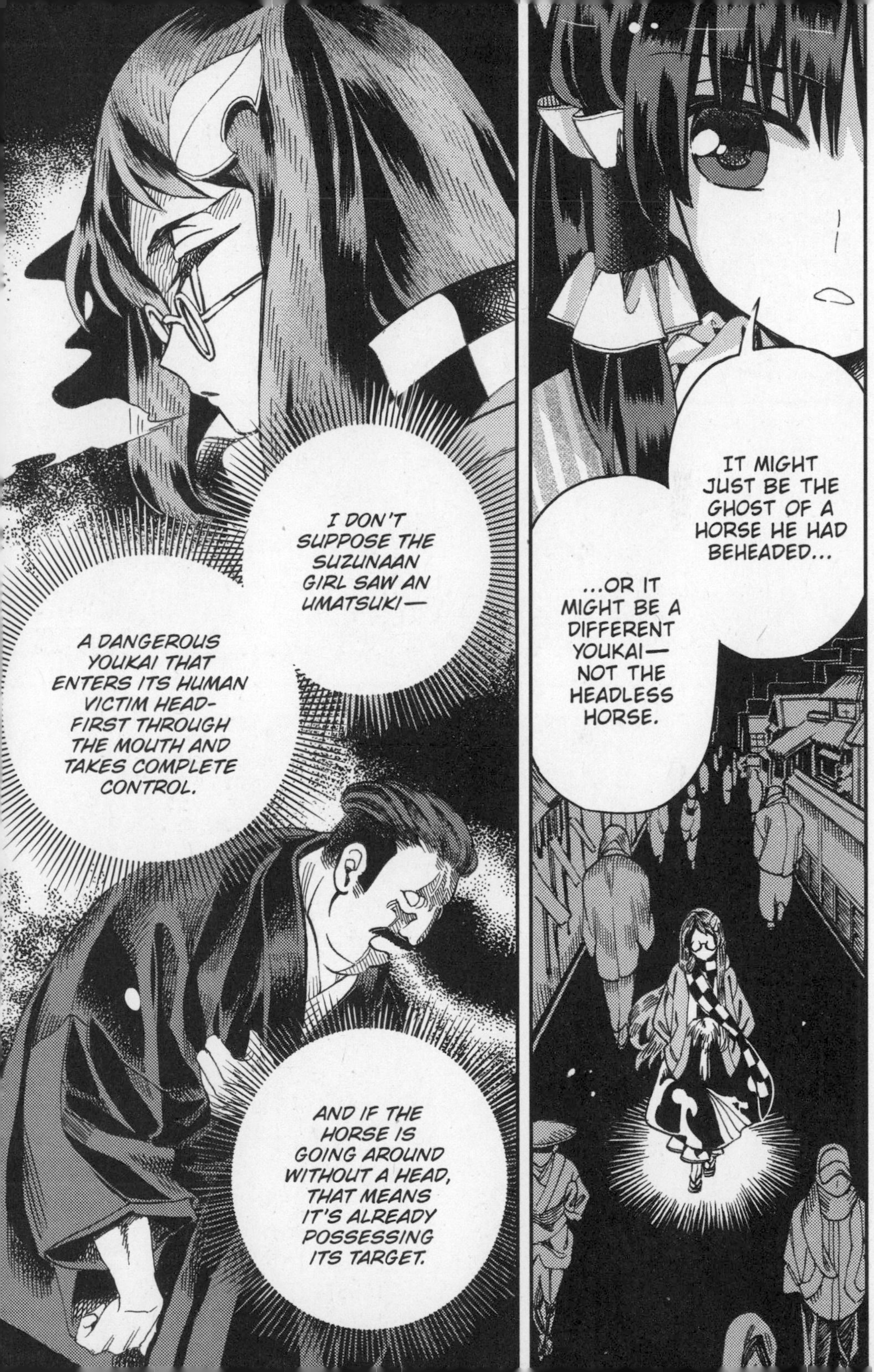
IT MIGHT JUST BE THE GHOST OF A HORSE HE HAD BEHEADED...
...OR IT MIGHT BE A DIFFERENT YOUKAI—NOT THE HEADLESS HORSE.
I DON'T SUPPOSE THE SUZUNAAN GIRL SAW AN UMATSUKI—
A DANGEROUS YOUKAI THAT ENTERS ITS HUMAN VICTIM HEAD-FIRST THROUGH THE MOUTH AND TAKES COMPLETE CONTROL.
AND IF THE HORSE IS GOING AROUND WITHOUT A HEAD, THAT MEANS IT'S ALREADY POSSESSING ITS TARGET.

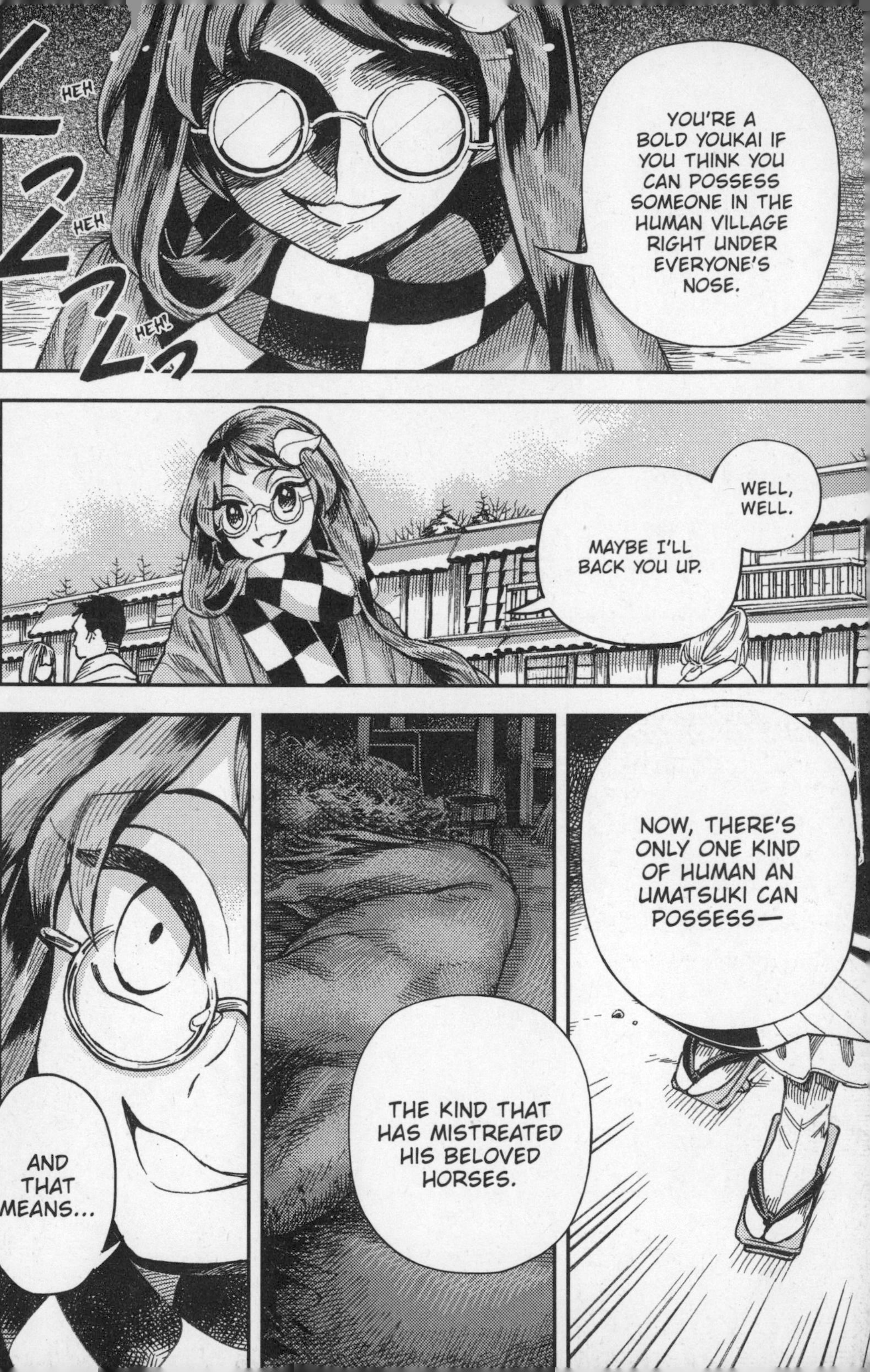
YOU'RE A BOLD YOUKAI IF YOU THINK YOU CAN POSSESS SOMEONE IN THE HUMAN VILLAGE RIGHT UNDER EVERYONE'S NOSE.
HEH
HEH
HEH!
WELL, WELL.
MAYBE I'LL BACK YOU UP.
NOW, THERE'S ONLY ONE KIND OF HUMAN AN UMATSUKI CAN POSSESS—
THE KIND THAT HAS MISTREATED HIS BELOVED HORSES.
AND THAT MEANS...

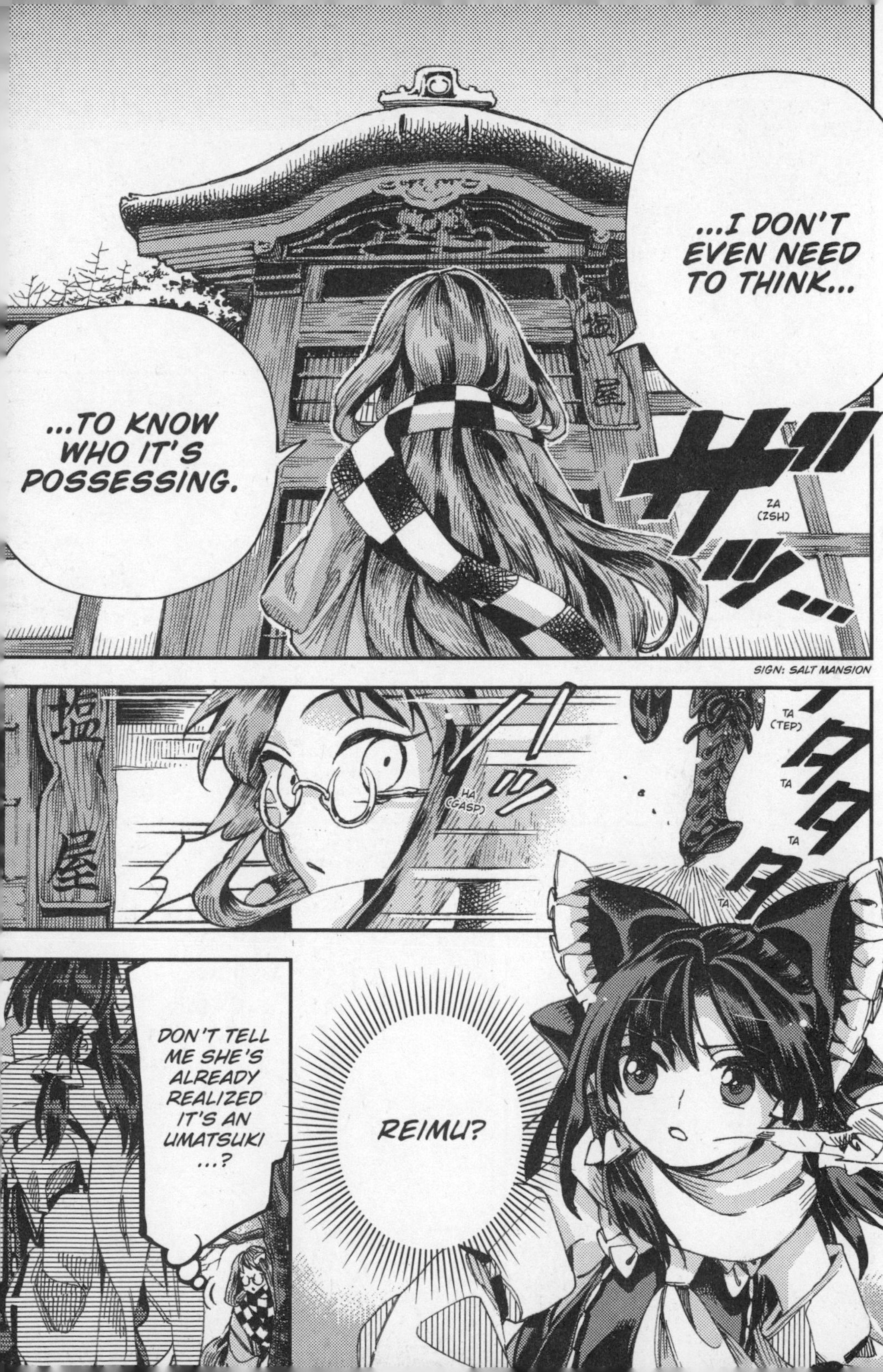
...I DON'T EVEN NEED TO THINK...
...TO KNOW WHO IT'S POSSESSING.
ZA (ZSH)
SIGN: SALT MANSION
TA (TEP) TA TA TA
HA (GASP)
REIMU?
DON'T TELL ME SHE'S ALREADY REALIZED IT'S AN UMATSUKI ...?

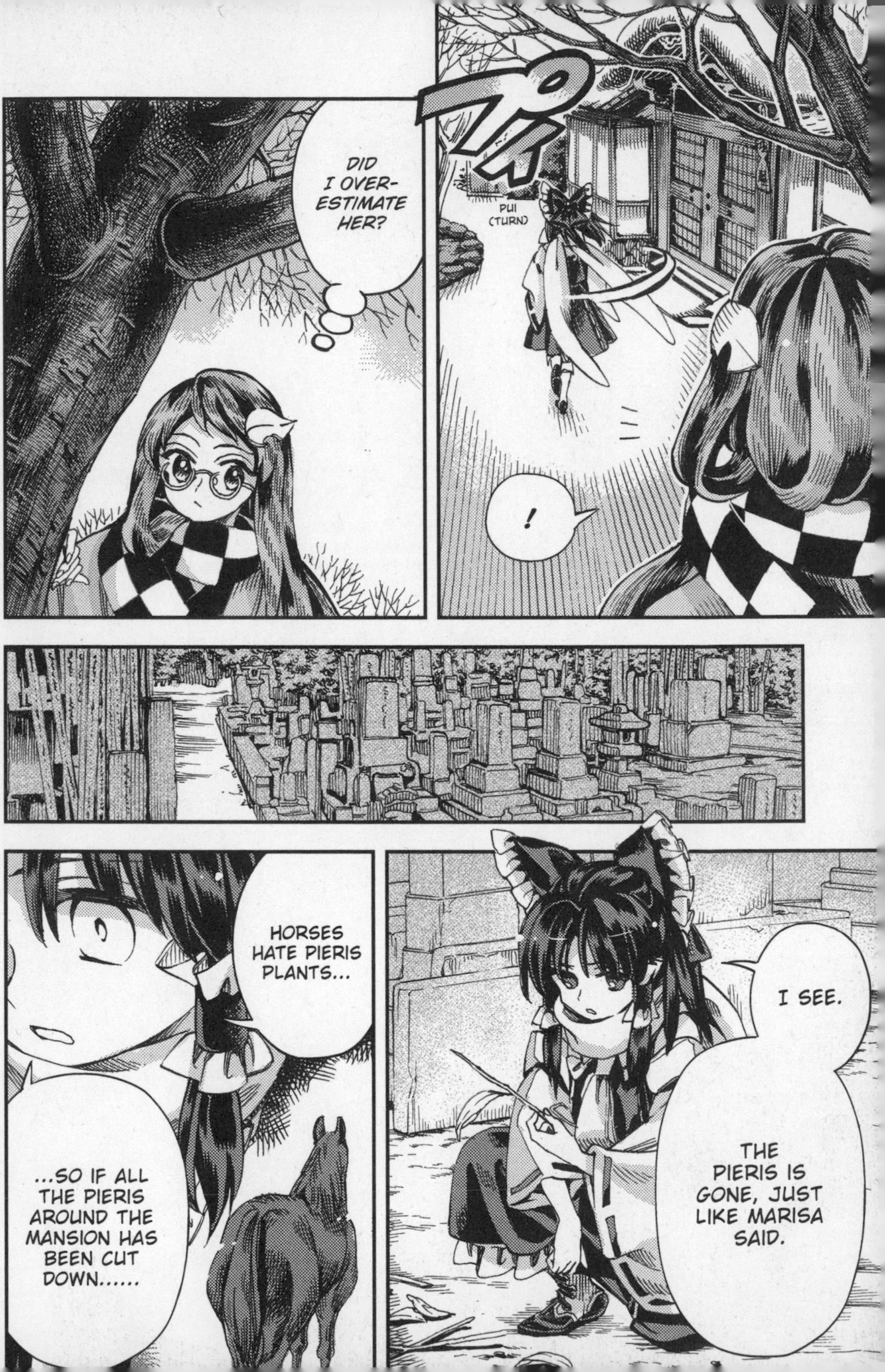
PUI (TURN)
!
DID I OVER-ESTIMATE HER?
I SEE.
THE PIERIS IS GONE, JUST LIKE MARISA SAID.
HORSES HATE PIERIS PLANTS...
...SO IF ALL THE PIERIS AROUND THE MANSION HAS BEEN CUT DOWN......

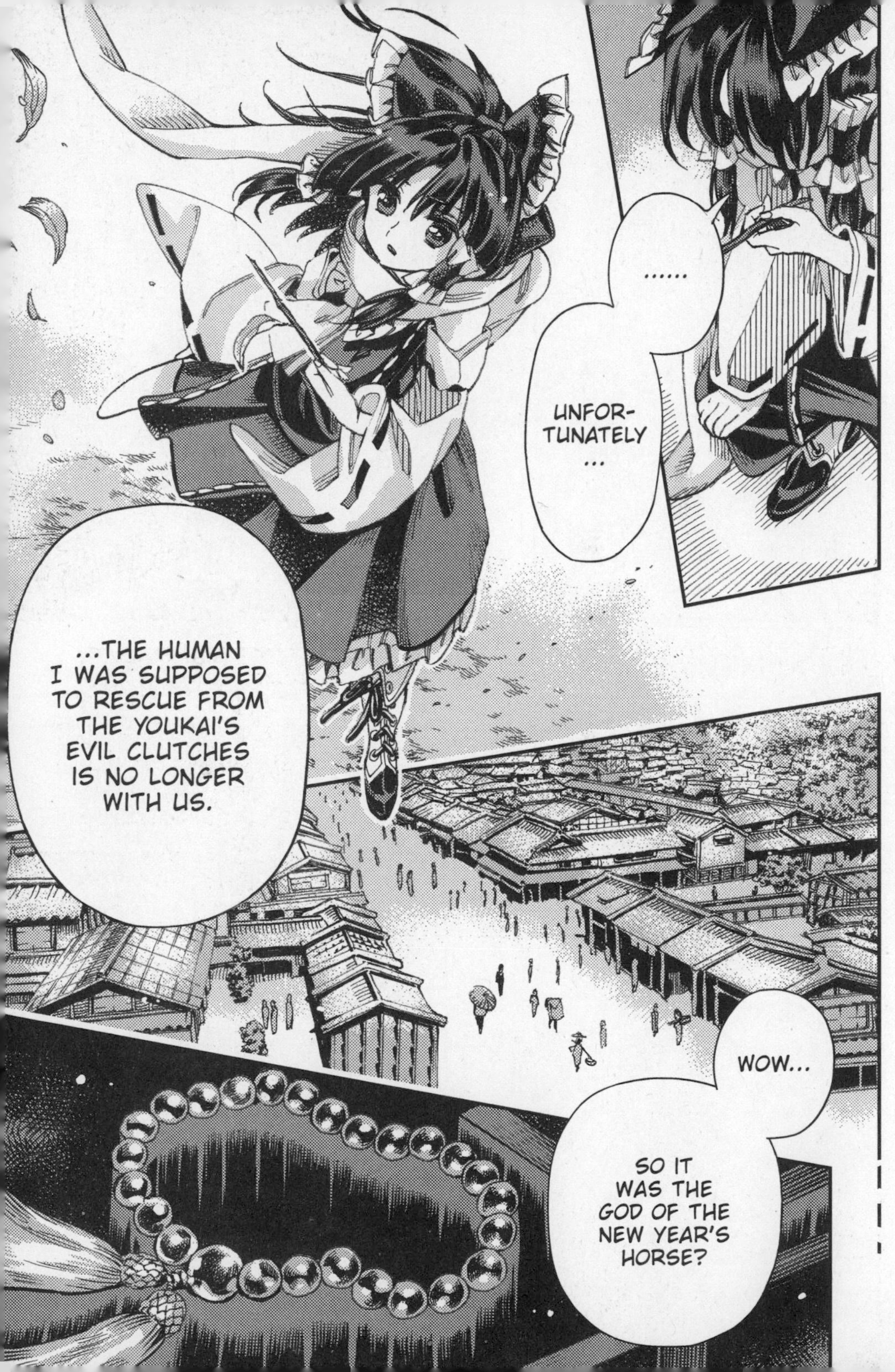
......
UNFOR-TUNATELY...
...THE HUMAN I WAS SUPPOSED TO RESCUE FROM THE YOUKAI'S EVIL CLUTCHES IS NO LONGER WITH US.
WOW...
SO IT WAS THE GOD OF THE NEW YEAR'S HORSE?

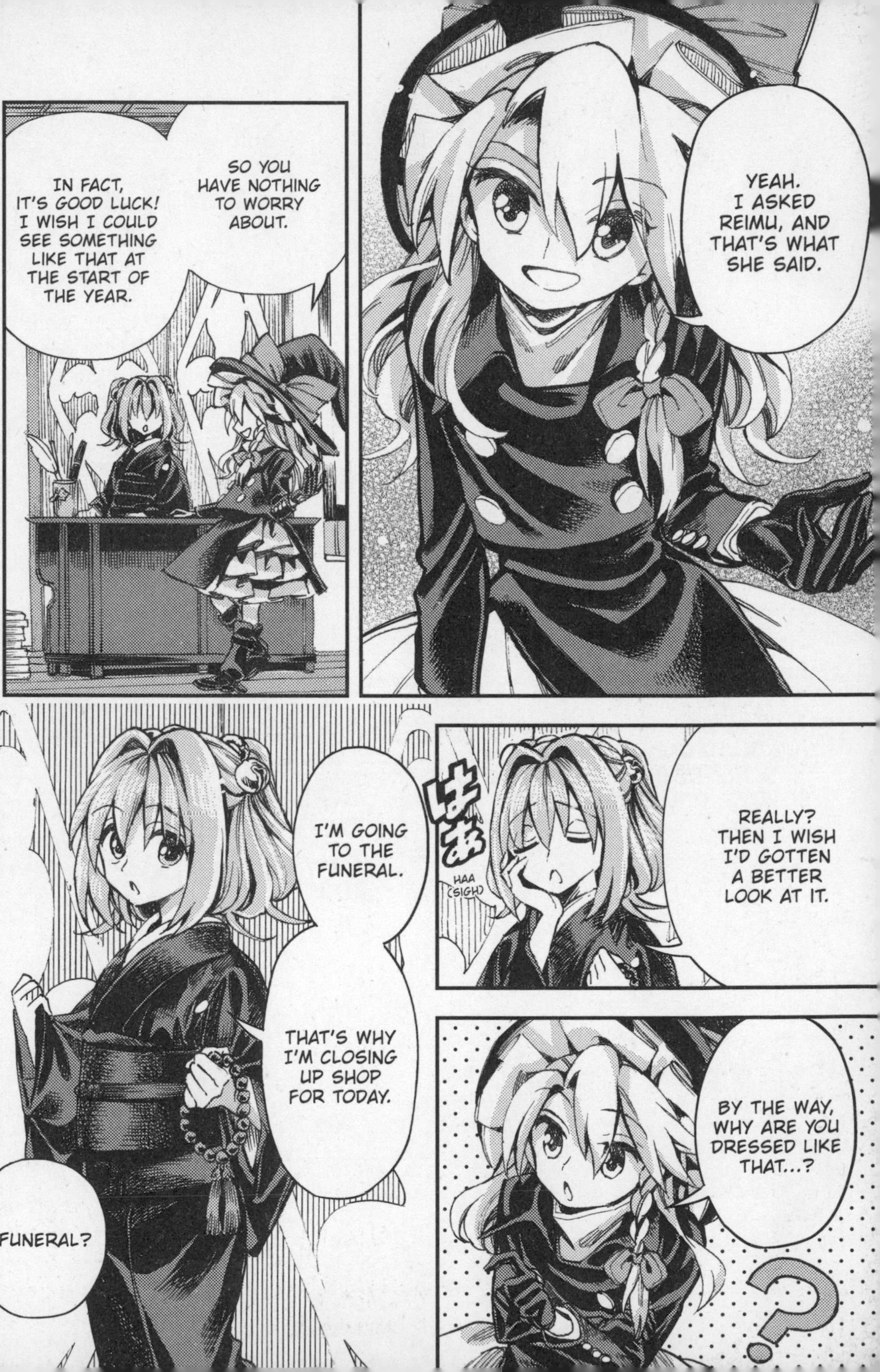
YEAH. I ASKED REIMU, AND THAT'S WHAT SHE SAID.
SO YOU HAVE NOTHING TO WORRY ABOUT.
IN FACT, IT'S GOOD LUCK! I WISH I COULD SEE SOMETHING LIKE THAT AT THE START OF THE YEAR.
REALLY? THEN I WISH I'D GOTTEN A BETTER LOOK AT IT.
はぁ
HAA (SIGH)
BY THE WAY, WHY ARE YOU DRESSED LIKE THAT...?
?
I'M GOING TO THE FUNERAL.
THAT'S WHY I'M CLOSING UP SHOP FOR TODAY.
FUNERAL?

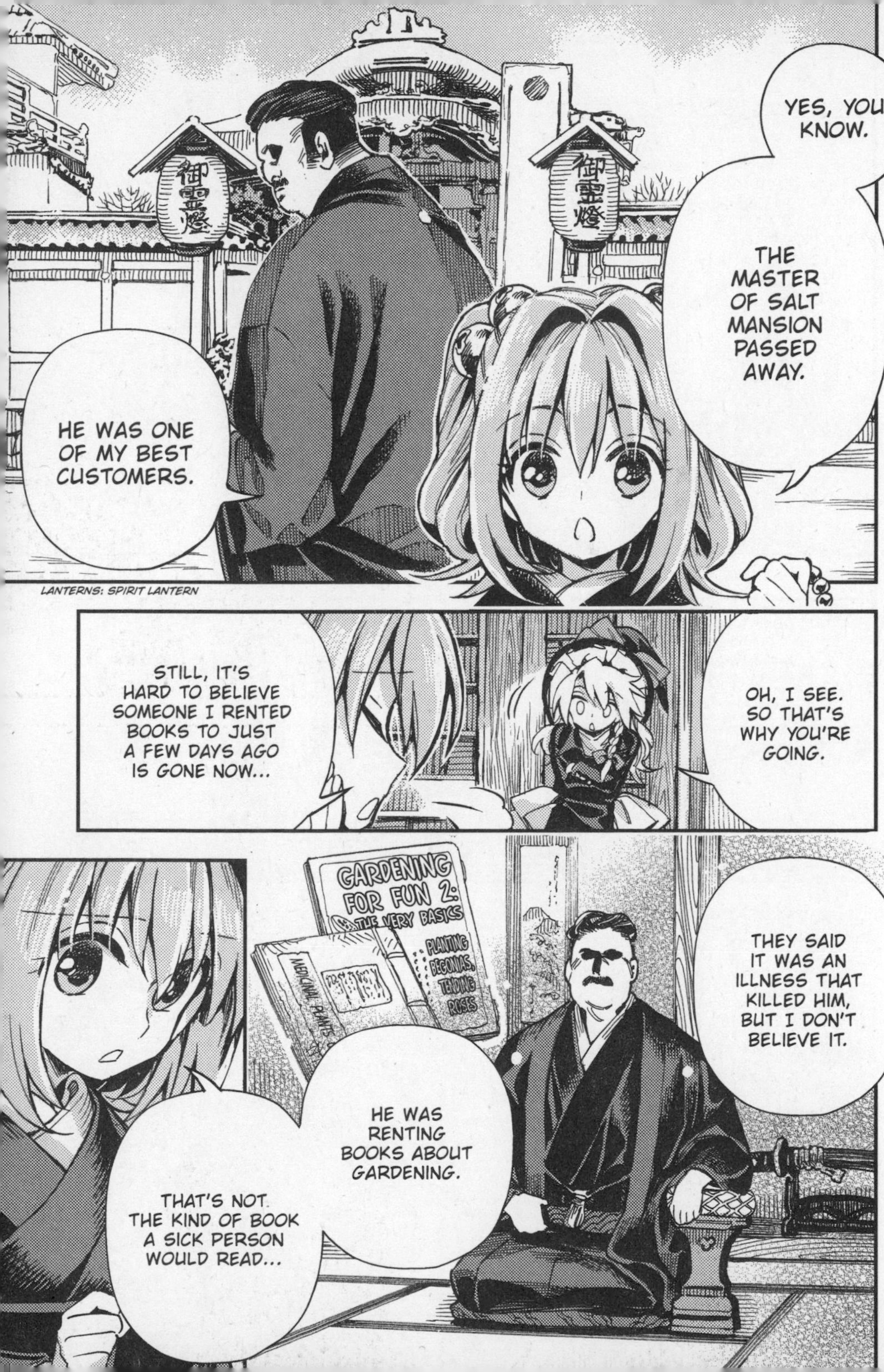
御霊燈
御霊燈
YES, YOU KNOW.
THE MASTER OF SALT MANSION PASSED AWAY.
HE WAS ONE OF MY BEST CUSTOMERS.
LANTERNS: SPIRIT LANTERN
OH, I SEE. SO THAT'S WHY YOU'RE GOING.
STILL, IT'S HARD TO BELIEVE SOMEONE I RENTED BOOKS TO JUST A FEW DAYS AGO IS GONE NOW...
GARDENING FOR FUN 2: THE VERY BASICS
PLANTING BEGONIAS, TENDING ROSES
MEDICINAL PLANTS
THEY SAID IT WAS AN ILLNESS THAT KILLED HIM, BUT I DON'T BELIEVE IT.
HE WAS RENTING BOOKS ABOUT GARDENING.
THAT'S NOT THE KIND OF BOOK A SICK PERSON WOULD READ...

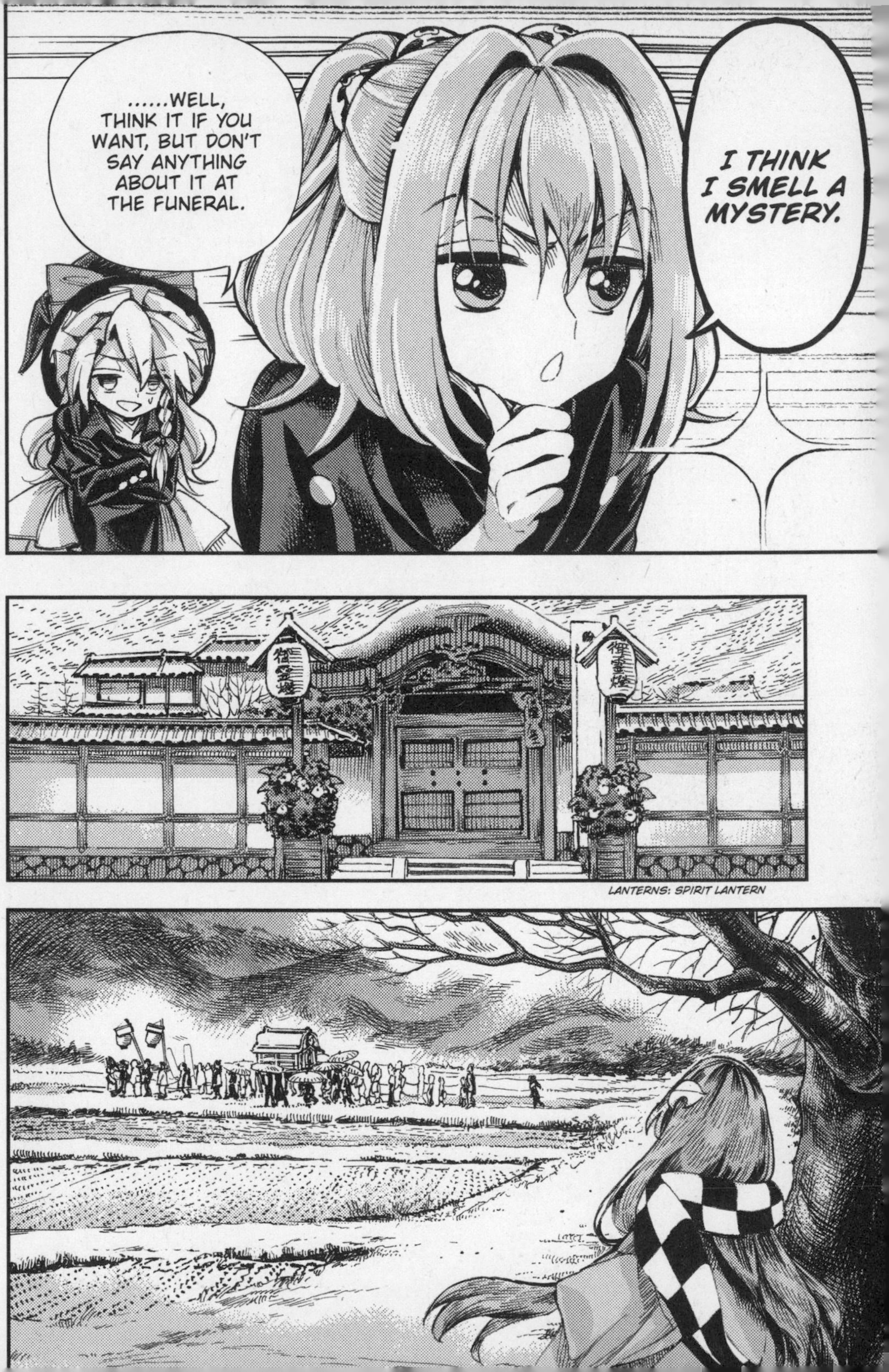
I THINK I SMELL A MYSTERY.
......WELL, THINK IT IF YOU WANT, BUT DON'T SAY ANYTHING ABOUT IT AT THE FUNERAL.
LANTERNS: SPIRIT LANTERN

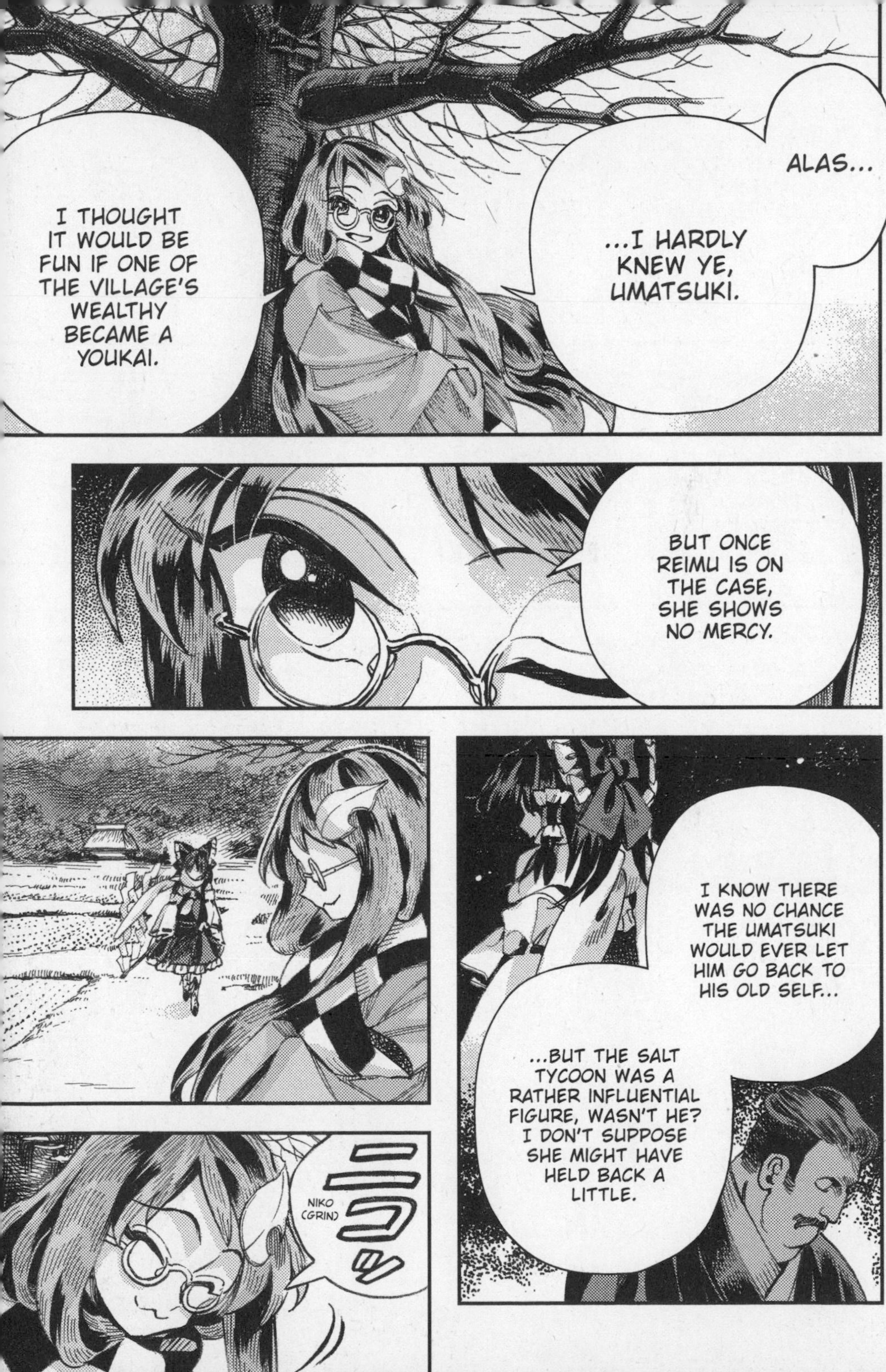
ALAS...
...I HARDLY KNEW YE, UMATSUKI.
I THOUGHT IT WOULD BE FUN IF ONE OF THE VILLAGE'S WEALTHY BECAME A YOUKAI.
BUT ONCE REIMU IS ON THE CASE, SHE SHOWS NO MERCY.
I KNOW THERE WAS NO CHANCE THE UMATSUKI WOULD EVER LET HIM GO BACK TO HIS OLD SELF...
...BUT THE SALT TYCOON WAS A RATHER INFLUENTIAL FIGURE, WASN'T HE? I DON'T SUPPOSE SHE MIGHT HAVE HELD BACK A LITTLE.
ニコッ
NIKO (GRIN)

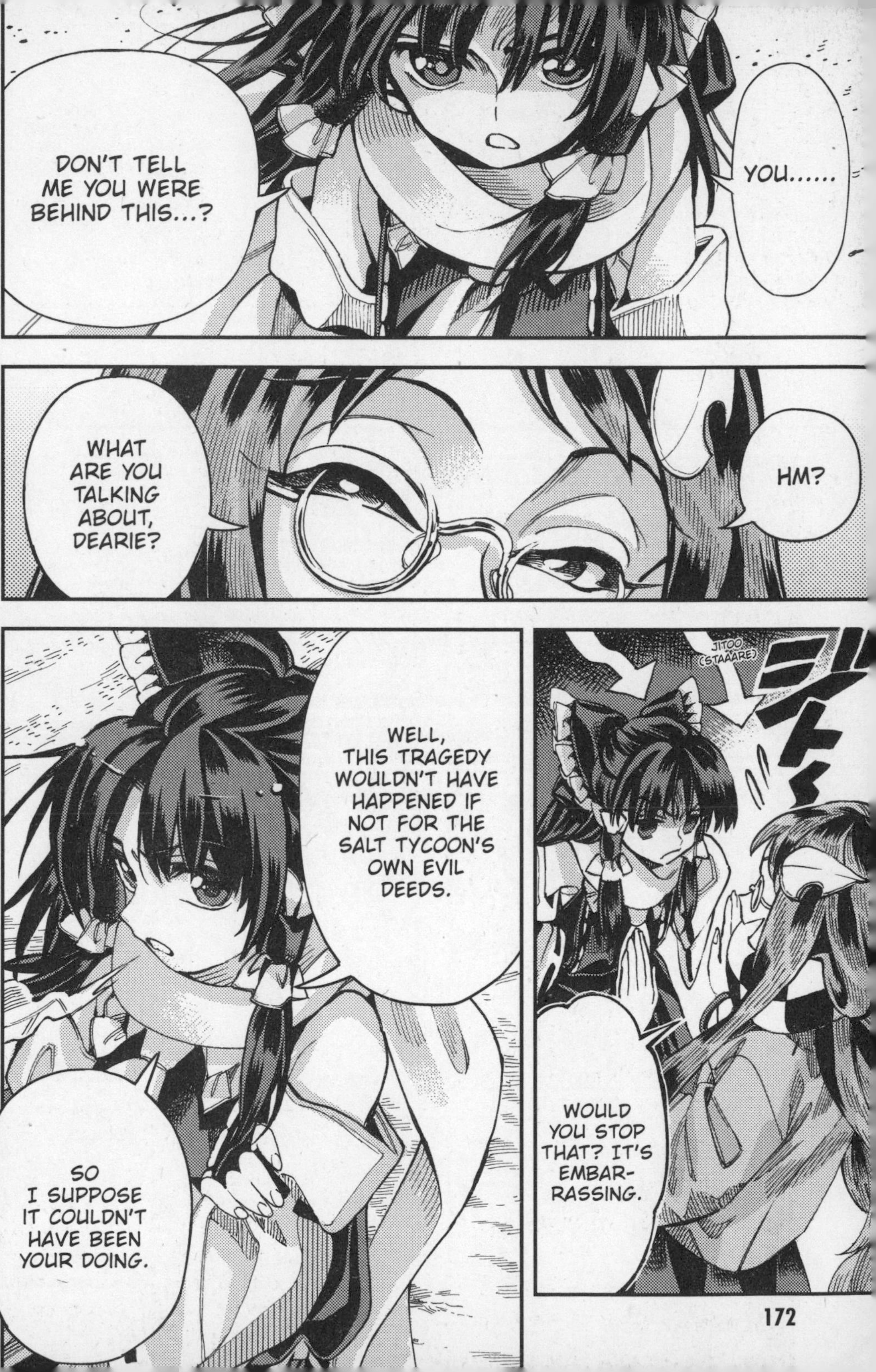
YOU......
DON'T TELL ME YOU WERE BEHIND THIS...?
HM?
WHAT ARE YOU TALKING ABOUT, DEARIE?
JITOO (STAAARE)
WOULD YOU STOP THAT? IT'S EMBAR-RASSING.
WELL, THIS TRAGEDY WOULDN'T HAVE HAPPENED IF NOT FOR THE SALT TYCOON'S OWN EVIL DEEDS.
SO I SUPPOSE IT COULDN'T HAVE BEEN YOUR DOING.

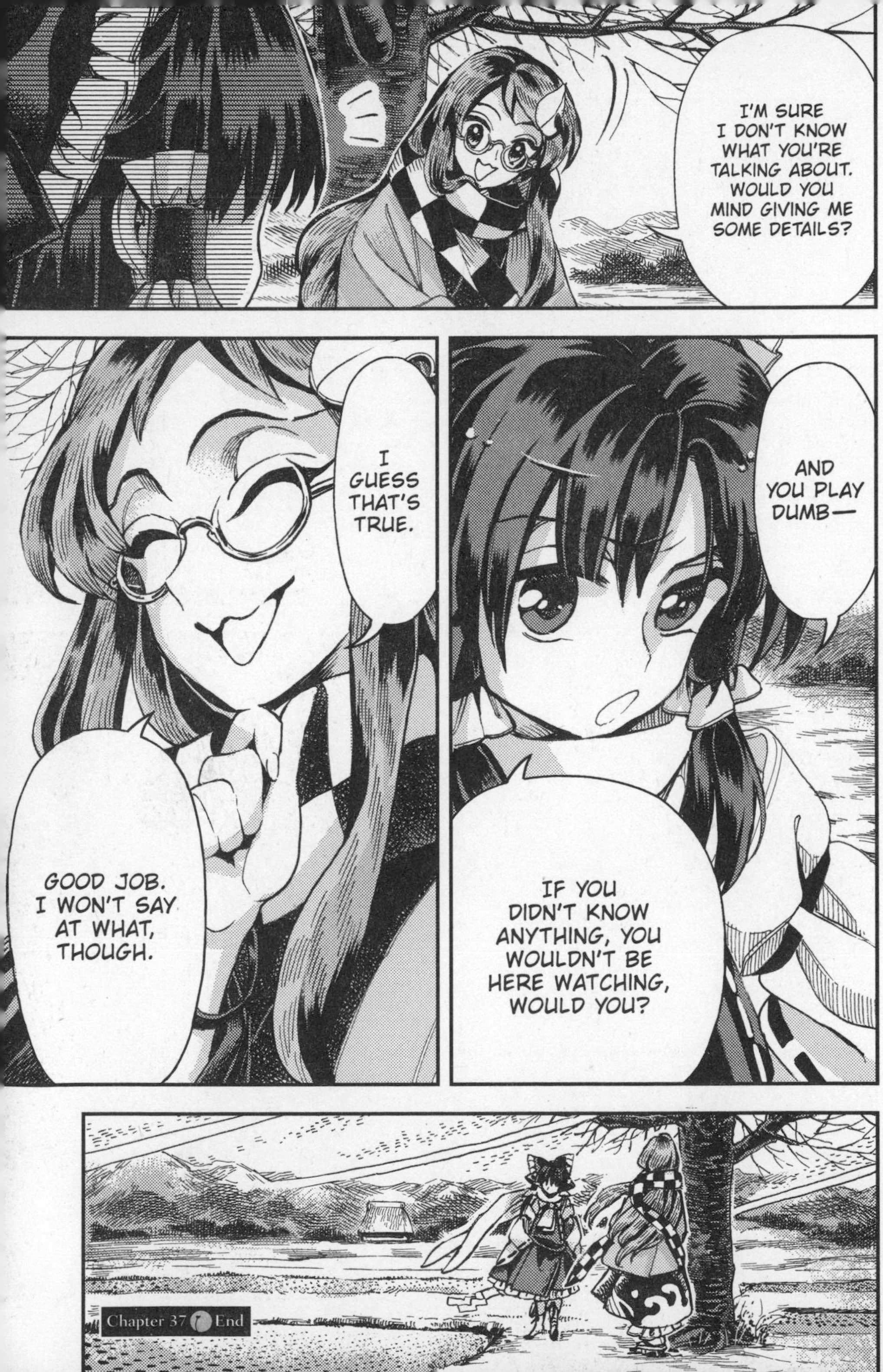
I'M SURE I DON'T KNOW WHAT YOU'RE TALKING ABOUT. WOULD YOU MIND GIVING ME SOME DETAILS?
AND YOU PLAY DUMB—
IF YOU DIDN'T KNOW ANYTHING, YOU WOULDN'T BE HERE WATCHING, WOULD YOU?
I GUESS THAT'S TRUE.
GOOD JOB. I WON'T SAY AT WHAT, THOUGH.
Chapter 37 End

TRANSLATION NOTES

GENERAL

Certain character names, such as Akyu Hiedano, are also commonly rendered differently, i.e., Hieda-no-Akyu, literally "Akyu of the Hieda." This English edition renders names as given name first in order to avoid confusion.

The character names also frequently contain references or certain meanings due to how they're written in Japanese.

Nue Houjuu: "Nue" is the name of one of the oldest recorded *youkai*. While it is said to be quite vicious, there is not much known about its habitat and lifestyle because throughout history there have been very few sightings. The kanji characters used for the surname "Houjuu" literally translates to "sealed beast."

Aya Shameimaru: Aya's name is written with the kanji for "text" or "writings," which is quite fitting for a journalist such as herself. Her surname, "Shameimaru," is written with the kanji for "arrow," "destiny," and "full," although it is likely to be adapted from "Sha-Mail," a term used in Japan for mail accompanied by pictures sent by cell phone or laptop.

Byakuren Hijiri: "Byakuren" directly translated means "white lotus" or "purity." Since she is a monk, it is likely her name is a reference to the *byakurenkyou*, or a type of Buddhist sectarianism called "White Lotus." The surname "Hijiri" carries the meanings of "highly virtuous monk" or "Buddhist missionary."

PAGE 24

Ushi-oni: The *ushi-oni*, or cow devil, is a *youkai* with so many different stories about it that it is difficult to define. Some say it is a cow with the head of a demon, and some say it is a demon with the head of a cow. Generally, it is a sea creature that likes to kill humans it finds walking on the seashore.

The Cow Woman: The cow woman is a variation of *kudan*. A *kudan* is a cow with a human face that appears in human society and prophesies of impending doom before it then dies. In appearance, the cow woman is inverse of the *kudan*, or rather, it is a woman with a cow's face.

PAGE 26

Mikoshi Nyuudou: Meaning "look past priest," the *Mikoshi Nyuudou* is a *youkai* that has the appearance of a tall priest. If an unfortunate victim were to look up to see its face, the *youkai* would grow taller and taller, and when the victim looked up so high that they fell over, the *youkai* would attack them. The simple way to get past a *Mikoshi Nyuudou* is to say, "I've seen past you," which, in Japanese, can be stated in one word.

PAGE 31

Turbo Granny and Hasshaku-sama: Nue is referring to urban legends that came to life in the Touhou Project game "Urban Legend in Limbo." The monk Byakuren Hijiri became Turbo Granny, an old woman who would surprise people driving through tunnels by knocking on their window to get their attention so they can see she is riding her motorcycle at the same speed as they're driving. Hasshaku-sama is a spirit who appears from under a hat and grows into a giant woman who seduces and kills men.

PAGE 64

Kawaraban: The *kawaraban*, meaning "tile print," is a form of newspaper that was distributed in Japan during the Edo period. As the name suggests, they were fliers made from clay printing blocks, and they were often used to advertise social events or report on natural disasters.

PAGE 89

Age of Maitreya: The Age of Maitreya refers to a time in the future when it is said the bodhisattva Maitreya will return to Earth. It is predicted that it will occur at a time when mankind has lost its way and has invited destruction upon itself.

PAGE 105

"The Strange Tale of Worldwide Upheaval": This is the heading of a real newspaper article that was printed in a Meiji newspaper in 1881. It was a translation of a European article about a prophecy of the end of the world.

PAGE 169

Spirit Lantern: *Goryoutou* in Japanese, offering lanterns are meant to help guide spirits of the deceased. They're also given as offerings to the gods.

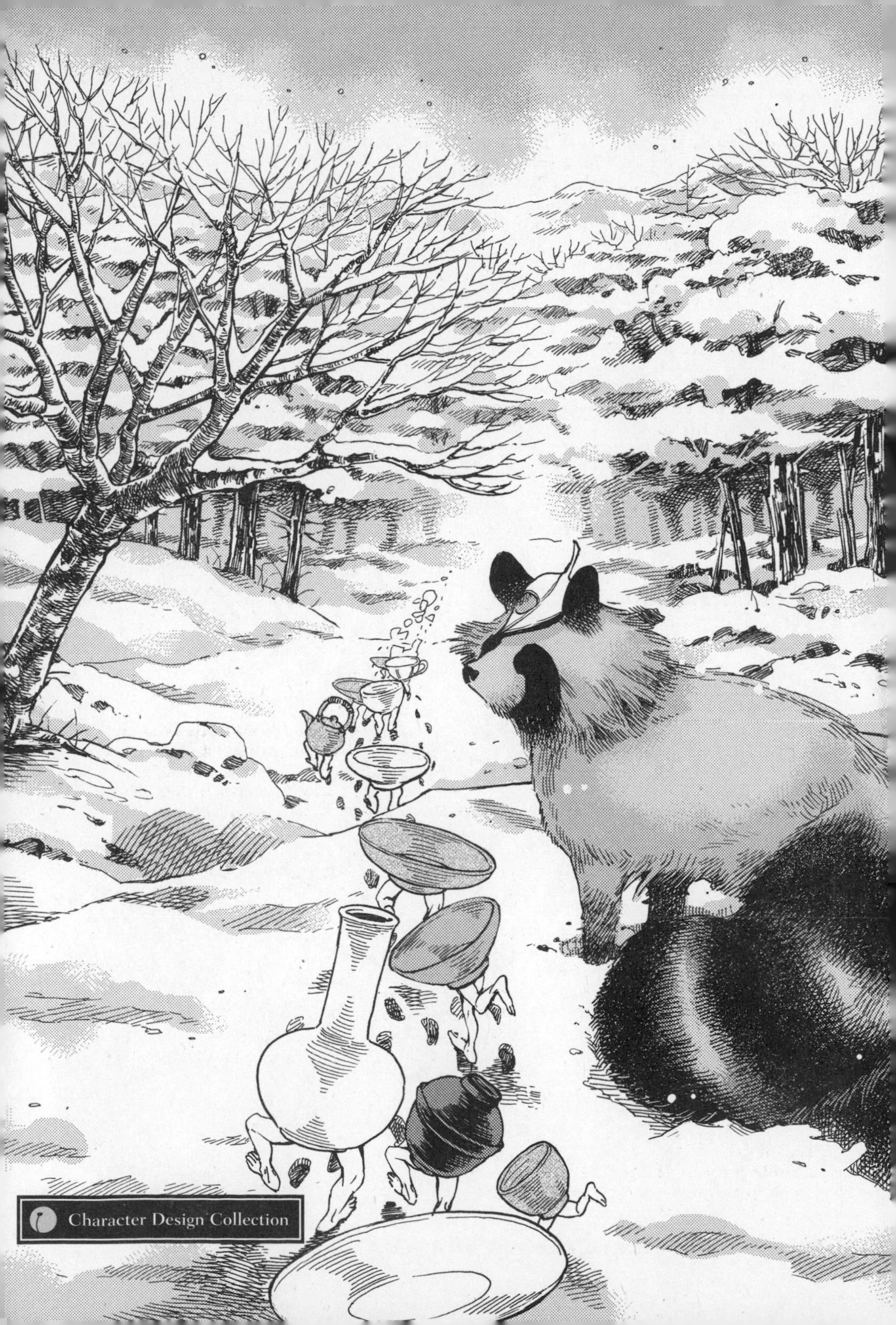
Character Design Collection

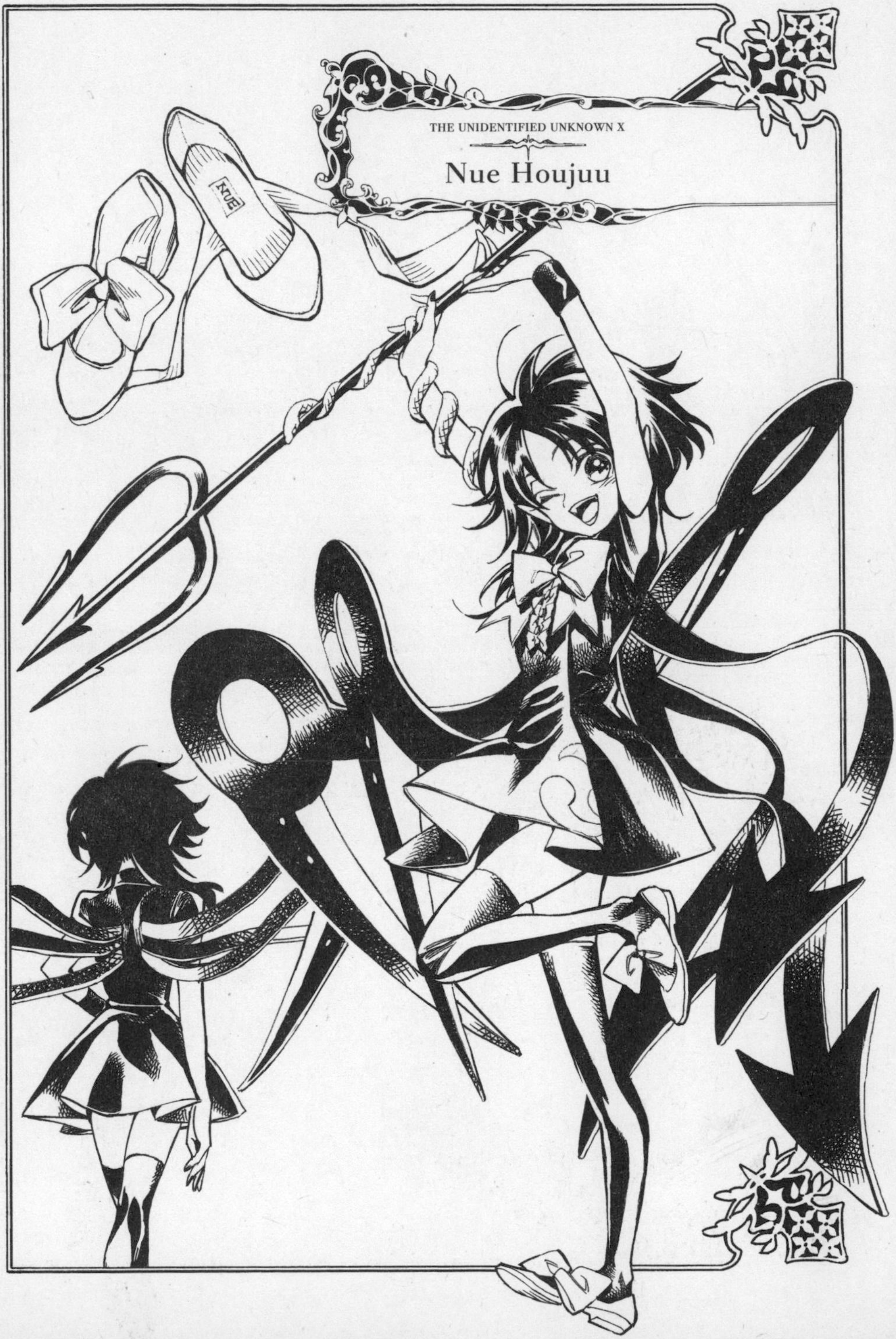
THE UNIDENTIFIED UNKNOWN X
Nue Houjuu
NUE

THE CROW TENGU JOURNALIST

Aya Shameimaru

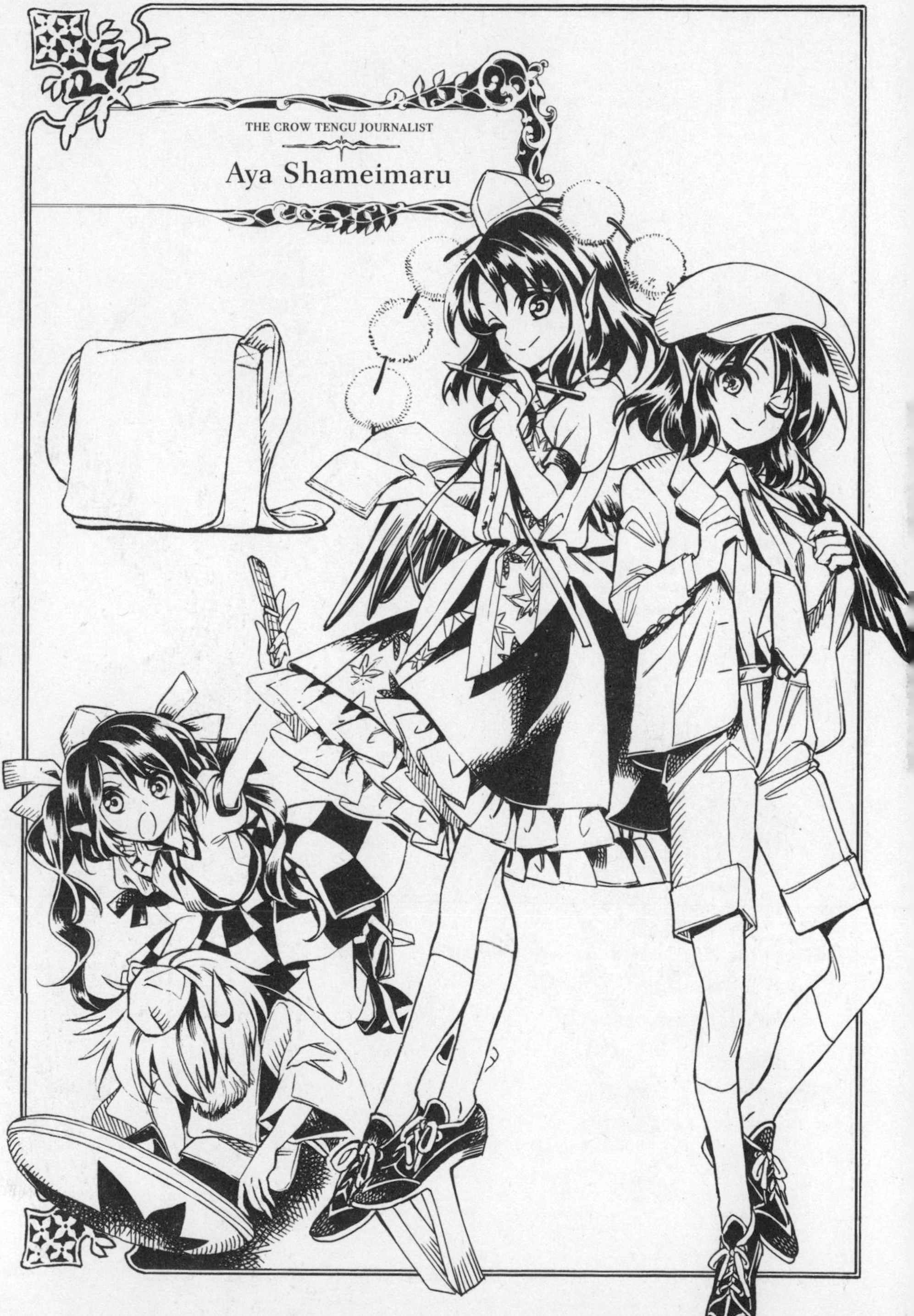

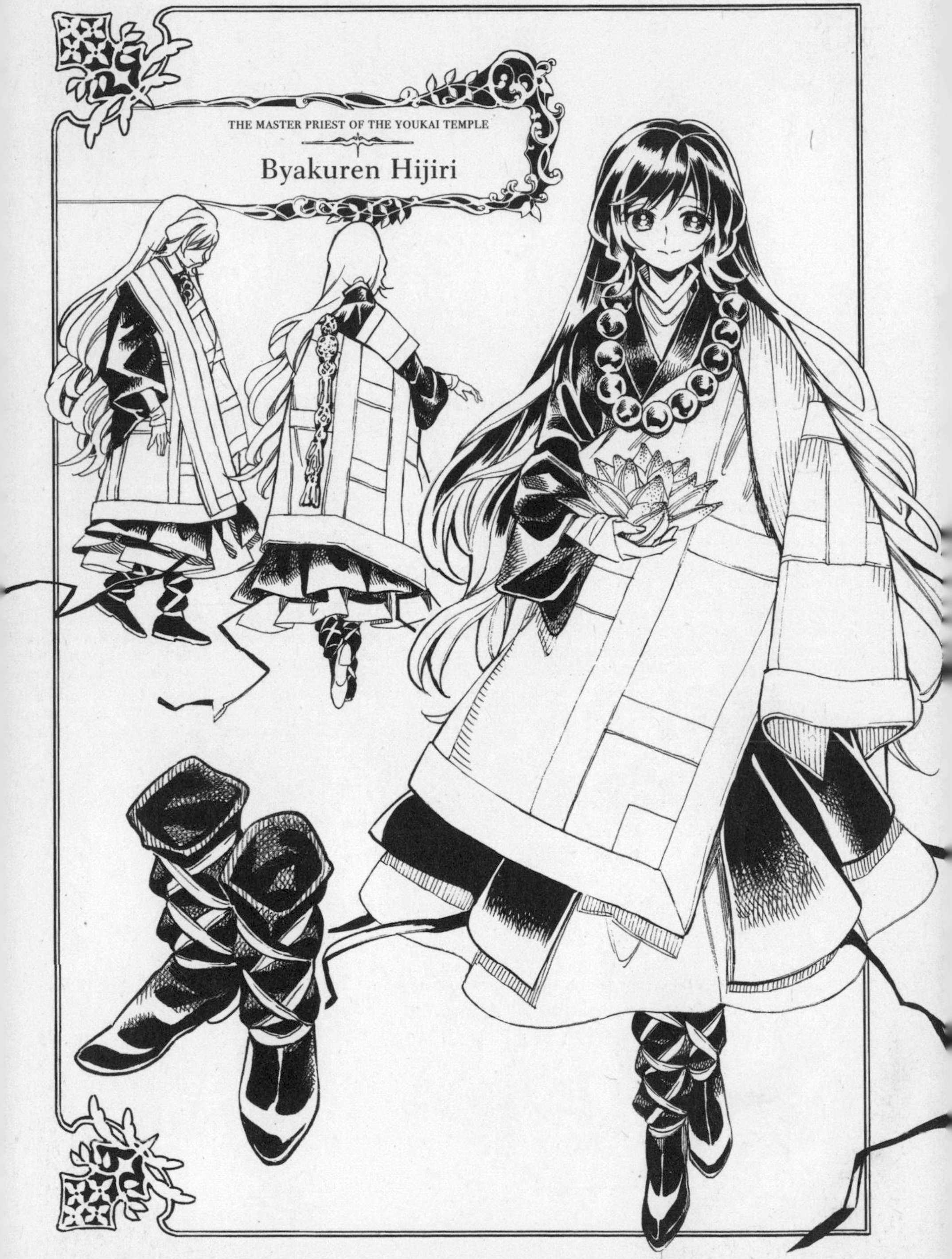
THE MASTER PRIEST OF THE YOUKAI TEMPLE
Byakuren Hijiri

ZUN

Hello, ZUN here. In no time at all, we present Volume 5.

In this volume, the *tengu* make an appearance, and we get a glimpse into the *youkai* power struggle. The *youkai* act like friends on an individual level, but apparently when they get together in groups, they're hostile toward one another and tend to quarrel. In other words, they're not much different from humans.

The story alluded to in "Where Is the Cow Head?" is an urban legend that really exists. It's an interesting one that turns the whole urban legend system on its head, because if anyone hears it, they die, so nobody knows what it's about. It would be fun if there were more stories created like that.

Well, I hope to see you again in Volume 6 or in *Comp Ace*.

Moe Harukawa

Hello. I am the artist, Harukawa.

I wonder if to you readers it feels like it's only Volume 5 or like it's already Volume 5? It's something I'm really curious about.

To ZUN-san, who writes up the story outline for me every month despite his busy schedule, my editor who deals with everything so quickly; and all of you who read this book, thank you very much.

Forbidden Scrollery

5

⁂STORY⁂
ZUN

⁂ART⁂
Moe Harukawa

TRANSLATION: ALETHEA NIBLEY AND ATHENA NIBLEY
LETTERING: ALEXIS ECKERMAN

TOUHOU SUZUNA AN ~Forbidden Scrollery. Vol. 5
© Team Shanghai Alice © Moe HARUKAWA 2016
First published in Japan in 2016 by KADOKAWA CORPORATION, Tokyo.
English translation rights arranged with KADOKAWA CORPORATION, Tokyo
through TUTTLE-MORI AGENCY, Inc., Tokyo.

English translation © 2018 by Yen Press, LLC

Yen Press
1290 Avenue of the Americas
New York, NY 10104

VISIT US AT YENPRESS.COM

facebook.com/yenpress yenpress.tumblr.com
twitter.com/yenpress instagram.com/yenpress

First Yen Press Edition: November 2018

Yen Press is an imprint of Yen Press, LLC.
The Yen Press name and logo are trademarks of Yen Press, LLC.

The publisher is not responsible for websites (or their content)
that are not owned by the publisher.

Library of Congress Control Number: 2017949553

ISBNs: 978-0-316-51195-7 (paperback)
978-0-316-51208-4 (ebook)

10 9 8 7 6 5 4 3 2 1

WOR

Printed in the United States of America